PSYCHOLINGUISTICS

PSYCHOLINGUISTICS

A New Approach

DAVID McNEILL
The University of Chicago

1817

HARPER & ROW, PUBLISHERS, New York
Cambridge, Philadelphia, San Francisco, Washington,
London, Mexico City, São Paulo, Singapore, Sydney

Sponsoring Editor: Leslie Carr
Project Editor: Joan C. Gregory
Cover Design: *WYCKOFF* Design
Text Art: Laura Pedelty and Robert Williams
Production Manager: Willie Lane
Compositor: ComCom Division of Haddon Craftsmen, Inc.
Printer and Binder: R. R. Donnelley & Sons Company

PSYCHOLINGUISTICS: A New Approach

Library of Congress Cataloging-in-Publication Data

McNeill, David.
  Psycholinguistics: a new approach.

  Bibliography: p.
  1. Psycholinguistics.   I. Title.
P37.M34   1987   401′.9   86–14593
ISBN 0–06–044387–1

87 88 89 90 9 8 7 6 5 4 3 2 1

Contents

Preface

The "new approach" I mention in my title is a synthesis of approaches that seem, superficially, in conflict: Saussure's conception of language as a system of static contrasts on the social level, and Vygotsky's conception of language as a dynamic process on the individual level. This conflict can be resolved by introducing the dimension of time. The Saussurian and Vygotskyian conceptions of language have validity at different points in the temporal development of the linguistic acts of speaking or understanding. The time in question is not the time it takes to say or listen to speech, but internal, developmental time. If speaking time is called "surface time," then the synthesis of the Saussurian and Vygotskyian approaches takes place in "deep time." The theme unifying this book is an extended analysis of the processes taking place in "deep time."

Pursuing such an analysis has given the book a distinctive flavor which I can best convey by listing some of its main featues:

1. There is throughout the book use of gesture data as a source of insight into linguistic and psycholinguistic problems. The gestures I mean are the unwitting semiconscious gestures that often accompany speech, not the familiar "Italianate" gestures (of which the "O.K." sign is one of the few citable examples). Although the term "paralanguage" is often used to label gesture phenomena, the spontaneous gestures of the kind I use in this book are, in fact, integral parts of sentences and belong to the early stages of sentences in "deep time."

2. There is systematic use of the concept of inner speech associated with the concept of a dialectic. These concepts make indispensable a clear regard for the central place of verbal thinking in acts of speaking and understanding. In Chapter 5 I explain inner speech and dialectic; but, as unifying ideas, these concepts lie behind the book in its entirety. The dialectic in question is that between individually and socially constituted sources of value. Value itself is a Saussurian concept. Values from the two sources merge through time into the final linguistic product. This results in a qualitatively changed form of thinking embodied in a word, phrase, sentence, or longer discourse spoken or understood by an indi-

vidual in a particular context at a specific time. The same dialectic analyzes speech production and understanding. From the viewpoint of the internal computations involved these are identical processes.

3. The central argument of this book incorporates the context of speaking from the start. Symbols are not assumed to have the same value in every context. Two early chapters are devoted to describing the context of speaking: one the social context and the other the informational context.

4. This argument also accepts the assumption introduced by Chomsky (1965) that linguistic performance (acts of speaking and understanding) incorporates linguistic competence (the state of linguistic knowledge). I propose a new and unobvious solution to the problem of explaining this incorporation.

Within the above framework I discuss many problems that occupy linguists and psycholinguists today: methods of language description and analysis; speech acts; conversational cooperation and implicature; turn-taking; cohesion and deixis in discourse; sentence understanding and production; speech errors; metaphors; word recognition; heuristic strategies and information processing; linguistic determinism; gesture and sign language; language use by children, chimpanzees, and artifacts; and linguistic consciousness.

In presenting these topics, I have divided the book into eight chapters, starting with an explication of the socially constituted and individually constituted aspects of language and linguistic actions (Chapters 1 and 2), proceeding to the context of speaking (Chapters 3 and 4), to speech production and understanding (Chapter 5), then to linguistic determinism (the Whorfian hypothesis—Chapter 6), to gesture and sign (Chapter 7), and finally to action, thought, and language, including linguistic consciousness (Chapter 8).

The book is meant to be a textbook on psycholinguistics, and I should say a few words about the principles on which I wrote it. It is meant for graduate students and advanced undergraduate students in psychology, linguistics, education, and allied fields. I have found that students, including undergraduate students, are quite capable of comprehending original sources once they grasp the arguments presented in this book. My impression is that linguistics students find getting into the book initially easier, but that by the third chapter all students feel equally at home.

As I have worked on this book I have been supported by the University of Chicago (Division of Social Sciences), the National Science Foundation (Linguistics Section), the Spencer Foundation, and two European institutions—the Netherlands Institute for Advanced Study in Wassenaar, to which I am eternally grateful for a year of peace and quiet in a lovely academic setting, and the Max-Planck-Institut für Psycholinguistik in Nijmegen for use of its wonderful specialized library. I am grateful to Ino d'Arcais for his help in arranging my visit to NIAS, and to Wolfgang Klein, Willem Levelt, and William Marslen-Wilson for their hospitality at the Max-Planck. Over the past six or seven years many colleagues and students have helped me with my gesture research. Mitsuko Iriye, Elena Levy, Laura Pedelty, and Debra Stephens have worked on this project virtually from the start. Together with Catherine Greeno, who studied the gestures of mathematicians, they are the keen observers who analyzed the video records and found the examples of iconic, metaphoric, and discourse-related gestures cited in Chapter 7. I owe special thanks to Laura Pedelty for her careful and artistic drawings in Chapter 7 and elsewhere; only a sample of her work appears here. William Eilfort and Anne Farley brought their gifts as linguists to bear on the narrations that are utilized repeatedly as illustrations in Chapters 5 and 7. To all these excellent people who have shared my enthusiasm and interests and have given so much of their time and energy I owe a tremendous amount of thanks. The drawings of children's gestures are by Robert Williams. The "Anaphora Workshop" between 1980 and 1983 at the University of Chicago had an influence on Chapter 4 far beyond what I can acknowledge through citations of the work of the participants: Elena Levy, Rebecca Schiffman, and Michael Silverstein. My great thanks to Melissa Bowerman, Joan Bybee, Robin Campbell, John Lucy, and Naomi Quinn for insights and material used in Chapter 6. From Adam Kendon I have received many suggestions, and Chapter 8 (the only chapter he has not read) owes its existence altogether to his comment that something was missing. I have had thoughtful letters about Chapter 5 from Mark Johnson and John Lawler. William Washabaugh kept up a correspondence about topics that have found their way into Chapters 3 and 5 and has had an influence over my presentation of deixis and the social foundations of language use. Finally, I want to thank, however inadequately, my family. More than anyone, they have lived through the thinking out and writing of this book. The book has taken what seems eons to finish. My children, Cheryl and Randall, I thank for their achievements in life; they have given me great pride and satisfaction. My wife, Nobuko, I thank most of all. She has given me far more advice, support, and love than I can ever repay, and she has been a colleague, whose ideas and taste permeate the book.

David McNeill

PSYCHOLINGUISTICS

chapter 1

Two Approaches to Language

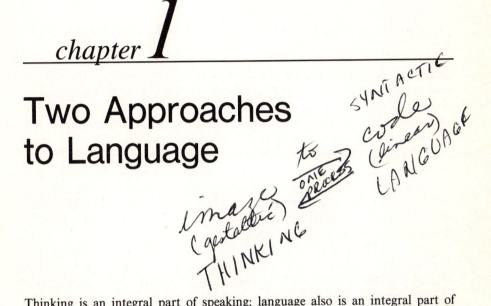

Thinking is an integral part of speaking; language also is an integral part of thinking. This is not as paradoxical as it looks. Sorting out the two poles of language and thought and studying how they interact is the special province of psycholinguistics. Thinking and speaking lie on a continuum. It makes no sense to ask where one ends and the other begins. Rather, there is a transformation of thinking from one type into another type. The transformation takes place in both directions: outward to speech and inward to speech understanding. At one end of the continuum thinking is more global and imagistic, and at the other end more segmented and syntactic. But a continuous process of transformation connects the two ends.

Virtually everything in this book is presented to explain the transformations that occur along this continuum. In this first chapter I begin by examining two approaches to language. The transformations of thinking that take place during linguistic activities can be explicated only by showing how the subject matter of these approaches can be synthesized into a single process. Considering only one approach or the other—linguistics or psychology—will never reveal these transformations.

The continuum that links thinking and speaking exists in time. It is a real continuum with earlier parts changing into later parts. This time I will call "deep" time, to distinguish it from the "surface" time that we directly perceive in the flow of speech. Deep time does not necessarily equal surface time. Deep time is the inner developmental time of a sentence, where thinking is undergoing transformations. It may run rapidly or slowly. Surface time is the outer time, where one kind of thinking—socially constituted and syntactic—is presented sequentially to a

1

hearer in the medium of the speech signal. Surface time tends to run at a constant speed. The same distinction is drawn for speech understanding. For hearers, deep time is the time it takes for a speaker's socially constituted syntactic thinking to be transformed into the hearer's own global imagistic thinking. Again, this may be faster or slower than surface time.

There are further oppositions. Linguistic actions are spontaneous. We say a word or sentence at some definite moment, but there is no input that is the trigger of the act and we may not know exactly where the act is going. Psycholinguistics has as a core problem the fact that individuals perform linguistic acts that even the individuals themselves do not foresee, but that must be instantly interpretable by others. Psycholinguistics is the science of how individual thinking, which is private and flows continuously, relates to a social institution that is public and the product of tradition—that is, language itself.

The relation of individual thinking to the social institution of language can be observed in many forms but appears most fundamentally in the real-time linguistic actions of speaking and understanding. A single linguistic action is perhaps the smallest interval over which a single change of mental state is observable. It is also one of the smallest intervals over which we are held to strict standards of well-formedness in our acts.

It is the institution of language that makes an individual's actions interpretable by others. When we perform linguistic actions that meet the permanent socially constituted standards of performance that we refer to as knowledge of language itself, our actions acquire a linguistic value that is the key to making the action interpretable. Yet the institution of language is timeless and unaccompanied by any context from the individual's point of view, whereas linguistic actions are contextualized and take place in real time.

Such subject matter invites us to combine two traditional approaches to the phenomenon of speaking, and this combination is the new approach I am using in this book. In this chapter I describe these approaches. In later chapters I prepare the ground for a synthesis, which I propose in Chapter 5.

TWO SOURCES OF VALUE

The lists on page 3 give some of the characteristics of the two traditional approaches to language phenomena, what I will refer to as the *linguistics of language* and the *psychology of language* approaches. If we inquire into a particular language phenomenon—for instance, how to define what a sentence is—we obtain answers that differ depending on the approach we use, and the differences sort out along the lines that these lists imply. Subsequent sections of this chapter will explain the words that appear in each list.

Since our knowledge of language, beyond the immediate intuitive grasp that everyone has by virtue of being a speaker, depends on the theoretical system we presuppose, these lists also characterize the *limits* of knowledge in each traditional approach. Moreover, since there are two lists, we are faced with a choice of which limited form of knowledge we shall have.

The theme of this chapter is that both the linguistics of language and the psychology of language approaches are incomplete for the goal of describing and explaining linguistic actions. Acknowledging the incompleteness of these approaches is the first step toward finding a way of combining them.

The differences between the linguistics of language and the psychology of language approaches are most sharply exhibited in their different concepts of *value.* In the linguistics of language approach the value of an object—a sentence or word—is determined by its position in a socially constituted system of language objects; without a place in this system the object has no value in itself. The value of the same object in the psychology of language approach is intrinsic to the object. The value depends on something inside the object ("meaning" or "thought") that does not derive from the system of language but from *the individual speaker.* Between these two kinds of value, one socially constituted and the other individually constituted, there seems to be no common ground. However, we shall see that they can be combined on the one dimension which they share: the dimension of time, or *diachrony.* If we ask what a sentence is or what some other linguistic object is, the answer we get depends on the approach we use. We can emphasize either of two sources of value in the linguistic action.

Linguistics of Language	Psychology of Language
Socially constituted	Individually constituted
Synchronic	Diachronic
Contrastive value	Intrinsic value
Context-free	Context-determined
Stable	Changing
Object	Process
Container metaphor	Act metaphor

Ever since Saussure (1959; originally 1916), linguistics has had the characteristics listed in the left column; psychology of language has had those listed in the right column. A full explanation of the production of value in speech acts, however, requires combining these two sources of value. The puzzle is seeing how to do this.

The immediate aim of the following section is to explain the linguistics of language approach and the concept in this approach of value based on exclusion. To do this I will begin with what is still the definitive statement of the linguistics approach—the revolutionary paradigm (as this term was used by Kuhn, 1962) that Saussure introduced nearly a century ago. In the next chapter I will discuss modern linguistics and show how recent work both remains within the tradition of Saussure and adds significantly to it. In fact, the significance of contemporary additions can be appreciated best in the context of the Saussurian paradigm. Within the present chapter, I will also explain the psychology of language approach and the concept of intrinsic value associated with it. To do this I will introduce a new source of data—the iconic and metaphoric gestures that spontaneously accompany acts of speaking. These are, I will argue, part of the speech act and comparable to the production of speech sounds. Finally, I will give a forecast of the rest of the book and the synthesis of the linguistics and psychology of language approaches that I will propose.

THE LINGUISTIC PARADIGM OF SAUSSURE

Saussure presents an interlocking series of contrasts, as follows:

1. Langue versus parole
2. Signifier versus signified
3. Synchronic versus diachronic
4. Syntagmatic versus paradigmatic ("associative")
5. Pure linguistic value versus intrinsic value

Langue–Parole

Langue–parole is a division of the total phenomena of human speech into mutually exclusive parts. One of these parts is langue, or "language" itself, which is the systematic part of human speech—systematic in that it contains the language system. It is the part that is not modifiable, deletable, or expandable by individual speakers working on their own. Langue exists as a *social* reality that is maintained through the contributions of all the individual members of the linguistic community, acting as a whole. An example of a socially constituted fact is the way we pronounce the words *pear* and *apple* in English. Among the restrictions on pronunciation in English speech is that the /p/ sound of *apple* is nonaspirated, whereas that of *pear* is aspirated. Writing /p/ signifies that we are referring to a phoneme—a type of sound—rather than to a specific sound that someone has produced. *Aspirated* means that /p/ is pronounced with a little puff of air, which can be felt if you hold your hand in front of your mouth. *Nonaspirated* means this puff is absent. Aspiration in English appears only in certain contexts and is excluded from other contexts such as the middles of words. This fact of English pronunciation is accepted by all and cannot be altered by an individual speaker. If you force yourself to say *apple* with an aspirated /p/ (as if you were saying *a pull*), the effect is not that you have changed the pronunciation of *apple,* but that you are just not saying *apple* any longer. The inclusion of nonaspirated /p/ is a socially constituted fact belonging to langue and cannot be changed individually.

All members of the English-speaking community accept and support the fact that *apple* is pronounced with a nonaspirated /p/, whether they know this fact consciously or not. Such facts are the proper subject matter of linguistics according to Saussure. Socially constituted facts exist at all levels of language, not only at the phonemic level seen in this example, and different branches of linguistics concentrate on different levels.

Parole, or "speaking," is what is left in human speech after langue has been removed. It is what is unsystematic about human speech—not in the sense that it is irregular, but that regularities are not caused by the language system. Parole is under the control of individual speakers; it can be and is changed by speakers at will, and therefore has reality at the individual level but not at the level of the language system. An example of parole is a person saying *this is an apple* rather than *this is a pear.* The individual chooses to say *apple* rather than *pear* because of some factor that is outside the system of language—because of the situational appropriateness of referring to apples rather than pears. Situational facts such as these are randomly sequenced as far as the structure of langue is concerned. They are significant and meaningful for individuals, but not for the community of speakers as a whole.

Saussure considered parole to be what is left of human speech after langue is removed. This conception sets up an absolute separation between langue and parole. Our goal in this book is different. We aim to see how the socially constituted and the individually constituted parts of human speech are synthesized in speech acts. Far from separating them absolutely, we wish to find a way to combine them in a manner that shows the contribution of each to the act of speaking.

Signifier–Signified

These terms denote two sides of linguistic symbols. The signifier and signified are inseparable in the sense that isolating one of them destroys the symbol, but they are still distinguishable parts of the symbol. Destruction of symbols can be experienced directly in a process known as *verbal satiation* (Fillenbaum, 1967). This is the experience of loss of meaning that comes from staring too long at a printed word. For example, gaze steadily at the following:

TREE

If we stare at this word for a reasonably extended period of time, the signifier form of the word will begin to occupy all of our attention, the signified meaning will recede, and the group of letters will cease to look like—or even be—a word. The symbol will be destroyed. The signifier and signified are the external and internal halves of symbols. The relation between them is called signification. The *signifier* is the sound-image of the symbol, the side of the symbol that can be made overt in speech acts. The *signified* is the concept that the signifier signifies; the side of the symbol that can never be made overt. It is incorrect to think of a word—*tree,* for example—as just the overt sequence of sounds or letters: t-r-e-e. The word *tree* is equally the concept of a tree. The concept *is* the word to the same extent that the sound sequence is the word—namely, in each case, one-half of the word. The following is a diagrammatic representation of a linguistic symbol:

TREE symbol =
> Signifier: the sound-image "tree"
> Signified: the concept of a tree

Linguistic symbols are necessarily part of langue. This is because the linguistic symbol is *arbitrary,* according to Saussure, by which he meant that the *form* of the signifier is not determined by the content of the signified. There is nothing in the form of the sound-image *tree* that the concept of a tree determines.

That these are paired in English is an arbitrary fact belonging to langue. There are, of course, degrees of arbitrariness. For example, *nine* and *ten* are absolutely arbitrary in the sense that nothing in the signified concept of nine or ten determines the form of the signifiers in these words, but *nineteen* is only relatively arbitrary: its form is predictable from the signified concept, but only in part. The particular method of combining *nine* and *ten* into *nineteen* (rather than **ten-nine,* for instance) is again an arbitrary fact of English (the *indicates a form not belonging to langue).

Because symbols are arbitrary, they must be socially constituted. The community of speakers must accept and support the arbitrary combinations. With a nonarbitrary "natural" symbol, where the form of the signifier *is* determined at least in part by the content of the signified (e.g., smoke as the sign of the proverbial fire), there is no need to socially maintain the combination of signifier and signifed. Similarly, drawings, despite cultural variation, have nonarbitrary connections with the objects being drawn. This is particularly evident with stick figures (Fortes, 1940).

A consequence of the arbitrariness of linguistic symbols is what Hockett (1958) called *duality of patterning* and semioticians call *double articulation* (Eco, 1976). The term *duality* refers to the fact that symbols must participate in two sets of patterns at once. One pattern is that of signifiers and the other that of signifieds—the level of sound-images and the level of concepts, respectively. Since these are combined arbitrarily, there have to be two separate patterns in the linguistic system. One pattern does not control the other when pairings are arbitrary.

Signifier patterns are contrasts between phonemes, and signified patterns are contrasts between word meanings. The difference between /b/ and /p/ is an instance of the former, and the differences among *dread, fear,* and *anxiety* are instances of the latter. These separate levels of patterning are predictable from the arbitrariness of linguistic symbols. With nonarbitrary symbols, where the form of the signifier is determined by the content of the signified concept, social regulation of the symbol could be exerted at the conceptual level, and duality of patterning would presumably not occur. (For details about the phonemic patterns of language see Gleason, 1955; for a more theoretical treatment see Chomsky and Halle, 1968).

Synchronic–Diachronic

These terms refer to opposite theoretical viewpoints toward language; whether language is regarded as static or changing. The static synchronic viewpoint was crucial to Saussure for defining the idea of contrast. The synchronic method and the idea of contrast are mutually supporting: each requires the other. Synchronic means that a language system is studied with all its elements regarded as a whole at a single instant—a theoretical fiction, but the foundation of Saussure's (and modern) method. This is the required method because, as Saussure said, in language there are only differences. All that matters for determining the linguistic value of a symbol are the other symbols that contrast with it. Choosing one symbol means excluding others that could have been chosen instead. This exclusion determines linguistic value.

The value of the English word *sheep,* for instance, is necessarily different from the value of the French word *mouton. Mouton* translates as *sheep,* but because English *sheep* has a contrast (the word *mutton*) that French *mouton* does not have, choosing the English word *sheep* means excluding *mutton;* this produces a linguistic value that is different from the value of the French word. Clearly a synchronic view of English is necessary to define the value of *sheep* and *mutton,* for it takes a synchronic view for these words to be seen in contrast in the semantic field of sheep-related things.

This kind of search for contrasts spans the entire language, making a synchronic view of the language system as a whole an essential methodological axiom (Greeno, 1981). By the same token, it is only because of exclusion that there is the necessity of a synchronic view of language in which excluded elements are seen in the analysis. Contrast and synchrony are mutually supporting axioms.

The diachronic viewpoint looks for change rather than choice. In its original use the word *diachronic* referred to historical change of language—the study of earlier states and the laws that governed how they changed. In general, diachronic can be used to describe any view of language that produces a temporal, dynamic interpretation. However, diachronic leaves out the idea of exclusion. Later in the book diachrony will be used to refer to much shorter intervals of time.

Saussure was emphatic about the need to separate sharply the synchronic and diachronic viewpoints. The processes of historical change, in their very nature, have altered synchronic contrasts. Each historical change is an isolated event that is initiated outside the system of language and erodes some contrast inside it. Saussure gave this example among many others: the French word for enemy, *ennemi,* is from Latin, where it was *inimicus,* literally "nonfriend." Through historical change the internal structure of the word eroded and became an indivisible whole. Thus it lost its contrast with the French word for friend, which changed along a different path and became *ami,* although in Latin it was *amicus.* (Compare *amicus-inimicus* to *ami-ennemi* to see the loss of contrast.) Thus, to study the contrasts of form that in the Saussurian and modern paradigms are the entire basis for studying linguistic systems, diachronic change had to be frozen: this was to adopt the synchronic viewpoint. Between the synchronic and diachronic viewpoints Saussure accordingly saw an opposition as profound as any in language.

However, we will have to blur this distinction. The key to the synthesis of linguistic and psychological value will lie in merging the synchronic and diachronic viewpoints. This is an argument I will give at the end of the chapter.

Syntagmatic–Paradigmatic

These terms denote the two main axes of contrast in which all linguistic elements participate. Saussure used the term *associative* for the paradigmatic axis. Elements that contrast define each other reciprocally: contrast implies resemblance. A mosquito and a syllogism differ but do not contrast because they cannot define each other reciprocally. *Dread* and *fear* do contrast, and the meaning that goes to one is taken from the other; if the word *dread* ceased to exist, its content (in part) would go to *fear.* The goal of synchronic analysis is to discover the contrasting elements of language—that is, the differences between elements reciprocally related to each other within a context of resemblance—and this is done on two axes at once. Because of the mutual support between the concept of contrast and the synchronic method, the entire Saussurian (and modern) method can be called the synchronic–contrastive conception of language.

An example of paradigmatic contrast is the relationship among the words *dread, fear,* and *anxiety.* What these words have in common is the semantic field of reactions to nasty situations and they divide between them the content of this field. On the phonemic level there is also paradigmatic contrast between /b/ and /p/. What they have in common is the manner of production: closure of the lips. The "paradigm" of a given paradigmatic contrast consists of two points: (1) the field in which the elements are similar, and (2) the manner in which the elements are differentiated. *Dread, fear,* and *anxiety* are similar in that each expresses a reaction to a nasty situation. The three words differ in that each conveys a different part of the content of this field. The phonemes /p/ and /b/ are similar in that they belong to a paradigm of bilabial-stop consonants. They differ in the manner of production, the first being voiceless and the second voiced. A duality of similarity and differentiation is found throughout language. Paradigms are organized sets of alternatives. Paradigmatically contrasting elements on any level are *choices;* to pick one means rejecting others. Thus paradigmatic values are based on exclusion.

An example of a syntagmatic contrast are the words *red* and *apple* in the noun phrase (NP) *the red apple.* What these words have in common is their membership in the same NP, which they jointly create. The reciprocal definition of value in the syntagmatic case is collaborative: *red* defines *apple* as the head, or main element, of the NP and *apple* defines *red* as the modifier, or secondary element. In other syntagmatic contexts these words could have other values. *Apple* is the modifier in *apple pie,* for instance (which is a kind of pie, not a kind of apple). The "syntagm" of a syntagmatic contrast is the higher linguistic object that includes the contrasting elements. A syntagm is an organized basis of combining elements. Syntagmatically contrasting words are *constituents,* and to pick one implies picking the other. Syntagmatic values are based on combinations.

Thus a paradigm is a basis for choosing, and a syntagm is a basis for combining. Accordingly, paradigmatic value is a function of what is excluded and syntagmatic value is a function of what is included.

Saussure put the difference between paradigmatic and syntagmatic contrasts in this way:

1. Paradigmatic contrasts imply one another but do not coexist in the same construction. For example, *dread, fear,* and *anxiety* imply one another whether or not they appear in the same context.
2. Syntagmatic contrasts imply a higher linguistic object and must coexist in the same construction. For example, *red* + *apple* imply an NP only when they appear in the same syntagmatic context.

The syntagmatic axis exists because of a fundamental property of langue—its unidimensionality. Meanings can be complex and multidimensional. Our idea of a certain kind of fruit is complex in the sense that it includes at least the dimension of fruitiness and the dimension of color (actually more dimensions than this are included). When we see the fruit, all the dimensions combine into a single mental event. In langue, however, only one dimension of variation is available, and the meaning, although grasped as a whole, has to be broken down into a succession of changes in time. We have to divide the meaning into segments and arrange these segments in order along the syntagmatic axis; thus we get *red apple*. This concept of dividing meaning-wholes into segments and arranging them in order is fundamental and plays a crucial role in the production of linguistic value.

The familiar phrase-structure tree of linguistic description is a summary of the syntagmatic values created by the process of segmentation and linear combination on the syntagmatic axis. *Red apple,* for example, looks like this:

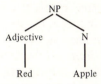

This diagram has a straightforward interpretation in terms of syntagmatic contrasts. Each element has a syntagmatic value that arises from how it combines with the other element. The diagram shows the contrasting words on the same level, while the higher NP that they jointly create is on a higher level and is connected to the objects that contrast within it. A phrase-structure tree thus diagrams the syntagmatic values of linguistic objects. A quite different method must be used to diagram paradigmatic values. (The far-reaching effects of this different form of diagraming will be shown in Chapter 2.)

Pure Linguistic Value–Intrinsic Value

These terms refer to different sources of value. The puzzle of synthesizing the linguistic and psychological approaches can be reformulated as how to synthesize pure linguistic and intrinsic values. Pure value comes only from contrasts (both paradigmatic and syntagmatic). Intrinsic value arises when symbols have a "natural basis." Pure linguistic value is pure in the sense that it arises only from the system of language. In langue there are no values that come from symbols themselves: all value is due to contrasts (as already argued).

Intrinsic values are nonarbitrary. They exist whether or not there is a community of speakers to support them. Although concepts can affect the form of some signifiers, this source of intrinsic value is intermittent. (For example, words denoting small objects are often "diminished," so *tiny* is small but *teeny* is very small—a phenomenon known as phonetic symbolism—see Sapir, 1929 and discussion in Chapter 6). A much more important and constant source of intrinsic value for linguistic symbols is the mental processes of speakers when they generate or interpret the symbols. These mental processes have a determining influence on signifier form. Consider a proud owner's declaration: *It's a Porsche.* This sentence is the nexus of various pure *linguistic* values: paradigmatic in the choices of lexical items (*it* which excludes *that, Porsche* rather than *Chevy,* etc.), and syntagmatic in the combinations of these items into larger constituents (*a Porsche* contrasts syntagmatically with *is,* and with *is* it jointly creates a predicate phrase; the predicate phrase contrasts with *it* and jointly *it* and *is a Porsche* create the sentence).

However, this sentence is also the embodiment of intrinsic values; that is, values that belong to this sentence itself at the time it was said, and are not derived from the linguistic system. The source of intrinsic values is the speaker's process of thinking. Intrinsic values imply that sentences are part of thinking itself. The speaker is thinking of the car as an object and is presenting it for admiration. This idea appears in the sentence, not from the system of langue, but from the speaker's own mental operations. If such value is part of the sentence, there would be in this sentence intrinsic value—value arising from the thought itself.

How does intrinsic value influence the signifier form of the sentence? The external or surface form of the example sentence is motivated by the idea of presenting an object; *it* denotes the object that is being presented, and *is a Porche* comments on this presented object. The sentence *structure,* a signifier property at the grammatical level, parallels this act structure. Its overall grammatical form is a nonarbitrary signifier of the act of presenting an object. A gesture that confirms this act-structure is, for example, holding up the hands as if supporting an object while saying what the object is. Such a gesture would exhibit an image that has the same intrinsic value the sentence is supposed to have. Gestures like this that accompany speech are a major source of data about the intrinsic values of linguistic symbols. Intrinsic values are an object of study in the psychological approach to language.

THE PSYCHOLOGY OF LANGUAGE APPROACH

In this section of the chapter I will explain the properties listed earlier under individually constituted values. This approach also has its origin in the writings of a great thinker of the past. Vygotsky (1962, 1978, 1985), working in the 1930s, discovered the basic insights of the psychological concept of language that I will now present.

A fundamental point for Vygotsky was the necessity of adopting a developmental viewpoint. This is a style of explanation in which a given fact is explained by showing how it arises out of earlier facts. Thus, to Vygotsky, unlike Saussure, explanation was to be diachronic. For example, the use of pictures to aid a child's memory of words (Vygotsky, 1978) is not completely explained merely by describing the associative process between the word and its picture (where W is associated with P, and P in turn helps to recover W):

This ignores the history of the ability in the child to utilize mediation that arises out of an earlier stage in which there was not mediation (where W is associated with P, but P leads to fresh associations that may never get back to W):

The first and second diagrams, taken independently, are all that a synchronic description of the child's memory performance could formulate, but a diachronic (developmental) description can relate these and can show how the first emerges out of the second. Such a developmental perspective was necessary to Vygotsky, since to him the goal was to understand processes, not objects, and change, not static states.

Another example of the developmental method is Vygotsky's (1962) discovery of "pseudo-concepts" as a bridge from developmentally primitive forms of categorization to adult levels of categorization. Pseudo-concepts are words that produce systematic reference classes but have the wrong conceptual content. Pseudo-concepts were demonstrated with artificial concepts, utilizing variously shaped colored blocks (known as "Vygotsky blocks"). A child or an adult would try to learn what a *mur* (a new word) was. The adult would try various combinations of blocks—all the red blocks, or all the triangular ones, or some other combination. When a mistake was made (this information was gained when a block was turned over, revealing what name was written on the bottom), the adult would question and remove all the blocks that had the property excluded by the discovery of the error. If the adult thought *mur* meant "red block," for example, and turned over a red block but didn't find *mur,* he or she would realize that red was not the concept and would question all the red blocks. In contrast, the child would remove the *single offending block,* but would not question or remove any other red block. In terms of the objects of the world to which they apply, pseudo-concepts may be indistinguishable from true concepts but differ crucially in the mental operations they imply. A purely synchronic approach could probably identify pseudo-concepts but could not relate them as a bridge from primitive thinking to advanced forms of thinking. Synchronically, pseudo-concepts would appear to be an isolated oddity, not an essential stage of development. The correct interpretation of pseudo-concepts presupposes a diachronic axis.

The intrinsic value of a linguistic symbol depends on what the speaker puts into it. Vygotsky's example of pseudo-concepts is appropriate. When pseudo-concepts lurk behind real words, the words may have the same references in the world for children as for adults and can be members of the same paradigmatic cast of characters. The words thus can have the same linguistic values. But since the mental operations are different, their intrinsic values must be entirely different. The question is how to relate intrinsic and linguistic value.

Diachronic Change

Development entails change, and change implies a temporal axis. The absolute amount of time is not a criterion and varies depending on the process being described. The historical shifts that Saussure was describing have one time scale, and the development of mnemonic devices or concepts in the lifespan of a child that Vygotsky described have quite a different time scale. Other developmental processes are over in a second or less. The production and understanding of sentences fall into this category. Yet on all of these vastly different time scales a diachronic perspective is required in order to describe change and process.

The diachronic axis divides into zones. Each zone includes its own phenomena, may require different explanatory principles, and sorts itself into its own scholarly specialty. In each zone, nonetheless, there is a diachronic perspective.

I	II	III	IV
Speech production and understanding	Language acquisition	Historical change	Bioprogram
0–10 seconds	c. 6 years	c. 1000 years	c. 2 million years

Over this vast span of time the principles and phenomena are quite different. Saussure's sharp division between diachronic and synchronic referred to zone III. He argued that the processes of change on this scale disturbed and muddied the synchronic system of langue. (For the "bioprogram," see Bickerton, 1981.)

In this book we are focusing specifically on zone I. The diachronic scale in this zone covers what is called *microgenesis* (Werner and Kaplan, 1963); that is, changes of state or form during a *single mental operation.* Here on the microgenetic level we will find that the synchronic and diachronic perspectives can be combined, that choosing the diachronic point of view does not exclude taking the synchronic view. The principle is very different from zone III. On the 0–10 seconds time scale there are alternative diachronic paths. The concepts of choice and change combine, for each new choice sets the process of change going along a new path. Rather than changes eroding synchronic contrasts in zone I, synchronic choices guide changes. Each choice (= a synchronic concept) produces a change (= a diachronic one). For example, the verb *is* set the microgenetic evolution of the sentence *(It's a Porsche)* along a path in which the act of presenting an object had to fit into the formula of equating things. *Is* is a verb of equation. Had the speaker made a different verb selection, the microgenesis of the sentence would have been along a different path, even though the intrinsic value (the act of presenting something) is the same. For example, *cost* could lead to *this cost a bundle* or some other sentence that unpacks the same initial idea of presenting the car for admiring view. By choosing *is,* then, the speaker excluded *costs,* and excluded the series of changes (the diachronic path) that the other verb would have produced. (See Chapter 5 for a discussion of "smart" words, particularly verbs, that are self-activating during thinking, and can be the nucleus of the internal development of sentences.)

The diachronic axis in zone I is not the time it takes to *speak* the sentence; *this* time is connected to pure syntagmatic value and is "surface time." The diachronic axis is the time of development during which mental processes are operating and changing; it is "deep time." The psychology of language approach applies, in particular, to deep time, the emergence in the developing sentence of individually constituted intrinsic values. However, out of this phase comes the final form of the sentence when there is a full complement of linguistic values and the sentence becomes a member in good standing of the socially constituted system of langue. Between these two ends of the diachronic axis the mental processes of the speaker undergo constant change. To describe this evolution is to describe the sentence internally. At every stage there is the same sentence, but a sentence developing.

Zone II of language acquisition is often included in psycholinguistics discussions, but differs from zone I in that there is change of synchronic systems during language growth. There is also only a single developmental path. The child, as he or she grows, is not constantly excluding alternatives but is following a single path by moving from one form of linguistic organization to another. In terms of the phenomena, therefore, zone II may have more in common with zone III than with zone I (Slobin, 1977).

Historical linguists working on changes in zone III (rather arbitrarily set at 1000 years) often call the events in zone I "synchronic." This term is completely misleading, although its use is understandable, given the great distance of these observers from the 1–10 seconds range of zone I. In fact, in all zones the approach is diachronic.

It is easy to observe the diachronic axis in zones II–IV, but there has always been a difficult problem with zone I, particularly for speech production. External speech output is easily observed, but where does the internal development of a sentence begin in deep time? There is no baseline to which the diachronic processes can be linked.

However, expanding the observational net to include *gesture data* makes external this internal development of linguistic symbols. In this book we will often use such data as an observational tool for uncovering the intrinsic values of symbols. Arguments are provided in a later section for regarding gesture, along with speech itself, as part of a single linguistic act.

Contextualization

Another point in connection with the psychological approach to language phenomena is the importance of context. The pure linguistic values of sentences necessarily are unchanged in different contexts. They are context-*in* sensitive. The necessity of this arrangement follows from the concept of linguistic value: value depends only on contrasts with other linguistic forms, and changing the context of one form does not change the other forms with which it contrasts.

Intrinsic value, however, is highly sensitive to context. We cannot infer this value without knowing the context of speaking. The intrinsic value of a sentence changes with context because of the developmental axis, which creates the potential for change. Intrinsic value also changes with context because it is individually constituted, and therefore alterable by the speaker under the influence of various perceptions and memories. *It's a Porsche* has the intrinsic value of an act of presenting an object in one context, but need not have this value in other contexts. (Because of the crucial importance of context for intrinsic value, two chapters are devoted to this topic—Chapters 3 and 4.)

Context also affects linguistic choices, but does so in a different way. Rather than context changing the value of the same linguistic structures, the syntactic structures themselves change. The following examples are based on Chomsky (1977, p. 53):

I mentioned that Sam died last night.

Last night, I mentioned that Sam died.

The syntagmatic contrasts are different in these sentences. In the first example, *last night* contrasts with *died,* whereas the shift of this phrase to the front of the sentence in example two brings *last night* into contrast with *mentioned.* Example one would be selected in a context where the time reference was Sam's dying, and the second example where the time reference was the speaker making the statement. These are changes in syntactic structure induced by changes in context.

In contrast, intrinsic value can change without changing the syntactic structure. For instance, the first example above can have, rather than Sam's dying, the statement itself as the time reference if there is gesture and intonational emphasis making it clear that the speaker is performing the act of presenting something. This can be demonstrated as follows (the brackets show the temporal extent of the gesture):

I *men*tioned that Sam died last night.
|_____|
(both hands reaching out as if presenting an object)

With this gesture and emphasis, the time reference can be altered to the moment of speaking (readers should try this for themselves).

USE OF GESTURE DATA TO INFER INTRINSIC VALUE

The linguistic analysis of a symbol gives us its pure linguistic value. Combining this form of observation with gesture data will be a basic methodology in this book. The effect is similar to the results of triangulation on perspective in vision —a new dimension of seeing becomes available.

The example above of a combination of gesture and linguistic data was artificial. An example that was actually observed and recorded on videotape during a narration of a story is the following:

He ignites himself and flies off out the window.
|_____|
(hand moves forward and fingers spread at same time)

The sentence structure embodies pure linguistic values—paradigmatic in the selections of *ignites, flies off,* and so forth, and syntagmatic in the way these are combined to make a higher linguistic object. In particular, the sentence was built around the conjunction *and.* The sentence also embodies intrinsic value in that there was an image of something flying out and expanding or exploding at the same time. This image was divided into two parts—exploding and flying—and apportioned to the two main parts of the sentence: exploding to the first clause *(he ignites himself)* and flying to the second *(and flies off out).* The conjoined structure of the sentence was a nonarbitrary choice given this image. The image produced an intrinsic value for the sentence structure that joined the pure linguistic value of conjunction.

The above example illustrates another important point. We will find that the two kinds of value (as inferred from the two forms of observation) have a *constant relation in time.* The gesture anticipates the corresponding linguistic segment of the sentence. This small interval directly reveals the internal development of the sentence along its diachronic axis. To observe this anticipation note the timing of the gesture with respect to the sentence: the hand movement showed something flying out, but was timed to *end* at the word *flies;* thus it had to begin before this word. In fact, there was an earlier movement that prepared the hand to make the flying out movement, and this earlier movement commenced at the very start of the sentence vocalization. Thus the image of flying out was affecting the speaker's gesture movements from the start, even though the linguistic segmentation of this image did not occur until (comparatively) much later.

ARGUMENTS IN SUPPORT OF GESTURE DATA

Chapter 7 gives a complete description of gesture production. In this section I will give arguments and examples to justify the use of gesture data for inferring the intrinsic values generated during speech acts. The basic conception that underlies these arguments is stated by Kendon (1980*d*) in the following manner:

> The "ideas" being expressed in speech are also encoded in the movement patterns being produced. It will be clear that the manner of encoding is, in each case, quite different. In gesticulation we see patterns of movement that are enactive or depictive of the ideas being expressed, yet such expressions are concurrent with, indeed they often somewhat precede, verbal expression. This suggests that the formulation of ideas, a form of action which is iconic or analogic to those ideas, is as fundamental a process as the formulation of ideas in verbal form (p. 209).

Movements of the hands and arms, called *gestures* or gesticulations, characteristically accompany acts of speaking. These can be interpreted as exhibiting imagery. The occurrence of gestures lets us observe a speakers' thinking in a form that is related to yet different from the speaker's linguistic expression. Arguments that justify using gestures for inferring intrinsic values are: (1) gestures are nonarbitrary with a natural basis in thinking; (2) gestures are noncompositional; and yet (3) gestures are part of the diachronic development of the spoken sentence out of thinking.

Gestures Are Nonarbitrary

The igniting-and-flying-out gesture discussed above is an example of what McNeill and Levy (1982) called an *iconic* gesture. It is iconic in that it exhibited in its form and manner of execution a meaning that was relevant to the concurrent sentence meaning. The gesture is a symbol like linguistic symbols in the capacity to carry meaning. In the example given, the hand did not represent itself, but represented a character from a comic-book story. The hand and its motion is the external aspect of a gesture-symbol—a signifier. The memory trace of the character and his explosive method of locomotion is the internal aspect—the signified concept.

In iconic gestures the hands are nonarbitrary symbols: shape and movement are determined by the meanings the hands convey. In the example, the hand moved forward and upward because of the meaning of upward and outward motion implicit in the concept of "flying out." The fingers spread outward at the same time because of the meaning of exploding in flames, à la a rocket, that is implicit in the concept of "ignites himself." In the terminology that Saussure introduced, the signifier form of gesture-symbols has a "natural basis" in the speaker's imagistic thinking. This is one indication that gestures, specifically iconic gestures, exhibit intrinsic values: values in the case of iconic gesture do not depend on contrasts with other gestures. The values of iconic gestures depend on contrasts of meaning, not on contrasts of gestures themselves (in fact, it is not clear how to apply the idea of contrast to gestures).

That iconic gestures are nonarbitrary can be seen in the manner in which gestures vary. The variations are clearly the products of meaning distinctions. For example, when the speaker is describing scenes that include downward movement, gestures tend to move downward, not horizontally or upward. On the other hand, if a scene includes horizontal movement, gestures tend to move horizontally, not downward (these correlations were studied systematically by McNeill and Levy; see Chapter 7 for details). Correlations of meanings and movement indicate that signifier form changes in iconic gestures as a function of signified content—and this is the hallmark of a nonarbitrary symbol.

A different type of gesture symbol, called "metaphoric," is similar to the iconic type. These gestures seem to be nonarbitrary signifiers of abstract concepts. Whereas the iconic gestures studied by McNeill and Levy had the speaker's memory image of a concrete event as their signified content, metaphoric gestures have for their signified content an intrinsically unpicturable concept. Yet metaphoric gestures exhibit an image: the image the speaker regards as similar to the concept. When there is a concept that motivates an image, and this image is exhibited in a gesture, we can also speak of a nonarbitrary symbol whose natural basis is imagistic thinking of the speaker entertaining this concept. Examples of metaphoric gestures are given in Chapter 7. The following is one of them:

It was a Sylvester and Tweetie cartoon.
|_____|

(hands appear to be supporting an object the size and shape of a watermelon)

The gesture, like the one for *It's a Porsche,* presents an object. However, this gesture presents the object as a metaphor of the concept of a cartoon. In the "conduit" metaphor (Reddy, 1979; see Chapter 5 for discussion of the topic of metaphor), abstract concepts such as works of art, language, knowledge, and so forth, are presented as if they are concrete objects. For example, we say *a heavy book,* referring not to physical weight but to conceptual weight. So it was in this example for the concept of a cartoon: the idea of a cartoon was presented as an object, and this object-image determined the form of the gesture. We can infer that the speaker was thinking in terms of some kind of object while referring to the concept of a cartoon, and the gesture was a signifier of this conceptual content.

If gesture data are utilized as evidence of intrinsic value, we can see how sentence structures are the result of synthesizing intrinsic values with linguistic values. In the case of the previous iconic-gesture example, the intrinsic value of the gesture was the image of the character exploding in flames and shooting off, up, and away. The synthesis of this intrinsic value with linguistic value is not hard to see: for each part of the image (exploding and flying), there was a separate clause (centered around the verbs *ignites, flies out*). To explain the occurrence of this sentence, we have to refer to both forms of value. In the metaphoric example, the intrinsic value of the gesture was the image of a concrete object that the speaker was holding up and presenting to the hearer. There was a synthesis of linguistic values with this intrinsic value in the selection of the sentence form *(it was something),* which was a nonarbitrary choice for the act of presenting an object (the *it*) and commenting on it. Again, to explain the sentence in all its aspects we must refer to both intrinsic and pure linguistic values.

Gestures Are Noncompositional

A complex word such as *unreadable* is composed of parts *(un-read-able).* Sentences are even more obviously composed out of parts. Each part of the word or sentence has its own status as a symbol and the whole is a compositional sum of these separate symbols. *Un-* means negation, *read* means read, *-able* means having the capacity; the meaning of *unreadable* is the combination of these separate meanings. The relationship of the parts to the whole is the reverse in a gesture. We can understand the meaning of each part only after we have determined the meaning of the whole. In the flying-out gesture, we know that the hand stands for a person (and not a plane), and that the spreading fingers stand for flames (and not an open mouth), only because we understand the meaning of the gesture as a whole—that it depicts a person who is exploding in flames and flying out.

Gestures are noncompositional because they are nonarbitrary. They do not require the support of a socially constituted system. Gestures are nonarbitrary because they are patterned directly after images. Noncompositional means gestures differ as wholes. Nonarbitrariness and noncompositionality mutually produce symbols with a "natural basis" whose value depends on global meaning contrasts.

Gestures are *global* in that the symbol depicts meaning as a whole (noncompositionally) and *synthetic* in that the symbol combines into one symbol meanings that in speech are divided into segments. The cartoon gesture illustrates these properties (but any iconic gesture could be substituted as an example). It is global in that it represents a whole, instead of each hand separately representing the idea of a side and then putting the two sides together to create the idea of a container. The gesture is synthetic in that it combines the image of an object with the image of presenting the object. The flying-out gesture shows the synthetic property even more strikingly: it combines in one symbol the body of the character, the process of bursting into flames, and the act and path of flying out (the only thing it omits is the window). This gesture also shows the globality property, though not so strikingly as does the cartoon gesture: the hand represents the character, and we understand this because of the whole gesture, not because the idea of a person is created from parts of the hand representing various parts of the person (e.g., two fingers representing two legs, the palm representing the torso, etc.).

When people use gestures deliberately for communicating meaning—that is, when they focus their attention on gesture as a medium of communication, gestures with global and synthetic properties are spontaneously replaced by gestures with linear and segmented properties. This proves that the global and synthetic properties are properties of the imagistic thinking behind gestures, not properties of gestures themselves. R. Bloom (1979) had subjects narrate fairy tales by utilizing only gestures. The narrator was free to utilize gestures as needed, but was prohibited from speaking. Compositional gestures that occurred under these circumstances were quite different from the global and synthetic gestures that appear unwittingly during speech. For example, a gesture for "king" was made in two steps—first the hand circled the head, indicating a crown, then the arms moved, as if showing muscles. Making two gestures for one concept constitutes a difference from speech-concurrent gestures. The gesture for "queen" was also made in two steps—the first gesture was the same circling of the head for the crown, the second gesture indicated another distinctive anatomical feature (breasts). These gestures were clearly compositional.

Thus speech-concurrent gestures show something different from speech. They are copresent with speech but convey meaning in a fundamentally different form—global and synthetic rather than linear and segmented. The meanings conveyed in the gesture and linguistic channels are related but are revealed in different manners. The difference is summed up with the two expressions intrinsic versus linguistic value. The intrinsic value of a sentence is shown in the gesture in a global-synthetic manner, and the pure linguistic value of a sentence in the choices of syntax and words in a linear-segmented manner. *It was a Sylvester and Tweetie cartoon* presents the same meaning as the gesture, but in the sentence this meaning is broken into segments and arranged in linear order according to grammatical rules. In the gesture it is presented as a global whole with all aspects combined into one image. Thus the gesture is a source of data that can be compared to the sentence structure, as our methodology requires.

Gestures Are Part of the Sentence

The copresence and shared meanings of gesture and speech have a deep source: the words and their order, and the gesture arise from two stages of a single process. One thinks of sentences in terms of what can be easily written down; anything that cannot be written down we tend to regard as not part of the sentence. However, this is really just a historical accident of the way writing developed, and tells us nothing about the true psychological composition of sentences. Several subarguments can be given for including gestures together with words and syntagmatic order as part of sentences, but the most important are that gestures and sentences are synchronized and that gestures take over linguistic complexity from speech when the speech channel is blocked.

Gestures and Sentences Are Synchronized   Gestures and sentences often coincide exactly, such as in this example:

and he bends it way back
L_____J

(hand appears to pull back object)

Other gestures, even if they do not extend through the full length of a sentence (e.g., the flying-out gesture), still synchronize in that: (1) There is not more than one iconic gesture per clause (a *clause* is one subject-predicate combination—a *sentence* is one or more clauses; see Chapter 2). (2) Gestures do not extend past a clause boundary; if two gestures are made in succession that have the same external form, there will be an indication of the boundary in the gesture movement itself.

The following excerpt demonstrates the one-gesture-per-clause rule:

and he goes up through the pipe this time
            L_____J

            (hand rises quickly and fingers open)

The iconic gesture depicting the character rising up coincides with just part of the clause; there was room for more gestures, but none were made. That is, the speaker did *not* do this:

and he	goes	up	through the pipe this time.
L____J	L__J	L_J	L_____J
(shows	(shows	(points	(hand rises and fingers open)
figure)	motion)	up)	

A second gesture did not occur because the sentence expressed the same image that the existing gesture displayed. A second gesture would have taken place only if there had been a second image. The one-gesture-per-clause rule therefore implies that each linguistically constructed sentence corresponds to just one image.

Consider the following three clauses:

and as he's coming down and the bowling ball's coming down
L_____J

(left hand drops—representing the bowling ball—while the right hand rises—representing the character)

he swallows it
L_____J

(left hand drops—again representing the bowling ball—while right hand rises and surrounds left hand, now representing the character's mouth)

There are three clauses here; the meaning of the right hand gesture in the first two clauses differs from its meaning in the third. The right hand is the entire character in the first two clauses; it is the character's mouth in the third clause. The gestural movement nonetheless is the same throughout. However, a small extra movement occurs at the boundary between the second and third clauses. This movement indicates the moment at which the gesturing hand changes meaning and the speaker is shifting from one image to the next:

and as he's coming down

and the bowling ball's coming down he swallows it

(both hands loop out and back)

Extra movements like these maintain the one-gesture-per-clause rule and are also explained by the hypothesis that each clause expresses just one image.

The synchronization of gestures with speech means speech and gesture occupy the same psychological moment. They can therefore be part of the same mental operation.

Gestures Take Over Complexity   That gestures and grammatical sentence structure compensate for one another is the second point in support of the idea that gestures are parts of sentences. Such compensation is quite frequent. It implies that speech and gesture share a computational stage during which semantic information may be shifted to appear in gesture form. In the following, the speaker transfers information to the gesture channel that would have required an additional relative clause in an already complicated sentence:

And he seeks to protect her

by hiding the glove and not telling any of the other
|_____|

(appears to remove glove from other hand and place it in pocket, then both hands return to lap)

detectives about this

The gesture showed the process of hiding the glove and was synchronized with just the part of the sentence describing this act. If there had not been the gesture, there would have been a relative clause embedded in the sentence at this point. For example:

And he seeks to protect her by hiding the glove *which he took from his hand and placed in his pocket* and not telling any of the other detectives about this

The extra burden of complexity was avoided by placing information in a gestural image. The gesture occurred just where it would relieve this burden. That such compensations are observed is an argument for regarding the gesture and sentence as having developed in the same process.

Another illustration of the compensation of speech by gesture is the behavior of subjects under delayed auditory feedback (DAF)—the procedure of playing back the sound of the speaker's own voice after a short delay (McNeill, 1985c). The effect of DAF is disturbance of speech to a high degree. Speakers make up for this disturbance by increasing the production of gestures and shifting semantic information from speech to gesture; the new gestures coincide exactly with those sentences with which DAF most interferes (see Chapter 7 for details).

The arguments presented here—that gestures and speech are synchronized, that gestures are noncompositional, and that gestures take over complexity from speech—indicate that gestures and speech develop together in deep time, and that we can rely on gesture production to provide data about the intrinsic values of the linguistic constructions they accompany.

chapter *2*

Linguistics of Language

The purpose of this chapter is to present modern linguistics in terms of Saussure's conception of langue as a synchronic–contrastive network of symbols, and show how this conception can be extended to complex structures—in particular, to phrases and sentences. These structures, both simple and complex, are used to "unpack" the speaker's global and synthetic images. It is this analysis that we need from linguistics in order to understand the synthesis of the socially constituted knowledge of langue with individually constituted thinking and context. Although what is written will be comprehensible to the reader on its own terms, the purpose of this chapter is not to provide even a partial summary of modern linguistics, which would be quite impossible. For introductory coverage of the generative grammar school (the school represented in this chapter), see Radford (1981).

In this book I am following a principle stated by Chomsky (e.g., 1968) termed the "weak competence hypothesis." This principle states that a grammar defines a function that is computed by speakers and hearers, but that the function stands in no simple relation to the mental operations of speakers/hearers. Functions defined grammatically are selected by individuals to "unpack" global–synthetic imagistic thinking. This process of unpacking is not what the grammar explains under the weak competence hypothesis. The weak competence hypothesis is contrasted with the strong competence hypothesis (Bresnan, 1978), which requires operations of the mental processor to correspond directly to the rules of the grammar. At the end of this chapter I will consider "realistic" grammars that try to meet the strong competence hypothesis.

The chapter is organized along the following lines. First, sentences and phrases are treated as symbols—complex and structured ones—which will be explained. Second, the principle of duality of patterning implies separate levels of structure of signifiers and signifieds, and how this works will also be explained. Third, a change in the relative emphasis placed on paradigmatic values compared to syntagmatic values is taking place, and this change and its implications for the concept of a linear and segmented linguistic symbol will be explained. Fourth, various constraints on grammatical contrasts are examined. The last section of the chapter discusses nontransformational grammars, including "realistic" grammars.

PHRASES AND SENTENCES AS COMPLEX SYMBOLS

Phrases and sentences have been treated as if they were symbols in Saussure's sense. Each sentence (and phrase—this should be assumed from here on) has a signifier and a signified half. To show that sentences are symbols, it is necessary to show that they are analyzed as having two major components—one a meaningless syntactic structure that corresponds to the signifier and the other a meaningful semantic structure that corresponds to the signified—and that these components, while inseparable from each other, are distinct. Moreover, it is necessary to show that the relation between the components is signification and that the connection between them is arbitrary.

In the outline of a transformational generative grammar (TGG) given in Chomsky (1977) and elsewhere, there is a basic division between a syntactic component that produces base structures and surface structures of sentences, and a semantic component that produces semantic representations utilizing semantic rules. This twofold character of sentences reflects an approach to sentence structure that is basically symbolic. Interpretive semantic rules apply to syntactic forms to produce semantic structures. The semantic rules are called interpretive because, in this type of grammar, they have no independent capacity to generate linguistic structures. Semantic rules are little understood, but their status as interpretive rules fits into the symbol schema quite neatly. For any given sentence the analysis in this style divides the structure into two parts corresponding to the original Saussurian division between signifier and signified, with the new insight (specific to complex symbols) that the *signifier* is the locus of generative capacity. The source of the "infinite productivity" of new yet ever comprehensible sentences is the formation of new signifiers.

The following example will be used to demonstrate these points:

Bill knows how to multiply.

(The absurd ambiguity of this sentence will be used later to make an observation.) The surface syntactic structure of this sentence (i.e., its signifier structure) is represented by the tree diagram shown in Figure 2.1.

The symbols in Figure 2.1 are generally obvious mnemonics: S means sentence, NP means noun phrase, VP means verb phrase, COMP means sentence complement, V means verb, Ø means a constituent of the sentence that is inferra-

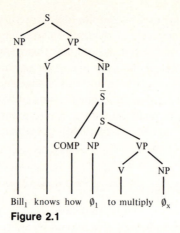

Figure 2.1

ble at this point but is not realized at the surface, and subscripts indicate coreferentiality; constituents indexed with the same number refer to the same thing. The S with a bar over it will be explained later.

This structure is produced by rules that operate exclusively on uninterpreted, semantically empty syntactic categories and arrangements. Three major rules, for example, are written as follows:

$$S\text{-----}\!\!\twoheadrightarrow \quad NP\ VP$$
$$VP\text{----}\!\!\twoheadrightarrow \quad V\ NP$$
$$NP\text{----}\!\!\twoheadrightarrow \quad \begin{bmatrix} N \\ S \end{bmatrix}$$

The final rule has two optional "expansions," one N (as in *Bill, numbers,* etc.) and the other S. The latter choice means that the first rule can apply again, as was done in the generation of *Bill knows how to multiply.* These rules and the tree diagram they produce show, via the node labels S, NP, VP, and so forth, the creation of syntagmatic values. These values are aspects of the signifier.

What is signified is difficult to specify, but about the signified meaning of grammatical structures we usually have definite intuitions. For instance, we understand intuitively that the *how to multiply* clause of this sentence is semantically the object of the first clause (a clause can now be defined as a section of the sentence dominated by an S node). The second clause S is shown descending from an NP in the first clause. NPs that contrast syntagmatically with Vs are the semantic objects of the Vs, and this applies to NPs that are internally Ss as well.

This is an intuition at the syntagmatic level; it is not an interpretation of any of the specific words. The same object relationship occurs with other complex symbols constructed according to the same plan—*Bill remembers how to multiply, Bill demonstrates how to multiply,* and so forth—the entire second clause being the semantic object of the verb of the first clause in each case; this arrangement attaches to the signifier as such, as a signified concept of the syntactic structure.

We will say therefore that sentences act as symbols. Sentences, like words, divide into signifier and signified parts. However, in contrast to words, sentences are complex constructed symbols. Whereas word-signifiers change only slowly and have, at any given time, a fixed form, sentence-signifiers are changeable from speech act to speech act. Nonetheless, the same principles of contrast apply to sentences as to words.

The use of interpretive semantic rules in the analysis of sentence structures implies an "autonomous syntax"—a syntactic component of the sentence that is autonomous with respect to the meaning of the sentence. This concept depends on the Saussurian concept of an arbitrary pairing of signifiers with signifieds. A theory of the organization of signified meaning is given by Montague (1974). In what is called "Montague grammar," each syntactic node of a sentence is linked with a constant specific semantic effect. (A readable summary of Montague's theory is provided by Johnson-Laird, 1983.) Syntactic constituents with the same role in the sentence structure—such as all the NPs—are treated as having the same semantic structure. This structure is expressible in terms of sets. Noun phrases denote sets of sets. The NP *Bill* denotes the set of all sets of which Bill is a member. Similarly, the NP *no man* denotes the set of all sets of which no man is a member. Thus a conundrum is solved about statements with negative quantifiers (*no man is an island,* etc.)—what they denote are the sets of all sets to which the negated entity does not belong. Verbs, on the other hand, denote sets of individuals. A given verb denotes the set of individual objects with the property conveyed by the verb. The meaning of the sentence is then composed by combining the meanings of its constituents. *Bill knows such and such* is true if the set of individuals denoted by *knows such and such* is contained in the set of sets denoted by *Bill.* This would be the case if one of Bill's properties is that he knows the particular thing in question. In the Montague theory a signified semantic structure is generated that parallels the signifier syntactic structure point for point. The complex symbol that results has signifier and signified components that are isomorphic. In Montague grammar the contrasts of a sentence can therefore be specified on the signified side of the sentence.

It is clear that Montague grammar remains a theory of pure linguistic value. Even though the signifier (syntactic form) of the complex symbol is composed out of the logical structure of the signified, and in this sense is not arbitrarily paired with the signified, the complex symbol still does not have intrinsic value. The logical structure of signifieds is, in fact, itself a contrastive structure completely formulated within a synchronic framework. The theory applies only to socially constituted linguistic objects, not to acts of speaking. One indication of this socially constituted character of the objects considered in Montague grammar is the insensitivity of the analysis to context variation. *Bill knows how to multiply* is ambiguous and the analysis captures both meanings equally; there is no process in the theory that automatically excludes the meaning that is inappropriate for the context. *Bill* denotes the set of sets that have Bill in them. *Multiply* denotes a set of individuals and this set includes Bill if the sentence is true. There are of course two senses of *multiply,* the mathematical and the procreative, and whichever set contains Bill will be a member of the set of sets that *Bill* denotes; the sentence *Bill knows how to multiply* is guaranteed to be true under either interpretation. This is just the kind of analysis that is synchronic and contrastive, and that displays pure linguistic value.

TWO LEVELS OF STRUCTURE

The concept of duality of patterning was originally applied to morphemes and phonemes (Hockett, 1958). These were the two levels referred to by "duality," and they correspond exactly, as levels, to the two sides of linguistic symbols, as pointed out in Chapter 1. Words enter into two patterns simultaneously. One of these is the set of phoneme contrasts on the signifier side separating *bottle* from *mottle, battle* from *tattle, goggle* from *bottle,* and so forth. The words that contrast on this level do not necessarily have shared semantic fields, and thus do not necessarily contrast in meaning (though they "differ"). The contrasts are in terms of sound category, or phonemes. The other pattern is the set of contrasts on the signified side separating *bottle* from *flask, cup, pot, barrel,* and so forth, where the words that contrast share semantic but not necessarily phonemic fields.

This same distinction between levels of structure extends to the complex structured symbols of phrases and sentences considered in modern grammars. Here, the patterning of signifiers is the system of syntactic structures, and the patterning of signifieds is the system of sentence interpretations already mentioned.

An example that nicely illustrates this duality of patterning of complex symbols are the differences—syntactic and conceptual—between the following sentences (examples from Chomsky and Lasnik, 1977):

Bill persuaded John to go.

Bill told John what to do.

Syntactically these sentences contrast in the selection of the main verb, *persuaded* or *told,* and in the presence of the COMP word *what* in the *told* sentence. Conceptually the sentences contrast in dividing a semantic field that is something like "controlling the behavior of others through verbal means." The two sentences denote contrasting parts of this field—*persuaded* denoting control via verbal *incitement, told* denoting control through verbal *instruction. Told* also implies a social stratification of speaker and hearer that *persuaded* does not imply.

The syntactic and conceptual contrasts in this example are two levels of patterning that are separate from one another, in congruence with the duality of patterning principle. On the signifier side the choice is between a surface COMP or not, and on the signified side between incitement or instruction. This principle implies that sentences behave as symbols that have a fundamental similarity to words, and that the syntax of sentences is an elaboration of the sound-image side of symbols. This implied continuum from word to sentence will be an important clue for the process of the production of speech, as discussed in Chapter 5 (specifically the concept of "smart" symbols).

That sentences are on a continuum with words implies the existence of other languages in which the generative power of the grammar is moved more toward the word end. There are such languages, termed "polysynthetic." Greenlandic Eskimo is a spectacular example. In this language very long complex words are built up by affixing parts to roots—a familiar morphological process, but one carried to an extreme in Greenlandic. The affixes are functionally equivalent to separate words in English. Darden (1984, p. 2) explains, "Just as there is an almost infinite number of potential English sentences, there is an almost infinite number of potential Greenlandic words. A speaker of Greenlandic cannot possibly know all the words necessary to converse in his language. He must spontaneously form and instantly parse words in the course of a normal conversation." Between English and Greenlandic we see the continuum mentioned—complex symbols that range from words to sentences without losing their essential symbolic character.

TRANSFORMATIONS

Regarded as a symbol, a sentence has linguistic value that can be analyzed into the two classic forms, paradigmatic and syntagmatic. These values arise from the position of the sentence in a network of other sentences. This network is the structure of the language, or langue. Modern grammars have developed very detailed analyses of the contrasts—both syntagmatic and paradigmatic—that create linguistic values for complex symbols. All of the analyses to be described below apply to the syntax of sentence structures; that is, to the signifier half of the symbol.

The basic goal of grammatical analysis includes specifying the syntagmatic structure of sentences. As pointed out earlier, this structure is summarized in the familiar tree diagram (see Fig. 2.1). Each node in the tree given for *Bill knows how to multiply* represents a higher linguistic object built out of lower objects that are in syntagmatic contrast. Since the tree is hierarchical, there are syntagmatic values at all levels. For example, NP and VP contrast syntagmatically and create S as the higher object, V and NP contrast and create VP as the higher object, and so forth.

The same element of the sentence can have one syntagmatic value at one level and a different value at another level. We see this in the *Bill knows how to multiply* example in the double classification of the clause *how to multiply* as NP and S. The S is said to be "embedded" in the NP and also in the higher S, since the NP is part of this higher S. That an S is embedded within another S is called "recursive self-embedding." This is the basic source of infinite productivity of complex symbols: it is always possible to add another S to an existing S.

The next example (Ross, 1967) also illustrates recursive self-embedding; the sentence will be used to demonstrate the concept of a transformation and to explain the related concept of "abstractness." The example comes with two tree diagrams. The first, Figure 2.2, shows the structure of *I believed that Otto was wearing this hat,* and the second, Figure 2.3, shows the structure of *this hat which I believed that Otto was wearing,* a relative clause related to the sentence.

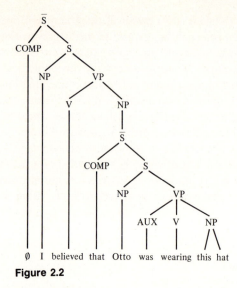

Figure 2.2

The tree structures shown in these two figures are the same except for three contrasts:

1. The topmost node of the "sentence" tree (Fig. 2.2), S̄ (the meaning of the bar is explained below), appears under an NP node in the "relative clause" tree (Fig. 2.3). This arrangement means that the relative clause as a whole can enter into syntagmatic contrasts as an NP, for example, with a VP to form a new S *(this hat which I believed that Otto was wearing is pink).* It contains within it two other constituents—one is another NP *(this hat)* and the other is an S̄ *(I believed that Otto was wearing this Ø).*
2. The NP *this hat* has been moved from its position at the end of the "sentence" tree to the initial position of the "relative clause" tree where it appears with the relative pronoun *which.*

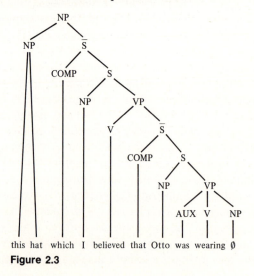

Figure 2.3

3. The position that the NP *this hat* formerly occupied in the "sentence" tree is still there and contrasts with the V *wearing* to form the higher VP; the NP Ø is a real element of the sentence that can combine with other elements to make higher constituents.

Points 1 through 3 state contrasts of the paradigmatic variety for complex symbols. The complex symbol itself is an assembly of syntagmatic contrasts. Thus points 1 through 3 state paradigmatic contrasts of syntagmatic values. The sentence *I believed that Otto was wearing this hat* is on the paradigmatic axis of the relative clause *this hat which I believed that Otto was wearing.* The sentence is one of the implicit contrasts of the relative clause (and vice versa). A rule of transformation summarizes these paradigmatic contrasts of syntagmatic values in the following way, by deriving the relative clause from the sentence. The transformation is the movement of the NP *this hat* leaving everything else the same:

COMP I believed that Otto was wearing [$_{NP}$ this hat]

[$_{NP}$ this hat] COMP I believed that Otto was wearing [$_{NP}$ Ø]

This is called a "movement transformation" because the contrasts summarized in points 1 through 3 are what bodily movement of the NP *this hat* would produce.

The transformation is thus connected to the paradigmatic values of complex symbols. The use of the transformation is that the movement of NP is part of the signifier of the complex symbol (part of the syntax). The "structural description" of the sentence specifies the transformations that relate a given linguistic object to other objects that are regarded as more basic. Sentences are more basic than relative clauses, thus *I believed that Otto . . .* is more basic than *this hat which I believed. . . .* The structural description of the sentence therefore contains both an explicit statement of its syntagmatic values (shown in the labeled nodes of the tree diagram) and an explicit statement of its paradigmatic values (the other tree diagrams to which it relates transformationally). A single sentence consists of a succession of contrasting transformationally derived trees, and each of these trees summarizes syntagmatic values.

Modern grammars have developed this very compact mode of analysis in which all the contrastive values of complex symbols can be expressed. An important insight that has made this compact mode of analysis possible is the role of linguistic abstraction in sentence structure. By the term "linguistic abstraction" we mean the presence of constituents whose existence is inferrable only—cannot be concretely known. These constituents are inferrable through deduction but are not externally visible. An example is constituent $\overline{S}$, above. The existence of $\overline{S}$ is inferrable from the structure of the relative clause. If the movement of [$_{NP}$ *this hat*] is to the front of $\overline{S}$ (rather than unbarred S), there is already a COMP in the sentence in the correct position to become the relative pronoun *which*. This relative pronoun is explained by postulating a node with the syntagmatic value of $\bar{S}$ that is constituted out of COMP and S. The same $\bar{S}$ explains the word *that* in *I believed that Otto . . . ,* which therefore requires no addition to the theory. $\bar{S}$ with COMP in it can be used to produce questions such as *what was Otto wearing?* All of these facts, and others, point to the hidden presence of the abstract element $\bar{S}$.

Other examples of linguistic abstraction are unrealized NPs (the Øs) and all the paradigmatically contrasting sentence structures implied by transformations. All of these are abstract in the sense that they are not observed but are inferred. Abstract linguistic elements are an essential part of the signifiers of complex symbols.

The relative clause *this hat which I believed that Otto was wearing . . .* (is pink) is the signifier of a complex idea that includes, as part of the signified concept, a semantic relation between *wearing* and *hat,* namely that what was being worn was that pink hat. The relative clause signifier, however, does not itself show any relation between *wearing* and *hat.* A consequence of the movement transformation was that the NP *this hat* was removed from the direct object position of *wearing* and placed in front of the COMP position. In order for the correct semantic interpretation to take place, that is, in order to pair the signified concept of wearing the hat with the relative clause signifier from which this exact relation has been deleted, the paradigmatic contrast between the relative clause and the untransformed sentence must be taken into account. This signifier–signified pairing could be retrieved in either of two ways. One relies directly on the paradigmatic contrast—detransform the relative clause and interpret the underlying source sentence. The other relies on a syntagmatic contrast—place a "trace" in the relative clause sentence at the original position of the NP *this hat,* and this trace could indicate the existence of the signifier–signified pair. Traces are the currently favored procedure (whereas earlier, detransformation was; see Chomsky, 1965).

Traces are said to "annotate" surface structures. They appear where, as a result of the movement of a constituent, the constituent appears in the surface structure sentence at a position other than the position where it can be interpreted semantically. Traces are conventionally indicated by *t,* [*e*], and Ø; in the following I will use *t.* Thus the annotated surface structure of the relative clause is:

[$_{NP}$ this hat] which I believed that Otto was wearing [$_{NP}$ t]

The significance of the trace is that the syntagmatic value of NP is still in existence and contrasts with *wearing* at the end of the relative clause. By keeping track of the traces and the constituents with which they link, semantic interpretations of the surface structure sentence can be made. Furthermore, by indexing traces, more than one trace-constituent pair can exist in the same surface sentence. *Bill knows how to multiply* is an illustration of this (writing *t* in place of Ø), and shows that the first trace links to [$_{NP}$ Bill]:

Bill$_1$ knows how t$_1$ to multiply t$_2$

An interesting demonstration of traces in surface sentences is the impossibility of contracting *want* and *to* in *who do you want to see Bill?* (where *Bill* is the direct object of *see*). It is impossible to say *who do you wanna see Bill?* with this meaning (Chomsky and Lasnik, 1977). This is so because there is a trace between *want* and *see* in this sentence that is the result of moving the subject NP of *see* to the COMP position of the sentence (where it becomes *who*):

[$_{NP}$ who] do you want [$_{NP}$ t] to see Bill?

Contraction of *want* and *to* is prevented by the trace, which is in fact an NP between the two words.

In a superficially similar sentence, *who do you wanna see, Bill?*, on the other hand, contraction is possible (the sentence means that Bill will do the seeing). This sentence also is derived by movement of an NP, but this time it is the NP direct object of *see* that is moved. Thus the trace is left after *see* rather than want, and there is nothing standing between *want* and *to* that blocks the contraction:

[$_{NP}$ who] do want to see [$_{NP}$ t]?

By postulating the existence of a trace one can therefore explain the possibility or impossibility of contraction in these cases.

The effect of the trace annotation of surface sentences is to multicode the syntagmatic values of complex symbols. This is done without adding to their paradigmatic values. Thanks to the movement of the NP *this hat,* the annotated surface structure of the relative clause *this hat which I believed that Otto was wearing* codes the same syntagmatic values at two places, one at the head of the clause and again at the end in the original position; but these NPs imply only one paradigmatic contrast—that which includes the full sentence *I believed that Otto. . . .* The annotation of surface structure by traces is an example of a growing emphasis on syntagmatic value in recent grammars. In the early days of the TGG school most of the attention focused on transformations—that is, on the paradigmatic contrasts of syntagmatic structures—and there were many transformations of specific types (e.g., negation, question, passive, etc.; Chomsky, 1957). More recently there has been a tendency to replace specific transformations with a single generalized movement transformation, and then to add other rules to restrict this generalized movement transformation to certain syntagmatic environments. One form of this restriction is the topic of the next section.

CONSTRAINTS

With a single movement transformation there is the theoretical possibility of overgeneration, of moving NPs and Ss to nongrammatical positions. There is accordingly a need for constraints on the formation of paradigmatic contrasts so that only actual members of the language appear in the paradigms of sentences.

These constraints limit the types of sentence structure that a given sentence contrasts with, and thus reduce the size of the set of implied complex symbols from which choices are made.

The "subjacency constraint" will illustrate this process (Chomsky, 1977). It limits the extent of the movement that is produced by a movement transformation. The constituents being moved are Ss or NPs. The subjacency constraint says that an S or NP may be moved either within the same constituent or to the next more encompassing constituent. Two trees cannot contrast if they differ by a movement larger than this. This constraint applies even if the two trees can be associated with the same meaning. The constraint, in other words, applies to the form of the complex signifier, not to the signified concept. For example, the first and second sentences below contrast in a way that fits the subjacency constraint, but the first and third sentences contrast in a way that violates it. The third example is ill-formed—meaning it is structurally not part of the system of langue, although if an interpretation is forced it is the same as in the first and second sentences (examples based on Chomsky, 1977; the asterisk indicates that the sentence is ill-formed).

The only one that I like of Illinois's wines is out of stock.

The only one of Illinois's wines that I like is out of stock.

*The only one of Illinois's wines is out of stock that I like.

Treating the first example as the source, the second example is the result of a movement of [$_S$ *that I like*] across one NP boundary. For example three, however, this constituent has to move across two NP boundaries (for clarity the start and end of each NP and S are indicated):

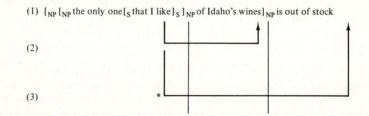

(1) [$_{NP}$ [$_{NP}$ the only one [$_S$ that I like] $_S$] $_{NP}$ of Idaho's wines] $_{NP}$ is out of stock

(2)

(3)   *

This restriction cannot be motivated by the signified side of the complex symbol in example three. The sentence, though weird, is interpretable. It is an arbitrary fact of the pairing of signifiers and signifieds in complex symbols that the third example is excluded but example two is permitted. Chomsky argued that subjacency should be regarded as a universal constraint that prevents children from learning grammars in which there are movements that cross more than one NP or S boundary.

Other constraints have been proposed that also limit the range of the possible paradigmatic sets of syntagmatic structures. I will not describe these, but they include the specified subject constraint, the complex NP constraint, the coordinate structure constraint, and others; see Radford (1981) for lucid descriptions. They can all be interpreted as restrictions on complex signifiers that exclude some theoretically possible signified–signifier pairings.

BINDING AND CONTROL

In *Bill spoke to himself* there are two NPs that refer to the same person. In *he spoke to Bill* there are two NPs that refer to different persons. This distinction has been made into the subject of an elaborate theory of "binding" (e.g., Chomsky, 1980). This theory, in turn, further illustrates the emphasis on syntagmatic contrasts in recent grammars. The purpose of the binding and control theory is to restrict the power of reference indication and eliminate overgenerated sentences in which *Bill spoke to himself* could refer to two persons or *he spoke to Bill* could refer only to Bill.

To keep coreferences and other references straight, it is useful to employ subscripts:

$Bill_1$ spoke to $himself_1$ (for *himself = Bill*)

He_2 spoke to $Bill_1$ (for *he ≠ Bill*)

"Binding" means that two NPs have the same subscript; they are coindexed. Then one of the NPs is said to be "bound" to the other. The NP doing the binding must be able to "c-command" the bound NP (the expression *c-command* is short for "constituent-command"; see Reinhart, 1983). An NP that is not bound is "free," that is, not coindexed with another NP. Another concept is "governing category." This is the smallest NP or $\bar{S}$ that contains the two NPs in question.

The rules for binding have been worked out by Chomsky as follows (see Radford, 1981):

1. A c-commanded NP is bound to its commanding NP in its governing category. Thus *himself* is coindexed with *Bill* in *Bill spoke to himself.*
2. A c-commanding pronoun must be free (not coindexed) in its governing category. Thus in *he spoke to Bill,* he and Bill cannot refer to the same person.
3. A lexical NP must not be coindexed with any c-commanding NP. Thus *Bill* must be free in *he spoke to Bill.*

The concept of c-command is crucial. If a pronoun is the c-commanding NP it must refer outside the sentence. This is the case with *he spoke to Bill.* The concept can be illustrated with the following tree diagram:

c-commands

In words, a node *b* c-commands another node *a* if the first branching node over *b*—which here is *B*—also is over *a* (although *B* need not be directly over *a;* here *A* is that node).

The tree structure shown in Figure 2.4 illustrates how this definition of c-command applies to *Bill spoke to himself* and *he spoke to Bill.* (PP stands for prepositional phrase.) When the leftmost NP is *Bill* and the other NP is *himself,* the leftmost NP c-commands the pronoun NP. Thus *himself* and *Bill* are co-indexed. However, when the leftmost NP is *he* and the other NP is *Bill, he* and *Bill* cannot corefer because the pronoun cannot coindex if it c-commands.

There are various refinements and elaborations of the binding theory (see Reinhart, 1983), but the above suffices to make the observation that is relevant here. When the subscripts are the same, the NPs denote different syntagmatic values for the same choice of referent. Coindexing thus joins the use of traces as a way of elaborating on the syntagmatic contrasts of the sentence without adding to the paradigmatic contrasts. This idea enriches the concept of the unidimensionality of speech.

As Saussure presented this concept, there is a linear string of words, and complexes of meaning are broken down into successions of changes along the time axis. However, both trace-annotation and coindexing reveal global properties of segment strings. The rules of binding are formal statements of limitations on these global properties that require that the global property of coindexing appear only in the same governing category, with the appropriate command relation, and so forth. Strings of symbols are not always successions of paradigmatic choices. Sometimes the same paradigmatic choices are made at more than one place. To keep the Saussurian metaphor, speech proves to be curvilinear at certain points where there are coreferring NPs or traces.

Complex symbols, described in these ways and implying grammatical meanings, provide tools for unpacking images and other forms of unitary undi-

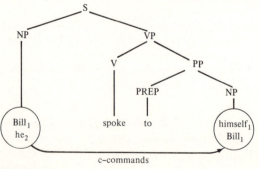

Figure 2.4

vided thinking. This process is discussed at length in Chapter 5. The next two chapters return to the theme of intrinsic value and describe the effects of context on the individually constituted aspects of thinking and speaking.

NONTRANSFORMATIONAL GRAMMARS

Nontransformational grammars have, of course, existed for a long time. But within the TGG school in recent years there has been an effort to devise formal grammars that do not employ transformation rules. Chomsky's own grammatical analyses have moved in the same direction, all transformations being now described by one rule (movement). However, other major efforts can be mentioned that have taken the last step, and removed from their grammars all forms of transformation. These grammars, nonetheless, are still within the synchronic–contrastive tradition. They are not retrograde; they must therefore find other nontransformational ways to express the paradigmatic contrasts of tree structures that transformations express, and each of these grammars has found a way to do this.

Gazdar (1981), for instance, has proposed a generalized phrase–structure grammar that contains only phrase–structure rules that, by themselves, express syntagmatic contrasts. To express paradigmatic contrasts there are "metarules." These are phrase–structure type rules that show how phrase structures are related to other phrase structures. For example, there is a metarule that states the contrast between VP and question formed with subject–verb inversion (Gazdar, p. 165), a contrast that in a transformational grammar is stated via transformation but here is stated via a phrase–structure-like metarule.

Another effort in this area is "realistic" grammar. Bresnan (1978) in particular has been interested in this type of grammar. A "realistic" grammar is one in which grammatical rules can be mapped more or less directly into conceivable psychological operations such as memory retrieval. Distinct grammatical rules in a "realistic" grammar should correspond to distinct mental operations. In particular, movement transformations are excluded in favor of a "dictionary" of sentence structures. Bresnan does not use transformations between contrasting sentence types, such as the transformational contrast between active and passive sentences illustrated below.

Sam swept Bill's floor. (NP_1 sweep NP_2)

Bill's floor was swept. (NP_2 was swept)

Instead, Bresnan utilizes dictionary entries in which "logical structures" are paired with surface sentence structures. For example:

Logical Structure	**Surface Structure**
NP_{agent} SWEEP NP_{object}	$----\!\!\!\to$ NP sweep NP (active)
$(\exists\ x_{agent})\ x_{agent}$ SWEEP NP_{object}	$----\!\!\!\to$ NP was swept (passive)

The passive sentence, *Bill's floor was swept,* would not be derived by a transformational rearrangement of *someone swept Bill's floor* in this grammar. Rather, the logical structure of the passive sentence—which is read "there exists an agent x, and this x swept Bill's floor"—would lead directly to an entry that specifies the frame of a passive surface structure. While there is indeed no transformational movement in producing the passive, the grammar still expresses the paradigmatic contrast between passive and active sentences. This can be seen in the contrast of the logical structures. In the passive there is an unspecified x_{agent}, while in the active there is a specified NP_{agent}. These form a paradigm of mutually defining contrasts. This paradigmatic contrast is exactly what is stated by setting up the active and passive logical formulas as above. In the common field of meaning corresponding to the relationship of agents to verbs, there is a contrast between specified and unspecified agents, between saying Sam swept it and "somebody" swept it. If there were no passive sentences in English, then the *NP verb NP* frame would presumably expand to include unspecified arguments, x_{agent}.

Moreover, there is nothing diachronic about these logical structures. The realistic aspect of "realistic" grammar does not directly explain the microgenesis of linguistic actions. This grammar assumes that thinking is already sorted into linguistic categories. For instance, the initial state of a passive sentence assumes the passive logical formula, and the contextualized thinking process of the speaker of a passive sentence itself must be already categorized as specified by the passive logical formula. Such categorization must be presupposed in order for the grammar to function as a processing model. The relation of the passive sentence structure to global–synthetic thinking (i.e., thinking not *yet* categorized) is not therefore explained by "realistic" grammar so much as this relation is assumed as an input. "Realistic" grammar does not depart from the fundamental restriction on all linguistic formulations: it analyzes socially constituted aspects of linguistic actions but the individually constituted aspects of the process are left out.

MORPHOLOGY

While not specifically part of the TGG (or any other) school, I will close this chapter with a brief explanation of morphology. The terminology of this subject will prove useful. A "morpheme" is similar to a word (words are discussed in Chapter 5), but is defined to avoid the ambiguities of the word as a concept about linguistic form. For example, is *cats* one word? If so, then is *cat* also a word, and how do the two words relate to each other? A morpheme is defined as a minimal meaningful unit in the synchronic–contrastive system of langue. *Cats* consists of two morphemes: *cat* + *s.* This makes clear the relation between *cats* and *cat* and avoids the ambiguity of what to call *cats* and *cat.*

In every language there are "root morphemes." These are morphemes that can be used singly, such as *cat.* Most freestanding words are root morphemes, although many are combinations of morphemes, like *cats.* Two root morphemes can combine, as in *catfood,* but more important from the systematic viewpoint are combinations of root morphemes with "affixes". An affix is another morpheme affixed to a root. Affixes cannot stand alone—they appear only attached to other morphemes. "Affix" is the superordinate term covering prefixes, infixes, and suffixes. These terms refer to the syntagmatic position of the affix:

prefix-[RO( )OT]-suffix
$$\uparrow$$
$$|$$
infix

In English there are prefixes (*pre*-fix) and suffixes (suffix-*es*), but no infixes. In many other languages, however, infixing is a common method of adding affixes (some examples from American Indian languages are presented in Chapter 6, p. 203). In American Sign Language (or ASL, the manual-visual language of the deaf in North America), there are what might be called "parafixes"—affixes that are added to the root sign but are not separate segments. For example, making a sign more quickly acts as an intensifier: "fast" becoming "very fast," and so forth (Klima and Bellugi, 1979).

In addition to the position of the affix relative to the root, affixes can be classified according to the type of syntagmatic combination they produce. Basically, there are combinations that do and combinations that do not change the grammatical category of the root. Among those that do not change this category are combinations of two roots: in *cat* + *food* two nouns produce a new noun. Another type that does not alter the grammatical class of the root are the affixes called "inflections": in English these include plural suffixes on nouns and verbs, and tense suffixes on verbs. Thus *cat* is a noun and *cat* + *s* is also a noun; *run* is a verb and *run* + *s* is also a verb. Thus inflectional morphology always leaves unchanged the syntagmatic value of the root. "Derivational" morphology, in contrast, does alter the syntagmatic value of the root. Here are some examples (both prefixes and suffixes):

V to N: $sing_V$ + er ($singer_N$), the "agentive" suffix

N to V: be + fog_N ($befog_V$)

N to Adjective: boy_N + ish ($boyish_{Adj}$)

V to Adjective: $bear_V$ + able ($bearable_{Adj}$)

For further discussion of morphology see Bybee (1985), Gleason (1955), or Hockett (1958).

chapter 3

The Context of Speaking I: Social

In explanations of linguistic actions, the context of speaking is a fundamental datum. This is because sentences are *situated,* and the context of speaking is one of the forces that must be considered in explaining how sentences take form. Like other actions, linguistic actions are adaptive. To describe the context of speaking brings into the picture the conditions to which linguistic actions adapt. Linguistic actions are modified by the speaker to conform to earlier actions and to the informational and social environment.

Two kinds of context can be distinguished, broadly speaking: social and informational. The intrinsic value of a sentence is affected by both, but for convenience I have divided the discussion of context into two chapters. By social context I mean aspects that can be traced to the fact that there are two or more participants in the speaking situation. By informational context I mean aspects that can be traced to the content of speech—the objects referred to (real or imaginary), presuppositions about reference objects, and the predications about reference objects that the sentence conveys. Every concrete act of speaking is shaped by both social and informational elements, and the separation of these contexts into two chapters is an expository convenience. The separation should not imply that there are pure social and informational contexts or that some linguistic elements are reflections of one contextual factor alone. In the present chapter I have gathered together—far from an exhaustive list—aspects of the social context that affect the pure linguistic and intrinsic values of sentences.

My purpose in this chapter is to present illustrations of how linguists, psychologists, and philosophers have thought about and described the social context of speaking: as speech acts, as cooperation, as theater, and, in a specific type of social interaction, as the mutual synchrony of speaker and listener roles during conversations. I will not attempt to synthesize these approaches into a single approach, something that would carry us far afield and may not even be possible. My aim is simply to acquire concepts that will be useful in thinking about the context of speaking.

EXAMPLE OF SOCIAL CONTEXT

While producing the following sentence (from Goodwin, 1981), the speaker directed successive clauses and phrases to different listeners, as shown by the speaker's shifts of gaze:

I gave up smoking cigarettes I uh one week ago today actually
    ↑   ↑   ↑
(looks at D)   (looks at B)   (looks at A)

The identity of the addressee at any point is an element of the intrinsic value in the sentence. The first clause presupposes a hearer who has no previous knowledge of the event being recounted. It would be strange for someone to make this statement to a hearer who already knew the speaker had quit smoking. In this situation person D, the speaker's dinner guest, in fact did not know the speaker had quit smoking. The next clause, in contrast, presupposes a listener who already knew about the event and could appreciate that the moment of speaking was an anniversary of it. The new addressee at this point, B, was the speaker's wife and so did know what the clause presupposes. The adverb *actually* is harder to pin down, but appears to apply to the sentence itself. It signals that the sentence has in fact conveyed the piece of information that this is an anniversary. Person B and person D could have been the target of this signal, but the speaker looked at A—the other dinner guest, and the only person not already included in this performance.

    The emerging sentence was thus reconstructed three times to fit the recipient of the moment. The intended recipient adds to the intrinsic value of the clause, and this blending of context and structure illustrates how pure linguistic (syntactic and semantic) choices are made that would have been different if the context —here, the addressee—had been different. There is a synthesis of the linguistic values of the sentence with the speaker's consciousness of the social context, his memory of the past, and awareness of the calendar. Although what the speaker was saying was choppy, something like a harmonious whole was constructed that blended the speaker's sense of the context with the emerging sentence. The sentence looks choppy because it changed its form to synthesize with new intrinsic values—the identity of each addressee—as determined by the social context. Taking into account this context and its effect on intrinsic value allows us to see that there was continuity of linguistic action through the three clauses.

    As demonstrated in this example, the effect of the context is very often diffuse—affecting the sentence in many ways at once. Nonetheless, it is possible to analyze the effects of context into different factors. These are not mutually exclusive but can be analyzed as quasi-independent processes. The shaping of sentences by the context of speaking covers a wide range of effects, from semantic value to choices of particular words and sentence frames. In what follows we will pass through this full range.

The order of topics in the following sections runs from the most specific factor in the social shaping of sentences to the most general. The first topic is the *illocutionary force* of the linguistic act, the second the *cooperative principle,* the third *the theater metaphor* for conversational interactions, and the fourth is the system of *turn-allocation.*

ILLOCUTIONARY FORCE

Let's look at some terminology. Actually saying something, producing utterances, is termed *locution,* which is distinct from two other aspects of linguistic acts. The *illocutionary force* is what the speaker *does* by saying the locution; an example is the illocutionary force of the sentence uttered in the example above. This was the act of telling a story. The *perlocutionary effect* of the speech act is its effect on somebody else. Locution and illocution refer to something the *speaker* does, while perlocution refers to something that happens with the *recipient.* The perlocutionary effect of a linguistic act is often difficult to discern. In the dinner table example it might have been as insubstantial as a mood of approval of the speaker's new-found resolve and the hope that it lasts. Interest in the topic of "speech acts" (as it is generally called; cf. Searle, 1969) has generally been focused on the illocutionary force (IF) of sentences.

There are two ways to analyze the IF of linguistic actions. These are not antithetical, but in most cases only one is adopted. The method to have been utilized first is the identification of performative verbs (Austin, 1962). The second method, derived from the first, is through an analysis of the conditions that must be met for linguistic actions to have an IF of a particular kind (Searle, 1969, 1975; Labov and Fanshel, 1977). The second approach, because it emphasizes conditions rather than just categories, most clearly shows the role of context in developing the IF of speech; to understand it we should begin with performative verbs.

Linguistic acts, in this tradition of analysis, are acts linked to performative verbs. Performative verbs are verbs of a distinctive type, the saying of which performs an action in the nonlinguistic world. (The title of Austin's (1962) monograph is "How to Do Things with Words.") An example is *to promise.* If I say *I promise to send you a paper,* I am performing the act of undertaking to do something in the future. I perform this act by *saying* that *I promise to A.* If I fail to keep my promise I can be reprimanded on the ground that I *said* I would. In contrast, if I say *he promises to send you a paper,* no act of promising is being performed. Similarly, if I say *I promised to send you a paper,* no act of promising is being performed, but rather only a reference to a past performance of the act. The verb *to promise* must be used with a rather specific linguistic formula— unmarked for tense with the subject of the verb in first person, indicating the speaker. It is also necessary to describe the act A that is being promised—to send the paper (*I promise something or other* also fails to promise). When all these constraints are met the performative verb can *perform* the act of promising.

It is also possible to promise in ways that are not so constrained. For example, *I'll send it to you by March* is a promise that uses a future tense verb, and *ok* can be a promise without using a verb at all. Moreover, in these examples the action A is not specified either. Such examples illustrate *indirect speech acts,* the definitive characteristic of which is that the speech form does not use the performative verb. The problem of specifying the conditions that indirect speech acts must meet to have an effect comparable to the use of a performative verb leads to the second method mentioned, which will be discussed shortly.

Austin (1962) identified a number of performative verbs and proposed categories for them. *To promise* is a member of the "commissive" category; this is because, by saying *to promise* (in the restricted way required), the speaker is committed to do act A. Below are the categories, each followed by some example verbs.

Commissive:	To promise, undertake, covenant, contract
Verdictive:	To acquit, convict, reckon, value
Exercitive:	To appoint, dismiss, excommunicate
Behabitive:	To apologize, thank, deplore (i.e., various reactions to other people's behavior)
Expositive:	To affirm, remark, accept, turn to

D'Andrade and Wish (1985) have used data from televised conversations to estimate the relative frequencies of the Austin categories plus two others. Expositives are by far the most common (79 percent), followed by "reactions" (answering questions, assent or dissent to requests, etc.) (52 percent), behabitives (28 percent), excercitives (22 percent), "questions" (15 percent), commissives (2 percent) and verdictives (< 1 percent). (A given utterance could be coded as belonging to more than one speech act category; hence the total is more than 100 percent.)

The second approach to analyzing IF is to specify the conditions that a linguistic utterance must meet in order for it to have the IF of a particular category. (These categories are those above, plus refinements proposed by Searle, 1975; and Labov and Fashnel, 1977.) The conditions state properties that any locution must have in order that the speech act not "misfire"—that is, fail to have the right IF. The following are necessary for a linguistic act to function as a request (Searle, 1969, pp. 66–67):

1. There must be *propositional content* that describes the future act A—e.g., remove the speaker from the present location and take him home.
2. There must be evidence of having met the *preparatory conditions* of the speech act of requesting something. Of these Searle has analyzed two:
   a. The hearer is able to perform this A, and the speaker believes it.
   b. The hearer will not perform this A of his own accord.
3. It is assumed that the speaker meets the *sincerity condition,* which is that the speaker wants this A to be performed.

4. Finally, there is the *essential condition,* which is that the locution *counts* as an act that has the desired IF: saying the sentence counts as an attempt to get the hearer to perform this A.

Different locutions can meet the conditions of the IF of a request, including:

I request that you take me home.

I want to go home.

Could you take me home?

I got lightbulbs today. (Said in a hardware store.)

Information showing whether these conditions in each case are met must come from either the context of speaking or the sentence itself. The most formulaic request form—*I request that you take me home*—states the propositional content and names the essential condition. It names the essential condition with the performative verb. Even the direct request is not fully explicit and leaves to the context the fact that the preparatory conditions are met; but what is present in the direct request is explicable in terms of the conditions on requests.

The "indirect" requests—*could you take me home?* and *I want to go home* —also have constraints of form that are predictable from the conditions that requests must meet. These are conventional indirect requests and rely on context to no greater an extent than the direct request in example one. However, examples two and three leave to context different conditions. Example three is a question about whether the first preparatory condition is met; that is, a question about the speaker's *ability* to perform the act A. The second example is a statement of the sincerity condition—that the speaker desires the act. Both indirect requests state the propositional content of the act. Gordon and Lakoff (1975) distinguished between *speaker-based* and *hearer-based* indirect requests. In the case of speaker-based, or "I," requests, the request *asserts the sincerity condition;* this is seen in example two. In the case of hearer-based, or "you," requests, the request *questions a preparatory condition,* specifically the condition that the hearer has the ability to perform the act. Both the second and third examples leave the other conditions of requests to context. There are also indirect requests that question the other part of the preparatory condition, that the hearer would do the act anyway (e.g., *Are you taking me home?* as a request to be taken home), and leave the ability and sincerity conditions to context. (For further discussion, see Searle, 1975, 1979; Labor and Fashnel, 1977; Davison, 1975; and Sadock, 1975).

Indirect requests are felt to be more polite than direct requests, and this impression can be related to the form of the request. Indirect requests of both kinds provide room for graceful refusals, and one of them actually suggests the means for its own refusal on the ground that the listener is not able to perform the act A. The speaker-based version, *I want to go home,* asserts that the speaker sincerely wants A but says nothing of any sort about the listener's ability to perform A. The listener-based version *Could you take me home?* is really a question about this ability. Both requests, in their very form, suggest a means of refusing the request, and this is particularly obvious with the listener-based request. Indirect requests seem polite because of the diffidence built into them. By the same token, a request that leaves no option for refusal should seem impolite. *You can take me home (now)* seems like a demand and negates all the "outs" that are implicit in the conditions for the request IF (the listener's ability is asserted, rather than queried or not commented on). For a similar reason, the listener-based request, which actually queries the listener's ability to perform A, seems more polite than the speaker-based request, which ignores the preparatory conditions altogether and simply asserts the sincerity condition. Thus we have two continua that are aligned—the degree of politeness and the degree to which the listener's ability to perform A is left open:

Request	Politeness	Listener ability
Could you take me home?	High	Left open
I want to be taken home.	Medium	Neutral
You can take me home now.	Low	Settled

Example four is a *nonce* request. *I got lightbulbs today* is also an indirect request, but one whose form is not specified by convention. This particular sentence provides none of the information needed to convey the IF of a request to be taken home, yet can still function as a request for this A in an appropriate context. An example of such a context would be where the speaker and hearer are standing before a display of lightbulbs in a hardware store. In this context the sentence could assert a state of affairs that negates a reason for not being at home, and thus convey the request to be taken home.

The point is that the IF of a request is not tied to any one type of sentence but arises from sentence-and-context *pairs.* The two parts of the pair can compensate for one another, one part supplying information where the other does not. The sentence is not an isolated atomic unit but is part of a whole that includes the social context.

Part of the intrinsic value the speaker imparts to the sentence is the IF of a request, and the hearer understands this IF in the context. The speaker does this and the hearer understands it even though the pure linguistic value of the sentence is unrelated to any of the request forms.

We also can now see the sense in which the *psychological structure* and the *linguistic structure* of sentences behave differently. The following diagram can be interpreted as showing the extent of difference between the pure linguistic values of sentences and the internal intrinsic values of the same sentences. In terms of pure linguistic value, *I got lightbulbs today* has the same form regardless of its context. Psychologically, however, the intrinsic value of *I got lightbulbs today* is not constant. It has a different intrinsic value when it occurs in a context where it has the IF of a request than it has in some other context where it is a propositional affirmation of the fact of having bought lightbulbs. What is special about explicit performative verb sentences is that their internal intrinsic values change very little but this stability is achieved at the expense of having to use a highly constrained linguistic code.

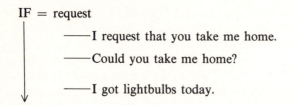

IF = request

       ——I request that you take me home.

       ——Could you take me home?

       ——I got lightbulbs today.

The scale begins at the apex with the most restrictive performative verb formula—*I request that you take me home.* That this formula is at the apex implies two properties:

1. It utilizes a performative verb that itself names the IF (*to request* names the IF of the speech act of requesting).
2. It utilizes a formulaic syntax that, by convention, is used to code this IF (tenseless verb, first-person subject).

Because of these properties, sentences at the apex change intrinsic value only in the most marked uses. "Marked" implies that the sentence calls attention to itself as unusual in the way it is being used. A marked use of saying *I request that you take me home* and not meaning by this "I request that you take me home" (i.e., to violate the sincerity condition) produces great irony or sarcasm.

As we move outward through the scale of possible sentences for a given IF, the potentials for disparity of pure linguistic and intrinsic value become greater. At the same time, the formulaic conventions that restrict the form of the speech act are relaxed. This means that the intrinsic value of the sentence is less and less constrained by the pure linguistic values embodied in its grammatical structure. At some point into the range there are no conventions at all, and any sentence can convey any IF. For this to be possible, however, the sentence must be totally contextualized and intrinsic value must play the decisive part in conveying the IF (*I got lightbulbs today,* etc.).

Thus, the diagram simultaneously suggests the scale of possible sentence forms capable of performing speech acts indirectly, and the significance of the context of speaking for conveying the IF of the speech act as a function of the disparity between intrinsic value and pure linguistic value. A study by Clark (1979) shows that there is variation in this disparity within the conventional indirect request class. Some of these requests are reacted to as if they could be understood in only one way (as requests), whereas others appear to be interpreted in two ways (as questions and as requests). The question interpretation is due to the pure linguistic value of the request form.

Clark telephoned merchants in and around Palo Alto, California, with questions about their closing times (one question per merchant):

| Could you tell me the time you close? | .00/1.00 |
| Would you mind telling me the time you close? | .24/1.00 |

Do you close before 7?   .72/0.81
I was wondering whether you close before 7?   .63/0.95

By noting how these were responded to, Clark could estimate the strength of the tendency to see the sentences as questions and as requests separately. For example, if to *do you close before 7?* the answer is *nine,* the hearer is taking the sentence purely as a request. If the answer is *no,* the hearer is taking it purely as a question. If the answer combines these, *no, at nine,* the hearer is taking it both as a question and as a request.

The *could you?* request was taken by the merchants purely as a request. The numbers to the right of the sentences show the proportion of replies that indicated that the sentences were taken as questions (before the slash) and as requests (after the slash). Every merchant said *at nine* or whenever they closed, but none said *yes, at nine.* In this particular context the *could you?* request was conventionalized to the point that it was understood immediately as a request and all its question potential was lost. In contrast the *do you?* and *I was wondering* requests retained nearly as much question potential as request potential. These indirect requests present a disparity of pure linguistic value and intrinsic value (based on the speaker's intent to request). The speaker, to be understood, was counting on the hearer to make the appropriate interpretation or, as it is termed, "implicature" (Grice, 1975). This type of cooperation between participants in linguistic interactions is the second aspect of the social context that can be analyzed and examined.

THE COOPERATIVE PRINCIPLE

A general principle by which speakers produce effects on hearers is to get the hearer to recognize that the speaker intends to have an effect on the hearer (Grice, 1957, 1975). One effect of this cycle of seeing the speaker's intentions is that it is not necessary for the speaker to make explicit every detail of these intentions. All that the speaker must do is get the hearer to see that he or she has an intention to have the hearer see the speaker's intention to produce some effect. The hearer, if cooperative, then tries to figure out, or "implicate," what the intended effect could be. For example, the speaker of *I got lightbulbs today* intended to produce an effect on the hearer, and did so by getting the hearer to see that the speaker intended to produce an effect. The hearer, from seeing this intention, then had to implicate the IF of a request to be taken home, rather than take the sentence in a literal-minded way as a statement of fact. Hence the layering of intentions in the formulation of the cooperative principle.

It is important for the reader to see that the need for implicature arises from the desirability of cooperatively sharing the burden of communication between the speaker and hearer. A layering of intentions is part of any conversation where the speaker intends to produce an effect and is not explicit about the effect that is intended.

Grice (1975) puts forth several *maxims of cooperation* that analytically describe the process of being cooperative in conversation. These are:

Maxim of quantity Be as informative as required but not more informative than needed.

Maxim of relation Be relevant.

Maxim of quality Do not say what is false.

Maxim of manner Be brief but avoid ambiguity.

These have an almost biblical tone, but if one *is* as brief, relevant, informative, and truthful as required, the listener can recognize one's intentions *directly.* This would be, for example, a speaker who says *Noting that you are able, I request that you take me home,* but not one who says *I was wondering whether you could take me home?* or *I got lightbulbs today* with the same IF. In these latter cases the speaker is obviously not being succinct or relevant, but is, in fact, *violating maxims.* However, this does not mean that the speaker is being uncooperative; on the contrary, the speaker is depending crucially on cooperation from the hearer.

An implicature is "to go beyond the information given," to suppose that the speaker is cooperative and make a deficient speaker's utterance meet the cooperative principle. Hearing an apparently irrelevant statement, *I was wondering whether you close at 7,* the hearer implicates something that will make this statement relevant: the IF of a request to find out when the store closes, in this case.

The maxims can be purposefully violated in a certain style of speaking; Grice gives these examples:

Violating the maxim of relation:

A: Smith doesn't seem to have a girlfriend these days.
B: He's been spending a lot of time in New York lately.

Violating the maxim of quantity:

REVIEWER A: Miss Smith sang "Un Bel Di."
REVIEWER B: Miss Smith produced a series of sounds that corresponded closely to the score of "Un Bel Di."

The apparent irrelevance of B's statement and the prolixity of Reviewer B's description call for implicatures by the hearer to restore the violated maxims. The hearer is forced to implicate what the speaker is unwilling or unable to say. The semantic–syntactic choices of the speakers in these cases must provide the hearer with a basis for making the implicature but the implicature is not mechanically derived from the speaker's sentence (hence it is called "implicature," not "implication," which is a logical inference). The context of speaking, general knowledge, and many other factors also must be considered.

THEATER METAPHOR

In informal verbal interactions where the sole purpose is simply to make one's way through a social encounter (Goffman, 1974, 1981), implicatures are guided by a metaphor for conversational interaction in which there is no other purpose than the performance of the conversation itself: theater. In these conversations the participants take turns being the performers and audience of a kind of theatrical production, and the intrinsic values of sentences derive from this guiding metaphor.

A sentence has a value that depends on the performance the speaker is staging. The cooperative principle still applies, but what is hidden behind the performance the listener does not implicate. Cooperation in the theater metaphor means abiding by the maxims of cooperative behavior, but violating the maxims of cooperation has a different meaning in a performance. It simply means the performance is a poor one. It does not mean that the performance is not what it seems.

The following excerpt illustrates one aspect of theater metaphor (from an actual conversation; see Chapter 4, pp. 56–57).

A_1: Oh, I have a good friend from Iowa. He's from Cedar Rapids—no, not Cedar Rapids. He's from the Amana area.

B_1: He—that's near Cedar Rapids, between like Dubuque and Cedar Rapids.

A_2: Yeah, yeah. He used to have some great stories about the Amanas.

B_2: Yeah.

A_3: An' uh well but uh he said it was the first socialist community in the United States or something.

There was something hidden behind speaker A's utterances (this will be described in later discussions of this conversation excerpt; see especially Chapter 4). It is well hidden at this point, however, and speaker A does not appear to be trying here to convey anything other than a story about his good friend from Iowa. The passage can be understood as a kind of performance by speaker A. This is in fact the way speaker B takes it. In A_1 through A_3, A is presenting a story for B. B responds—in B_1 with a supplementary contribution of his own, and in B_2 with a "back-channel" signal, *Yeah* (Yngve, 1970)—but these do not take over the performance. B remains "audience." Again, as in the theater, the utterances of A are "preformed," not because (as in a real play) they have been written by somebody else, but because they are remembered episodes from A's past; there is minimal new "literary" creation. These sentences illustrate another parallel to theater—namely, suspense. Suspense is in fact the most obvious theatrical effect in the above example. A series of sentences, in which what Silverstein (1984) calls "poetic" use of repetition of surface forms, builds up drama:

I have a good friend from Iowa
 —he's from Cedar Rapids
 —he's from the Amana area
 —he used to have some great stories
 —he said it was the first socialist community

This bit of conversation is theatrical in several ways, therefore, and illustrates Goffman's statement that "often what talkers undertake to do is not to provide information to a recipient but to present dramas to an audience" (1974, p. 508). The intrinsic value of *he said it was the first socialist community in the United States* is in part a function of the resolution the sentence provides of the suspense build-up during the preceding chain of sentences.

In any conversation, whether it is or is not guided by a theater metaphor, the participants must alternately orient toward and respond to utterances or acts of the other person. Several axes of orientation are seen in the following example from Goffman (1974); these add to the intrinsic value of the sentences:

> A: [enters wearing a new hat]
> B: No, I don't like it.
> A: Now I know it's right.

B's remark gets its wiseacre quality because it orients toward A's nonverbal act, and presupposes that A, by entering, was asking a question. A's *Now I know it's right* included two further lines of orientation, one to B's *No, I don't like it* and the other to A's own action of entering the room. These two axes explain the adverbial *now,* a word rich in intrinsic value in this context. *Now* conveys at least three ideas that provide a natural basis for its selection by A: the idea of a temporal boundary (now vs. before entering), of change of state (now A has achieved certainty of knowledge), and of the effect of B's remark on this certain knowledge (now that B has said what was said). The linguistic contrasts of *now* do not produce any of this (*now* vs. *then,* for instance). All of these values of the word are determined by context, not by the word acting alone.

There are also social contingencies exemplified by the question–answer pattern, as in the following example (also from Goffman, 1974):

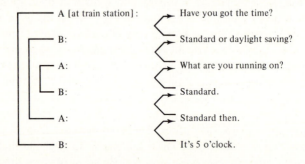

To know what to do next in this exchange, it is necessary for the participants to take into account two parallel series. One series is the questions and their answers embedded into one another; this embedding has to be traced and remembered (shown on the left side of the example). The other series is the succession of oriented statements shown on the right. Every sentence is a member of both series and the two have an effect on intrinsic value at every point. For example, when A said *Standard then,* it was because this sentence not only was oriented toward the immediately preceding statement, *(standard),* but also because it answered a question three steps earlier *(Standard or daylight saving?).* Both series affect the intrinsic value of *Standard then.* The pure linguistic value of this phrase, on the other hand, arises from its contrasts with linguistic alternatives, Standard *time* then, among others.

TURN-TAKING

A particularly obvious case of cooperation in conversation is the smooth alternation of speaking turns. The speaker and listener must coordinate their impulses to speak, so that their talking neither overlaps nor stops altogether. These twin evils are avoided only through *joint* action of the participants. The following illustrates what can be regarded as a pathology of turn-taking in which unintended joint actions take place repeatedly:

> A: (to self) It's incredible!
> SON: (in next room) What's incredible?
> A: (to son) Oh, nothing.
> WIFE: (in other room) What?

The first line violated the usual rules of turn-taking, because there was no intended addressee although there was a *de facto* listener. In the third line there was an intended addressee, but he was inadequately selected and a different person responded.

Conversational units, linguistically, may be sentences, clauses, phrases, words, or sometimes subwords. These units are constructed so as to "project" their own ends as units of conversation. Two rather different approaches to explaining the smooth management and control of turn-taking in conversation can be adopted, but I will try to combine them utilizing the concept of intrinsic value. The ethnomethodological ("ethmeth") approach to conversation tries to analyze it as an everyday activity that defines its own units as it is being carried out. The mode of constructing the conversation allows the hearer to forecast possible turn-switching points, and the observer can do no better than discover what the cues were in specific instances of conversational "talk." Sacks, Schegloff, and Jefferson (1974, p. 707), who pioneered this viewpoint, give examples such as the following:

> **(1)** A: Well, if you knew my argument
>   why did you bother to a: sk?
>   B: Because I'd like to defend
>   my argument.
>
> **(2)** A: Well, it wasn't me.
>   B: No, but you know who it was.
>
> **(3)** A: Sixty-two feet is pretty good si: ze.
>   B: Oh: :boy.

In two of the above exchanges there is a brief overlapping of speakers, in each case because A unexpectedly extends the final vowel nucleus. But apart from this rather mechanical form of synchronous vocalizing, the listener in each case quite accurately anticipates the end of the other person's turn. Sacks et al. are interested in finding the units of the conversation that B is reacting to such that B can tell when a unit is coming to an end. If A's sentences represent within themselves the end of the turn, participant B, having projected the end of this turn, can know exactly when to start talking. In the first example, a question demanding an answer, the unit is a pragmatically coherent whole easily projected to its end (except for the final vowel lengthening). In the second example, the unit is a denial of a previous statement, and the end of the logical unit of denial is also projectable from within. The third example is less obviously the end of a conversational unit. Sacks et al. do not say what the referent of this comment was, or whether the comment followed further comments about the same referent (facts that would have been available to the participants). If the example followed other comments it might have been the conclusion of a chain of inferences, and this logical role could have been the basis for projecting the end of the speaking-turn.

In these examples, there is a basis in the intrinsic value of the sentences—logical, semantic, or pragmatic—for projecting the end of the speaking-turn. Such information is recoverable by the hearer, and could have been incorporated in the first place into the intrinsic value of the speaker's sentence via an implicit inner speech dialogue.

A rather different approach to the coordination of speaking turns is found in Duncan and Fiske (1977). In their scheme the speaker is regarded as emitting to the hearer signals that coordinate events during the conversation. These signals point out relevant aspects of the social context of speaking. In contrast to the Sacks et al. approach, this approach emphasizes independently describable signals that comprise a repertoire independent of any particular conversation; in the Sacks et al. view the conversational units are functional units that can be recognized only within the framework of a particular concrete activity. For example, the speaker gazing at the listener has a significance specifiable in advance for Duncan and Fiske, but could be described for Sacks et al. as a signal only in the context of a specific conversational act where intentions can be judged.

Three of the signals discovered by Duncan and Fiske—head-turning, gesture production or cessation, and grammatical-clause completion—are not arbitrary choices. The two head-turning directions are linked and have opposite meanings, suggesting that head-turning is a single signal with paradigmatic + and − values. The speaker's turning away from the hearer is associated with asserting an intention to speak, and turning toward the hearer with inviting a back-channel response. Nearly all back-channel responses in conversations take place just after the speaker has looked toward the hearer. Conversely, most new turns start with the (new) speaker looking away. To look at the other person is to orient one's perceptual apparatus toward this person: it is preparation to *receive* something. Because the signals are linked into a system of oppositions, in preparing to *offer* something the speaker turns away.

Gesture production and gesture cessation are also linked signals with opposite meanings. At the beginning of a turn, gesture production is associated with asserting one's intention to speak and, at the end of a turn, with suppressing premature turn-taking attempts by the hearer. Correspondingly, ceasing a gesture signals willingness to give up the turn. Gestures are closely connected with the ideational content of speech. Not surprisingly, therefore, gestures appear as signals of the intention to speak or continue speaking. Because of a system of oppositions in which there are again linked + and − values of the same signal, cessation of gesture production signals relinquishment.

Grammatical clause completion, finally, is associated both with relinquishment of the speaking turn and with inviting a back-channel response—situations in which the hearer is being asked to say something. Hearing a complete grammatical clause is obviously an opportune moment to try interrupting the speaker. Starting a grammatical clause, the opposite signal, should have the opposite meaning of the speaker's intention to speak. But in this case the speaker is already speaking—thus, only one grammatical clause signal can have meaning, which is the − value of completing the clause.

These signals, although elements in a socially constituted system, are signals of intrinsic values and of what is individually constituted during the ongoing conversational act.

To summarize this chapter, we can ask: What does the social context of speaking contribute to the intrinsic values of sentences? To answer, we have emphasized three points: (1) The IF of a request (or other IF) is incorporated into sentences that are not, on the surface, requests. For example, "I got light bulbs today" can be a request to be taken home, and this IF is intrinsically a value of the sentence in an appropriate context. (2) The model of a theatrical performance adds values of dramatic effectiveness. For example, "He's from Cedar Rapids. . . . He's from the Amana area. . . . He used to have . . . and so forth," have a crescendo effect that arises from the context of speaking. (3) Sentences in conversations project a state of readiness to exchange or not exchange speaking turns, and this value can be revealed in signals that arise during speech output.

chapter 4

The Context of Speaking II: Informational

In this chapter I continue the discussion of the context of speaking begun in Chapter 3. Now we turn to the second main set of conditions to which linguistic actions adapt: the informational context. By this term I mean context that pertains to the referential domain of speech—the reference-indicating, predicative, presuppositional, and associative aspects of sentence generation and understanding. The informational context consists of both nonlinguistic and linguistic environments, and includes environments that past linguistic acts have created.

TWO WAYS OF CONNECTING TO CONTEXT

There are two kinds of connection between individual sentences and the information context: these are *cohesiveness* and *deixis* (pointing). Pointing has an obvious function when there are physical objects or events in the referential domain. In pointing out concrete events, the use of the demonstrative pronouns *this* or *that* almost requires an accompanying gesture in order to be well formed (Levelt et al., 1985). Deixis also can be used for abstract references. If, for example, a speaker asks *Is this your first year here or where did you come from before?* and points, not at the addressee, but at empty space, this abstract form of deixis can be understood in terms of pointing out a new *theme* or topic of conversation, as will be explained later. Pointing, both concrete and abstract, always implies a vantage point, or *origo* (written ⊕), and this origo is the distinctive quality of deixis.

Cohesiveness is the sense of connectedness that speakers and hearers have of a given reference with the theme or topic of discourse. A cohesive reference is one that presupposes some earlier reference in order to be understood (Halliday and Hasan, 1976). Some references seem closely connected with the theme in the sense that they presuppose it. The opposite of cohesiveness is *discontinuity*. Discontinuous references do not presuppose some earlier reference in order to be understood. Some references are well embedded in the ongoing conversation or narration and these are felt to be cohesive, whereas others are new introductions and are felt to be discontinuous. Pronouns are one means of conveying a sense of cohesiveness, and full NPs convey a sense of discontinuity. For example (from Levy, 1984):

1. The main character$_1$ walked out, he$_1$ didn't care

2. And he$_1$ says well, and then his father$_2$ made—told some kind of story

In the first example, the two references are coreferential (as indicated by having the same subscript), and the use of a pronoun signals this cohesiveness of the second reference with the first (if instead of *he* the speaker had said *Bill,* there would have been a signal of discontinuity instead). In the second example, the signal is discontinuity. The second reference, a full NP, conveys the introduction of a new referent object (if instead the speaker had said *he,* the two references would have seemed coreferential). The pronoun in example one presupposes the earlier reference—*the main character*—in order to be understood completely, whereas the full NP *his father* in example two presupposes nothing in the earlier discourse. (Binding does not apply in these cases and in many others since the references are not in the same governing category in either sentence.)

Cohesiveness and deixis are in complementary distribution in narrations and conversations (Marslen-Wilson et al., 1982; Levy, 1982, 1984). This term means that cohesiveness and deixis are not used at the same places. Pointing gestures appear at the beginnings of narrative episodes or conversational topics, whereas cohesive references appear with well-embedded referring forms, exactly where new references are not being made. Pointing gestures do not occur with embedded references (this is illustrated later in the chapter). Thus the two forms of connection between sentences and the information context appear at systematically different positions in the discourse.

Deixis and cohesion also differ in the expectations they engender. Deictic pointing induces no expectation of a connection between successive sentences. Each sentence must be connected to a vantage point, but need not be connected to other sentences. Cohesion, in contrast, induces the expectation that sentences will be connected to each other (with possible interruptions). Thus the two forms of connecting sentences to the information context have different effects on the flow and organization of information as this is built up during discourse. Cohesiveness connects sentences together, whereas pointing connects sentences to a vantage point. If there is more than one vantage point each must be indicated in order that their sentences can be connected to the correct one. Illustrations of these differences will also be seen later in this chapter.

The two kinds of connection between sentences and the information context correspond to intrinsic and pure linguistic values in the following ways:

1. The information context contributes to the intrinsic value of the sentence, respectively:
   a. the feeling of how cohesive with the context the particular sentence is, and
   b. the orientation of attention the sentence embodies toward an external reference object (either concrete or abstract) (Pechmann and Deutsch, 1980).
2. The information context is coded by linguistic values. These operations code the contextual sources of information that affect the intrinsic values. The linguistic coding of cohesiveness exploits the characteristic of presupposition, and the coding of deixis requires the implicit presence of a vantage point.

The use of linguistic devices for coding the information context thus is a specific instance of a synthesis of intrinsic and linguistic values. The final sentence may be a synthesis of many different intrinsic and linguistic values; in this chapter, however, we are considering just those linguistic choices that unpack the speaker's global feeling of connectedness with the information context on the two dimensions mentioned.

Taking into account just this single kind of linkage of sentences to context, nonetheless, is often enough to show that the developmental path of sentence production or understanding is overdetermined. Producing and understanding speech requires very limited new effort in many cases. This is because cohesiveness excludes many paradigmatic alternatives in advance. The following passage —discussed earlier as an example of theater metaphor—also illustrates the enhancing effect of the information context on linguistic production and understanding. The final sentence from speaker A is the one we are analyzing.

> *A:* Oh, I had *a good friend from Iowa. He*'s from Cedar Rapids, no not Cedar Rapids, *he*'s from the Amana area.
>
> *B:* *He*—that's near Cedar Rapids, between like Dubuque and Cedar Rapids.
>
> *A:* Yeah, yeah, *he* used to have some great stories about the Amanas.

If we add up all the effects from the context on the final sentence, we will see that almost nothing was a free choice in constructing it. Virtually every segment was determined by the whole of which it was a part—*yeah, yeah, he, used to have,* and *the Amanas;* only *some great stories* was new.

The pronoun *he* that appears throughout this passage cohesively links all the sentences. These inexplicit *he*s presuppose the explicit reference with which the sample begins, *a good friend from Iowa,* and can appear because of the speaker's feeling of cohesiveness during the sentences with *he*s in them with this theme. The production and understanding of the *he*s is due to the speaker's sense of cohesiveness with the initial sentence. Such a feeling of cohesiveness is part of the intrinsic value of these sentences. It is noteworthy that even speaker B briefly shows some sign of the same cohesive sense (but cohesiveness does not last long for B; this example is analyzed later).

The sentence was restricted by the context in other ways as well. The NP, *the Amanas,* in A's final sentence utilizes a definite article, and this is possible because there was an earlier mention of the Amana area. The definite NP is another presupposing linguistic operation—in effect, directing the hearer to find an earlier reference to the same thing mentioned in the definite NP (Chafe, 1976). That mention, in this sample, was contained in *he's from the Amana area,* a sentence whose own definite NP linked cohesively to the sentence that introduced the friend in the first place (which employed an indefinite NP, *a good friend from Iowa*— the connection of the Amanas to Iowa being implicit). On this point as well, therefore, the sentences were altered by the information context.

The original sentence specified the narrative present tense *(I have a good friend),* but by the time A reached the final sentence he wanted to make clear that the friend was not present. The choice of *used to* introduces past time and conveys this fact. If instead the original sentence had been *I used to have a good friend,* the final sentence could have been in past tense without an additional clause: *he had some great stories. . . .* Finally, the form in which the final sentence was introduced reflects an aspect of the social context: A's initial *yeah, yeah* acknowledges the back-channel comment of B without comment, therefore without risk of losing the turn.

The extent of novel creation by speaker A at the point of the example sentence was distinctly modest: only one additional idea was introduced. We see from this example the crucial part played by the context in the development of speech acts. Many of the linguistic alternatives were predetermined by the sense of cohesiveness the speaker felt with the earlier reference to the good friend from Iowa. The diachronic path of the speaker's mental operations was also largely predetermined. The impression of ease that speech production often gives depends on such extensive contextual determination of speech. We will encounter other examples of overdetermination in Chapter 5, pages 105–109.

The example discussed above illustrates the effect of felt cohesiveness over the shape of sentences. Other sentences are shaped by the other type of connection to the context—deixis. Deixis exists whenever there is an implied origo, whether or not there is also a pointing gesture. The following is an example:

Is this your first year here?

This sentence contains almost nothing other than pointing. As noted earlier, the sentence was also accompanied by a pointing gesture, but this is not what makes the sentence deictic. Virtually every linguistic segment of the sentence has an implicit origo, and not all of them are the same. Only the grammatical form of the sentence as a question does not point to the information context. This form is the sole new element in the sentence, an appropriate choice for the opening phases of a conversation, which is where the sentence appeared. All the other features of the sentence point to parts of the external context available to both the speaker and hearer. The second word, *this,* points to the time of speaking; the third word, *your,* to the addressee himself; the fourth word, *first,* to a particular place in a temporal sequence; and the fifth word, *here,* to the place of speaking. All of these except *first* imply the speaker himself as the origo, and *first* implies an ordered course of study as its vantage point (the speakers were students). The intrinsic value of this sentence consists in part of these vantage points. From the origos the words point at the information context of the sentence, a context that must be taken into account in order to understand the sentence. The amount of contextual determination of the developmental path is again large, and this hyperdetermination by context may, again, explain the impression of ease of linguistic production and understanding.

THE AMANA CONVERSATION EXCERPT

This section presents an excerpt from a conversation (parts of which I quoted above and also used in Chapter 3). This excerpt will be a source of examples throughout the chapter; for the sake of clarity, I will refer to the excerpt as the "Amana conversation." The excerpt is from a longer conversation between two previously unacquainted male graduate students at the University of Chicago (recorded and transcribed by S. Duncan). The part of the conversation shown here is the early phase (but not the absolute beginning), when the participants were still groping for a common theme to which both could orient themselves (in Goffman's sense of this term, 1974). The conversation is transcribed so that speaker A's and speaker B's lines are synchronized. The places where gestures occurred have been indicated with G_p for a pointing gesture, and G_m for a metaphoric gesture (no other kinds occurred; for an explanation of metaphoric gestures see Chapter 7 and the introduction in Chapter 1).

A: Is this your first year here, or where'd did you come from

           (G_p)   (G_p)

B: mmmhm

A: before? o-o-o   Oh, I have a good friend
B: um Iowa. I lived in Iowa.

A: from Iowa. He's from Cedar Rapids, no, not Cedar Rapids. He's
B: Oh, yeah?

A: from the Amana area.   Yeah, I guess it is.
B: He—that's near Cedar Rapids, between

$$(G_p)$$

A: Yeah, yeah. He used to have
B: like Dubuque and Cedar Rapids.

A: some great stories about the Amanas. And uh, well but uh,
B:

A: he said it was the first socialist community in the United

$$(G_m)$$

B:

A: States, or something.
B: I really don't know that much about it.

A: Oh, yeah.
B: I really—I've never been there. I've just heard about

$$(G_m)$$

A:
B: I've wanted to go there. They have—they make excellent

A: Do they? I . . . I
B: bread.   They make bread an' a lot lot of food that you

$$(G_m)$$

A: Uh-huh. An' how do you like Chicago
B: can buy there, yeah.

A: compared—did you go to school there or uh what?

$$(G_p)$$

B: I did go to

A:
B: school there

$$(G_p)$$

COHESIVENESS

Related to the concept of cohesiveness is the concept of "theme." The theme is that with which references are felt to be cohesive, and what cohesive linguistic operations presuppose. There can be more than one theme, and cohesiveness can vary in degree. The extent to which a referring form is thematic reflects its current syntactic role and also its history in the discourse (Schiffman, 1985). The subject slot is usually reserved for what the speaker considers to be the current theme; in the following line from the Amana conversation the theme has already been established as the Amana area in Iowa:

> B: *that*'s near Cedar Rapids.

The predicate slot, on the other hand, usually contains information that the speaker considers to be other than the theme—information that is being offered about the theme. In the example, speaker B predicates information about the location of the Amana area.

Coding Procedures

Because the linguistic coding of cohesiveness relies on presupposition, a variable in the linguistic code is the explicitness of the referring forms themselves. In the Amana conversation speaker B made use of an inexplicit referring form, a pronoun, in the subject position to refer to the theme, and an explicit NP in the predicate to convey additional information. Since the pronoun is inexplicit, the reference can be interpreted only by connecting it to some earlier reference, that is, by cohesively linking the reference to the context. An explicit referring form, in contrast, adds nothing to cohesion since it is interpretable on its own. Explicitness of reference is thereby part of the linguistic code for cohesiveness.

Levy (1984) found that explicitness of referring forms varied predictably depending on the estimated degree of cohesiveness. This estimation was based on objective text criteria: (1) The *immediate discourse context,* which reflects whether a given referring form is *coreferential* with *the most recent* and *most structurally parallel* reference of *the same semantic category* (e.g., singular human male). "Structurally parallel" means that the target referring form has the same syntagmatic value as the context referring form with which it is cohesive. (2) The *local density* of reference, which reflects the total frequency of mention of the reference in the immediately preceding context. Levy found that inexplicit referring forms were more likely to appear in sentences that met these criteria of cohesiveness; that is, the more parallel and the more dense the references, the more likely the form was to be inexplicit. Here are some examples from Levy's thesis (taken from narrations; 1984):

1. *The most cohesive context:* Here the target referring form has every critical point: its context is the most recent, most structurally parallel reference in the same category. In these cases the referring form (indicated by the arrow) strongly tends to be inexplicit:

The main character$_1$ walked out

→ He$_1$ didn't care

The target is an elaboration on the context, and a high degree of cohesiveness is expected.

2. *Less cohesive context:* Here one or more *non*coreferential forms intervene between the target reference and the context. In this intermediate case the referring form tends to be of intermediate explicitness. In the following a generic NP is used:

He$_1$ gave him$_2$ (i.e., a noncoreferring form)

an extra 5 pence or something

→ and the guy$_1$ went on to his class

In the next two categories of cohesiveness the referring form is coded as discontinuous with the context, first moderately discontinuous and finally strongly discontinuous.

3. *Next-to-most discontinuous context:* Here the last parallel referring form in the context is *noncoreferential,* and moreover a coreferential form that is *nonparallel* intervenes:

He$_1$ said something to the man$_2$ you know real formal

→ and the guy$_2$ took off his hat

The last parallel referring form is *he* in the first clause (like *the guy,* it is the subject of its sentence and the reference is singular human male). However, *the man* intervenes and this form is coreferential with *the guy* but not parallel to it (it is in the predicate). Again the target referring form is a generic NP of intermediate explicitness.

4. *Most discontinuous context:* Here the last parallel referring form is noncoreferential, but there is no other form intervening:

and he$_1$ says well

→ and then his father$_2$ made—told some kind of story

The second clause introduces a new reference. It is accordingly discontinuous, and the referring form chosen is explicit.

In addition, *local density* has an effect separate from the immediate context variable. If references to something are dense in the context, inexplicit forms might appear even though the reference is noncohesive by the other criterion; for example:

Charles$_1$ gives the guy$_2$ a tip

and Ø$_1$ says that "I'm$_1$ sorry"

the guy's$_2$ muttering

→ so he$_1$ goes out

That is, an inexplicit referring form is used in the final sentence even though the situation here is the maximally discontinuous one of case number four. This *he* immediately follows a structurally parallel noncoreferring form, and so should be explicit (*the guy* is in the subject slot of its sentence and belongs to the same semantic category).

If variations in explicitness also occur in inner speech, the internal dialogue would mesh with and organize the speaker's own memories and sense of cohesiveness. Thinking with pronouns (e.g., "it") has a different effect on the course of thought than does thinking with explicit nouns (e.g., "the Amana area"). With "it," attention turns to earlier context, but with "the Amana area" thinking is almost inevitably discontinuous with the context that came before and attention turns in some new direction. (See Chapter 5 for further discussion.)

Rules of Introducing and Maintaining References

The following rules cover a number of situations in which cohesiveness varies in strength.

1. Existing themes are weak and appear in subject position. "Weak" means they are indicated with inexplicit forms, are phonologically unmarked, and are grammatically unelaborated. In contrast, predications about themes are conveyed in a strong and differentiated manner (Clancy, 1980).
2. New thematic references are strong and appear in the predicate slot of sentences and later are shifted to the subject slot in weak form (Levy, 1982).
3. Repeated mentions of the same thematic references are weak in any position (Levy, 1982).
4. Switch-reference is accompanied by no weakening, and possibly an increase of strength of referring form (Clancy, 1980).

These rules for shaping sentences push the attenuated and elaborated parts of sentences in opposite directions. The rules thus have a powerful influence over the paradigmatic choices of the speaker. For example, when the theme is also the agent of an action, a subject-verb-object object sentence has the appropriate form, but when the theme is not the agent, some specialized syntactic form, such as the passive, must be introduced instead. For instance, the following sentence indicates that the theme is the object of the action:

It got bent back.

If part of the intrinsic value of the sentence includes the speaker's feeling of cohesiveness with the theme, the passive could unpack this value and arise out of a synthesis of linguistic and intrinsic values. Paradigmatically contrasting complex symbols (such as the SVO active sentence) would be excluded in advance.

The following sentences occurred at the beginning of one of the "Pear Stories" (Chafe, 1980). They illustrate the use of explicit referring forms to introduce a new reference and inexplicit forms to show cohesiveness; they also illustrate the rule that new themes are introduced in the predicate slot but thereafter are indicated in the subject slot:

The movie opened up on this nice scene.

It was in the country.

It was oaks.

It seemed like West Coast.

The theme is the opening scene of a movie. In the first sentence the theme is introduced with an explicit form in the predicate; in the remaining sentences, it is referred to with inexplicit forms in the subject that indicate cohesion.

There is a certain logic to the rule for introducing the theme in the predicate. By placing it in the predicate it can be described—obviously desirable for the first mention of something—and because it is new, it cannot be presupposed —the property desired of the reference in the subject.

As a consequence, however, there is a problem of what to do with the subject of the first sentence: to fit the normal pattern of discourse structure, the subject should be less elaborate and more presupposing than the predicate. The speaker of the above example used "the movie" for the initial subject, and this choice solved her problem. The speaker had just seen the movie, and the hearer was aware of this. The movie itself could therefore act as a temporary theme while the real reference point—the opening scene—was being introduced.

The speaker's choice of a definite NP for this subject—*the* movie—shows that she was regarding the subject slot of the first sentence as indicating something that could in fact be identified by the hearer. The definite article invited the hearer to look in the context for something already known (Chafe, 1976). The speaker employed the definite article to create an interim reference point, and she took care to do this with a reference point that she knew the hearer could identify from knowledge of the nonlinguistic situation. In a self-actualizing manner typical of much conversation, the speaker was able to manipulate the information context and provide the desired asymmetry between the subject and predicate slots of the opening sentence.

Obviously, from a purely linguistic point of view, it is possible to have an elaborate subject followed by an attenuated predicate. For example:

This nice scene was the thing.

Such a way of constructing the sentence would appear, however, only if the emphasis were on discontinuity. If, for instance, the speaker had been talking about some situation in general and now wanted to introduce the nice scene as the specific topic, this reversed order, precisely because it is deviant, or marked, could be used to do it (Levy, 1984).

The theme in the above examples was indicated four times, the second through fourth times by means of inexplicit pronouns. Such a process can pass through still more steps. The first mention might be, as above, a full NP, and later mentions progressively less explicit forms, as in this example from Marslen-Wilson et al. (1982):

> so then it cuts back . . . to *The Hulk and the Thing* and *they*'re still battling and Ø knocking down chimneys

This passes from full NPs (proper names), through a pronoun, to "Ø" (see pages 23–24). Still other subdivisions are possible; for example, between full NPs and pronouns in the scale of explicitness there can be generic NPs (e.g., "these guys," "one or the other of them").

There are examples of theme indicators in the Amana conversation that have weak and attenuated form, and appear in the subject position:

> A: I have *a good friend from Iowa*
> *He*'s from Cedar Rapids . . . No, not Cedar Rapids
> *He* used to have some great stories about the Amanas
> *He* said it was

Similarly from B:

> B: *They* have excellent bread
> *They* make bread and a lot lot of food

On the other hand, there are sentences in which inexplicit theme indicators occur in predicate position without breaking cohesiveness. Such inexplicit referring forms in the predicate give the impression of being back-channel verbiage. In the following, the Amanas remain the reference point but are referred to with pronouns in predicate position:

> B: I really don't know that much about *it*
> I've never been *there*
> I've wanted to go *there*

These sentences suggest diffidence and reluctance on B's part to continue talking about the Amanas. In fact, they were the last sentences on the topic and induced in A, perhaps because of their peculiar back-channel form, a return to the question of B's origins.

Switch-reference means that the subject of the current clause is different from the subject of the immediately preceding clause. The switch-reference rule counteracts the rule which states that repeated mentions of a reference should be more and more inexplicit. An inexplicit referring form would be ambiguous in the switch-reference situation. Even though the subject refers to something that has been mentioned already, when there is switch-reference, the subject should not refer inexplicitly.

The following, taken from a narration, is an example of switch-reference:

So he's₁ looking through binoculars

and Tweetie's₂ looking back at him₁

In accordance with the switch-reference rule, a new subject (Tweetie) is referred to explicitly. Although this sentence was not the first mention of this reference in the narration, to have used an inexplicit form would have been ambiguous:

So he's looking through binoculars

and he's looking back at him

Switch-reference passes through an interesting developmental history that Karmiloff-Smith (1982) has investigated. She had children describe sequences of pictures that presented a story of a little boy and a balloon-man. The following is a five-year-old's version, a child for whom there is no linguistic coding of cohesiveness at all. The asterisks (*) indicate points at which switch-references occur.

He's walking away

*He gives him a green one

*He walks off home

*It flies away into the sky

*So he cries

The child consistently uses the pronoun *he* in a way that seems *deictic*—the pronoun points to the externally presented picture before him. These uses of the pronoun are like pointing gestures in verbal form. The pronoun, although inexplicit, does not seem to code cohesiveness with previously mentioned linguistic objects. It does not seem ambiguous to the child to use the same pronoun to indicate in one sentence the little boy *(he sees a balloon-man)*, in the next sentence the balloon-man *(he gives him a green one)*, and in the third sentence the little boy again *(he walks off home)*.

With children who are slightly older the problem has shifted. The child of five years or so who told the following story appears to be sensitive to ambiguity and uses pronouns to indicate cohesion, but does not yet make use of the switch-reference rule. To avoid ambiguous pronoun uses, the subject slot has to be reserved for references to a single character (the most prominent, the little boy).

A little boy is walking along

He sees a balloon-man

*The balloon-man . . . he asks for a balloon

And Ø goes off happily

*The balloon . . . he lets go of the balloon

And Ø starts to cry

The evidence for the inexplicitness rule in this narration is clear and convincing. The intitial reference to the little boy is with a full NP and indefinite article, the next reference is by a pronoun, and later the child twice shrinks the pronoun to "zero."

The child, however, does not yet know how to coordinate two reference points. For this he needs the switch-reference rule. In two places the child attempted to use the subject slot to indicate another character but then rejected it. These "repairs" are convincing evidence that for this child there is not yet a switch-reference rule. Cohesiveness can be coded in such a narration, but the same theme must be maintained continuously.

Constructing Cohesive Discourse

A study by Marslen-Wilson et al. (1982) found that very explicit referring terms in which there is a full NP plus a descriptive phrase, like *the Hulk, the green fellow,* were limited to contexts where the speaker was introducing characters into the story for the first time. Inexplicit referring terms, in contrast, appeared in contexts from which extensive cohesive connections emerged to other parts of the narration. The following table from their report (p. 344) shows this correlation:

Degree of embedding	NP plus description	NP alone	Nonspecific NP or pronoun	Third person pronoun	Ø
Story	3	2		1	
Episode		7	6	2	
Event introduction	1	14	1	2	
Event maintenance		4		30	15
	With pointing gestures			None with pointing gestures	

In this table, the terms listed under "Degree of embedding" can be explained as follows: "Story" is one unit unto itself; references at this level introduce characters for the first time and take the form of the example above—*the Hulk, the green fellow.* "Episodes" are comparable to scenes of a movie, a parallel actually used by the narrator with such phrases as *so the scene cuts back to.* Referring terms at the episode level are simple NPs without supplementary descriptive phrases, and generic NPs, like *one or the other of the two.* "Event introductions" are sequences of actions within an episode. The referring terms used are NPs and 3d person pronouns. "Event maintenance" are also sequences of actions where the participants have already been introduced in the event. The referring forms here are third person pronouns and "zeroes." Thus, as the speaker reaches the more deeply embedded levels of the narration, and experiences cohesive links that are stronger, there is a shift in the type of referring term. Explicit terms that presuppose little are replaced by inexplicit terms that presuppose more. (Pointing gestures are discussed in the section on deixis, pp. 73–74.)

In the Amana conversation there are also referring forms that run in a sequence from full NP, through pronoun, to "zero." Simultaneously, references become more and more embedded in the information structure being built up:

> A: He's from *the Amana area*
> B: He—*that*'s near Cedar Rapids, Ø between like Dubuque and Cedar Rapids

Cohesive Devices

The term "cohesion" has already been extensively used in this discussion. In what follows I will illustrate some of the devices of language that Halliday and Hasan (1976), the authors of this term, call "cohesive devices." Cohesive devices code links from the sentence (part) to the information context (whole). They indicate the position of each part in relation to the whole. Among the cohesive devices are: *third person* and *demonstrative pronouns, substitution* and *ellipsis, discourse conjunctions,* and what I will call *polarity.*

Third Person and Demonstrative Pronouns   An outstanding cohesiveness feature of pronouns is their ability to form long chains in which one pronoun links back to another pronoun, this to another, and so on, until the chain reaches what all the pronouns presuppose—a word or phrase that has an independent meaning. Both participants in a conversation can contribute to the same chain. The following is a pronoun chain to which both speakers contributed in the Amana conversation excerpt (including "there," which functions cohesively.):

A: from *the Amana area*	Source
B: *that*'s near Cedar Rapids	1 word back
A: *it* is	9 words back
B: I've never been *there*	53 words back
B: I've wanted to go *there*	62 words back
B: you can buy *there*	85 words back

A pronoun chain is a store of information about the coreferent (Lesgold, 1972). If one wished to determine the factual yield of a conversation, the information stored in coreferring pronoun chains would be a good way to uncover it.

Substitution   Substitution of one word for a group of words not only links two places in discourse, but also "repudiates" part of the earlier discourse. The sole example of substitution in the Amana conversation is the following:

> A: *He's from*   Cedar Rapids, no
>   not   Cedar Rapids

In this example the word *not* substitutes for the affirmative sense of *he's from* and repudiates *Cedar Rapids*. All substitutions have these two components —linkage to a source and repudiation of some part of the source. A negative word is not necessary for repudiation, but there must be a sense of contrast.

The substitution in the Amana conversation is probably best regarded as a type of clausal substitution; it means "he's *not* from," changing the clause from affirmative to negative. (Halliday and Hasan also describe nominal and verbal substitutions.)

Ellipsis   Ellipsis is like substitution in that it simultaneously adds to cohesion and repudiates a part of the source. Ellipsis can, in fact, be regarded as substitution by "zero." Ellipsis, therefore, is not a short-circuiting of speech, but a positive force for increasing cohesion. It is restricted to syntactically parallel constructions.

In the Amana conversation, ellipsis appears in several places. For instance, in the utterances:

A: *Where did you come from* before?
B: Ø   Iowa

the clause, *where did you come from?,* is ellided and *before* is repudiated—that is, replaced by *Iowa.* In the utterances:

B: That's *near Cedar Rapids*
A: Yeah, I guess it is   Ø

the locative *near Cedar Rapids* is ellided. *That,* which is replaced by *it,* is the repudiated element. The precise discourse significance of this repudiation is rather hard to see, but the shift to a nondemonstrative pronoun seems quite fluent. Finally, in the utterances:

B: *that's* near Cedar Rapids
B: Ø   between like Dubuque and Cedar Rapids

that's is ellided. *Near* is repudiated and replaced by *between.*

When there is ellipsis of nouns, the ellisions and repudiations follow a systematic order that depends on the conventional order of constituents in NPs (see Bever, 1970, for discussion). The following is from Halliday and Hasan:

Here are my two white silk scarves
Where are yours   Ø
I used to have three   Ø
Can you see any black   Ø
Or would you prefer cotton?   Ø

The substitutions repudiate, in order, *my, two, white,* and *silk.* So, for example, saying *I used to have three,* after saying *here are my two white silk scarves,* presupposes *white silk scarves* and repudiates *two.*

Substitution and ellipsis rest on relations of contrast and replacement. When these cohesive devices are used, the part is opposed to the whole. For example, *I used to have three* opposes *two* but preserves the other contextual aspects.

Conjunctive Association   The conjunctions *and, or, but, no, yet,* plus others, tell the hearer that segments of discourse on either side of the conjunction are connected and how this connection is to be made. Conjunctions in discourse are loosely related to the same conjunctions within propositions. In discourse *and* does not indicate the summation of two assertions, it indicates that there's more to come:

> A: He used to have some great stories about the Amanas *and* uh but

In this case, *and* signals that there is more to be said about the Amanas.

Or directs the hearer to treat two segments of discourse as alternatives, as in:

> A: Is this your first year here, *or* where did you come from before?

In this example, *or* signals that the hearer has a choice of questions to answer.

No in discourse means "the following denies what preceded it," as in:

> A: He's from Cedar Rapid, *no,* not Cedar Rapids

The remaining conjunctive example from the Amana conversation excerpt is *but,* the function of which is to signal that the segment following *but* conflicts with the segment just before (somewhat like *no*). In the excerpt the conflict exists at a metalinguistic level—at a level above, and commenting on, the speech level:

> A: And uh well *but* he said it was the first socialist community in the United States or something

Speaker A signals that the segment initiated with *but* will be, in contrast to the word salad just preceding, uttered in a relevant and interpretable manner (implying that the speaker was able to foresee a successful production of the next clause). Because *but* and *and* are on linguistic and metalinguistic levels, the *but* did not cancel the *and,* which remained in force to signal that more was to come.

Polarity   This is a term for the cohesive effects of pragmatically negative or positive verbs and adverbs that tie together successive clauses when they express the same attitude. This attitude is the whole of which the clauses are parts. In the Amana excerpt there is a stretch with cumulative negative effect:

> B: I *really don't know that much* about it. I *really*—I've *never* been there. I've *just heard* about it.

Really, don't know, that much (implying contrast), *never, just,* and *hear* reduce the speaker's obligation to make any serious contact with the preceding content (the Amanas); they achieve this by negative polarity. All of these clauses are linked by virtue of expressing the same attitude. Positive polarity would have had the opposite effect of establishing the speaker's authority over the topic:

> B $^{-1}$: I know *quite a lot* about it. I've been there *often.* I've *actually* see . . ..

It is interesting to note that the positive version uses adverbs of quantity and frequency—*quite a lot* and *often*—and a verb that refers to seeing. In our folk epistemology enumerating, measuring, and seeing (rather than hearing) are the royal road to definite knowledge. One wonders about other cultures where, perhaps, knowledge comes in dreams.

As the name implies, cohesive devices tie a discourse together into a structure beyond a succession of sentences. When cohesive devices are removed or tampered with, the hearer's ability to understand can be greatly impaired. Garnham et al. (1982) have shown that children are better able to remember stories in which the cohesive devices do signal cohesion with the context, compared to stories with the same content and succession of events in which the devices do not signal cohesion.

Information Hierarchies

Sentences in discourse exist in a hierarchy of relative informational importance. Informationally less important sentences can occur successively with more important ones, and are interpreted in relation to the surrounding sentences of greater importance. A hierarchy of informational importance can be inferred from the coreferences of the cohesive devices that appear in the discourse text. Presupposing devices are hierarchically subordinate to the referring forms that they presuppose.

The information hierarchy for speaker A in the Amana conversation is shown below. (Italics indicate the themes that are inferred by this method; indentation indicates themes that are more embedded in the hierarchy.)

B's origins (1) Is this your first year here or where did you come from before? (B: from Iowa)
  Friend (2) I have a good friend from Iowa
      (3) He's from Cedar Rapids
        Iowa geography   (4) no, not Cedar Rapids
    Friend (5) He's from the Amana area (B: That's near Cedar Rapids)
        Iowa geography   (6) Yeah, I guess it is
  Friend (7) He used to have some great stories about the Amanas

(8) He said it was the first socialist community in
        the United States

B's origins: (9) an' how do you like Chicago compared—did you go to
                      school there or uh what?

In graphic form speaker A's information hierarchy looks as follows:

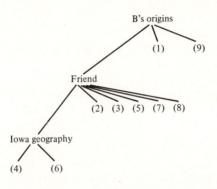

According to the hierarchy as reconstructed, sentences adjacent to one another in speaker A's speech were not always equally important. Conversely, sentences of equal importance were not always adjacent to each other. The most important sentences were those directly related to B's origins (dominated by *B's origins* in the graph), of intermediate importance were those about the friend from Iowa, and of least importance were the sentences directly about Iowa geography. Of the latter, only one (number four) was autochthonous; the other was directly evoked by a comment by speaker B. Despite variations in cohesiveness, however, all the sentences related to a single thematic whole, which can be designated as: Where did B come from? Relatively unimportant sentences are interpreted in relation to the more important sentences bearing directly on this main theme. Cohesion explains how speaker A could jump, apparently discontinuously, from the Amana area as a topic, to B's origins: B's origins had actually been A's principal topic all along. (A similar hierchical structure seems impossible to construct for the social context; in social context there may not be a structure of this form.)

For speaker B, the information hierarchy looks quite different:

                    (A: Where did you come from before?)
B's origins   (1) I lived in Iowa
                    (A: Did you go to school there?)
                (9) I did go to school there

*Iowa
geography*   (A: the Amana area)
                (2) That's near Cedar Rapids between like
                      Dubuque and Cedar Rapids
        The Amanas   (3) I really don't know that much
                                about it

(4) I really—I've never been there
(5) I've just heard about
(6) I've wanted to go there
(7) They have—they make excellent bread
(8) They make bread an' a lot lot of food that you can buy there, yeah

In graphic form there are two separate branches for B:

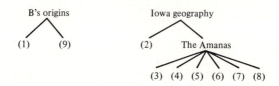

Comparing A's and B's information structures, we see that for the two speakers this part of the conversation had quite different forms and significance. To speaker A the conversation was about B's origins, and all other topics were subordinated to this. For B, however, the topic of origins was taken up only as a direct response to A's questions. Speaker B in fact gives the impression of trying to avoid the topic of where he came from. For B the conversation dealt chiefly with Iowa geography. Thus a somewhat comical, but hardly atypical, situation arose in which speakers A and B were exchanging turns talking about different topics. The absence of a common thematic reference point for A and B was not obvious because there was a factual relation between A's friend and Iowa. This allowed a loose association between A's topic and B's topic to substitute for a true shared thematic reference point. (A and B, shortly after this stage in their conversation, came across a topic about which both were willing and able to predicate new information.)

Gestures of Cohesion

There are gestures, called *cohesive gestures,* that connect the sentences with which they occur to the preceding information context. In cohesive gestures the same gesture form appears twice on separate occasions. The gesture re-establishes a reference introduced earlier. There can be cohesive gestures in the absence of linguistically coded cohesiveness, and in these cases the gesture is the principal clue for coreference.

In the following excerpt from a narration of a film, the speaker describes a character who, while lying in bed holding a newspaper, is looking at another character through a mirror. There is thus a complicated intermeshing of action streams. The speaker uses pronouns to refer to both of the characters, but avoids ambiguity through cohesive gestures that separate the streams (the streams are indicated by the right and left arrows):

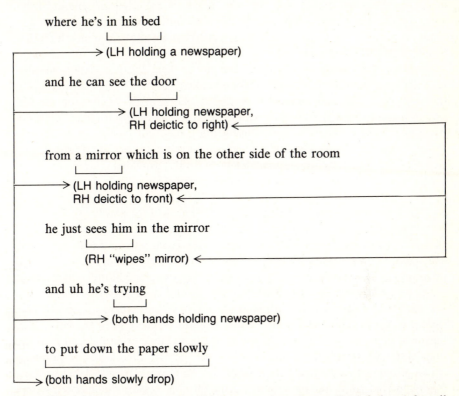

The right hand is used for all references to the mirror, the left hand for all references to the character in bed holding the newspaper. In the final clause the first *verbal* reference to the newspaper is by means of a definite NP—presupposing a previous reference; but the only previous references were by gesture. Thus we see that the linguistic and gesture channels were utilized cooperatively to structure the narration at this point.

DEIXIS

Most words have references that do not depend on an ⊕. The references of *cat, book,* or *deviousness* can be the same from every standpoint. In what Bühler called *primary deixis* the ⊕ is a complex of time, place, and personal identity centered on the speaker: the locus expressed with "I," "here," and "now." In *secondary deixis* the ⊕ is arbitrary. For example, *to the left of the post* has the post as the ⊕ and points in a direction relative to this origo.

Deictic references contrast with cohesive references (also called *anaphoric* references). Some writers have proposed that anaphoric references are special cases of deixis in which the reference object is verbally introduced (Klein, 1982,

p. 177). It would be necessary in this case to assume that an ⊕ is implied by the anaphoric reference and the hearer is able to work this origo out from the discourse. In most treatments, however, deixis is regarded as separate from cohesiveness. The relationship of pointing is not considered to be the same as that of presupposition. To my knowledge, there has been no analysis of anaphora that would supply the necessary ⊕.

Among pronouns, *I* and *you* are the prototypical deictics. They have shifting references (and therefore are sometimes called "shifters"; cf. Jakobson, 1960) that depend on the particular speaker—that is, choice of ⊕—of the moment. *He, she, they,* and *it,* on the other hand, are regarded as the prototypical cohesive pronouns. They corefer by presupposing the target, not by linking an ⊕ to a target. However, not all first and second person pronoun uses are deictic. Cohesive uses occur in direct quotations. Klein (n.d.) has provided a neat example of a cohesive first person pronoun in the following:

The goalkeeper ran out and thought, What do I do now?

In this sentence the *I* cohesively presupposes the goalkeeper and does not deictically point at the speaker. It is also possible to have deictic uses of the third person pronouns, as we saw in the use of pronouns by the youngest children of Karmiloff-Smith's (1982) study (see pages 63–64), and deictic third person pronouns also occur in adult usage, as in *he's the man who did it, officer,* where a referent object is pointed to by *he* and the speech situation is the implied ⊕. In the latter case, however, there is a strong compulsion to make a deictic pointing gesture at the same time. The strength of this urge is much greater than with the normally deictic pronouns *I* and *you*. The gesture may help overcome the cohesive functioning of the third person pronoun, and for this reason the speaker feels a compulsion to include it.

Implicit Deictic Words

Some verbs, particularly those describing motion and other kinds of transferals, carry an implicit ⊕ in their meaning. Some examples are *come/go, tell/hear,* and *sell/buy*. Use of one of these verbs automatically introduces an ⊕ from which the direction of motion is reckoned. In well-known but unpublished lectures on deixis (often called the "Santa Cruz lectures"), Fillmore (1971) analyzed the deictic relationships built into a number of verbs like *come, go, take,* and *bring*. *Come* and *bring* code that motion is toward the origo, either at speaking time or at a reference time. Speaking time is, obviously enough, the time of speaking. An example of motion toward origo at speaking time would be:

Come here.

Reference time is the temporal focus of the event. This can also be speaking time but is not necessarily so. An example of the use of a deictic verb whose origo is reference time is:

He came home at midnight.

This implies motion, not at the time of speaking, but at the time of some previously established event frame.

Other possibilities include a moving ⊕, such as a moving person:

Is Alice coming with you?

In this question both the point of departure and the destination are irrelevant to understanding the deictic reference (example from Tanz, 1980). Finally, *come* can code an origo that is assumed for the central character of the discourse as a kind of "home base." This is its use in the following, by one citizen to another (cited by Tanz):

So Solzhenitsyn isn't coming to the White House after all.

(If this were uttered by the residents of the White House, the origo would be the current speaking situation.)

Pointing Gestures

The table from Marslen-Wilson et al. on page 64 indicated that pointing gestures occurred with some referring forms (the speaker was holding on his lap pictures of the main characters). As the box showed, these gestures occurred at explicit levels of reference only. There were no pointing gestures with the least explicit referring forms. Pointing gestures and cohesion thus appeared at complementary places in the narration. The two kinds of connection that link the context to individual sentences—cohesiveness and deixis—appeared in different places.

In the Amana conversation there were also pointing gestures (marked G_p). They occurred specifically when the speakers were attempting to introduce chains of coreferring forms. The start of such chains are also places of minimal cohesiveness. For speaker A all pointing gestures occurred when he was introducing the (not as yet accepted) thematic reference point of speaker B's origins. For B, likewise, a pointing gesture occurred when he was introducing the topic of Iowa geography. A second pointing gesture by speaker B occurred when, at last, he took up speaker A's offer to talk about his own origins. For B this was the beginning of a coreferring chain (the rest of which I have not reproduced: it was at this point in the conversation that A and B finally found something they could jointly orient toward). The other type of gesture, metaphoric (marked G_m in the transcript), was never produced at the beginning of a chain of coreferring forms. Metaphoric gestures occurred only inside these chains and suggest an image of a palpable substance, rather than lines running out from the sentence to the theme (the hand in these gestures appeared to grasp and support objects). These gesturally created objects accompanied the mention of a product—*he said, I've heard, a lot of food*—the first two being abstract products of speech. The two types of gesture thus had different places in the discourse (metaphoric and pointing gestures are discussed further in Chapter 7).

Pointing gestures occur in conversations at places analogous to first introductions of characters in narrations, where Marslen-Wilson et al. observed pointing gestures. The gestures in both of these situations appear to indicate the speaker's attempt to orient his own and the hearer's attention to the new reference object (i.e., the character being introduced, or the new conversational topic).

Fundamentally, the pointing gesture assumes the same metaphoric "entification" of abstract meanings that the metaphoric gestures display. Pointing differs from metaphoric gestures in that rather than depict this "substance" they point it out.

Pointing gestures also imply an origo, which can be inferred by tracing the gesture backward. In the Amana conversation this origo shifted systematically depending on the content of the concurrent speech. When it was about the other participant, the origo was shifted away from the speaker's own locus, whereas when it was about the speaker himself, it was at the speaker's locus. Figure 4.1 illustrates two gestures that occurred at the end of the Amana excerpt—when A reintroduced his theme of B's origins and asked *Did you go to school there?,* and when B replied *I did go to school there.* Both gestures point at a space that represents where B came from, but the origos are different.

Inherent Versus Deictic Reference

Words that refer to spatial arrangements, such as *left,* have two uses, one of which is not deictic. The drawings in Figure 4.2 (from Levelt, 1984) illustrate what is involved. In (a), sphere A is "to the left" of sphere B. This is deictic reference with an origo that the symbol V indicates (the V represents the speaker's lines of sight looking at the spheres). In (b), person A also is to the left of person B, from the same vantage point. This is deictic reference as well.

In (b), however, person *B* is *also* to the left of person *A.* The phrase *to the left of* can be used in two contradictory ways in (b). This is because people (and

A: did you go to school there or uh what?   B: I did go to school there

(origo at side)   (origo at self)

Figure 4.1 Examples of gestural deixis and shift of origo to correspond with viewpoint of sentence.

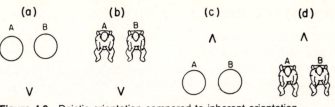

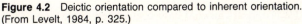

Figure 4.2 Deictic orientation compared to inherent orientation. (From Levelt, 1984, p. 325.)

other entities with canonical orientations—cars, buildings, furniture, etc.) have an inherent nondeictic orientation that is independent of vantage point. If the speaker moves behind the spheres, then sphere B is to the left of sphere A (c) and person B is to the left of person A (d). The inherent and deictic reference systems now correspond. Spheres do not have inherent orientations; hence there is never a contradictory use of *to the left of* with them. People do have an inherent orientation, however, and when the point of regard faces the inherent front (b) contradictory deictic and inherent usages occur.

Things become still more complicated when we consider furniture. Figure 4.3, also from Levelt, shows a desk and chair in a typical arrangement. For the chair the relationship of the left, front, and right sides is as with a person whose front is facing in the same direction as the chair. However, for the desk the left and right sides are reversed. If a person's front were facing the same direction as the desk's front, what is the left side of the person would be the right side of the desk, and vice versa. The difference between the chair and desk can be explained by referring to the canonical position of a person using these objects. In both cases what is "front" is what is next to the person's front. The same correspondence determines what is left and right. (For yet more complications and a number of amusing examples, Levelt's paper of 1984 should be read.)

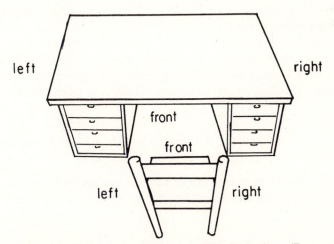

Figure 4.3 Deictic and inherent orientation with furniture. (From Levelt, 1984, p. 335.)

Discourse Structure by Deixis

In discourse deictic references appear in a variety of places. The conversational excerpt began with the deictic references in *Is this your first year here?,* as already noted. In that excerpt, however, deixis was not the principal form of information organization. In other situations, the information structure is almost completely organized around the concept of an ⊕.

Primary deixis appears in what have been called "gaze tours." Carrying out a type of investigation initiated by Linde and Labov (1975), Ullmer-Ehrich (1982) had university students describe their rooms and noted how the choices of referring terms depended on the assumed ⊕. The most common ⊕ was the doorway entering the room. This was the imagined locus of the speaker, and from it proceeded the gaze tour: the succession of objects and locations that one would see from that vantage point when running one's eyes along the walls. This tour is described in a different way from what, at first glance, looks like a highly similar situation, a walking tour. The descriptions differ because the ⊕s are different. A walking tour (in this sense) is also an imagined tour, but one in which the speaker imagines the hearer or some other secondary ⊕ moving through space (Klein, 1982). Klein's subjects were passers-by in a German city who were stopped and asked to give directions for finding a well-known building a few blocks away. The ⊕ of the walking tour is the position of the hearer as he or she is imagined to move through space.

In both kinds of tour there was no expectation that successive sentences would be connected cohesively. In this regard wholes structured deictically and wholes structured cohesively are completely different. This difference is particularly obvious in the gaze tour. Each successive sentence relates to the position of the viewer in the doorway. If sentences relate to other sentences, this is not essential for understanding the relation of the sentences to the whole. In the walking tour there is an order imposed on the successive sentences that corresponds to the order of locations along the tour, but neither does this induce cohesiveness of one sentence with another. The sentences relate to the moving ⊕ rather than to one another.

The different origos of the gaze tours (GTs) and walking tours (WTs) induced alterations of surface sentence structure. Different kinds of sentences comprise a kind of code for the type of deixis: (1) different subject NPs, (2) different verbs, (3) different advervbs, and (4) different word order.

1. Different subject NPs:

> GT: and then between the window and the wall is *this bookshelf*
> WT: and shortly *you* will be at the Old Opera

That is, the GT sentences had as subjects the objects to be seen in the room, whereas the subjects of the WT sentences were the hearers.

2. Different verbs:

> GT: . . . *is* this bookshelf
> WT: *go up* that way, always straight on

That is, the verbs of GT sentences described states of being, whereas those of WT sentences described movements.

3. Different adverbials:

> GT: as you enter the door *to the right* is . . .
> WT: you come *directly* to the Old Opera

That is, the adverbials of GT sentences described locative states, whereas those of WT sentences described directions.

4. Different word order:

> GT: . . . between the window and the wall is this bookself
> WT: you come to the Old Opera

That is, the word order of GT sentences had references to places before references to objects (idiomatic in German), whereas that of WT sentences had references to subjects before references to places.

The different choices of subject NPs and verbs are easy to understand: for the moving ⊕ of the WT there are the listener and the verbs of motion, for the static ⊕ of the GT there are the objects in the room and verbs of state.

The adverbs likewise refer to obvious differences between the two kinds of deixis: directional adverbials for the WT structure, in which someone is moving about in space, and locatives in the GT structure, in which nonmoving objects are encountered in a spatial array.

The word order difference is more subtle. Ullmer-Ehrich (1982) explains it as follows. In the GT the most predictable elements are the places. Given a standard shape and size of student room, there are few surprises in this domain. References to predictable elements tend to go into the initial, more presupposing positions of sentences. What the person will find *in* these places, however, is not predictable. References to unpredictable objects tend to be made in later sentence positions; whence the place-object word order of the GT. In the WT the most predictable element is the person who will do the walking, and the least predictable the places he or she will pass through; whence the subject-place word order of the WT.

OTHER RELATIONS TO INFORMATION CONTEXT

Information Space

Besides the two principal means of connecting individual sentences to information context that have been described, three others should be mentioned. *Focus spaces* (Grosz, 1981), *conversation spaces* (Reichman, 1978), and *scripts* (Schank and Abelson, 1977) are examples of information spaces that restrict the scope of possible cohesive connections. These differ from each other in the social context of speaking and the way the boundaries are formed. In focus spaces the boundaries reflect the structure of a task that the speaker is performing and explaining to a hearer; in Grosz's study it was an actual mechanical operation (disassembling an air compressor). The social context of focus spaces is thus one-way exposition. In conversation spaces the boundaries are determined by the participants' mutual focus of attention. Here the social context is conversation. In scripts the boundaries are defined by standard activities; for example, the activity of dining at a restaurant. The script itself defines a social context. All of these can be called "focus spaces" in a general sense, meaning a structured area of information on which the participants jointly focus their attention. Insofar as referring terms direct the attention of the speaker and hearer to the environment, the focus space will be an important determinant of the referring terms the speaker chooses and of their interpretation. The focus space provides the limits, in terms of information, on the sense of cohesiveness and the control of attention.

In Grosz's study data were collected by having an expert teach a novice how to perform a complex sequence of actions on a mechanical device. The dialogue between the teacher and student turned out to be analyzable into a hierarchical structure that closely matched the structure of the task itself. If steps B and C were necessary to perform step A, the dialogue explaining this was also organized hierarchically (the description of B and C organized under that of A). Referring terms stayed within the specific focus spaces. Cohesive connections did not cross boundaries into other focus spaces. If there were two identical potential reference objects for a particular referring form, it would be possible to refer without ambiguity to one of the objects with an inexplicit referring form if the objects were in different focus spaces. For instance, a speaker could say *I'm picking them up* and refer unambiguously to one set of screws rather than another set also visible, as long as the task structure clarified the focus space and called for only the one set. On the other hand, if both objects were in the current information space an explicit referring form would have to be used instead. Similarly, one can use a definite NP *the menu* just on the strength of the information space boundaries created by the restaurant script, even though there has been no prior mention of a menu.

Foreground and Background

A different form of information structure is the distinction between foreground and background (Hopper, 1979; Hopper and Thompson, 1980). This contrast is important particularly in narrations. Sentences are foregrounded if they mention events in the chronological order in which the events are depicted as occurring. To change the order of mention of foregrounded sentences would be to code a change in the order of events. Background sentences are not so tied to the storyline. They set scenes, introduce characters, summarize what has already gone on, and so forth. Their characteristic property is that they do not belong to a defined chronological sequence. Accordingly, background sentences theoretically can be moved to other places in the narration and this will not code a new order of events.

In some languages foreground and background sentences are constructed differently. In Swahili, for example, there is a special prefix, *ka-*, which attaches to the verbs of foregrounded sentences (Hopper, 1979). In English there is no such fixed formal feature, but the foreground-background distinction is expressed, rather, through features that cluster differently in foreground and background sentences. Foreground sentences tend to be constructed with nonprogressive verbs; for example, from Hopper (1979):

We *journeyed* several days

Background sentences, in contrast, tend to be constructed with progressive verbs; for example,

passing through several villages

Foreground sentences tend to be high on what Hopper and Thompson (1980) call transitivity—that is, the kinetic aspect of events—whereas background sentences tend to be low on this dimension, emphasizing, rather, unchanging states.

The foreground–background distinction is a dimension that divides the contents of a single focus space into two parts, and these parts are then differently coded.

The following is a narration in Swahili illustrating the use of *ka-* to mark the foreground.

Tu-*ka*-enda kambi-ni, hata usiku tu-*ka*-toroka, tu-*ka*-
we   went camp- to, and night we   ran off, we

safiri   siku kadha, tu-ki-pita   miji   fulani,
traveled days several, we   passing villages several,

na   humo mwote hamna mahongo
and them all   wasn't   tribute

This can be translated as: "We returned to the camp, and ran away during the night, and we traveled for several days, passing through several villages, and in all of them we did not have to pay tribute" (from Hopper, 1979). The foreground statements contain *ka-* and appear in the narration in the same order as the sequence of events. The background statements lack *ka-* (one has a *ki-*) and are contained within the "traveled several days" step of the narration:

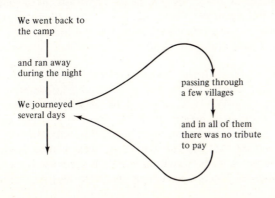

The foreground sentences are higher on kinesis. Each describes an action taken by the characters. The background sentences are lower on kinesis. In *there was no tribute to pay* the sentence describes a state, and in *passing through a few villages* the sentence is specifically marked as timeless and without temporal boundaries; *ki-* does this in the Swahili original, and the progressive verb *-ing* does it in the English translation.

McNeill and Levy (1982) discovered that the gestures made with foreground statements also tend to be kinetic—iconic gestures that exhibit in action form the situation that the statement is describing. With background statements the gestures tend to be "beats"—they tend to be punctuated movements that have no semantic quality of their own and that emphasize only the occurrence of the statement as a statement (see Chapter 7). Hopper and Thompson (1980) present evidence for the transitivity dimension in a large number of languages, suggesting that the same foundation of actionlike and statelike representations appears in language after language.

GIVEN AND NEW INFORMATION

The distinction between given and new information is simply the cohesiveness-discontinuity continuum by another name. New information can be equated with *nonpresupposed* and old information with *presupposed,* and this distinction covers what appears to be the spirit of the given–new distinction. Although "given–new" are in widespread use, they lead to inconsistent classifications. There have been proposed at least five different definitions of "given" and "new," and they are not always compatible.

1. *A speaker-based definition: New information is what the speaker thinks the hearer does not already know.* According to this definition (which was expressed by Haviland and Clark, 1974, for example), when speaker A said "I have a good friend from Iowa," everything except the pronoun "I" would be counted as new.
2. *A hearer-based definition: New information is newly activated in the hearer's consciousness.* It is possible for information that the speaker thinks the hearer already knows (hence "given" in the first sense) to be reactivated in consciousness, hence "new" in the second sense (Chafe, 1976). For example, if someone says "You remember our conversation yesterday," the entire clause is new if the hearer wasn't then thinking of the conversation, although the hearer would necessarily have known of it.
3. *New information is the least predictable information in the sentence on the basis of context.* Relatively unpredictable information is not necessarily out of consciousness or previously unknown. There can be independent variation of predictability (Grimes, 1975). For example, speaker A's saying *an' how do you like Chicago?* directly after speaker B had said *a lot of food that you can buy there,* was relatively unpredictable and could be classified as new, although B gives evidence of being highly conscious of Chicago as a topic and even had been trying to avoid it.

4. *New information corresponds to the answer to an implicit question.* The question itself corresponds to the given information (Grimes, 1975; Keenan and Schieffelin, 1976). For example, *I have a good friend from Iowa* answers an implicit question—*what do you have to do with Iowa?* The new information in this statement, according to the definition, is "the friend."

5. *New information is the semantic focus of the sentence.* This focus is the element to which all the other information in the sentence points (Halliday, 1967*a,b*). For example, in *I have a good friend from Iowa,* the *I have* and the *from Iowa* constituents point to *a good friend.* Both modify and circumscribe this friend and their occurrence makes a space for the friend, which is the new information.

As can be seen, these definitions are partially incompatible, partially overlapping. In the sentence, *I have a good friend from Iowa,* we have these designations of *new* information:

By *definition 1:*   Everything except *I.*

By *definitions 4 and 5:*   Only *a good friend.*

By *definitions 2 and 3:*   Variable portions depending on the context and the contents of the hearer's consciousness.

The definitions also differ in how easily operationalized they are, with definitions 2 and 3 seeming to be particularly inaccessible to operationalization. On the other hand, the definitions that lend themselves to operationalization are not necessarily the best motivated in terms of discourse function. A model of discourse structure may not be best formulated in terms of, for instance, what the speaker has grounds to believe the hearer already knows.

The essential fact of discourse organization toward which all these definitions tend seems adequately expressed in the concepts of cohesiveness—presupposed and nonpresupposed information. These concepts can be operationalized using the text-based scale of cohesiveness devised by Levy (1984) and described earlier in the chapter.

EXPERIMENTS ON PRONOUN INTERPRETATION

Pronoun interpretation is usually viewed as a kind of memory test. The pronoun is a *probe* presented to the hearer, who is then supposed to retrieve from memory information associated with the probe. The functional viewpoint of the concept of cohesiveness has played essentially no part in these experiments. Nonetheless, they can be related to the concept of cohesiveness. Pronouns can code cohesiveness only if they can be interpreted. Thus the limits on this process constrain the expression of cohesiveness. There is also a connection with intrinsic value. It is possible that the same variables that have been found to limit pronoun interpretation also influence the speaker's sense of cohesiveness with earlier linguistic events and thus constrain the contribution of the information context to intrinsic values of sentences.

The main conditions that have been examined for an effect on information retrieval are *recency* (Clark and Sengul, 1979), *parallel function* (Grober et al., 1978), *verb causality* (Garvey et al., 1975), and *plausibility* (Hirst and Brill, 1980).

1. *Recency.* Clark and Sengul (1979) reported a difference of about 200 milliseconds in the speed with which hearers felt, subjectively, that they could understand sentences that contained pronouns whose coreferring nouns were in the just preceding clause, compared to identical sentences and pronouns whose sources were two or three clauses earlier—the nearer sources were faster. This difference, though small (approximately the duration of a single syllable in ordinary speech), indicates a recency effect, and implies that recent speech is kept in a state of higher availability for the duration of about one clause and then becomes increasingly inaccessible for retrieval (see Jarvella, 1971, for a similar conclusion; also, see Chapter 5, pp. 129–131). Such a recency effect would favor directing attention to the just preceding clause. In the Amana conversation, despite forming long chains, nearly every pronoun is linked to a source in the just preceding clause (usually another pronoun).

2. *Plausibility.* The search for a coreferring NP initiated by a pronoun is guided by a sense of what makes a plausible scenario. For example:

Henry went to the party while John minded the store; he ate all the canapes.

In this example, the *he* is, strictly speaking, ambiguous (Hirst and Brill, 1980). Nonetheless, the scenario in which the coreferring NP is *Henry* rather than *John* is more plausible (although *Henry* must be retrieved from a less accessible state of memory). The greater the difference in plausibility between alternative pronoun interpretations, the faster the interpretation. As Hirst and Brill point out, this result suggests that the hearer first tries to integrate sentences with information from the context; and if this is possible, then assigns the pronoun to the NP that makes the most plausible scenario. Attempts at integration, therefore, precede attempts at interpretation, or assignment of reference.

3. *Causality.* Certain verbs code the direction of cause and effect (Garvey et al., 1975). *Criticize,* for example, implies that the cause of the action lies with the recipient, whereas *apologize* implies that it lies with the agent; so *she* corefers with different NPs in the following:

John criticized Mitsuko because she wanted a favor.

John apologized to Mitsuko because she wanted a favor.

Garvey and associates observed that subjects interpret pronouns in such sentences according to the implied cause-effect direction.

4. *Parallel function.* All other things equal, people prefer to avoid the switch-reference situation. This preference Grober et al. (1978) called "parallel function." However, verbs, such as *criticize,* that imply that the recipient is the cause force switch-reference. Grober et al. tested the effects of adding modal verbs to verbs like *criticize*—both what they called "strong" modal verbs (e.g., *must*), and "weak" modal verbs (e.g.,

may). They also tested the effects of changing the relationship between the clauses from one that is specific to causality *(because)* to one that is neutral *(but)*.

Their findings showed that strong modal verbs reinforce the switch-reference effect:

Toshiko must criticize Kimiyo because she wants a favor.

Toshiko may criticize Kimiyo because she wants a favor.

In the second sentence *she* can corefer with *Toshiko* or *Kimiyo,* but in the first it corefers only with *Kimiyo.*
    The relationship between clauses is also important:

Machiko criticized Yoshiko because she wanted a favor.

Machiko criticized Yoshiko but she wanted a favor.

In the first sentence *she* and *Yoshiko* corefer, but in the second sentence *she* can also corefer with *Machiko.*

What can we conclude from the experimental studies of pronoun interpretation? In terms of the contribution to intrinsic value, the results present a very reasonable picture: the information context is a more powerful influence over intrinsic value when it is recent, is connected to the current sentence in a plausible manner, can rely on basic cognitive relations like causality, and when the information in the context and in the sentence is structured in parallel ways.

Nonetheless, the conditions under which the experimental results have been obtained are highly restrictive and not well met by natural occurrences of pronouns. The most fundamental of the artificialities is a complete absence of thematic reference points that extend over more than one sentence. In no experiment has there been a theme, artificial or genuine, to which the pronouns under test are cohesive. Instead, the pronouns in these experiments were interpreted by matching to a single prior NP.

The findings are also limited to ambiguous pronoun uses; for example, *he ate all the canapes* or *Machiko criticized Yoshiko because she wanted a favor.* In contrast, pronoun uses in actual discourse are often not ambiguous, as examination of the Amana conversation excerpt shows (see pp. 56–57).

The findings are also limited to single-link cohesive connections. This contrasts with natural pronoun use, in which pronoun chains extend across many clauses. The underlying processes might be quite different.

In some experiments the findings are limited to *pragmatically nonsensical* uses. Lesgold (1972), for example, tested the cohesiveness of pronouns in sentences such as:

The uncle ate the pie and he was senile.

Does this mean that the pie *made* him senile? Such unnatural uses, not found in normal discourse, may be handled by people in unique ways.

chapter 5

Producing and Understanding Speech

The goal of this chapter is to bring out some of the processes by which speech is produced and understood. I include in this topic not only the production and hearing of speech sounds, but also—and this is the central topic of this book— the synthesis of individually constituted (intrinsic) and socially constituted (pure linguistic) values. This synthesis is obscure in the case of simple linguistic symbols, but can be shown clearly in the case of complex symbols. Sentences are products of linguistic acts and are structured linguistically in these acts to exhibit the speaker's thinking. This is the natural basis for sentences as symbols with intrinsic value.

Viewed as products of linguistic acts, symbols—sentences in particular— have four properties that must be considered in a complete psycholinguistic description:

1. Symbols are affected by the contextual whole of which the symbol is part.
2. Symbols have linguistic, or contrastive, value.
3. Symbols are affected by the person's processes of thinking.
4. Symbols have spontaneous generativity, that is, the ability to occur without inputs that trigger them (this property is described in the present chapter).

These factors have not hitherto been combined into a single approach. The topics of speech production and understanding have traditionally been conceived of in terms of selecting spoken symbols in the light of their contrasts. Speech understanding also has been conceived of in terms of reconstructing the speaker's mental representations. Very often the determinative influence of the context has not been considered at all, and the property of spontaneous generativity has not even been recognized as a property of linguistic activity.

In this chapter an integrated approach will be taken that includes all of the above factors. We will consider speech production and speech understanding jointly within this context. The closer one gets to the organs of speech perception and articulation, the more the processes of production and understanding appear to differ. At the level of process in which we will be involved, however, there is only the faintest of lines between them. Were this book about the dynamics of articulatory movements (Fowler, 1977) or the auditory aspects of speech perception (Denes and Pinson, 1963), the topics of speech production and speech reception would require different chapters altogether. But with respect to the internal psychological computations that are taking place, the building up and the understanding of speech are virtually the same process and are treated least redundantly in the same chapter.

As I have shown in Chapters 3 and 4, there are specific indexing codes for picking out parts of the context and for establishing a perspective toward the context. These codes can be studied from a synchronic point of view. But, in order to understand why this or that contextualized code was selected during the course of speaking, the best approach is through the contextualization of thinking. That will be the direction taken in this chapter.

As described earlier in Chapter 1, we will make use of a new source of data about the internal structure of linguistic acts: referential gestures that spontaneously occur with speech. These exhibit the same or overlapping propositional content as the surface sentence, but show this content in quite different forms.

SYNTHESIS OF IMAGISTIC AND SYNTACTIC FORMS OF THINKING

Concurrent gestures reveal that the speaker is engaging in two types of thinking simultaneously: syntactic (segmented and linear) and analogical (global and synthetic). The linguistic act is a synthesis of syntactic with imagistic thought. It

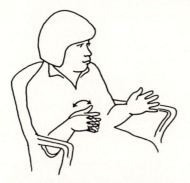

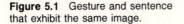
and they wanted to get where Anansi was

Figure 5.1 Gesture and sentence that exhibit the same image.

reveals this synthesis in a mutual penetration of imagistic and syntactic properties; images are shaped by the system of linguistic values (this is the specific topic of Whorfian hypothesis discussed in Chapter 6), and sentences are shaped by the images they unpack. The following example is offered to illustrate this interpenetration and the preservation of global-synthetic properties in surface sentence structure. The sentence and gesture occurred during a narration of one of the Anansi stories—folktales of the Ashanti people of Ghana—that the narrator had learned from a film. Anansi is a spider who is constantly getting into dangerous situations but always can count on salvation by his six wondrous sons (the referent of the subject pronoun *they*). The speaker is a 9-year-old boy who had been shown a film about Anansi in his school; the point of the example does not, however, depend on the fact that the speaker is a child. Figure 5.1 illustrates the example.

At the point in the narration where the example occurred, the boy had already explained that Anansi had been swallowed by a fish and that the six sons were setting out to rescue him. The gesture exhibited two objects that stood apart; one object moved in a wavy fashion as if in water, whereas the other walked back and forth ineffectually. The nonwalking object (indicated by the left hand) appears to be Anansi imprisoned inside the fish. The walking object (the right hand) is the sons collectively setting out on the rescue mission. The lack of closure of the objects depicted by the two hands shows the inaccessibility of Anansi inside the fish. Thus, the gesture can be interpreted as having created a compact concrete symbol that is a metaphor of all the ideas we ponderously express with the words *pursuit* and *inaccessibility*.

The following are some of the global-synthetic parallels that can be found between the surface grammatical form of the Anansi sentence and the synchronized gesture:

1. Two hands appear in the gesture; two participants are mentioned in the sentence *(they* and *Anansi).*
2. The right hand (dominant for this speaker) becomes the thematic reference point of the sentence; correspondingly, the sons are referred to with *they,* a presupposing pronoun.
3. The hands are held apart in the gesture; the references in the sentence to the two participants are contained in different clauses: *they wanted to get (somewhere); Anansi was (somewhere),* with syntactic distance reproducing the spatial distance of the gesture. (Mention of the participants within a single noun phrase would have been possible; e.g., *Anansi and the sons couldn't get together.*)
4. The right hand is walking; the corresponding participants in the sentence are the subject of the verb *get,* conveying movement. (Alternatively, the movement could represent the number of participants, coded with a plural pronoun.)
5. The left hand is moving passively as if in water; the corresponding participant in the sentence is contained in a locative stative *where Anansi was,* emphasizing lack of active movement.
6. The two hands do not close on one another, despite the movement of the

right hand; the subject of the movement verb is also the subject of *want,* the use of which presupposes that the action denoted by *get* has not taken place. (The choice of this verb also permitted the two-clause structure of the sentence.)

The surface form of the sentence, in other words, had many of the same properties as the global-synthetic representation of the gesture. In addition to coding the intentions of Anansi's sons, the surface sentence *exhibited* in its linguistic choices the meaning of pursuit plus inaccessibility. Rather than replacing the metaphoric image of two nonclosing objects, the constituents of the sentence *unpacked* this image, presenting the same image in a new way. The surface sentence has both pure linguistic (contrastive) and intrinsic value. Its intrinsic value has a natural basis in the image of two nonclosing objects. It is a synthesis of the two forms of value.

Other examples also show preservation of global-synthetic properties in surface structure; for example, the image of an object that was held up to view and predicated upon was unpacked with a choice of *it* plus predication in *It's a Porsche* or *It was a Sylvester and Tweetie cartoon* (from Chapter 1), and others of a similar type. The pronoun *it* indicates an object and the predicate *(is a Porsche* or *was a Sylvester and Tweetie cartoon)* articulates what the object "contains."

Not only do gestures co-occur with their sentences and exhibit imagistic thinking, but gestures and sentences are, to a degree, interchangeable. Complexity shifts between them. They exist in the same form at an early stage of deep time and can take one another's place in the developing sentence after this stage. The evidence for this conclusion is that the speaker's meaning can appear in either channel depending on the tactical problem of expressing it in spoken rather than gesture form. Evidently the sentence and gesture are, at one stage, a single process that appears at the surface in gesture or linguistic form. An example of a gesture that takes over complexity from the linguistic channel is the following:

and she chases him out again
└─────────────────────────┘
(hand swings "object" as if hitting a target)

The gesture depicts the weapon with which the chasing out described in the linguistic channel was carried out. To have placed a description of the weapon in the linguistic channel would have been possible, but would have required an extra phrase.

The converse phenomenon is speech taking over complexity from gesture. This was seen in an experiment in which we had subjects narrate a videotape of another speaker's narration, instead of a cartoon or film (McNeill, 1986). The narration, unknown to the subjects, had been performed with deliberate mismatches between the gesture and linguistic channels. In one part of the narration the speaker said *and he comes out the pipe* and performed an up-and-down motion. The gesture normally made for this scene by speakers who have seen the original cartoon is wide and sweeping. Subjects later retold the story from this videotaped performance. We found the subjects describing scenes with words that contained information first presented in gesture form, as in this example:

Our narration:

> Sylvester ingests the bowling ball . . . comes back out the drain pipe and goes rolling down the street
> |_____|
> (hand bounces up and down)

Subject's narration:

> Sylvester ate . . . ingested the bowling ball . . . falls back down to the bottom of the drain pipe and bounces down the street
> |_____|
>   (hand sweeps to side)

The up-and-down movement that had been originally presented in a gesture was expressed in spoken form as *bounce.* At the same time, what had originally been presented in speech *(rolling down the street)* became a sweeping gesture. The two channels traded places with one another.

Yet another demonstration of the interchangeability of gesture and speech is in a study reported in McNeill (1985c). Subjects were asked to narrate stories from memory under conditions of delayed-auditory-feedback (DAF). The experience of DAF is highly disruptive of speech. The speaker hears his or her own voice slightly delayed (in our experiment, it was 200 msec, or the approximate duration of a syllable). One tested subject, in particular, is interesting in this context. He produced no gestures *at all* under normal speaking conditions and commenced to gesture only under DAF. DAF itself was not the cause of the speaker's gesturing, but was the cause of linguistic simplification. When this speaker's sentences were syntactically less complex (less embedded) under DAF they were accompanied by gestures. Sentences under DAF at this speaker's normal level of embedding were not accompanied by gestures at all. Evidently, gestures took place to carry semantic complexity when this was blocked from the speech channel. It is conceivable that speakers, such as the speaker described, who habitually produce few gestures are able to transfer semantic complexity to the linguistic channel that other speakers usually convey gesturally. The above speaker is, in fact, the only one who ever *mentioned* rather than demonstrated in a gesture the destination of the character described at a certain point in a cartoon narration (this was a sentence produced under normal, non-DAF, conditions):

> then he proceeds to clamber up inside a drain spout which eventually will lead up to Tweetie's window

In contrast, all other subjects we have observed omit the destination and produce a pointing gesture instead.

Thus an argument can be put forth that gestures reveal a stage deep within the speaking process. At this level two kinds of thinking are being coordinated: imagistic (thinking that is global and synthetic) and syntactic (thinking that is linear and segmented). This dialectic is suggested by the concept of unpacking a global-synthetic representation with a linear-segmented string that exhibits the same global-synthetic sense. Imagistic thinking is not an "input" to a speech formulator (Kempen, 1977) but is a continuing part of the linguistic act. Imagistic thinking remains in the surface sentence, contributing intrinsic value, and is unpacked out of its global-synthetic form into a linear-segmented form that possesses linguistic value. The sentence is, at all stages, both imagistic and syntactic. An expression of this dialectic is that there is no system break between thinking and speaking. Grammatical features exist in thought (in this example, agentivity, transitivity) and thought features exist in grammar (a global-synthetic image of two objects not closing in the surface form of the sentence). There is no distinction between "input" and "output" in this situation, but only different developmental stages of a single process. If this reveals the language of thought, this language is much more imagistic than Fodor (1975) believed. Yet imagistic thought is capable of explaining the impression of ease and speed of action that one has of normal speech generation. Kendon (1983) has proposed related and supporting arguments.

Considering the diachronic axis of the linguistic act, at the start the syntactic contribution is implicit whereas the image is explicit, and then the syntactic aspect of the sentence becomes explicit and the image becomes implicit. We can still observe the image in the final linguistic product when we are guided to it by a concurrent gesture, as in the Anansi example.

The implicit syntax of the sentence in its primitive form is evident in several ways. There is congruence between thinking in terms of nonclosing objects and the syntactic concepts of agent and recipient of the action, of an object in motion and an intransitive verb choice, of nonclosure of objects despite motion and a major syntactic separation via a dual clause structure. All of this syntax is implicit and not yet actually present. It lacks linguistic value. To demonstrate how it could be implicit in germinal form and could guide the development of the sentence to attain its final external form, I will introduce the concept of inner speech. This is a concept that is well suited to expressing a dialectic between individual thinking and socially constituted values.

Inner Speech

Despite the use of the word "speech," inner speech is a form of thinking rather than speaking (Vygotsky, 1962, 1984). Inner speech is the smallest unit in which imagistic and syntactic thinking come together, yet is not itself a complete syntax. It is important because it builds access to socially constituted knowledge, including implicit linguistic choices, into thinking. At the same time, imagery grounds and gives meaning to inner speech. What I try to show in this chapter is that thinking that is imagistic and also utilizes inner speech symbols is able to unpack thinking into linear and segmented speech by means of its own internal resources. Such a self-organizing ability is the key to the spontaneous generativity of linguistic acts (property number four, above).

In addition, inner speech, when it is fragmentary, is inherently contextualized via its sense (as described below). Thus thinking in inner speech symbols brings with it adaptation to the environment of speaking, both internal and external.

The production of *they wanted to get where Anansi was* is a continuation of the same thinking process that produced the image of two nonclosing objects with the identity of Anansi and his sons, and their spatial relationship. Our task is to show how the surface sentence could have unfolded itself out of the image by utilizing the appropriate inner speech symbol. I will return to the question of how the inner speech symbol itself was aroused in the section on "smart" symbols, below.

What might this symbol of inner speech have been? The best method for tracing it is to assume that the inner speech symbol and the image remained together through the entire diachronic development of the sentence. On this assumption, the inner speech symbol can be inferred from the part of the external speech stream with which the gesture synchronized. In the Anansi example this was *and they wanted.* Thus our theory is that the speaker thought in terms of the image of two unclosing objects and utilized *and they wanted* to categorize and give meaning to, direct, and ultimately unpack this image into syntactic form. At the same time, the image grounded and specified *and they wanted.*

We must recognize that the above assumption cannot be directly validated. There is no independent method of observing the inner speech symbol to check that it was *and they wanted.* The validity of the assumption can, however, be indirectly supported. If plausible descriptions of the person's thinking and speech result from the assumption, then this is indirect validation of the assumption itself. If implausible descriptions result, the assumption is challenged. In the Anansi example and others to be presented, plausible accounts can be derived if inner speech symbols are identified via surface segments with which gestures synchronize.

Therefore, from the initial cognitive state (image + *and they wanted*), how could the full sentence *and they wanted to get where Anansi was* have come out as an inevitable unfolding? *And they wanted* divides the image into linguistically codable parts corresponding to the two objects. The inner speech symbol affects the image by forcefully separating the objects, one of which does not have a place in the symbol. For this object a new place must be found. The absence of closure in the image matches the inner speech symbol in that the symbol with *wanted* presupposes absence of action. This absence of action itself is unpacked by fitting together *want* with *get,* a movement verb, which in turn creates the two-clause structure that is the linguistic analogue of the physical separation of the two objects. The remaining object, Anansi, finally fits into this two-clause structure. Considered as a whole the lexical and syntactic choices of the surface sentence were made along the lines that are found in the global image when this image was initially interpreted in terms of the inner speech symbol *and they wanted.* (This process is considered in more detail later in the chapter, in the section headed "Analysis of Two Examples)."

Inner speech is thinking that utilizes words and other linguistic symbols as "cognitive tools" (Vygotsky, 1962, 1978, 1984). A cognitive tool "crystallizes" (Leont'ev, 1979) mental operations that are connected with the symbol. Inner speech is thinking carried out by means of these mental operations. In the intended use of the concept, the symbols of inner speech are purely mental representations and do not necessarily engage the movements of the speech articulators. Dysarthric patients—individuals incapable of moving their tongue, lips, and vocal chords in order to articulate speech, but who otherwise understand speech and read and write—show evidence of inner speech representations (Baddeley and Wilson, 1985). For example, they can match as having the same pronunciation *dough* and *doe,* or *ocean* and *oshun.* These words are presumably compared on the basis of purely mental sound images. If there are pure mental representations of signifiers, there should also be pure mental representations of signified content. The same mental representations of inner speech are assumed for normal speakers as well.

The following example was taken from a videotaped narration. The narrator produced a gesture at the same time he used the word *finds.* His hand, taking the form of a grip, groped behind him as though picking something up (in the narration what was found was a knife). The following is the example in full (from McNeill, 1985):

and finds a big knife
    |___|
(hand in grip shoots out to rear and grasps "knife")

We infer that the inner speech symbol was *finds.* This is based on the assumption that the symbol and image remained together through the entire development of the surface sentence. The gesture showed (1) the act of picking up the knife, (2) that the knife was picked up from the rear, and (3) that the shape of the knife's handle was round. Yet the gesture synchronized with the single word *finds,* a word that conventionally carries none of this information. The gesture image is plausibly interpreted as the intrinsic value of the word on this occasion.

This example shows to a maximum degree the abbreviated and predicative form of inner speech that Vygotsky (1962) described:

finds

Thinking that utilizes *finds* as a cognitive tool would employ operations associated with the concept of an action. There is also the presupposition that the action is accidental. Thus, the thinking crystallized in *finds* would include operations associated with the idea of an accidental discovery. Also crystallized in the symbol is a form of thinking in which, even though left open, there are logical slots for an agent and object and the syntactic relation between them that the symbol conventionally describes.

A property of the inner speech symbol is what is termed its *sense,* a term that refers to all the mental operations that are active at the same time with the inner speech symbol. "A word's sense is the aggregate of all the psychological facts that arise in our consciousness as a result of the word" (Vygotsky, 1984, p. 283). Sense gives intrinsic value. The sense of *and they wanted* would have included the global-synthetic image of two nonclosing objects. The sense of *finds* would have included the shape of the object being found, the posture of the character, the location of the object, and so forth. The conventional meanings of words, the pure linguistic values, are only "zones" of the total sense of the word, the maximally stable and socially constituted aspect of what is, from Vygotsky's developmental viewpoint, the momentary sense. The sense is dynamic, individual, and sensitive to context. Sense makes thinking context-sensitive. Sense has uniqueness and internal complexity, two qualities necessary for the the surface sentence to possess spontaneous generativity—to be able to organize itself without input.

If the word with which the gesture synchronizes is the cognitive tool utilized by the speaker on this occasion, we can infer the speaker's thinking during the production of the clause that was carried out with the mental operations attached to *finds.* These operations were carried out in the context of a visual-kinesthetic image of the character being described leaning back and grasping a round-handled object. This complex thought process is plausible as a mental predication about the character referred to, who in the story grappled with another character, leaned back, and by accident came across a knife, with which she then dispatched the second character. *Finds* would have been an appropriate cognitive tool for remembering and organizing thinking about this event, particularly in view of the narrator's wish (which was evident in many places in the narration) to portray sympathetically the character who "found" the knife. Compare in this regard a different choice of inner speech symbol, *grabs for.* This verb would describe the same movements of the character and same effect on the knife (that it got picked up), but would have implied a deliberate and culpable act, not an accidental one.

In the case of *finds* inner speech implied that a linguistic agent and object would be found in the image of a hand reaching out to grasp something. The object, moreover, would be small and round (the knife handle) and in the shape of the hand, which could have helped select the lexical item *knife.* The agent and object would be related by the logic of the cognitive tool *finds.* Thus the information required to produce the outer clause *and Ø finds a knife* was already present in thinking. Like the Anansi sentence, this clause has an intrinsic value that can be traced to an image—in this case, an image of a character groping behind her and coming across a kinfe. Yet this intrinsic value depended on the inner speech cognitive tool of *finds* for being brought into sharp relief. The main structural choices of the sentence were thus implicit in the organization of the speaker's ongoing thinking.

It is in Vygotsky's spirit to consider the linguistic act as including a diachronic axis. The person's thought is unpacked or unfolded into external speech; inner speech plays a vital role in this process because it is the starting point, and the entire process is one of diachronic change along the lines implied by the sense of the inner speech symbol and its mental operations (the amount of time is brief but not negligible).

> Thought does not immediately coincide with verbal expression. Thought does not consist of individual words like speech. I want to express [a] thought. . . . I see all this together in a unified act of thought. In speech, however, the thought is partitioned into separate words. Thought is always something whole, something with significantly greater extent and volume than the individual word. . . . It does not arise step by step through separate units in the way that his speech develops. *That which is contained simultaneously in thought unfolds in sequence in speech* (Vygotsky, 1984, pp. 289–290).

Gestures illustrate the unified act of thought that Vygotsky describes— thought as something whole that includes all its parts simultaneously. Gestures combined with the concurrent linguistic evidence thus show as it is happening (in "real time") the full developmental passage of speech from a unitary undivided thought to an externally articulated utterance.

The theory of this chapter is that between inner speech and outer speech exists a relation that can be described as a developmental transition from a more primitive state to a more finished state. The transition requires developing the syntactic implications of the cognitive tool and breaking up the sense into segments that fulfill these implications. All of these syntactic implications already are included in inner speech and its sense; thus this inner speech symbol and its sense can be regarded as a verbal plan. In the case of *finds* and *and they wanted,* passing from inner speech to outer speech required *only* the information that was part of the speaker's thinking process when thinking had utilized these linguistic symbols as cognitive tools.

This theory of verbal planning explains the intuition that, to a speaker, speaking seems to embody the same choices as thinking: thinking turns into speaking; speaking is actually thinking in a new form. The original cognitive tool turns into an ever more elaborate cognitive and increasingly social tool as it passes to the outside, but remains continuous with the original tool. The same transition occurs in understanding. To a hearer, his or her own thinking embodies the choices of the *speaker;* the hearer's thinking is someone else's thinking in internalized form. In one kind of satisfactory communication the hearer ends up performing the same mental operations that are crystallized in the inner speech symbols of the speaker. We can use this standard to explain the success of conversations in which there is no agreement over purpose or theme. The Amana conversation excerpt in Chapter 4 between speakers A and B, for example, was a partial success by this standard since the difference of conversational topic would not have been enough to prevent the speakers from carrying out similar mental operations.

Analogical Symbols

I have invoked a concept—the mental image—over which there has been much debate in recent years (see, for example, Kosslyn, 1975; Shepard, 1978; Pylyshyn, 1981; Anderson, 1978; and the papers collected in Block, 1981). It is useful to locate the present discussion in relation to this debate. Much of what has been disputed has neglected what is, for my purposes, the single most essential feature of mental images; namely that they are, no less than words and other linguistic forms, *symbols.* Images are analogical symbols that carry with them fragments of knowledge expressible in visual and kinesthetic form. The image itself can be regarded as the signifier that represents some conceptual material—its signified. If I have an image of the Eiffel Tower, this picture in my head may have a definite size, distance, color, perspective, and background. I may be able to zoom up to it and, if I want, rotate it upside down. However, the most important aspect of the picture before my mind's eye is that it signifies the actual Eiffel Tower and crystallizes within it the various things I remember and believe about the Eiffel Tower; and it probably crystallizes this knowledge in more compact and accessible form than would having a completely unfaded percept combined with memories and beliefs of the actual Eiffel Tower.

Much of the debate over mental images has focused on the pictographic quality of the image (Kosslyn, 1975; Pylyshyn, 1981). Regarded as a symbol, however, an image's pictographic quality is not its most essential factor. Rather, the manner of symbolization is most essential. Images symbolize analogically: this means that the signifier side of the image is felt to exhibit some property of the signified side. To use a term introduced by Werner and Kaplan (1963), the signifier of an analogical symbol shows little "distance" from its signified. Quite poor images in a pictographic sense can still be the signifiers of analogical symbols. Kinesthetic images are not properly described as pictographic at all.

The dimension that is pictographic-nonpictographic is in fact separate from the dimension that is analogical-nonanalogical. There are analogical symbols that have signifiers of poor pictographic quality and still function analogically. Introspective reports on the quality of imagery are of little value precisely because the pictographic and analogical dimensions are separate. The report reflects the person's impression of pictographic quality, but this could be poor and the symbol would still be analogical.

Another criterion is continuity in the signifier. An analogical symbol is said

Figure 5.2 Analogical symbol composed of discrete elements.

to represent by means of continuously variable signifiers, whereas a nonanalogical symbol represents by means of discrete signifiers. Figure 5.2 shows a drawing of a face that is a counterexample; a rather cheery looking person in a brimmed hat is represented analogically by means of discrete binary elements (| and). The use of discrete elements does not prevent this representation from being analogical.

Rather than asking whether a symbol is a faded perceptual trace or a continuously variable depiction, one can test whether a symbol functions analogically by asking whether it shows duality of patterning (Hockett, 1958; also see Chapter 1 of this book). Because they are nonarbitrary, analogical symbols necessarily lack this design feature. They function symbolically through parallels of structure between the signifier and signified halves. In such symbols, therefore, all that is systematically patterned in the signifier is due to differences of signifieds (of meaning). In a nonanalogical symbol, in contrast, there is a level of structure —the phonological—that is not part of any meaning pattern but is indisputably part of the symbol. The word *mat,* for example, is organized on two levels, one the level of meaning differentiation (where *mat* is distinguished from *rug*), and the other the level of sound differentiation (where *mat* is distinguished from *cat*). An analogical symbol—a drawing or gesture—exists only on a level where meaning is differentiated. There is no patterning of lines and spaces in a stick-figure drawing, for instance, *except* what is generated by the meaning of the symbol (Fortes, 1940). In analogical symbols patterning of the signifier is either regarded as due to meaning contrasts or is seen as random. This absence of duality of patterning is an index conceptually more justified of analogical representation than the extent of pictographic quality, the presence of continuous variation of depiction, or any other exclusively signifier-based criterion.

Limits on This Theory

This section aims to define the boundaries within which the present theory can apply. These boundaries exist because the theory requires the existence of inner speech in a context of analogical symbols. However, not everyone experiences inner speech at all times. When people lack inner speech, they report that they are thinking in terms of pure visual and actional images. Hadamard (1945) claimed very strong intuitions on his part that mathematical reasoning is carried out without the utilization of either linguistic or mathematical symbols, but instead makes use of visual images. Other mathematicians reported similar introspections. Einstein, for example, wrote the following in a famous reply to a questionnaire Hadamard had circulated:

> The words or the language, as they are written or spoken, do not seem to play any role in my mechanism of thought. The psychical entities which seem to serve as elements in thought are certain signs and more or less clear images which can be "voluntarily" reproduced and combined (quoted by Hadamard, 1945, p. 142).

Usually these images are rather vague but are definitely present, and are correlated with the mathematical content of thought. The vagueness is in fact a desirable property, Hadamard argued, since it protects the thinker from being overly dazzled and consequently misled by the image. He believed the function of images was to give the mathematician a visual concept of the argument as a whole.

In ordinary thinking the experience of inner speech also varies in explicitness; the less explicit the inner speech, the greater the dominance of visual images. I presented the following statements to a group of university students who were asked to introspect on their own thinking and say which statement or statements best described their typical experiences of inner speech. (I have no doubt that better statements could be formulated.)

Wordless thought (no inner speech)	10%
Single words and short phrases	33%
Sentence skeleton	33%
Full sentence, no phonology	7%
Full sentence, with phonology	18%

People report inner speech experiences at every level of explicitness, but for the majority the favorite level was single words and short phrases, and sentence skeletons. An example of a single word is *finds*. Sentence skeletons are telegraphic sentences consisting of nouns, prepositions, or verbs arranged in order but not including articles, plurals, or tenses. Wordless thought also was reported, but not frequently. Nearly all of the full sentences, with or without the impression of phonological form, were reported to have occurred on occasions in which the person was preparing to give a set speech, a situation in which fresh thinking would be minimal.

An observation of the upper, or explicit-speech, limit on inner speech is Sokolov's (1968) discovery of measurable subvocalizations—small soundless movements of the speech musculature detected through direct electromyographic recordings from the tongue—that occur when individuals are carrying out mental arithmetic operations. While Sokolov's method of recording does not reveal linguistic content or its extent, muscular reactions imply thinking in terms of phonologically represented linguistic forms. Mental arithmetic is much like verbal rehearsal in that it is thinking in which remembering namable segments (numerals) is crucial. For mental calculation, stating the problem in linguistic form and speaking the linguistic form to oneself provides assistance in holding the segments of the problem clearly in mind, and repeating the numerals to oneself promotes memory of them. Mathematical reasoning and mental calculation therefore appear to be totally different kinds of activities. Similarly, the students responding to my survey reported thinking in complete sentences when the sentence form itself was the object of thought and they were trying to form clear memory traces. This is another case where segmentation is crucial. Hadamard, in contrast, described reasoning in which grasping the whole of the problem was the crucial aspect, and it was this kind of reasoning that was aided by the presence of images.

Another question asked of the students was whether they experienced inner speech mixed with graphic-imagistic cognition and, if so, where in the above sequence. The replies here are important for understanding the variations of explicitness of inner speech. The experience of visual imagery was reported to be the greatest in the least explicit inner speech contexts: with wordless thought, images were strongly present; whereas with full sentences, visual imagery was almost totally absent.

From wordless thought, through inner speech, and on to outer speech, there is a certain continuity. As we pass upward along this dimension, two changes seem to be taking place reciprocally: visual-imagistic cognition declines and verbal elaboration increases. Such are the results of comparing the habitual experiences of different individuals. The inner speech explanation of speech production would apply in the middle of this range. Clearly, it cannot (for different reasons) apply to either wordless thought or full sentences.

We can also suppose that the same reciprocal relation appears within a single person when we compare different contexts of thinking and speaking. With thinking that is highly intense and concentrated, inner linguistic symbols may be completely replaced by images. This is the situation that Hadamard described for himself and other mathematicians. Under these circumstances the person may actually feel incapable of speaking, a phenomenon of which physicists and others engaged in sustained mathematical reasoning often complain. With verbal rehearsal just prior to emitting a set speech, on the other hand, images may disappear to be replaced by fully developed sentences. Whether one is actually incapable of thinking under this circumstance, the production of new mental relations is certainly not at the forefront of consciousness. The theory of inner speech applies, then, to the middle range of these contexts in which all persons find themselves from time to time.

The more structurally complete the linguistic tool, the less room there is for further developmental changes of thinking. The function of the cognitive tool thus can explain its form—the appearance of complete phonological symbols in thought when segmentation and memory for segments is at issue, and the appearance of analogical symbols when the formation of new connections in thought is the function.

Ordinary directed thinking occupies an intermediate place along this dimension. Both memory and segmentation and a global overview are important and are a source of flexibility. In ordinary directed thinking/speaking there is an interplay between two forms of symbolization that are being utilized simultaneously. Here the symbols of inner speech appear in an environment of images. Such a mixture of symbolic forms is what synchronized gestures exhibit, and it is on this part of the continuum from wordless thought to thoughtless speech that the highly abbreviated forms of inner speech seem to occur. It is here, then, that we believe the production and understanding of utterances also is taking place.

William James on Two Forms of Thinking

Two forms of thinking during linguistic acts also are described in the following passages by William James (1890):

> An analysis of what passes through the mind as we utter the phrase *the pack of cards is on the table* will, I hope, make this clear, and may at the same time condense into a concrete example a good deal of what has gone before.

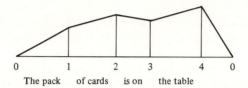

0   1   2   3   4   0
The pack   of cards   is on   the table

> It takes time to utter the phrase. Let the horizontal line [in the figure above] represent time. Every part of it will then stand for a fraction, every point for an instant, of the time. Of course the thought has *time-parts*. The part 2–3 of it, though continuous with 1–2, is yet a different part from 1–2. Now I say of these time-parts that we cannot take any one of them so short that it will not after some fashion or other be a thought of the whole object "the pack of cards on the table." They melt into each other like dissolving views, and no two of them feel the object just alike, but each feels the total object in a unitary undivided way (p. 279).

James's insight was, therefore, that *during the production of speech two forms of thinking are taking place simultaneously:* one form is analytic and syntactic, corresponding to the time-parts of meaning, and the other is global and synthetic, corresponding to the unitary undivided whole of the meaning. These two forms of thinking overlap temporally and interact, but they are different in form.

The thinking carried out with inner speech symbols operates with both of these forms. The unitary undivided aspect is present as an image, which we see exhibited in synchronized gestures. The image of a character bending back and groping for an object (e.g., a knife) is an example of a unitary undivided thought, as is the image of two nonclosing objects, the image of an object held up to be viewed and commented on, and many other images. The time-segmented parts of thinking are present in the inner speech symbol itself and in its syntactic frame implications. The surface sentence unpacks itself from this interplay of two forms of thinking in inner speech.

Metaphoric gestures show that images are also constructed for abstract concepts. The speaker who said (in Chapter 1) *It was a Sylvester and Tweetie Bird cartoon* and simultaneously held up a gesture-object had (we infer) a unitary undivided thought of the cartoon as an object that could be manipulated. The abstract concept of a work of art was conceptualized, via the metaphoric image, as this single object. This was the unitary undivided thought. (I will consider the role of metaphors in inner speech thinking in the section on metaphor later in this chapter.)

Comparison to Dual Coding

There is an interesting contrast between the inner speech hypothesis put forth in this chapter and what is known as the dual coding hypothesis. Pointing out this contrast will sharpen our understanding of inner speech as a tool of thought. Although the dual coding hypothesis seems similar to the argument of the present chapter, it in fact states something quite different. According to dual coding there are two coded forms of memory: "Some information is stored in long-term memory in imagistic form. . . . Other information is stored in long-term memory in some kind of linguistic format" (Bucci, 1984, p. 151; also see Paivio, 1971). Here Bucci places verbal and analogical representations into separate categories. Later she goes on to say: "The crucial implication of this model [dual coding] is that if there are two (or more) representational codes, then it is necessary to postulate a system of referential connections between them" (Bucci, p. 151).

This concept of separate imagistic and verbal codes and the consequent necessity of referential linkages between them is the critical difference between the dual coding and the inner speech theories. An inner speech symbol does not *stand for* an analogical representation; the connection between them is not referential. Rather, in this theory, linguistic and analogical symbols interact in a dialectic that can change both the analogical and linguistic representations as the speaker's thinking develops into spoken form. In the dual coding hypothesis, in contrast, the verbal and analogical codes are separate and noninteracting, and thinking carried out in one code has to refer to the other code.

What evidence can be brought to bear on this distinction? One important fact is that information perceived in a gesture can be later retrieved in the form of a word and, conversely, information perceived as a word can be retrieved as a gesture. Information readily shifts between the linguistic and gestural formats. Such fluidity implies a single memory store that gesture and speech access interactively (influencing one another). It does not suggest separate imagistic and verbal stores with referential connections between them, as envisioned in dual coding theory. The analysis given earlier of the Anansi example illustrated an interaction of analogical and linguistic thinking. A direct demonstration of information exchange between linguistic and gesture formats was provided by the experiment mentioned earlier (pp. 87–89) in which we found subjects describing scenes with words that contained information first presented only in gesture form, and producing gestures that contained information first presented only in spoken form. At the time of the internal computations that generate both speech and gesture, there is no clear distinction between imagistic and verbal formats and, as predicted by the process of a dialectic, the two channels mutually influence one another.

"SMART" SYMBOLS AND GENERATIVITY

Within a theory of linguistic acts we will explain the spontaneous emergence of inner speech symbols in thinking, and from this the spontaneous emergence of sentences in speech. Spontaneity of inner speech symbols is the key to generativity, the ability of surface sentences to occur without inputs. Thinking is not the "input" to some other process that evokes the inner speech symbol. Rather, the symbols of inner speech are what, along with imagery, *constitute* thinking. Imagery might seem to be an "input," but it cannot serve this role either. Imagery itself is influenced and categorized by the same forces that evoke the linguistic symbols it accompanies. The linguistic symbol and image emerge together. The image particularizes the symbol; the symbol codifies the image.

Rather than "responses" to "inputs," the symbols of inner speech appear to be self-activating in appropriate environments. Words that are self-activating are candidates for being designated "smart" words. The hypothesis is that "smart" symbols tend to be inner speech symbols. In keeping with the observation that the size and complexity of inner speech symbols varies, we should include "smart" phrases and "smart" clauses as well; however, even less data can be found that bear on the activation of these larger units than on words—I will concentrate here on words. (The process of word recognition will be considered in detail in several sections later in the chapter.)

Words that can be called "smart" have two important properties that earn them this name and that they must meet in order to play the role assigned them in the self-organization of the speaking process. These properties arise from the word's context-sensitivity, which extends in two directions. First, "smart" symbols are self-activating in appropriate environments. This means they are sensitive to the existence of thought patterns that are not yet coded in linguistic form or to thought patterns that are already coded but are changing into new thought patterns. Such a capacity explains the spontaneous emergence of symbols in the person's conscious experience. Second, "smart" symbols can select other symbols. This means they are sensitive to linguistic potentialities. Such a capacity is important for the unpacking of the image into the final linguistic product. "Smart" symbols are thus context-sensitive in two directions—to the evolving thought environment not yet coded linguistically and to the potential linguistic environment.

In contrast, a "dumb" symbol is relatively difficult to activate until it has a specific linguistic context into which it can fit. This type of symbol refers to its conventional reference category but does not self-activate. Such a word is less sensitive to context in both the conceptual and the linguistic directions, and provides a way of thinking only about its reference category (apples or whatever).

Not only do "smart" symbols switch on in appropriate environments, they *take in* environments. The symbol is altered as it alters. Verbs are potential "smart" symbols. When, for instance, *swallows* self-activates, two things happen: (1) the uncategorized image resolves into a mouth and food, whereas without this categorization the image would consist merely of blobs; and (2) *swallows* itself becomes a particular incident of swallowing with a specific context.

A "smart" symbol interacting with an image is the minimal psycholinguistic unit according to this theory. It is the minimal unit in which a dialectic of syntactic and global thinking occurs. From the first moment the term "thinking" can appropriately be invoked at all, linguistic thinking is a synthesis of syntactic with imagistic thinking. There is not a pre-verbal or a pre-imagistic phase. The balance between imagistic and syntactic thinking changes progressively until, at some point, thought achieves a form that can be spoken. The concept of the inherently linguistic nature of thought is stated forcefully by Sokolov (1972):

> The illusion is then created that the flow of thought forestalls speech, that thought precedes words. But this is nothing but an illusion. Thought can indeed be antecedent to oral and written speech since both develop relatively slowly; it also can forestall inner speech if the latter involves reasoning, but it never forestalls the abbreviated form of inner speech which expresses semantic complexes (p. 121).

As this discussion should make plain, "smart" symbols would be powerful cognitive tools. Both the first and second properties of "smart" symbols are reasonable if these symbols are conceived of dynamically as processes (Lenneberg, 1967). A "smart" symbol such as *swallows* maintains its stable zone of contrastive value even while its sense is altered by a specific image and context. "Smart" symbols explain generativity—the capability of surface sentences to unpack themselves on the basis of their internal resources. A "dumb" word, in contrast, can be selected by the linguistic context created by a "smart" word, but a "dumb" word cannot select a "smart" one.

It is possible that a "dumb" word cannot be readily selected by its own reference object. Winnick and Daniel (1970) found no priming of noun recognition when subjects were shown pictures illustrating the nouns' reference objects, a surprising result replicated by Morton (1979). ("Priming" refers to the speeding up of word recognition that is caused by showing a picture or another related word—the "prime"—just before flashing the target. The extent of priming is defined in relation to a separately measured baseline; see Meyer and Schvanevelt, 1971.) When someone says *apple* in the presence of an apple, this performance may be more difficult than thinking of *apple* in a framework provided by a self-activated "smart" symbol working in conjunction with an appropriate image (e.g., *Bill bit into the*_____ together with an image of a blob entering an opening). Moreover, ostensive acts of naming may implicitly contain their own "smart" symbols. If you say *apple* in the presence of an apple you are really saying "this is called *apple.*"

The second property of "smart" words, the sensitivity to linguistic potential and ability to select other words, is shown by verbs, prepositions, and other linguistic symbols that convey an implicit syntax. These elements are often conceptualized as frames (this idea is discussed in many places in the literature on artificial intelligence). *Finds,* for example, implies a transitive action in which there are two arguments. Regarded as a process, this can be conceptualized as a frame that selects two other words. These words are NPs that fill the designated slots of *finds* as agent and object. Thus *finds* provides a framework into which "dumb" NPs can fit, creating syntagmatic value in the global image that the NPs segment. Thinking in terms of *finds* as an inner speech symbol introduces mental operations associated with a transitive-act syntax.

Mitchell and Holmes (1985) provide a demonstration with verbs in which an implicit syntax is in fact introduced during sentence understanding. Mitchell and Holmes found that the subjects in their experiment took substantially longer to read the final prepositional phrase (PP) *(in his hand)* in the first sentence below than in the second:

The groundsman noticed the girl waving a stick in his hand.

The groundsman chased the girl waving a stick in his hand.

Changing the verb (from *notice* to *chase*) altered the speed at which a phrase that followed the verb at the end of the sentence could be read. Evidently, selecting either *noticed* or *chased* could alter the implicit syntax of the complex symbol. *Chased* provides a syntax that psychologically accommodates *a stick in his hand* (with the masculine possessive pronoun), whereas *noticed* does not. The lack of a slot provided by *noticed* pushed the phrase *a stick in his hand* into the slot invitingly but treacherously offered by *a girl waving,* and the subjects were "led down the garden path." At the end the subjects found themselves facing an unassimilable third-person masculine pronoun. Thus it took the subjects longer to read the phrase when *noticed* was the main verb.

Whether words that have an implicit syntax also show sensitivity to not yet categorized imagistic thinking (property one) is the empirical question I shall address in this section. The predictions stemming from property one are that context-sensitive "smart" words can be evoked by noncategorized imagistic contexts, whereas "dumb" words can be evoked only by linguistic contexts. Further, "smart" words might not be as easily evoked by linguistic contexts as by noncategorized contexts (a very strong prediction). This would also fit the self-activating property of "smart" words. I will describe three studies that provide partial evidence for the validity of these predictions. The experiments were all designed for other questions and extending them to this demonstration of "smart" symbols leaves a number of conditions untested. I am assuming that verbs and prepositions are "smart" and that nouns are "dumb." This assumption may be incorrect in a number of cases, independent of the correctness of the "smart"- "dumb" symbol distinction and the two predictions just derived.

A complete experiment would compare verbs or prepositions and nouns on their activation in linguistic and appropriate noncategorized contexts. An example of a noncategorized context would be an undifferentiated image prior to any choice of words to classify it. Verbs or prepositions should be more readily activated by such noncategorized contexts and nouns more readily by strictly linguistic contexts, provided the linguistic context is "smart." This experiment apparently has not been carried out, but experiments that approximate parts of it have been conducted for other purposes.

Gentner (1981) found that nouns, both as cues for the recall of other words and as the words being recalled themselves, are better performers in cued recall experiments than are verbs. This difference in favor of nouns seems to show both that nouns are comparatively easy to evoke in linguistic contexts and that verbs are comparatively hard to evoke in these contexts. The better performance by nouns than verbs does not reveal, however, that nouns are less easily evoked by noncategorized contexts.

De Groot (1983) also referred to the activation of verbs and showed that they are primed, if not by noncategorized contexts then by contexts not specifically categorized for the verb. De Groot showed that in lexical decision tasks verbs are primed by the general meaning area to which the verb belongs. ("Lexical decision" is a task in which the subject has to say whether a visually presented letter string is or is not a word—this is meaningful since on some of the trials a nonword letter string is presented; see Meyer and Schvanevelt, 1971.) An example of de Groot's result is the priming of the verb *to pose* by the noun *answer.* This noun is not a word directly associated with the meaning of *to pose,* but *answer* is associated with *question,* which can be associated with the verb. Thus presenting *answer* could have activated the semantic field of words having some connection with questions, but the "pose" categorization of this field would not have been activated until the verb *to pose* became active; and this verb became active faster when the field was already activated. While this procedure might be construed as an example of a noncategorized context sensitizing a verb, it is a specific verbal context rather than an undifferentiated imagistic one.

A further complication arises from what de Groot calls "lexical-coherence-checking," by which she means that subjects might have recognized both the prime word and the target word but then taken more time to search for a meaningful relation between them. Subjects might not have responded to the target until they had carried out this check. When the prime was *answer* and the target was *to pose,* the subject soon found the relation and responded. However, checking was slower when the prime and target were not related, since for unrelated words there is no natural stopping point for coherence checking. Faster response vis-à-vis an unrelated prime word is the evidence for priming. By masking the visual prime a moment later with a series of x's in the same place, de Groot was able to make the priming effect disappear: recognition of targets after related and unrelated prime words became equal. The mask presumably interfered with the subject's attempts at checking (perhaps by obliterating memory for the prime).

The question remains whether this coherence checking is part of activation in the sense of a "smart" symbol that self-activates. Interfering with checking could mean interfering with self-activation as well. Checking in de Groot's sense would seem to correspond to using the target to classify the context. In both checking and classifying, a word is related to the context and the meaning connection between them is determined. If this equivalence is adopted, the masking operation in de Groot's second experiment can be described as interrupting part of the context-sensitivity of "smart" symbols and thereby, perhaps, "lobotomizing" them—converting them to "dumb" symbols (to which they became equal in terms of activation). Nonetheless, the first described experiment does show that calling a person's attention to the general area of meaning of a verb is enough to prime it.*

Potter and Faulconer (1979) showed that nouns are not responsive to reference objects that fall outside a limited stereotypic range. Potter and Faulconer had subjects hear sentences of the following kind (a given subject hearing one kind or the other):

It was already burning when the man first saw the house.

It was already burning when the man first saw the burning house.

Immediately after the sentence a drawing of a house was flashed before the subjects, who were to say whether this drawing was of something mentioned in the sentence (there were also negative trials). The drawing sometimes showed a typical house and sometimes a house in flames. For subjects who heard the first sentence, response times were markedly faster when the drawing showed a typical house than when it showed a burning house. This was the case even though the subjects had been told emphatically that "the picture did not have to match the meaning of the sentence but only had to match one word, the name of the object" (Potter and Faulconer, 1979, pp. 512–513). For subjects who heard the second sentence, despite its peculiar repetition of *burning,* response times were nearly the same when the drawing showed a burning house and when it showed a typical house. In other words, the meaning of *house* could not readily be matched with a picture of a burning house unless it was grammatically integrated into a phrase (with *burning*).

This experiment demonstrates comparative unresponsiveness by single "dumb" nouns to contexts categorized in nonstereotypic ways (e.g., a house in flames). Only when the noun acquired syntagmatic value through combination with a modifier did it respond to nonstereotypic contexts as quickly as to stereotypic contexts. It may not be the case that even reference objects within the noun's stereotypic range easily activate the noun (Winnick and Daniel, 1970; see description on p. 101). Only if the noun is modified does it become responsive to a wider range of objects (both types of picture). Modification provides a context for the noun and might make the noun more context-sensitive, thus "smarter."

These three experiments show that (1) nouns are comparatively easy to evoke by linguistic context, and verbs are comparatively hard to evoke; (2) verbs are evoked by general areas of meaning that do not depend on specific linguistic connections; and (3) unmodified nouns do not connect to pictorial contexts that are categorized outside of a limited stereotypic range.

The remaining sections of this chapter will show how various major phenomena of psycholinguistics can be analyzed by the theory presented above.

*I am grateful to C. J. Tassoni for discussing with me many of the points raised above.

ANALYSIS OF TWO EXAMPLES

We are now ready to attempt a detailed analysis of how concrete utterances, situated in their context, might have been generated.

I have chosen two rather different examples. The first is the sequence of statements made by speaker A during the Amana conversation in which he introduces his "good friend from Iowa" as a conversational topic. This example lacked a gestural accompaniment but illustrates the role played by social context. The context actually begins with speaker A's earlier question about where B lived before and B's answer, *I lived in Iowa.* It continues with A's statements *Oh, I have a good friend from Iowa; He's from Cedar Rapids; No, not Cedar Rapids; He's from the Amana area.* The example ends when A starts to describe the friend and his relation to the Amanas, a new thought pattern.

The second example is the statement *They wanted to get where Anansi was,* described earlier in this chapter. This sentence was accompanied by an interpretable gesture and illustrates the relation between thinking and speaking more clearly than do the sentences from speaker A.

The "good friend" example illustrates four main points: (1) To understand the intrinsic value of sentences we have to explain the speaker's thinking; this is a basic claim of all the preceding analyses. (2) We must consider a series of sentences, rather than one sentence at a time. A speaker can take over a basic thinking pattern from the social context, and this pattern can continue for several additional sentences. (3) In the resolution of tension between unitary undivided thinking and syntactic thinking, "smart" inner speech symbols play an essential role. (4) The speaker's thinking and speaking are highly channeled by discourse and inner speech constraints.

While we cannot observe a "smart" word activating itself, we can see the consequences of such a word. Also, if a context-sensitive word is carried through successive utterances there is, in this fact, reason for saying it is being used as a cognitive tool. Its reiteration suggests that the speaker is working and reworking the conceptual framework embodied in the word. Speaker B's statement *I lived in Iowa* introduced for speaker A a framework for thinking. This framework was crystallized in a "smart" word, *in,* with two implied syntactic positions (object-location). This symbol might be self-activating and implies a syntax in which there are two elements, an object and a location, related as described by the preposition: _____ in *Iowa.* If we describe this as a frame it can be illustrated as follows (after Charniak, 1981):

Frame: *in*

        isa: locative relation (containerhood)

       slots: location *(*e. g., *Iowa)*

           object *(*e. g., *ego)*

Speaker A's subsequent thinking process was organized in terms of "from Iowa," which also is an instance of the _____ *(preposition) Iowa* framework. The unified undivided thinking that A organized with this syntactic form of thinking was something like: speaker A, too, had a connection with *(preposition) Iowa*— his good friend. Speaker B thus provided A with the key for structuring the thought. In his speech production speaker A changed just one element of the *from* syntax at a time—confirming the psychological reality to him of the implicit structure of an object and location—and clearly pointing to the essentially social origin of this line of thinking.

There were no gestures accompanying these sentences, but we can describe what appropriate gestures would look like. The schema built around *from* provides two slots, one for the object and one for the source, and the preposition itself describes the relational connection between them. A very natural gesture to go with *I have a good friend from Iowa* would be for the speaker to move his hand away from his body to a location in space, and then move his hand from that location to another location. That is, in the gesture would be an object (the hand) that moves from the speaker to a source location for this object (the first location), and then there would be movement of the object from the source. The *from* schema would thus segment the three elements of this hypothetical gesture and the *I have* phrase would segment the gestured relation of the speaker himself to these elements. The opening sentence, *I have a good friend from Iowa,* would be a syntactic unpacking of this plausible image.

Once the syntactic thinking pattern had been introduced, speaker A began repeating the syntax of *from* to bring out different parts of the global idea of his connection to Iowa through his friend. He first introduced his friend as the object in the *from Iowa* symbol. This symbol, A's inferred tool for thinking, was then used a second time to bring out another part of the global idea in *he's from Cedar Rapids.* This time the location slot takes in the new data and the object—the good friend—is held constant. Speaker A next discovered that Cedar Rapids was not the right location. Thus, the constituent structure was repeated a third time but supplemented with negations *(no, not)* and Ø for the nonrefuted parts *(he* and *from)*.

Finally, the constituent structure was repeated a fourth time with attention still focused on the location slot and retrieval of *the Amana area.*

Note how the cognitive use of the *from* symbol provided successive predications of new information about the location slot, cohesive connections to the theme of the good friend through the object slot, and provided the mental operations by which speaker A's memories about Iowa were articulated in syntactic form.

The details of these sentences include, in addition to operations with a cognitive tool, specific discourse signals relating the successive sentences to the contextual whole. These include the initial *oh* of speaker A's first statement, which signals that the relation to the previous context is one of discontinuity and that a new theme is about to be introduced, and the *he*s in the second and fourth statements that signal cohesiveness with this theme.

The NP-verb *I have* of A's first statement is probably best explained as a metaphor of thinking in which the good friend is regarded as a cognitive object. *I have* performs a discourse function understandable in terms of this metaphor: speaker A "has" this object (his friend) and proceeds to predicate information about it.

There is also a crescendo effect leading up to *the Amanas,* an example of the theater metaphor (Goffman, 1974), and an illustration of the poetics of prose in the fourfold repetition of the prepositional phrase structure (Silverstein, 1984). (These aspects of the example were discussed in Chapters 3 and 4.) The fourfold repetition of _____ "from" _____ illustrates production units formed out of idea units and stress-groups that relate speech control to context: *a good friend from Iowa, hé's from Cedar Rápids, nót (from) Cedar Rápids, hé's from the Ámana area* reveal not only repeated use of the same "smart" inner speech symbol, but also the influence of stress-groups on the unpacking of meanings. (These stress-groups form what have been called "syntagmas," and are discussed later in the chapter.)

The illocutionary force of these utterances is subtle and illustrates the importance of regarding the basic operating unit as a sentence-context pair. Superficially each sentence was an assertion, but informing speaker B about his connection with Iowa was not speaker A's exclusive interest. There was an ulterior motive, which was to discover where B came from and where he had been a student. Speaker A's sentences were also, therefore, *requests* for further information about B. This is a natural occurrence similar to the artificial example in Chapter 3 (*I got lightbulbs today* also functioning as a request). The effect intended by speaker A was more or less this: "I have a connection with Iowa which I will tell you about—now tell me more about yours." Speaker B had been less than forthcoming in the conversation heretofore about where he had been a student and this aspect of the social context must be taken into account in an explanation of what directed speaker A along the path he followed (cf. Silverstein, 1984). It explains, in particular, A's readiness to adopt B's prepositional thought-pattern: It was exactly this thought-pattern of B about himself that A was after.

In all, then, a number of details in A's speech can be explained as having derived from the social context as this influenced thinking. Speaker A unpacked a unitary undivided thought by reusing the same schema and surface syntactic pattern that he obtained from the other speaker. He did this by making minimal substitutions in one slot or the other but never in both slots simultaneously in this example. Speaker A's thinking was channeled by the inner speech use of *in* and the conversational situation. Presumably such limited degrees of freedom are typical of casual conversations; limits like these are part of what make conversations casual.

The second example is the production of *They wanted to get where Anansi was,* a sentence in a narration that was accompanied by an interpretable gesture. This example illustrates the claim that speaking is a form of thinking and memory. The speaker's individual mental operations were transmuted into socially constituted forms that were communicable. The individual and social forms coexist, and to explain the intrinsic linguistic values of the sentence both forms must be considered and their interactions understood.

The gesture depicted two objects separated in space, one moving or "walking," the other moving as if in water, and there was no closure despite this motion (see Figure 5.1). Similarities between the syntactic form of the sentence and the image displayed in the gesture were attributed to the surface sentence being an "unpacked" version of the image. This idea implies that the gesture and sentence developed together as parts of the same linguistic act. The following is how the "unpacking" process could have taken place.

The speaker's memory was embodied in an image of two separated objects, one standing for the imprisoned Anansi, the other for the sons, so classified by the inner speech symbol inferred from the synchronized gesture, *and they wanted.* This composite of image and verbal symbol was the form of the narrative in the speaker's thinking, and the course of the speaker's thinking over the next few seconds was an elaboration and differentiation of this composite. For the purposes of the example I have artificially frozen a dynamic situation by picking (though not completely arbitrarily) one moment as the starting point.

Thus we want to see how the speaker, thinking in the form of an image of two unclosing objects plus the verbal symbol *and they wanted,* was able to say *and they wanted to get where Anansi was* by continuing to think in two forms simultaneously, with a drive to make his thinking socially accessible.

The word *wanted* plays a crucial role in this pattern of thinking in that (1) it implies the continuing separation of the two objects of the image, and (2) it makes it easy to unpack this image by providing a linguistic mechanism by which the referring forms can be as far apart as possible in separate clauses.

The want _____ $_S$ option of *wanted* was the obvious choice since it produced the two-clause pattern that unpacked the nonclosing image. There are two distinct *wanted*s. Because of their high frequency they would probably be learned and remembered as separate words: want _____ $_{NP}$ (*want a book,* etc.) and want _____ $_S$ (*want to get,* etc.). What the sons "wanted" was "getting to" the Anansi-object. The self-activation of *get* depended on the joint presence of *wanted* and the image of unclosing objects. Once activated, it brought into the evolving situation a new syntactic frame that had a slot for an NP patient: get _____ $_{NP}$.

The syntactic contrast of the sons and Anansi in separate clauses was supported by a further contrast that also can be traced to the image and that filled the NP slot of *get.* The sons were active and Anansi was inactive in the image. The sons appeared in a syntactic frame that applies to active things (in construction with a motion verb), whereas Anansi appeared in a syntactic frame for inert things (in construction with *where* in a locative). The nominalization of the locative finally created the NP that the *get* frame was seeking.

Finally, there was cohesiveness between the stream of thinking and the sons as the theme. This cohesiveness was coded in the discourse conjunction plus referring form, *and they,* while the explicit reference *Anansi* arose for Anansi who was not the current theme. There was also a "poetic" influence met by stress-groups: *they wánted, to gét,* and *where Ánansi was* are all plausible "packages" of speech output that have the same metric structure and also correspond to idea units in the unpacking process.

The linguistic product in this example was a synthesis of two forms of thinking. There was the initial memory as represented in the composite of an image and verbal symbol, the syntactic slots brought in with *wanted* and *get,* and the previous discourse with which the sons were cohesive. As can be seen from the limited degrees of freedom for each of the choices outlined above, the surface sentence was almost completely determined by the requirement of producing this synthesis. In both the Anansi and the "good friend" examples, although the processes are intricate, there were limited degrees of freedom constraining the diachronic path of the sentences. This kind of constraint would play a role in explaining the apparent ease of speech production in these examples.

In the Anansi example, the initial inner speech symbol also appeared initially in the surface sentence, and later refinements of thinking were performed by linguistic symbols that actually appeared later in the sentence. A *strategy* of speech production is to attach new nodes to the right. This strategy could have been a factor promoting ease of production. (There is further discussion of strategies later in the chapter.) Presumably there is nothing necessary about a correspondence in real time between the diachronic axis of the sentence and the dimension of speaking time. When correspondence does not occur (e.g., when the initial inner speech symbols correspond to surface consitutents which appear later), there may be hesitations in the surface flow of speech and other symptoms of lack of correspondence, such as syntactic false starts and speech errors (Maclay and Osgood, 1959).

The nature of the analysis of these two examples has been to show the conditions that exist in a speaker's thinking and speech at successive stages of their joint development. The analysis does not attempt to reduce the generation of the sentence to the inputs and outputs of processors that do not have the properties of thinking or speech, as would an information processing analysis. Information processing theories and some of their limitations are discussed later in the chapter.

WORDS

The next major topic to consider is, logically, word recognition. Recognition obviously takes place during acts of understanding. But if "smart" words self-activate during speech production, there is also implicit word recognition during linguistic acts of *speaking.* The topic of word recognition can be viewed as an illustration of the common processes that exist between speech production and speech understanding. In this section we will ask: How are words recognized in (external or inner) speech? A great deal of research has been devoted to the question of external word recognition. A specific proposal for extending the results of this research to inner speech recognition will be discussed at the end of the section on theories of word recognition later in this chapter.

Words, phrases, and full clauses are examples of linguistic symbols. In the theory of inner speech, speaker/hearers utilize these symbols without drawing any fundamental distinction between them. A continuum of inner speech symbols was described on page 96. All levels of this continuum provide cognitive tools; all crystallize mental operations that guide and shape thinking. Words are merely one end of the continuum. The word end is the best studied from a psychological viewpoint, however, and many of the conclusions we reach in this section of the chapter will be extended up the symbol continuum to complex symbols (phrases and clauses).

Word Construction and Word Recognition

Words can be described from multiple perspectives. To Sapir the word was "one of the smallest, completely satisfying bits of isolated 'meaning' units into which the sentence resolves itself. It cannot be cut into without a disturbance of meaning, one or other or both of the several parts remaining a helpless waif on our hands" (1921, p. 35). To see the correctness of this, try to cut up a word I have just used—*part.* Divide it into *p* and *art,* which leaves helpless waifs, *p* and *art,* one of them another unrelated word.

The word is also a linguistic element that can be brought readily into consciousness. Again, Sapir has a pertinent observation: "Linguistic experience . . . indicates overwhelmingly that there is not, as a rule, the slightest difficulty in bringing the word to consciousness as a psychological reality" (1921, p. 34). This accessibility to consciousness sets the word apart from its technical linguistic counterpart, the morpheme, which (unless it happens to correspond to a word) is often remote from consciousness. Whereas it is easy to become aware of and focus attention on *finds,* it is difficult to become aware of *s* as a separate meaning entity in *finds.* Nonetheless, *s* is a valid morphological element of the English language. Its contribution to the meaning of *finds* is due to a definite and repeatable process. The psychological salience of the word swallows up the morpheme *s* within *finds.*

From the viewpoint of speech production and understanding, words have at least four important qualities:

1. They are cognitive tools (they crystallize mental operations that the person can utilize in inner speech).
2. They are segments, or time-parts, of meaning complexes.
3. They provide syntactic structures for other words.
4. They enter into semantic contrasts.

In the following sections I will discuss these qualities. The first was the topic of previous discussion, but the following sections add other observations.

Words as Time-Parts

To Saussure (1959) a fundamental point about language was its unidimensionality. Meanings can be multidimensional, but linguistic expressions are limited to successive variations along the one dimension of time. James (1890) presented the same point with the difference between unitary undivided meaning and the division of meaning into time-parts. This dividing up of the undivided is carried out fundamentally by means of words, either words acting in isolation or words that also introduce frames.

Children have to discover for themselves the function of words in breaking down complex meanings. To have attained mastery of a word a child must have discovered at least three things: (1) that it has referents—for example, that *cat* picks out cats in the world; (2) that it contrasts with other words—for example, that *cat* contrasts with *dog, cow, shoe,* and so forth (the learning of properties one and two by children have been the focus of interest of developmental psycholinguistics investigators; see, for instance, Bowerman, 1978; Barrett, 1978, 1982); and (3), that words break down meaning complexes. Theories that explain properties one and two will not necessarily work for property three. At the end of the process of differentiation that Barrett (1982) analyzes in one child's speech, the word *pussy* denoted cats as contrasted with cows, horses, and dogs (all of which had once been part of the referential domain of the word that the child used initially to refer to cats). Although these contrasts had been formed, and the word now picked out cats and not other animals, nothing in this development would tell the child to limit her references in *cat-events* to just those parts that are *cat-entities,* that is, to categorize only cats rather than categorizing entire ongoing phenomena in which cats are the most salient namable parts. The semantic contrast of *pussy* to *doggie* and other like words would rarely help the child in segmenting events; only if cats, dogs, horses, and so forth happen to appear in the *same* ongoing events, would the subdivision of the semantic field of animals imply a segmentation of the event as well. In general, the referential and contrastive properties of words imply little about the segmenting property. I believe a case can be made that a child has not learned a word until the word has all three properties.

The segmentation of complex meanings is often imperfect. Errors of metathesis, anticipation, and perseveration are the results of inadequate segmentation, not to mention specific syntagmatic errors (haplologies). In all of these cases a unitary undivided meaning has not been broken down properly and words interact or combine in ways not allowable in the grammar. (Speech errors are discussed later in this chapter.)

Context Sensitivity

"Smart" words that convey an implicit syntax or frame are by definition context-sensitive in that they provide context for other words. Such words may also be sensitive to not yet categorized thought contexts. A type of verb that clearly is able to categorize thinking is shown in such examples as *blanket the bed* and *cocktail the diners* (Clark and Clark, 1979). These verbs are derived from nouns, hence are called "denominal" verbs (the opposite process creates nouns out of verbs, such as *(a) shield;* these are called "deverbal nouns"). The mental processes of the speaker who said *cocktail the diners* would indeed seem to have been visited by the spontaneous emergence of a symbol.

The significance of denominal verbs is that they illustrate a way of making "dumb" words intelligent—that is, more context-sensitive and able to codify thinking: "To decide what they mean on a particular occasion, we must know not only the meanings of their parts, but also something about the time, place, and circumstances in which they are uttered" (Clark and Clark, 1979, p. 767). If nouns are to become capable of self-activation, it is presumably through the addition of processes exemplified by denominalization that give them the power to sense and classify their context. Having become verbs, they also provide an implicit syntax for other words.

Clark and Clark's paper includes extensive lists of denominal verb examples classified to indicate the role in the action of the object denoted by the parent noun. The following gives a small sample from each class (one example is considered to be a newly created verb and one a well-established verb):

Locatum verbs are verbs whose parent nouns denote an object that is put at a location: *blanket the bed* (Bill did something so that the blanket was placed on the bed), *roof the house* (an established verb).

Location verbs are verbs whose parent nouns denote the locations where objects are put: *youth-hostel in Europe* (Bill stayed at youth hostels in Europe), *cellar the wine* (an established verb).

Duration verbs are verbs whose parent nouns denote the time period of an action or state: *daylights as a barber* (Bill works during daylight hours as a barber), *winter in California* (established verb).

Agent verbs are verbs whose parent nouns denote the agents of actions: *agent a book, jockey the horse* (both established verbs).

Experiencer verbs are verbs whose parent nouns denote persons who "experience" but who do not cause or receive the direct effects of actions: *witness the accident* (Bill was a witness to the accident—i.e., Bill neither caused nor received the accident, but did experience it as a witness). (All examples in Clark and Clark are established verbs.)

Goal verbs are verbs whose parent nouns denote the goals of an action: *tent the blanket* (Bill did something to make his blanket into a tent), *dwarf his enemies* (an established verb).

Instrument verbs are verbs whose parent nouns denote the instrument with which an action is carried out: *sports-car to Boston* (travel to Boston by sports car), *thumb to LA* (an established verb).

For the hearer, such verbs might lodge in memory as syntactic frames but be lost as individual words. For example, hearers of the last examples above might retain the idea that the method of travel was by sports car or by hitch-hiking, but forget that it was the verb that contained this information. What remains in memory is the semantic content, or "gist," of the sentence (Fillenbaum, 1966).

Experiments on Word Recognition

Experimental findings suggest that, based on context and perceptual data, words are recognized by eliminating alternatives. Word recognition is in effect word *selection,* and on this score, recognition and production are fundamentally similar. The selection of words for thinking and for speech production/understanding is a topic of obvious importance for the conception of linguistic performance that is presented in this chapter. The processes described in this section are crucial, both in the selection of cognitive tools in inner speech and in the selection of words to fill the time-parts of outer speech. In this section I will summarize a body of work on word recognition that has been built up over many years by psychologists.

In keeping with the concept of paradigmatic contrast, word recognition implies selecting one word from a set of words that share a common field of meaning and/or phonetic form. (Both the signifier and the signified sides of symbols are relevant.) This means that paradigms must be activated during word recognition. The factors that affect word recognition affect the recognition of contrasts, and discovering these factors is the way research on word recognition has proceeded.

Effects of Word Frequency   Word frequency refers to the number of times a given word occurs in a sample of text (spoken or written). Massive word frequency counts have been published on several occasions (Thorndike and Lorge, 1944; Kučera and Francis, 1967). How frequently a word occurs reflects the probability of finding the word in a sample text, and is taken to reflect the psychological variable of familiarity. Many psychological experiments have shown this to be a powerful variable. It affects the rate of learning or forgetting, the guessing preferences of subjects, and many other aspects of performance.

Familiarity also accounts for the historical preservation of irregular lexical items. Bybee (1984) reports that of the 30 most frequent past-tense English verbs listed in the Kučera and Francis word count, 22 are irregular. Of the next 30 past tenses, only 8 are irregular. (The irregulars are verbs such as *was, sat,* and *came,* as distinguished from verbs such as *distinguished.*) Moreover, Bybee reports that irregular verbs become regular when their frequency of use drops. When irregular verbs lose their protective mantle of familiarity, they no longer resist change, but shift over to regular forms. Bybee gives the following list of frequencies of modern verbs, all of which have descended from irregular Old English verbs. (The numbers are the frequencies per one million words of text according to Kučera and Francis; "strong" means irregular in past tense; "weak" means regular.)

Verbs That Are Still Strong		Verbs That Have Become Weak	
Drive	208	Bide	1
Rise	280	Reap	5

Ride	150	Slit	8
Write	599	Sneak	11
Bite	128	Rue	6
Choose	177	Seethe	0
Fly	119	Smoke	59
Shoot	187	Float	23
Lose	274	Shove	16
Flee	40	Wax	19
Fall	338	Weep	31
Hold	498	Beat	96
Know	1227	Hew	1
Grow	257	Leap	42
Blow	81	Mow	1
Average	304	Sow	3
		Flow	95
		Row	53
		Average	26

With only a few exceptions the current frequency of the still irregular verbs is higher than the current frequency of the no-longer irregular verbs, and the average frequencies of the two classes are far apart. The same protection from regularization occurs in the speech of individual learners of language. Bybee and Slobin (1982) found a negative correlation ($-.67$) between the number of times adults used irregular verbs in talking to children and the number of times the children regularized the same verbs in their own speech (e. g., whereas *blowed* might occur, *knowed* probably would not).

The *word frequency effect* in word recognition is that the threshold of recognition is lower for more frequent words. This threshold is conventionally defined as the signal-to-noise (S/N) ratio or the stimulus duration (for visually presented words) at which the subject recognizes half the words presented to him or her. The lower the threshold, the more sensitive the recognition process. This definition of the recognition threshold does not mean that every detail of a recognized word is discernable. For example,

CATASTROPHE

can be recognized as "catastrophe" even though the letters are not, in themselves, completely recognized. (In this example and the next I try to simulate the perceptual experience of seeing a word flash for a brief instant in a tachistoscope.)

More frequent words can be recognized on the basis of lower grade stimulus information—lower S/N ratios or shorter durations (Howes and Solomon, 1951; Postman and Rosenzweig, 1957). To what is this reduction of threshold due? A far-reaching explanation, which applies to many other phenomena as well, is that in word recognition what is really taking place is word selection or reconstruction (Savin, 1963; Neisser, 1967; Catlin, 1969). According to this explanation, even when a stimulus lacks enough clarity to specify a single word, it can reduce the set of contrasting words in a paradigm by a significant amount. From this restricted set the subject reconstructs or selects the stimulus, and in so doing tends to try more familiar words first. Thus when the stimulus is a more frequent word, in fact, it will have a better chance of crossing the 50 percent threshold and will tend to do so at a lower S/N ratio or shorter exposure duration. At a given level of stimulus quality the same fragmentary perception of frequent and infrequent words may exist, but a more frequent word will have a better chance of being correctly selected.

For example, suppose the stimulus word is *tap* (lower case). At a certain exposure duration only some of the letters are recognizable:

tap

Even this much data, however, eliminates long words such as *dinosaur* or *manifesto*. The subject still might try *cap, cat, can,* and so forth. Several of these choices are more probable than *tap.* More detailed stimulus information would be required, in general, before the subject would reconstruct *tap* rather than *cat, cap,* or other possibilities. If it were available, more detailed stimulus information would narrow the set of possibilities by elminating some of the high (as well as low) frequency alternatives. Improvement of stimulus quality comes from increasing the S/N ratio or prolonging the stimulus presentation; thus the threshold of *tap* is raised. If the high frequency alternatives of *tap* did not exist, the threshold would be lower. The point about selection as a process of word recognition is that the level of the 50 percent threshold depends on several factors that interact reciprocally—the quality of the stimulus, the number of alternatives in the paradigmatic set of the stimulus, and the relative likelihood of the stimulus within this set of alternatives.

Effects of Length   The length of a word also affects the recognition threshold. In this case, the effect differs depending on how the word is presented to the subject—whether aurally or visually. When presented aurally, greater word length lowers the recognition threshold. In Savin's (1963) experiment, for example, one-syllable words whose probability of occurrence in texts was three words out of a thousand crossed the 50 percent at 0 db S/N (i.e., there was equal loudness of signal and added white noise), two-syllable words of the same probability at −5 db (i.e., 5 db more noise than signal), and four-syllable words at −10 db (see Licklider, 1951, for an explanation of the decibel, or db). An explanation of this effect is that accumulating the information available in a long word, even when the stimulus quality is low, removes many alternatives from the paradigmatic set of the word, thus allowing the threshold to be lower. With short words this accumulation of information is bound to be less.

In contrast, when a stimulus word is presented visually, words with more letters per syllable have higher recognition thresholds, given equality of frequency. For example, *knowledge* (4.5 letters per syllable) has a higher threshold than *amicable* (two letters per syllable) (Howes and Solomon, 1951). It is not clear what causes this effect. Savin (1963) and Gough (1972) believe that in a recognition test with tachistoscopically presented words, subjects attempt to read the words in the usual left-to-right order. When the exposure duration is very short, the subject cannot read the entire word, and thus sees fewer long syllables than short syllables. Words with long syllables may therefore have a double disadvantage when seen at short durations: both the quality of the stimulus is low, and fewer syllables can be seen. Words with short syllables have less of the second disadvantage. For example, seeing *amic* (of *amicable*) is more useful in selecting a word to report than seeing *know* (of *knowledge*). Seeing *amic* might suggest *amicable,* but seeing *know* leaves open a high-probability alternative—*know* itself. This explanation assumes that, when trying to remove contrasting words, knowing additional syllables is more useful than knowing simply an equal number of additional letters. The assumption that useful information is operated on perceptually in the form of syllables, however, apparently has not been investigated in a separate study.

Effects of Information Load　　Increasing the information load on a word raises the recognition threshold (Miller, Heise, and Lichten, 1951). Information load varies directly with the number of alternative words with which the word to be recognized contrasts. Thus the larger the paradigmatic set of contrasting words, the higher the recognition threshold (all other factors being equal).

The concept of information load refers to the reduction of uncertainty achieved by identifying the word. This depends on how many other words there are that might have occurred instead. If this number is (by some prior arrangement) just two or three, the initial uncertainty is one-half or one-third, and the amount by which recognizing the stimulus reduces uncertainty cannot be more than $1 - \frac{1}{2}$ or $1 - \frac{1}{3}$. If the number of possible words is 500, the amount of uncertainty reduction—and therefore the amount of information load—is much larger, $1 - \frac{1}{500}$. The information load on one word out of 500, in other words, is much bigger than that on one word out of two or three.

It is easy to see that the results of Miller et al's experiment are consistent with word selection as the process of word recognition. Before each trial Miller et al. told the subject the list of words from which the stimulus on that trial would come (not revealing the identity of the stimulus). This established a temporary contrastive set of words. The size of the contrastive sets ranged from 2 words to 256 words. Inasmuch as the contrastive sets were artificial, it was possible to test the recognition thresholds of the same words in sets of different sizes. Less stimulus quality was needed to eliminate a single alternative from a set of 2 words than to eliminate 255 alternatives from a set of 256. The S/N ratio at the 50 percent threshold with just two alternatives was -14 db, whereas with 256 alternatives it was -4 db. A difference of 10 db means that only about one-third of the stimulus intensity was needed to cross the threshold for words in the two-word sets (the absolute sensitivities in this experiment and others depend on the specific conditions of the experiment).

Effects Within Words　　The minimal context for word recognition is the word itself. Pillsbury in 1897 found that people would "recognize" visually presented words that were not actually present; for example, they would perceive *forever* when they were really shown *foyever.* From this finding it follows that the recognition threshold of *forever* (when actually presented) would be lower than the threshold of *foyever.* The context, in this case, is the rest of the word, *fo ever.*

With acoustic presentations, also, missing or distorted elements are restored by subjects. Such effects, called phoneme restorations, have been studied by Warren (1970) and Warren and Obusek (1971). They replaced speech sounds with nonspeech sounds, such as a cough(*); for example, *legi*lature* (without disturbance of rhythm). Though people could hear the cough, 90 percent of the subjects could not identify its location. Apparently they did not notice the absence of /s/ and that the cough had taken its place. Other substitute sounds not animately derived, such as buzzes and tones, also could not be accurately located; only a brief silent interval could be located reliably.

These observations suggest that there is within the word itself pressure to reduce the recognition threshold. A deviant letter or sound will not be incorporated if it conflicts with the other evidence for recognizing the word. The utility of this arrangement is apparent. In natural situations there are many distortions, both large and small, of the speech signal. Thanks to word-internal redundancies these distortions are often overlooked. The same process explains the notorious difficulty of spotting errors during proofreading. The reason that distortions do not raise the recognition threshold is that the presence of one deviant element will not necessarily increase the size of the paradigmatic set that has to be considered. The set that includes *foyever,* for example, is probably only one item larger than the set that includes *forever* (the extra item being *foyever* itself, and within this set *foyever* is radically less probable).

Not only does the word-internal context help the reader recognize *words* at lower thresholds, but *single letters* can be recognized at lower thresholds when they are part of a word, in contrast to when they are part of a nonword or are presented alone (Reicher, 1969). For example, *s* can be identified at a lower threshold when it is part of *snob* than when part of *sbjt.* This phenomenon has been called the *word-superiority effect* by Johnston (1978). Although the word-superiority effect shows an influence of word-internal context on letter recognition, the process by which it is produced is not one in which alternative letters are eliminated because they are inconsistent with the rest of the word. Johnston found no difference in accuracy of letter identification when the number of alternative letters was deliberately varied. Johnston proposed, rather, that when a letter appears alone or in a nonword it rapidly fades from the subject's perceptual memory (Sperling, 1960).

Such a fading trace, however, cannot account for the letter and phoneme restoration effects. In Pillsbury's, Warren's, and Warren and Obusek's experiments, resistance to losing a letter in a word context would lead to a *reduction* of the restoration rate. Subjects should have been *more* able to see the *y* in the stimulus. (Unless the subject had already seen that the stimulus is not a word; but then why restore the *r*?) The upshot of these considerations is that the word-internal context has two quite separate effects: at the level of the word as a whole, restoration of a distorted word; at the level of the elements, enhanced discrimination of the elements. These tendencies clearly work at cross-purposes when there is distortion, but support one another when there is an undistorted signal.

The process of eliminating alternatives implies that the hearer/viewer can identify the paradigmatic set of the word before having identified the word itself. "Cohort theory," described in the section below on theories of word recognition, explains a process by which this could be done, and also how a selection from the paradigmatic set could be made in real time. At this point I will discuss the problem of identifying paradigmatic sets of words in general. There are several lines along which this can be accomplished, corresponding to the multiple paradigmatic sets of which words are naturally a part. A fragment of the stimulus is sufficient to locate a word among its phonemic contrasts (Savin, 1963) or graphemic contrasts (Howes and Solomon, 1951). For instance, perceiving just curved bits of letter are enough to place a stimulus among words starting with *s* (Johnston, 1978). Arbitrary paradigms can be created (Miller et al., 1951). Semantic and pragmatic information from context also can activate paradigms. A context in which the theme is medicine is enough to activate a paradigm of medical words (*doctor, nurse, patient, hospital,* etc.).

In general, one can suppose that the phonemic, graphemic, and semantic paradigms that contain a word are distinct but correlated. Selecting words from these paradigms clearly is different but can converge on the same target, insofar as semantically related words are phonemically or graphemically related. Depending on the size of the paradigm, however, the same word may have higher or lower information loads and hence recognition thresholds. Phonemic similarity within semantic fields is not negligible, as word families like *medico, medicine, medical, medicinal* or *education, educator, educational, educative* show. J. Bybee, in an unpublished paper (1984), states this principle concisely: "Morpho-phonemic alternations tend to diagram morphological relatedness: the more closely related two forms are semantically, the more likely they are to be similar morpho-phonemically" (p. 16). The size of any given morpho-phonemic paradigm seems rather small (like the two indicated), and the information load on its members seems therefore not great; this would further speed word recognizability, including the recognition of self-activating "smart" words in inner speech.

Irregular Verbs

As we have already seen, words of very high frequency tend to preserve their unique morphological characteristics, which narrows the size of the paradigm even further. Narrowing could be carried to the logical extreme of a paradigm of one, which would imply direct recognition, but in fact irregular words, too, fit into small paradigms that can be identified in advance of the word itself. English "strong" verbs are often lumped indiscriminately together as irregulars, but they fall into paradigms that reflect regularities in their manner of being irregular. Conforming to one or another of these patterns could provide the basis for selecting irregular verbs from activated paradigmatic sets during speaking, thinking, and comprehending. The high frequency of these irregular verbs implies that they belong to small paradigmatic sets, which in turn implies a light information load on each verb and therefore high accessibility during word recognition (including the recognition of inner speech that takes place during speaking). This in turn enhances the frequency of their use.

The regular past-tense pattern of English is described by a single rule,

$$\text{verb}_{past} \rightarrow \text{verb} + ed; \text{ (e.g., } walk + ed)$$

The *ed* form in this rule appears in different versions depending on the exact phonetic context, but all include some form of dental consonant—either a /t/ (*laughed*—/læft/) or a /d/ (after a voiced consonant, *lived,* or after a vowel, *weighed*—/weyd/).

Bybee and Slobin (1982) divided English irregular verbs into eight classes, none of which is exactly the same as this rule (other schemes have been proposed with larger numbers of classes: Jesperson, 1942, had 10 classes, and Bloch, 1947, had 20). The eight Bybee–Slobin classes are the following:

/t/ and /d/ Paradigms

1. Verbs that end in dental consonants and do not change form in the past tense; for example, *beat, cut, hit.*
2. Verbs that change a final /d/ to /t/; for example, *send → sent, build → built.*
3. Verbs that have an internal vowel change and add a final /t/ or /d/; for example, *feel → felt, lose → lost, say → said, tell → told.*
4. Verbs that undergo an internal vowel change, delete their final consonant, and add a final /t/; for example, *bring → brought, catch → caught.*
5. Verbs that end with /t/ or /d/ and change an internal vowel; for example, *bite → bit, find → found, ride → rode.*

Vowel Paradigm with /æ/ or /ʌ/

6. Verbs that indicate the past tense by changing /ɨ/ to /æ/ or /ʌ/ plus a nasal or velar consonant, /ng/, /n/ or /k/; for example, *sing → sang* = /sæng/, *drink → drank* = /drænk/, *sting → stung* = /stʌng/.

Vowel Paradigm with Final Consonant

7. Verbs that indicate the past tense by changing the vowel of a word that ends in a consonant: *give → gave, break → broke.*

Vowel Paradigm with Final Diphthong

8. Verbs that indicate the past tense by changing the vowel of a word that ends in a diphthong: *blow → blew, fly → flew.*

Note that each of the first five paradigms makes use of dental sounds *(d, t)* to signal the past tense, the phonemic signal also used by the regular past-tense rule. If there is a front-consonant paradigm for past tense, all the irregular verbs in the first five classes could be selected from this common set. The sixth, seventh, and eighth paradigms are totally different, consisting of vowel changes. The paradigms of the vowel past tenses differ, depending on whether their verbs contain velar consonants and end in consonants or in diphthongs, but as a loose set they contrast with the *t/d* verbs. Bybee and Slobin found that /æng/ in the sixth paradigm was even applied incorrectly under time pressure by adults to produce such nonattested alterations as *string → strang* (= /ing/ → /æng/). That the nasal consonant is essential in this paradigm is shown by the fact that there were no erroneous past tenses produced under time pressure like *dig → dag* or *stick → stack,* where the consonant is nonnasal, though it is made in the back of the mouth; this fails to produce /i/ → /æ/. Evidence for other vowel changes as indicators of the past tense are such erroneous past-tense productions under time pressure as these:

lean → lent (/i/ → /E/)

flow → flew (/ow/ → /uw/)

snooze → snoze (/uw/ → /ow/)

Theories of Word Recognition

The problem of word recognition is often conceived of as one of mapping an incoming phonetic string onto a remembered lexical item. Theories thus have emphasized the "bottom-up" or "data-driven" aspects of the process of recognition. This formulation often seems to have in mind the situation in the typical word recognition experiment, that is, where there is recognition of isolated words on the basis of signal properties alone. Theories have not focused on the effects of context on word recognition and they are not particularly illuminating on this point. In this section I will describe three theories: Forster's lexical search theory, Morton's logogen theory, and Marslen-Wilson's cohort theory.

Forster (1976) described a model in which *search* (rather than direct access) is the core operation. Given a phonemic signal already processed into distinctive speech sounds, the word recognition process goes to a file of words arranged in the order of the frequency of occurrence of words in speech. It searches in this file for a word that matches the input signal and when a sufficiently good (not necessarily perfect) match is made, then finds an address to a second, master file in which is stored everything else about the word that the speaker/hearer must know for appropriate usage (meaning information, syntactic properties, sociolinguistic information, etc.). The word recognition process thus operates serially and autonomously: from the input signal it eventually reaches a store of semantic-syntactic-pragmatic information about the word, but is not able to relate the input signal to this kind of information until the word has already been recognized. Marslen-Wilson (in press) has criticized Forster's model on this point. In various studies he and colleagues have demonstrated powerful effects of context on word recognition (some of these are summarized below). Such effects seem impossible to incorporate into Forster's theory without fundamentally altering the search mechanism.

In Morton's logogen theory (Morton, 1969), the acoustic input (again assumed to have already been segmented into phonemes) triggers one or more "logogens"—receptors that are tuned to particular phonemic features. The logogens that respond to a given phonemic feature constitute one paradigmatic set based on phonemic similarity. When a logogen reaches a preset threshold, it "fires," that is, notifies other mental processes that its particular phonemic pattern has been sensed. The logogen is thus a species of "demon" (Selfridge and Neisser, 1960; Lindsay and Norman, 1977), a mechanism that constantly scans the range of input to which it is sensitive and acts whenever an input event within its range occurs. In contrast to the search that dominates Forster's theory, in Morton's logogen theory the process is one of *direct access.* The input is in direct contact with all the logogens; there is no search at all. Logogens differ in their sensitivity and in their interconnections. The logogens of more frequent words have permanently lower thresholds; thus the word-frequency effect follows directly. Logogens also can have their thresholds lowered temporarily by other logogens and by the results of perceptual (nonlinguistic) analysis; thus influences from both the verbal and nonverbal context are accommodated.

Closely related to the logogen theory is the "cohort" theory of Marslen-Wilson (Marslen-Wilson and Welsh, 1978; Marslen-Wilson and Tyler, 1980; Marslen-Wilson, in press). As with logogens words in this theory are thought of as reactive devices to which access by the phonemic input proceeds in parallel. While many different paradigmatic sets can be defined for a given word, a cohort is a paradigmatic set of phonemically contrasting words. The word is recognized out of this set. To this extent cohort theory is similar to the view of word recognition that has guided most modern research in this area. What is novel in cohort theory is that it takes into account the surface time required to hear the speech signal. When speech arrives, it (or the phonemic analysis of it) is broadcast to the word detectors in parallel. If a detector is sensitive to the acoustic pattern it turns itself on. This is a logogenlike feature. Detectors also turn themselves off as soon as there is phonemic data inconsistent with them. The full paradigmatic set of words consistent with the input at any moment is called the cohort. Because the word detectors respond simultaneously and in parallel (independently), a cohort is brought to life very quickly—within the first syllable. Because word detectors also turn themselves off in parallel, words that are incompatable with incoming speech data turn off simultaneously and only as much bottom-up sensory information is absorbed as is needed to reduce the cohort to a single word. This survivor is the recognized word.

The semantic and grammatical context has an effect on the winnowing of the cohort but not, Marslen-Wilson maintains, on the initial activation of the cohort itself (Marslen-Wilson, in press). Thus priming the recognition of a word by presenting a semantically related word in advance (Meyer and Schvaneveldt, 1971) operates by speeding the selection of the word from the cohort, but not by shrinking the cohort itself.

The removal process can move fast enough to reach a single word before the whole word has been read in. Such winnowing can take place for longer words, but also for short words if the cohort is small enough. One can therefore predict the point, called the "recognition point," *within* the word at which recognition should take place. If the first sound is /k/, the cohort of /k/-initial words, *cap, king, catalogue, catastrophe, cat,* and so forth, could be reduced to one word, say, *catastrophe,* upon completion of the second syllable. Before this time *cap, king,* and other one-syllable words will have turned themselves off, and by the end of the second syllable *catalogue* will have done the same. *Catastrophe,* then, is recognized, although only *catas* has been heard (for the sake of the example I am ignoring derivations from *catastrophe–catastrophic,* etc.). If top-down information is inconsistent with some of the words of the cohort, the winnowing takes place even sooner.

The recognition point can be estimated a priori from dictionaries (making allowance for the fact that it is how words are pronounced rather than spelled that matters), and empirically by a procedure known as "gating" (Grosjean, 1980). In this technique subjects hear successively longer pieces of a word (in increments of 30–50 msec, where a syllable typically lasts 200 msec). After each presentation they say what they believe the word is. The amount of the word needed to identify it corresponds to its empirical recognition point (Tyler and Wessels, 1983).

Taking into account the recognition point allows Marslen-Wilson to make a number of unique predictions. For example, the time to detect in ongoing speech a phoneme target that has been given to the subject in advance should depend on where in the word the target appears in relation to the recognition point. The closer the target to the recognition point, the faster the response should be. If the word is *catastrophe,* the subject's response latency (delay) should be less if the target is /s/ than if it is /k/ (response latency is measured from the moment the target occurs). Marslen-Wilson (1984, in press) found very high correlations between response latency and distance of the target from both the a priori recognition point (r = .89) and the empirical recognition point (r = .92). (The two methods of identifying recognition points themselves correlate highly.)

In another experiment Marslen-Wilson (1978) had subjects listen for *non*-words that deviated from real words at earlier or later points in the input. For instance,

*s*thoided (nonword deviates after initial /s/)

*feath*orn (nonword deviates after initial /feath/)

The subjects responded to the presence of the nonword a constant 450 msec after the first point at which there was evidence of the nonword. The subjects could have at this point (and not before) reduced the cohort to zero members. Their response required another 450 msec after this regardless of where in the input the "nonrecognition" point occurred.

In a further experiment of the same type, Marslen-Wilson (in press) varied the size of the set of real words of the initial cohort that were still in the cohort at the point at which the evidence of a nonword first occurred. If the recognition process takes place in parallel, it should not matter how large this set is; all contenders are removed simultaneously by the same deviation from a real word. On the other hand, a serial search model such as Forster's (1976), in which all the candidate words have to be tested one after another, predicts a correlation between the latency to say there is a nonword and the size of this set. With sets of contending real words ranging from one to seventy, however, the latency was constant.

This result appears to conflict with the finding of Miller et al. (1951) that the information load on a word—the size of its paradigmatic set—had a major effect on recognition. One difference between the experiments is the response value that was measured. Miller et al. measured accuracy of recognition in noise, whereas Marslen-Wilson measured reaction time. If information load affects primarily a long-duration process like guessing, there would be no correlation expected with information load and reaction time.

On the other hand, it is possible that in Marslen-Wilson's experiment there was still an effect of information load on real-time processes. This could happen if the appropriate variable for information load is the size of the initial cohort, rather than the terminal cohort. If a nonword is *robent,* for example, the word initial cohort is 40+ words, but the terminal cohort is only about 3 words; thus the two cohorts give quite different estimates of the information load. If these estimates are uncorrelated in size, as is likely, a noncorrelation with reaction time and size of the terminal cohort is then expected. The size of the initial cohort would be the more relevant variable on the argument that the size of a word's paradigmatic set is a stable, socially constituted property of the word; it is a causal factor in determining linguistic value, and changes slowly only when words are added to or lost from the paradigmatic set. This property of a word would still exist when most of the paradigmatic set has switched off (in fact, it would exist when all of it has switched off). The experiment therefore does not appear to exclude information load as a stable property of words that could affect word recognition speed.

In an earlier series of experiments, Marslen-Wilson (1975) obtained data that showed at what point during the perception of words the word is related to the sentence structure of which it is a part. Subjects "shadowed" (i.e., repeated concurrently while they heard) passages of prose that had been planted with mispronounced words, such as *univert* in place of *universe* (a mispronunciation in the third syllable). Other words were mispronunciations in the first or second syllable; for example, *eeniverse* or *unipurse.* Shadowers frequently detected mispronunciations in the first syllable (i.e., they accurately repeated *eeniverse*), but missed mispronunciations in the second or third syllable (i.e., they inaccurately said *universe* for *univert*). This fact implies that the hearer ceased taking in bottom-up data after the recognition point, which would have occurred after a single syllable in these words. When the sentence was semantically uninterpretable, mispronunciations were equally well detected in every position. Thus, having a basis for interpreting the sentence was necessary for the hearer to know when to cease taking in bottom-up data. When an interpretation is possible, the hearer reacts very quickly. It follows that in normal speech understanding hearers are relating bottom-up data to the word's semantic-syntactic context during the 0.2

seconds or so that it normally takes to turn off the cohort. (For an exchange of papers about cohort theory, see Norris, 1982, and Marslen-Wilson and Tyler, 1982.)

As now formulated, cohort theory is limited to the phonemic paradigms of words. However, words in fact belong to multiple paradigms including, in particular, semantic paradigms. The assumption in cohort theory that only sensory input is allowed to activate the cohort seems critical for predicting the recognition point of a given word, but otherwise appears to be an arbitrary limitation. Recent findings by others (Huttenlocher and Goodman, in press, summarized below) in fact call into question the concept of a recognition point. Thus, to include contextual and semantic factors among the forces capable of activating cohorts may not entail any further sacrifice.

Intersecting phonemic and semantic paradigmatic sets could greatly reduce the size of the initial cohorts that have to be winnowed. For example, assume that a phonemically activated paradigm is all the words in set P below and a semantically activated paradigm all the words in set S. If P and S intersect and are not coextensive, activating the cohort that meets both semantic and phonemic criteria (the area filled in) creates an information load that is significantly smaller than that of a cohort that meets just one criterion.

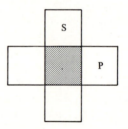

It remains to be seen if cohort theory can be extended to include semantic paradigms of words in the definition of cohorts in a nondestructive way.

Troubles with Recognition Points

One aspect of cohort theory that has not been well supported by other research workers is the hypothesis that, after the words of a cohort encounter incompatible stimulus information, they are able to switch themselves off in real time. The concept of a cohort itself as a paradigm of words activated during word recognition has not been challenged, nor has the idea that the process of recognition operates in parallel on all the words in a cohort simultaneously. However, the idea of a recognition point within a word has been called into doubt.

Huttenlocher and Goodman (in press) noted that the Marslen-Wilson (1978) study mentioned above made use of sound sequences that broke the phonological sequencing rules (phonotactic rules) of English. For example, *sthoided* violates a prohibition against the /s/ + /th/ sequence. Thus, they argue, a string like *sthoided* could be identified as a nonword without going through the process of rejecting alternatives from a cohort. In their experiment, care was taken to make the nonword sequences phonologically legal, and they found that the time to detect a nonword was not equal after early and late nonword points. Responses were about 30 percent faster after late nonword points. This difference in favor of late points implies that listeners waited until hearing the complete wordlike string of sounds before deciding it was not a word, even though this decision could have been made earlier. The same inference is made from a comparison of the amount of time subjects took to say that a string of sounds was a word. Since a word decision definitely requires waiting until the end of the word (the last sound might make it into a nonword), people should, if there is real time switching off of words, take more time to say that something is a word than to say it is a nonword. However, the times for declaring a string a nonword were the same as saying it was a word.

Another negative result bearing on the recognition point has been reported by Slowiaczek et al. (1985). They found that word recognition was facilitated by priming the *ends* of words. For example, recognition of *hand* was sped up by a previous exposure to *sand* (overlap of three phonemes from the end). This priming was greater than after *send* (overlap of two phonemes), which in turn was greater than after *dried* (overlap of only the final /d/). The priming of targets from the end contradicts the early-to-late processing order assumed by cohort theory and on which its prediction of recognition points depends.

Both of these studies challenge the idea of recognition points *within* words. They do not bear on the concept of the cohort itself or on the idea of parallel processing. Moreover, if there are no recognition points, a reason for not countenancing cohorts defined by semantic paradigms disappears. It is difficult nonetheless for an outsider to evaluate the empirical situation with regard to the recognition point. The two negative studies, Huttenlocher and Goodman's in particular, are convincing in their negativity, but other studies by Marslen-Wilson and coworkers have provided striking findings in support of the concept of a recognition point. It does not falsify cohort theory, or course, if there is some other process of word recognition that operates from the rear of words, as Slowiaczek et al. have found.

Extension to Speech Production

What can we say on the basis of cohort theory about speech production? It appears that a straightforward application is possible. If inner speech symbols are "smart" and self-activating, these symbols must also be recognized. Inner speech symbols would also evoke a cohort of possibilities. These inner cohorts could then be winnowed in the same manner as externally evoked cohorts. The survivor would be the inner speech symbol that is utilized as a cognitive tool. Recognition of inner speech symbols through winnowing of cohorts would be a way of ensuring that the linguistic value of the inner speech symbol is the same as that of the symbol in outer speech.

One type of speech error, the stress-placement error, is evidence of cohorts that have been activated during speech production. Saying *énvelope* (noun stress pattern) where *envélope* (verb stress pattern) was intended (Cutler, 1980) is evidence of a cohort during speech production that included both of these words. A cohort could be quite small if both semantic and phonological paradigms are active and intersect. Assuming the concept of a recognition point is valid, it may even be possible, via stress-placement errors, to define speech production recognition points. In the case of *énvelope,* for instance, the confusion took place between the first and second syllable stress—that is, early in the word and in advance of the presumed recognition point for *envélope.* On the other hand, an error such as *envelópe,* where there is no possible cohort source, should not be observed.

In the list of examples gathered by Cutler (1980) the great majority of stress-placement errors involved competitions of words in which both phonological and semantic paradigms could have been active. That there are real cohorts during speech production is suggested by a striking statistical result apparent in Cutler's tables—a symmetry in terms of the frequency with which grammatical forms appeared as intended and as erroneous words. This symmetry could arise when words belonging to different grammatical classes are part of the same cohort. A word is selected out of this cohort but with a certain probability that the selection will be wrong. However, since every member of a cohort has an equal chance of selection until it is eliminated by new data, this tendency toward error would be unbiased; particularly when the selection occurs too early, before all the necessary data for accurate winnowing of the cohort is available, error would affect one type of word as much as another type within the cohort. The example above consisted of giving a noun form where a verb was meant, but equally often there are errors that consisted of other grammatical categories taking the place of noun forms. Erroneous and correct verb and erroneous and correct adjective forms were also symmetrical in terms of frequency, as illustrated by the following. (The two columns, "intended" and "error," do not add up to the same number because one error had an unclassifiable stress pattern.)

	Intended	Error
Noun	20	18
Verb	7	9
Adjective	13	12

These errors and other errors of speaking are further discussed in the section on speech errors.

Some of the exceptions to a cohort interpretation discovered by Cutler might also be explained if we assume that ad hoc cohorts can be generated in particular contexts. One error for which the context was recorded was saying *ádj-* when *adjústed* was meant. There is no source word for this stress placement but, as Cutler observed, the immediately preceding context consisted of another word containing the same initial vowel in which stress was on the first syllable. This context was:

there's such a thing as level of expectation and level of áspiration and ádj-adjústed people

If there was a temporary cohort carried forward that included *aspiration* when the speaker started to think in terms of *adjusted,* the stress-placement error could have occurred before the recognition point in this ad hoc cohort (after the first vowel). This explanation predicts that whereas *ádujsted* is an error that could be induced by *áspiration, adjustéd* would not be an error that could be induced by *expectátion,* because the stress shift in this temporary cohort would have to occur after the correct recognition point for *adjústed.*

SURFACE PHENOMENA

Three phenomena of speech production/understanding that can be interpreted by reference to the surface texture of speech are grouped here. They are: (1) all the signified meanings attached to a particular signifier-shape are retrieved at the same time; (2) speech output is packaged into small stress-group units; and (3) exact memory for perceived speech detail exists but is fleeting.

Automaticity

If cohorts were defined on the basis of phonetic information alone, it would be necessary to select the correct word from a set of contrasts that includes semantically improbable alternatives. Such an expectation may be correct. Experiments have demonstrated that even though one meaning of an ambiguous word is clearly inappropriate contextually, such words are first activated in long-term memory with all their meanings intact (Swinney, 1979; Seidenberg et al., 1982). I will describe Swinney's experiment. He had his subjects listen to short passages like the following:

> Rumor had it that, for years, the government building had been plagued with problems. The man was not surprised when he found several spiders, roaches, and other bugs in the room.

At the same time the subjects had to make a lexical decision about a visually presented stimulus. The experimenter measured the priming effect of *bugs* on this stimulus. On some trials nonword letter strings were presented and on other trials real words were presented. On any given trial one of the words or the nonword letter string would be shown while the subject was listening to the passage. The words and nonwords were timed to occur just after the occurrence of *bugs.* The real words were of three kinds:

Contextually appropriate: ant
Contextually inappropriate: spy
Unrelated baseline: sew

The question was, does *bugs* prime both *ant* and *spy?* If it does, then the contextually inappropriate sense of *bugs* must have been active at the moment the visual stimulus was presented; this was the clear result of the experiment.

In another condition, Swinney delayed the visual presentation until the occurrence of *room* at the end. The additional three syllables evidently provided enough time for context to remove the inappropriate meaning, for by then only *ant* was primed.

This transitory influence of the listening-device meaning rules out one obvious alternative explanation of the main result—namely, that the very mention of the government is enough with some suspicious subjects to prime the word *spy.* If this were the case, however, the effect would have persisted already for 28 syllables and should have been able to persist for another 3 syllables.

When someone is thinking with inner speech symbols there could also be a transitory presence of inappropriate meanings contained in a phonological paradigm while the inner speech symbol is being recognized by the thinker. Since these words are excluded in parallel very quickly, they may never reach a level of conscious awareness. Yet they might still have an influence over thought. In certain states of consciousness the cohort may reach awareness. Inappropriate members of cohorts can get into consciousness and the resulting swarm of dissimilar meanings can redirect thinking. This phenomenon might be important in some kinds of schizophrenic speech where bizarre semantic incongruities occur. For example, explaining the meaning of "when the cat's away the mice will play," one patient replied as follows (Benjamin, 1946):

> The last supper of Jesus, all of those that kissed the novitia, the covitia. The political world is too much, we can't fight it, we can't see murder (p. 75).

Weird though this undeniably is, there are possible sound associations between *cat* and *covitia, mice* and *murder, play* and *political, mice* and *kisssed, covitia* and *novitia,* and others. The bizarre statement might have been the rather desperate attempt to linearize meaning segments that have nothing in common except random linkages of sounds.

Speech Programming "Packages"

How is the verbal plan, produced by synthesizing linguistic value with images, translated into movements of the speech articulators? A series of careful experiments by Sternberg et al. (1978, 1980) shows that the "package" of articulatory movements is the stress-group (for a recent summary, see Monsell, in press). A stress-group is a word or very short phrase that contains one primary stress. If we apply these findings to the theory proposed in this chapter, we can say that speech production requires unpacking an image into segments and matching these meaning segments with stress-groups. When these two orders of packages correspond there is what has been called a "syntagma"*—defined as one meaning unit pronounced as a single output (Kozhevnikov and Chistovich, 1965; see also McNeill, 1979).

In a typical experiment of Sternberg et al. a well-trained subject is given a short list of words to repeat from memory when a "go" signal appears. The idea is to finish saying the list as quickly as possible. The length of the list to be repeated is one of the variables. The words on the list might be, for instance, monosyllabic nouns. In experiments utilizing materials of these kinds subjects have been found to take longer to begin saying the list when the list is longer. This is true even if the list consists of saying the same word repeatedly: *Monday-Monday-Monday* takes longer to start than *Monday-Monday,* for example, even though the lists differ only at the end. The rate of increase of the starting time is a linear function of the number of items to be said. Even more astonishing, the same linear increase occurs in the amount of time taken to produce each successive item on the list. Each *Monday* on the three-item list takes slightly, but measureably, longer to say than each *Monday* on the two-item list.

The type of evidence that reveals the stress-group to be the control package in this situation is as follows: When the list consists of monosyllabic words each separated by an unstressed conjunction—*ONE-and-TWO-and-THREE,* for instance—the linearities described above hold only if length is expressed as the number of stressed syllables (so, in the example, the length is three, not five). The output unit is, therefore, *ONE-and, TWO-and,* and so forth.

Monsell (in press) describes a new experiment in which the utterances were grammatically structured; for example, *Barbara tricks a (rather rueful) dean,* with the long version including the words in parentheses. This contains three or five stress-groups, and the same linear increases appear as a function of length calculated over the number of stress-groups.

The need to find stress-group packages for idea units, thus forming syntagmas, establishes a constraint from below on the development of verbal plans. This is one of the ways in which "poetic" factors play a role in speech planning (Silverstein, 1984). If each control package is matched with a single segment of meaning from an image, there would be several syntagmas for a grammatical sentence that unpacks the entire image, one for each of the segments. This estimate of the size of a syntagma is smaller than assumed in McNeill (1979), but is the size empirically estimated in the Sternberg et al. and Monsell experiments.

Rapid Amnesia of Surface Detail

A curious phenomenon, first discovered by Sachs (1967), is hearer's amnesia for the surface details of speech. Memory of exact surface structure is quite short-lived. Listeners to speech are presumed to keep a fairly exact record of what they

---

*The term "syntagma" is similar to "syntagm," which is Saussure's word; a syntagma is a hypothetical psychological unit of processing, whereas a syntagm is a unit that results from items contrasting syntagmatically, and is purely linguistic.

hear until they understand the underlying linguistic structure; then they purge their memory. Sachs showed that there is detailed initial memory for speech but that within a short time, less than 80 syllables, this disappears and only memory for the semantic content of speech remains. She demonstrated this with the following passage to which subjects listened:

> There is an interesting story about the telescope. In Holland, a man named Lippershey was an eyeglass maker. One day his children were playing with some lenses. They discovered that things seemed very close if two lenses were held about a foot apart. Lippershey began experimenting and his "spyglass" attracted much attention. He sent a letter about it to Galileo, the great Italian scientist. Galileo at once realized the importance of the discovery and set about to build an instrument of his own. He used an old organ pipe with one lens curved out and the other in. On the first clear night he pointed the glass toward the sky. He was amazed to find the empty dark spaces filled with brightly gleaming stars! (pp. 438–439).

At this point the tape was stopped and the subject had to say which of the following sentences appeared in the story exactly as written (try this yourself without looking back):

1. He sent a letter about it to Galileo, the great Italian scientist.
2. Galileo, the great Italian scientist, sent him a letter about it.
3. A letter about it was sent to Galileo, the great Italian scientist.

Although only 80 syllables (about 27 seconds) intervened between the original sentence and the test, subjects could no longer tell whether they had originally heard an active (number one) or passive (number three) sentence. They could identify only the test sentence that altered the meaning of the original (number two). Other subjects who were tested right after the critical Galileo sentence also could distinguish numbers one and three.

The next step in investigating the amnesia of surface detail narrowed the region of exact memory to the current clause or sentence. This was shown by Jarvella (1971), who again had subjects listen to interrupted narrations. Jarvella's subjects were told to recall verbatim as much as they could of the 20 words preceding each interruption. The materials had been constructed so that, in some passages, there had been a sentence break 7 words before the interruption and, in other passages, a sentence break 13 words before. Ingeniously, identical word strings were used in both passages. Therefore any differences in the subjects' ability to recall words could not be due to differences between the words themselves. The following are two such passages (p. 140):

> That he could be intimidated was what *McDonald and his top advisors hoped. This would keep Rarick off the ballot.* (7 words)

> He and others were labeled as Communists. *McDonald and his top advisors hoped this would keep Rarick off the ballot.* (13 words)

The result of the experiment was clear. Recall of the word right before the interruption was essentially perfect in both passages. In both passages there was a slow decline back to the seventh word, at which point accuracy was about 85 percent. Then there was an abrupt drop of accuracy. The eighth word back was recalled accurately 70 percent of the time in example two and only 50 percent of the time in example one. At the thirteenth word back recall in example two was down to 40 percent plus, and in example two to barely more than 10 percent. Recall of the twentieth word was identical for examples one and two, about 5 percent. There was thus a loss of surface detail in both sentences that had been presented just prior to the last preceding clause boundary (the word *this*), and this loss was more severe when this boundary was also a sentence boundary (example one). There was further loss of sentence detail that had been presented still earlier, but the loss was less severe in example two until its sentence boundary was reached, 13 words back. Material presented before the thirteenth word back was recalled poorly for both examples one and two.

We learn from this experiment that surface detail disappears rapidly at clause and sentence boundaries and is lost more slowly between these boundaries. The identical words are kept for shorter times in narrations that have the more recent sentence boundary. Equivalent results have been obtained by Caplan (1972).

The next step was taken by de Villiers (1974) who found more substitutions of equivalent words in recalling lists of sentences when subjects regarded the list as forming a story than when they did not. Subjects who believed they were remembering a story recalled more words and sentences, in all, but also made more word substitutions. In other words, although the quantity of recall was less, subjects had more accurate recall of individual words if they did not expect cohesive links between sentences. Put the other way around, surface detail was retained if the person did not see an overall structure behind the verbal input.

Listeners thus retain surface detail until they synthesize what they are hearing with an idea unit, and then remove the surface detail from memory. There is a functional advantage to this way of managing memory, particularly when, as appears to be the case, the synthesis and memory purge take place at clause and sentence boundaries. If the surface details of earlier sentences were accurately remembered during the producing or understanding of later sentences there would be the likelihood of errors from efforts to synthesize these old details into the person's new thinking; that is, risk of a blend of rhythmically parallel *advisors* and *ballot* is avoided if *advisors* is promptly forgotten. Gernsbacher (1985) has shown rapid loss of surface detail for memory of the left-right orientation of drawings that is quite parallel to the loss of linguistic detail from sentences, suggesting that idea units are indeed the critical factors.

INFORMATION-PROCESSING APPROACHES

In this section of the chapter I will discuss what is currently the predominant school of thought in psycholinguistics and in cognitive psychology in general. My purpose is to relate the idea of information processing to the inner speech theory presented earlier in this chapter. I am particularly interested in showing how *heuristic strategies* are recruited by linguistic thinking and utilized in linguistic actions. Out of this discussion will emerge not only an understanding of the place of heuristic strategies in linguistic performance, but also an understanding of some of the theoretical limitations on the information-processing approach.

Heuristic strategies can be thought of as devices recruited for generating parts of linguistic trees. They create linguistic values, particularly syntagmatic values. Strategies apply to both global imagistic ideas and to strings of words. In the case of global imagistic ideas, they pick apart ideas bit by bit and arrange the parts into syntactic sequences. In the case of word strings, they find the syntagmatic values hidden in the strings. Thus, in the Anansi example, a strategy of attaching new nodes to the right enabled the speaker to utter the sentence in the same order as he unpacked the image. Another strategy, minimal attachment, in which new nodes are attached in the syntactic tree as high as possible, was called forth to help unpack the image property of separating the participants (the sons and Anansi). By attaching the Anansi reference as high in the syntactic tree as possible, the sons and Anansi were put into separate clauses, rather than into the same subject noun phrase (NP), thus mirroring the imagistic separation of the participants (minimal attachment is discussed in detail later in this section).

A single strategy may create only a small part of the sum total of the linguistic values of a sentence, and a number of strategies will be called on to complete the linguistic action. A given strategy alters the environment for other strategies and in the microdevelopment of a sentence there will be a series of reactions and adjustments of strategies to one another. To be useful in this kind of process, strategies should ideally be automatic and reflexlike (an insight attributed by Fodor, 1980*b,* to M. Garrett). They should, like a reflex (conditioned or innate), blindly produce effects under specific conditions. Mutual adjustments among strategies can be accomplished through changing the conditions of application, not the operations of the strategies themselves. If everything goes smoothly, the effects of the strategies invoked in creating or understanding a sentence will accumulate without conflicts into a fully structured linguistic tree. If things do not go smoothly, various disasters can occur. Some of these will be illustrated in later sections.

Traditionally, strategies have been formulated for the speech understanding problem, but strategies are equally involved in producing speech as well. Strategies in both situations have the same effects; they differ only in what triggers the strategy. Given a string of words, an understanding strategy produces part of a linguistic tree; given an image, a production strategy also produces part of a linguistic tree. The difference is that the production strategy, rather than applying to a word string, applies to a global image. Given an image and "smart" inner speech symbol for thinking about the image, the same strategies would be utilized by both listeners and speakers. Children would have to learn a single set of strategies, and, for us to paint a picture of the role of this kind of process in linguistic actions, only one collection of strategies need be formulated.

Foremost of the built-in limitations on information-processing analysis is that this theory does not explain, or even formulate as a problem, spontaneous generativity: the ability of linguistic structures to take shape in speech production without inputs that trigger them. This limitation is a product of a number of underlying assumptions of information processing. The most basic is that information-processing operations are carried out on signifiers alone, on *contentless* symbols (Fodor, 1980*a*). Given this limitation the only way to take account of "meaning" and "context" is to treat them as inputs that are needed as triggers to get the machinery moving, but that are not modeled by the information processor itself. From this follows what can be called the linear "input-output" logic of information processing. Atomism and reductionism also follow, as does a curious kind of premature closure of the theoretical problem before the question of how speech and thinking interact can be stated.

The analysis of these limitations on the information-processing approach will be taken up later. In the discussion that follows I first consider the positive role of heuristic strategies and the extent to which they might approximate syntactic reflexes.

Parsers and Heuristics

Although many parsers have been proposed, a succinct definition of one rarely seems to be given. Here is an attempt: A parser is a device that converts an input string of words into a grammatical description according to rules stored in the device. Given *the + cat + is + on + mat* or some other string of words, the parser computes syntagmatic linguistic values expressible as a tree. For example, *the* and *cat* combine syntagmatically to produce the value of a NP; *is* (a verb paradigmatically) and *on the mat* (a prepositional phrase, or PP) combine syntagmatically to make a verb phrase (VP), and so forth through many combinations. Actual devices of this kind for parsing sentences and larger texts have been instantiated on digital computers (e.g., Winograd, 1972; Marcus, 1980; Johnson-Laird, 1983; Schank, 1980), but much of the discussion of parsers by linguists and cognitive psychologists concerns parsing principles formulated in terms of purely hypothetical devices. Some references to this literature include Kimball (1973); Frazier and J. D. Fodor (1978) and J. D. Fodor and Frazier (1980), who have proposed a parser whimsically named the "Sausage Machine"; Wanner (1980), who defends from this Sausage Machine a different type of parser—the ATN, or Augmented Transition Network; and Berwick and Weinberg (1983).

Parsers could, theoretically, operate by carrying out grammatical rules in reverse. Since there is a rule that states NP→Det + N, the word string *the + cat* could be replaced by the symbol NP if this rule could be applied in reverse. However, most parsers have not been organized in such a straightforward manner. A difficulty with backward rule application is that, for a given string of words, it is quite possible that many different grammatical rules could have generated the string; thus the parser would have to apply and reject many rules that give an incorrect parse. For instance in *the cat chasing dog, the + cat* has no syntagmatic value, since *the* combines with *dog*. Thus, it has been deemed necessary to postulate for parsers heuristics that guide the parse toward more probable linguistic values. At the same time, the parser also must be able to parse strings whose structures are less probable. The term "heuristic" implies this kind of tentative, reversible, and probabilistic solution.

Some Heuristics The first major discussions of heuristic strategies were by Bever (1970), Fodor, Bever, and Garrett (1974), and Kimball (1973). More recent discussions utilizing similar ideas are by Frazier and J. D. Fodor (1978), J. D. Fodor and Frazier (1980), and J. D. Fodor (1984).

Rather than list all the strategies that have been proposed in these discussions (the proposals are somewhat overlapping), I will discuss a few heuristic strategies that clearly function to build linguistic values. Some operations that have been proposed as strategies are purely processing in character and do not contribute to value. While processing generalizations about limitations on our capacity for linguistic understanding appear to be valid, they do not refer to devices for constructing linguistic value. In this discussion I will restrict the term "strategy" to devices that actually build up pieces of linguistic trees. As an example of a purely processing generalization, it is costly in terms of difficulty to go back and reorganize a part of a sentence that has already been parsed (this was first proposed as a strategy by Kimball). This generalization applies to every type of linguistic value and is therefore not a "strategy" in the sense of a specific value-building operation of the type to be described next.

Strategy One In $NP_1 \ NP_2$ (VP), the first NP is the internal object and the second NP is the internal subject of the clause (Bever, 1970, p. 337). This strategy could function for both hearers (as presented by Bever) and speakers. For a speaker, it provides a specific complex symbol of the type shown here:

The boy the girl saw

This type of symbol unpacks images in which one part (here the boy) appears in a dual role. Such a sentence is contextually most natural in situations in which the boy is both the thematic reference point and the object of the verb *saw*. If this strategy is activated automatically whenever this contextual situation arises, the unpacking of the image would also be automatic insofar as the dual relationships of the thematic reference point are concerned. This unpacking, in turn, could create conditions that evoke other strategies, in particular strategy two.

Strategy Two In $V_1 \ V_2$, the second V is the main verb and the first V is a subordinate verb (Bever, 1970, p. 337). With this strategy, along with strategy one, the speaker could completely unpack an image if it contained just two parts with one of them the thematic reference point; for instance:

The boy the girl saw ($=V_1$) was dropping ($=V_2$) all his books

This sentence is a product of both strategies working together. Listeners to *The boy the girl saw was dropping his books* could reconstruct syntagmatic values by drawing on the same strategies and thus be in a position to recreate the speaker's undivided global image.

If the conditions are slightly altered, however, strategy two will not be evoked even though it creates the correct values. The experience for the hearer (in reality, the reader) is to be led down the "garden path," as in this example (Bever, 1970):

The horse raced past the barn fell

Here V_1 is *raced* and V_2 is *fell.* They are, respectively, the subordinate and main verbs of the sentence as strategy two specifies. The sentence contains a *reduced* relative clause from which the relative pronoun and underlying subject have been deleted. In unreduced form strategy two could apply without difficulty (e.g., *The horse that the jockey raced past the barn fell*). In its reduced form the relative clause appears to fit another pattern (noun-verb-location) and the condition for strategy two is not met. Being "garden-pathed" is one disaster that can befall the microdevelopmental process of speech understanding when it utilizes heuristic strategies.

Despite the use of the word "speech," however, in spoken sentences the risk of a garden-path trap is considerably less than in sentences in written form. Intonation contours are not well represented in written English, and this contour brackets and makes quite obvious the subordinate, relative clause value of *horse raced past the barn,* which is uttered with lowered intonation (tone) and reduced stress (loudness). In the spoken version the application of strategy two would not, therefore, be as easily blocked.

For speakers, on the other hand, something comparable to a garden-path trap may be quite common. If a speaker is trying to unpack an image in which one thing seems to topple over while it is moving in front of another thing, it is quite easy to lose track of where in the image the various segments are to come from. If strategy two tries to unpack part of the image with *the horse fell,* but strategy one has already unpacked another part of the image in which the horse-object also appears into *the horse the jockey raced,* conditions are produced in which it may be hard to see what the two roles of the horse object are. A speech blockage can result: *The horse raced past the barn . . . well uh.* This blockage is a disaster of speech production that seems to be the counterpart of a garden-path trap. Where the blockage occurs should correspond to the activation point of a new strategy (whose activation fails to take place). Such would be the case in this hypothetical example (strategy two is blocked).

Strategy Three   Attach new nodes as high up in the tree as possible. This strategy was referred to as *minimal attachment* by Frazier and J. D. Fodor (1978). It creates a specific syntagmatic value by combining V *(bought)* with PP *(for Susan)* in the following:

Joe bought the book for Susan.

This string of words corresponds to two surface sentences, each of which has its own signified meaning. One, however, is more salient given the minimal attachment strategy. The phrase *for Susan* is preferentially attached to *bought;* that is, it forms the surface sentence that means the same as "Joe bought for Susan the book." The phrase is so attached even though, grammatically, *for Susan* could have been attached to *the book,* meaning that "Joe bought the book that was meant for Susan" (examples from Frazier and J. D. Fodor, 1978). As a production strategy, minimal attachment implies that the string of words in *Joe bought the book for Susan* is salient for unpacking an image of the Joe-object obtaining a book and giving it to the Susan-object (the propositional content of "Joe bought for Susan the book"). This string of words is not salient, however, for unpacking an image of the Joe-object obtaining a book that is already presupposed as belonging the the Susan-object (the propositional content of "Joe bought the book that was meant for Susan"). Trying to unpack the latter unitary undivided meaning with this string of words should be more difficult and more subject to mistakes, because the complex symbol that segments and linearizes it is less salient.

Minimal attachment is called such because the attachment of *for Susan* directly to *bought* is simpler by one NP node, as can be seen in the following (Frazier and J.D. Fodor, 1978):

For the meaning "Joe bought for Susan a book":

Joe ($_{VP}$ bought ($_{NP_1}$ the book) ($_{PP}$ for Susan))

For the meaning "Joe bought a book that was for Susan":

Joe ($_{VP}$ bought($_{NP_2}$($_{NP_1}$ the book) ($_{PP}$ for Susan)))

Where *for Susan* is attached to *the book,* the syntagmatic structure is more complicated because there is a second NP_2 that contains the PP *for Susan* and the NP *a book.* The more salient alternative where *for Susan* is attached directly to *bought* by minimal attachment lacks this extra NP node.

Strategy Four   Make semantic and pragmatic assumptions congruent. For example, if there is a pragmatic assumption that the listener does not intend to comply with a request, it is more natural to utilize a negative verb:

Wouldn't you mind passing the salt?

If there is no particular pragmatic assumption about the listener's intentions, a positive verb is more natural:

Would you mind passing the salt?

Strategy four can be evoked in inappropriate circumstances with quite disastrous results for understanding. Misuse of the strategy in effect produces a verbal illusion. Wason and Reich (1979) discovered a remarkable example of this:

No head injury is too trivial to be ignored.

What this means, in terms of the signified content that must be constructed on the basis of the syntactic form of the signifier, is:

All head injuries should be ignored.

However, Wason and Reich found almost zero acceptance of this interpretation; presumably the reader also finds such an interpretation unacceptable. Compare this sentence to another that is syntactically identical:

No missile is too small to be banned.

This has the same signifier structure and leads us to construct the same kind of signified meaning:

All missiles should be banned.

If the meaning of *banned* seems appropriate, then, by consistency of reasoning, so should the meaning of *ignore* in the corresponding illusory sentence. But *No head injury is too trivial to be ignored* appears to unpack a quite different concept: That every head injury should be *noticed* rather than ignored. Wason and Reich showed experimentally that the pragmatic infelicity of wanting to ignore all head injuries is a factor in creating this illusion. The sentence unpacks a thought so incongruent with pragmatic assumptions that we substitute without noticing it the opposite meaning. That the meaning that is substituted is pragmatically felicitous and exerts its own attraction on us is undoubtedly also a factor.

The Reflex Ideal   The verbal illusion discovered by Wason and Reich (1979) appears to show the operation of a blind, automatic linguistic reflex. Likewise the strategies of minimal attachment and the procedures for differentiating the functions of successive NPs (strategy one) and successive Vs (strategy two) seem to run off automatically once triggered. However, the clearest example of a process that works reflexively is what Cowart (1986) has called the *pronoun bias effect*. In this process the mere occurrence of a plural pronoun sets the hearer to seek a plural verb. This reflex was demonstrated in an experimental situation where subjects heard fragments of sentences such as the following:

1. Unless the ideas amount to a definite proposal, inviting suggestions. . . .
2. Unless they amount to a definite proposal, inviting suggestions. . . .

At the end of the fragment, either the word *is* or *are* was flashed on a screen and the subject had to read it. Either the plural or singular verb can go with the immediate antecedent in both sentences (this method of tapping on-line processes was first used by Tyler, 1977). However, the speed of reading *is* was slowed after

the second fragment. The speed of reading *are* was unaffected. Evidently the plural pronoun *they* interfered with the subjects' sensitivity to the singular verb.*
Whether other heuristic strategies attain the reflex ideal so completely is open to question. Other strategies are more dependent on context. Contextual conditioning does not necessarily make the strategy any less automatic once the device is in operation, but does mean that the context of speaking must be taken into account in predicting whether the device will operate at all. Minimal attachment, for example, is easily reversed by conflicts with pragmatic congruence. Wanner (1980) presented this example in which *yesterday* attaches to *died* rather than to *said* (the higher node):

> Tom said Bill died yesterday.

The proposition located in past time by *yesterday* is "Bill died," which pragmatically is more salient than the other proposition, "Tom spoke." In other words, this sentence is not a likely unpacking of the meaning of Tom speaking at a past time point, even though it is grammatically possible with this meaning. For this latter meaning one would want to use a different structure that is more salient for it, such as *Yesterday Tom said Bill died.* Other examples show that minimal attachment is also conditioned by semantic factors. Examples of this kind were provided by Steedman (1985):

> The woman positioned the dress on the rack.

This means *on the rack* attaches to the higher node in the sentence, *positioned,* as in the pseudo-German "the woman positioned on the rack the dress."

> The woman wanted the dress on the rack.

This means *on the rack* attaches to the lower node, *the dress,* not, as in the pseudo-German "the woman wanted on the rack the dress," to the higher node. The type of action or state that is being denoted—whether positioning or wanting —thus affects where in the tree structure the phrase attaches.

These examples argue against Frazier and J. D. Fodor's (1978) more mechanical hypothesis that minimal attachment is applied whenever the hearer can jointly retain in short-term memory the higher node and the new node. People surely are able to remember jointly *said* and *died* in *Tom said Bill died yesterday,* yet minimal attachment is not preferred. Frazier and J. D. Fodor's hypothesis is

---

*In a second experiment Cowart attempted to show that the reflex could be triggered in the face of pragmatic infelicity. He presented sentences in which the plural pronoun and *is/are* could not sensibly be combined. Even so, the plural verb proved easier to read after the plural pronoun. For example, *If they eat a lot of oil, frying eggs...* was followed by *is* or *are,* and *are* was easier for subjects to read. There is, however, a problem that robs this example of its force. The deverbal noun *frying eggs* (as in *Frying eggs is a common way of cooking*) may be, in general, less salient to subjects than the modified noun *frying eggs* (as in *Frying eggs are louder than boiling eggs*). The preference for the plural verb *are* could thus reflect the greater availability of the modifier meaning and not the pull of the plural pronoun *they.*

meant to explain the nonpreference of minimal attachment in long sentences, such as:

Joe bought a book I had been trying to obtain for Susan.

In this sentence, *for Susan* attaches to a lower node, *a book,* rather than to *bought.* (The sentence means that Joe's buying the book prevented Susan from having the book, rather than that it made it possible for her to have it—the minimal attachment meaning.) Both minimal attachment and nonminimal attachment create valid syntagmatic values. Frazier and J. D. Fodor argued that the distance between *bought* and *for Susan* causes *bought* to disappear from a short-term memory "window." Thus *bought* would have to be recalled from long-term memory in order for *for Susan* to attach to it. However, Wanner's and Steedman's examples show that minimal attachment is not triggered in some short sentences when pragmatic and semantic factors would be altered. In the long Frazier and J. D. Fodor sentence, pragmatic congruence is also a factor. This example is more felicitious when minimal attachment is avoided. Such a sentence would naturallly have *a book* as its thematic reference point; this is the effect of the reduced relative clause, *I had been trying to obtain.* The relative clause promotes the NP, *a book,* by modifying it, into thematic focus; the crucial phrase, *for Susan,* cohesively links to the theme that the relative clause has created. Readers of the sentence accept this thematic context and thus do not activate minimal attachment. Under this explanation the extra length of the nonminimal attachment sentence is a noncausal factor in the attachment of *for Susan* to the lower node.

To summarize, although the pronoun bias effect (Cowart, 1986) might be immune to contextual influences, other strategies are, like minimal attachment, affected by the context. They do not perfectly attain the reflex ideal, but are conditioned by the context of speaking. In such cases it is necessary to consider not the understanding or production of isolated single sentences, but the operation of sentence–context pairs. Parsing explanations of the kind proposed by Kimball (1973), Frazier and J. D. Fodor (1978), Wanner (1980), and others assume that a sentence structure has a fixed effect on the operations of the parser. The ability of the context of speaking to alter attachment preference and other strategy uses, however, implies that the crucial unit for the sentence understanding process is not the sentence but the sentence-context *pair.*

The special context of the citation form in most linguistics and psycholinguistics publications reduces context to zero and only the sentence half of the unit remains. Reducing context to zero produces what looks like idiosyncratic behavior in Wanner's and Steedman's examples. However, taking into the picture the likely contexts of speaking (those that speakers would impute in the absence of a real context) returns these examples to the realm of the orderly and well behaved.

In the early history of psycholinguistics, experiments were conducted to determine the relative difficulty of different sentence types. Thus passive sentences were discovered to be more difficult on various measures than active sentences, negative sentences more difficult than affirmatives, and so forth (Miller, 1965;

Mehler, 1963; Savin and Perchonock, 1965). Other experiments, however, showed that these differences appeared only in some contexts and could be reversed in others (Wason, 1965; Slobin, 1966; see Fodor, Bever, and Garrett, 1974, for a review).

The early experiments took the crucial unit of processing to be the sentence alone, and ignored the sentence-context pair. This pair, however, is what is difficult or easy, and the source of difficulty is the ease with which the sentence combines with the speaker/hearer's contextualized thinking. To take one of the favorite examples of the early period, whereas the sentence structure in the following is complex:

> Jack was surprised that two plus two equals four, and this astonished Ingrid, which bothered Frank

the sentence articulates a thought process in a more or less straightforward manner; someone might actually think this way. On the other hand the following center-embedded sentence is cumbersome and ineffectual as a tool of thought and is psychologically far more complex (example from Kimball, 1973):

> That that that two plus two equals four surprised Jack astonished Ingrid bothered Frank.

This construction requires the reader/hearer to complete and interrelate three clauses entirely in memory. No clause can be completed until its verb is encountered and all the verbs are withheld until the dreadful end. The more salient (though still clumsy) alternative sentence above is more thoughtlike. The clauses are ordered so that each clause can be resolved on-line before the next clause has to be dealt with. The demands on memory capacity are therefore smaller and the ability of the sentence to structure thought in a natural way greater.

Production of Discourse by Machine

The performance of a program written by Davey (1974) and described by Davey and Longuet-Higgins (1978) is my example of an artificial speech producer (also see the description and commentary by Steedman and Johnson-Laird, 1980). The program generates well-structured discourse samples about a restricted domain —games of tic-tac-toe. It proceeds on stored knowledge of the game and various strategies for playing it, as well as total recall of all the moves made by it and its opponent in particular games. For any game it has played, the machine is capable of generating a verbal description in which connectives, referring terms, choices of clause types (coordinated, subordinated) appear in appropriate places and structure the discourse. Figure 5.3 shows each stage of a match the machine won against a human opponent (the machine played noughts).

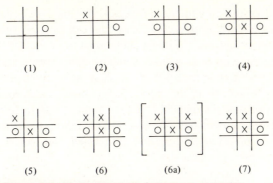

Figure 5.3 Tic-tac-toe game between a computer program (playing 0) and a human opponent. (From Davey and Longuet-Higgins, 1978, p. 126.)

The machine's description of the game is the following (numbers have been added to refer to the steps of the game):

> I started the game by taking the middle of an edge (1), and you took an end of the opposite one (2). I threatened you by taking the square opposite the one I had just taken (3), but you blocked my line and threatened me (4). However, I blocked your diagonal and threatened you (5). If you had blocked my edge, you would have forked me (6a), but you took the middle of the one opposite the corner I had just taken and adjacent to mine (6) and so I won by completing my edge (7)'' (Davey and Longuet-Higgins, 1978, p. 127).

Some of the features of this description are fixed routines of the program—*I* and *you,* for example, are simply stored in memory as codes for referring to the machine and the opponent respectively. But in general the program constructs its sentences; they are not stored in memory. The machine chooses words to describe the game—verbs (*take, block, threaten,* etc.) and nouns (*edge, line, corner,* etc.)—on the basis of the placement of noughts and crosses on the board. Pronouns like *one* that relate moves to other moves require memory of previous moves and this is available through the running record the machine keeps of every move of the game.

The machine constructs its description from this running record. From this it forms groups of moves that are tactically related. For example, the machine sees that after move 3 another of its noughts on the same line would have won the game and that the cross the opponent put there on move 4 keeps this from happening. Thus the machine groups moves 3 and 4 in the description with conjoined clauses: "I threatened you by taking the square opposite the one I had just taken (3), but you blocked my line and threatened me (4)." Different moves are described in separate clauses. This segmentation is determined by the play of the game, so the issue facing the machine is to decide when to link clauses together. Moves 3 and 4 are described in their order of occurrence and the *but* conjunction linking them codes the challenge–reply relation of the two moves.

These clauses illustrate further processes. The machine's move 3 is referred to both on a tactical level *(I threatened you)* and descriptively on the move level *(by taking the square opposite)*. The machine links these tactical and descriptive references to the same move as main and subordinate clauses, respectively. That was the method also used in the opening sentence of the description *(I started the game by taking the middle of an edge)*. On the other hand, when the order of mention is reversed and the tactical reference comes second, the two clauses are conjoined rather than embedded. The description of the opponent's move 4 shows this method *(you blocked my line and threatened me)*. Thus, depending on thematic relations, the machine can switch the order of mention in appropriate ways.

The machine picked this second order because the description of the opponent's move had been grouped with the machine's own previous move. If the opponent's move had been perceived as freestanding, the opposite tactic-first, description-second order would have been selected. This in turn would have specified an embedded rather than a conjoined clause *(you threatened me by blocking my line)*.

Tactical significance is something the machine determines by replaying the game from both sides (which it can do because all the moves are stored in memory). During this process it can discover moves that the opponent failed to make but that would have been superior from the opponent's point of view. Move 6a is an example: had the opponent played 6a instead of 6, he could have won the game in two more moves. The machine constructs a counterfactual clause to refer to move 6a: "If you had blocked my edge you would have forked me (6a), but you took the middle one of opposite the corner I had just taken and adjacent to mine (6) . . ." The counterfactual *if . . . you would have* is the machine's response to the fact discovered in replaying the game that despite its tactical superiority no move 6a appears in memory.

The program keeps a list of all the possible referents at every point in the description and from this list chooses pronoun usages. For example, the *one* of the first sentence connects to *edge,* and *one* in the second sentence connects to *square.* The principle seems to be to go back to the most recent syntactically parallel reference in the same semantic category. Although Steedman and Johnson-Laird (1980) point out that a verbatim list of potential referents is not a true model of discourse topics, the method of choosing inexplicit referring forms is similar to that used in human discourse production (Levy, 1984; also see Chapter 4, pp. 52–54). The first pronoun substitution also produces a refutation (Halliday and Hasan, 1976)—a definite description, *the opposite one,* refuting an indefinite description, *an edge.*

This program is outstanding for the impression of fluency in creates in human observers. It works by looking for the specific conditions under which to apply linguistic rules. Specific board configurations call for particular verbs and nouns. The machine relies on a record of the game in memory to choose clause types. More narrowly delimited conditions call for rules that specify the details of clauses, such as whether it should be conjoined or subordinated. Finding a legal move of higher worth of which no record exists in memory evokes the counterfactual. Pronouns (other than *you* and *I*) are chosen by a cohesiveness principle not too different from that used in natural discourse production.

Limitations of This Type of Program

Although the machine produces text that resembles human discourse, we cannot conclude directly from this fact that the steps the machine was programmed to follow are like those that a person generating the identical text would have taken. What could be different? The most fundamental change, I will argue, is that the program alters the relation between thinking and speaking: it is built on a basic cleavage between thinking and speaking. By accepting such a cleavage, the program can state a relation between thinking and speaking as a successivity of input and output. This, in turn, is a fundamental logical commitment of the program. Accordingly there can be no procedure in the logic of the machine for having mutual interactions of thinking and speaking. The clearest illustration of these assessments is the manner in which the tic-tac-toe machine produced the counterfactual clause. It reacted to a specific condition in memory:

(move of higher value not in memory)→*if . . . you would have . . .*

If there is a principled reason why an information-processing system cannot accommodate two forms of thinking simultaneously, we must ask what the price is of excluding this feature from our theory of mental activity (I leave to those committed to the issue, one way or the other, to dispute whether the machine was "thinking" at all). In the Amana excerpt and the Anansi example, the analysis tried to avoid separating thought/memory from linguistic unpacking. There was no "input" or "response," but two forms of thinking were carried on together and synthesized to make the final utterance. In the case of a counterfactual statement a similar process would be inferred. A speaker of *if . . . you would have . . .* would be regarded as unpacking with this phrase a global and synthetic image of "what might have been but was not" (Curme, 1931). (A spontaneous gesture that exhibits such an image is illustrated in Figure 7.11.)

The next section argues that the limitation to linear input-output logic is fundamental to current information-processing approaches.

The Inevitability of Input-Output Logic in the
Information-Processing Approach

The reasons for input-output logic in the information-processing (IP) approach are clear from an analysis and defense of the approach by Palmer and Kimchi (1986). Palmer and Kimchi present IP in terms of five central tenets (the last three are flow continuity, flow dynamics, and physical embodiment, none of which is directly relevant to this discussion). The first two are most crucial for our purposes.

1. *Informational description.* This means that mental events are described as informational events. Each such informational event has its own input that starts it operating; an operation that it performs on the input, and an output that it produces from this operation. The counterfactual *if . . . you would have* of the tic-tac-toe machine was the output of an informational event in this sense. The input was the discovery that memory did not contain a more highly valued move and the operation was either a look-up or a computation of the *if . . . you would have* formula.

2. *Recursive decomposition.* This means that implicitly complex events at one level of description are specified by explicit networks of simpler events at a lower level of description. For example, the absence of a move (6a) was decomposed into the simpler events mentioned—a certain situation in memory, locating this situation on a scale of value, looking up or constructing *if . . . you would have,* and then outputting the result. None of these simpler events corresponds to the counterfactual, which has been decomposed into a network of elements. The implicit complexity of the counterfactual situation has been replaced by the explicit complexity of the network (the goal of decomposition, as Palmer and Kimchi point out).

A central tenet of IP is this second step of decomposition, or reduction. It is called recursive decomposition because earlier decompositions can themselves be decomposed. However, eventually the process of decomposition must come to an end, and this necessity implies a set of primitive operations that are not decomposable by any other operation (in this IP theory). For example, the following steps constitute a search for a specified target T in a given list L (from Palmer and Kimchi):

1. Get the next element, E, from the list L.
2. Compute the similarity, S, of E to T.
3. Is S greater than C (some critical value)?
4. If S is greater than C, then the output is + , but if it is not greater than C, then go back to 1.

Searching for a target is not what any of these steps consists of individually; searching is an emergent property of the four steps working together.

Palmer and Kimchi give two noteworthy properties of decomposition. The first they call *complexity reduction;* this means that in an IP theory one tries to specify complex mental operations in terms of a concatenation of simpler processes. In other words, decomposition is the method of analysis employed in the IP theory. The second property is *emergence:* lower operations should be qualitatively different from higher operations. This is to remove from the theory all risk of a homunculus—the little man within the man of perceptual theory who looks at pictures inside the head. If this homunculus explains vision, there must be another still smaller man inside the first little man also looking at pictures, and so forth. In IP theories a homunculus problem would arise if lower mental operations were as intelligent as higher ones: some other operations would then be needed to decompose these operations, and so forth.

Together complexity reduction and emergence create the fundamental role of input-output logic in IP. The complexity of a higher level operation is reduced —that is, made explicit—on the lower level by replacing each higher-level operation with concatenations of inputs-outputs. Each decomposition is of this form. Thus input-output logic is inherent in decomposition. Figure 5.4 shows one illustrative decomposition. The boxes would be labeled with the names of the operations carried out (e.g., choose drink). The boxes on the lower level would bear the names of different less intelligent operations than the box of the higher level (each lower box, for instance, has only a single output arrow).

In-principle language machines, that is, machines conceived in terms of but not actually implemented on computers, also rely on input-output logic. Many of these have been explicit in the assumption that "meaning" and "thought" are realities outside of "language" and must be inputs to it. For example, Fromkin (1971) presents a model of speech performance in which there is a succession of steps, each of which reformulates the level about it. The output at the end of the succession is a phonetic code and the first input at the head of the succession is "meaning." Garrett (1976, 1980) has proposed a model similar in spirit that starts with an input of a "message" (see Fig. 5.5). Kempen (1977) and Levelt (1982) have proposed another model resting on the same assumption of a "message" that is input to a linguistic "formulator." These models all incorporate into their fundamental design a cleavage between thinking and speaking.

Information Processing Compared to the Theory in This Chapter

Information-processing models all *presuppose* input from the outside. This input is not explained by the model and, apart from triggering, it plays no role in the operations of the model. Information-processing models lack spontaneous

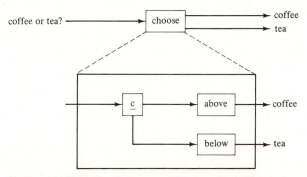

Figure 5.4 Example of decompositional analysis. The device takes the waiter's question, "coffee or tea?", and responds either "coffee" or "tea". This choice is decomposed into steps: find the value of *c*, or strength of coffee urge; if this is above a threshold value respond "coffee"; if not respond "tea". The step of finding *c* could be further decomposed.

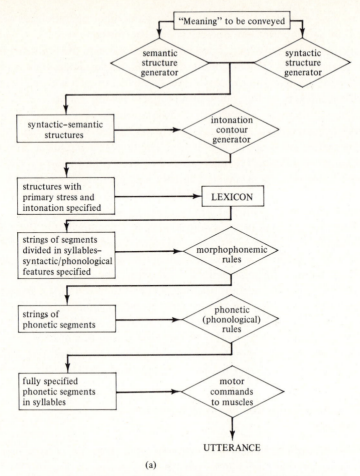

(a)

Figure 5.5 Two theoretical models of speech production that presuppose "meaning" as an input. *(a)* From Fromkin (1971, p. 50); *(b)* from Garrett (1976, p. 239).

generativity as a necessary consequence of their design. In Fromkin's and Garrett's models the ultimate input was "meaning" or "thought." The models were not models of meaning or thought and did not make use of meaning or thought in the operation of the model. Fodor's (1980*a*) concept of "methodological solipsism," Pylyshyn's (1980) concept of "cognitive impenetrability," and "modules" of every type have been invoked to exclude meaning by IP theories. Pylyshyn writes, for example: "Functions that are part of the basic fixed functional architecture of the mind . . . cannot be influenced in their operation by what might be called informational or cognitive phenomena. Such functions remain . . . *cognitively impenetrable*" (p. 127). Methodological solipsism asserts a radical separation of computational operations from interpretation: the operations featured in "computational psychology" should be limited to only uninterpreted symbols. In all these theories there is necessarily a *presupposed* ultimate input of "informational or cognitive phenomena," that is, meaning or thought.

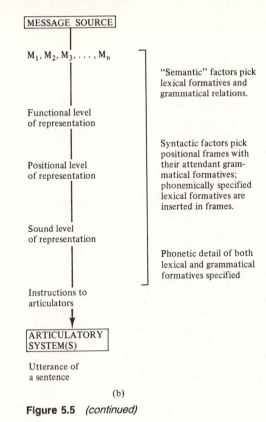

MESSAGE SOURCE	
$M_1, M_2, M_3, \ldots, M_n$	"Semantic" factors pick lexical formatives and grammatical relations.
Functional level of representation	
Positional level of representation	Syntactic factors pick positional frames with their attendant grammatical formatives; phonemically specified lexical formatives are inserted in frames.
Sound level of representation	
Instructions to articulators	Phonetic detail of both lexical and grammatical formatives specified
ARTICULATORY SYSTEM(S)	
Utterance of a sentence	

(b)

Figure 5.5 *(continued)*

If symbols are integrated with thinking, however, there cannot be this kind of separation. For practical reasons we may stop tracing back the web of thinking at some point and have what looks like a boundary, but this is not because we have to *presuppose* a thought process beyond what the theory is describing. It is only for theoretically neutral reasons, because we have run out of data or patience, that we stop the analysis.

"Smart" inner speech symbols are said to self-activate in an "appropriate environment." This underlies the phenomenon of generativity—the spontaneous emergence of sentences. A "smart" symbol is context-sensitive in two directions. It selects and classifies an environment of thinking not yet linguistically coded, and it implies a syntactic pattern into which other symbols can fit. It also takes in its environment, altering itself as it alters the environment. The appropriate environment of the symbol is not an "input" in the IP sense, and its role is not that of a trigger. Whereas an IP "input" triggers an operation but does not further participate in it, an "appropriate environment" becomes part of the mental operations carried out by the symbol. The environment is the setting in which the "smart" symbol self-activates, but in turn the environment is altered by the symbol and the symbol is altered by the environment. The stream of thinking is gathered up, bundled, selected, and codified by the symbol. Some aspects of thinking are emphasized and others suppressed; some are connected and others pulled apart. This classified environment of thinking enters into the mental operations of the "smart" symbol.

For example, in the Anansi narration the memory of Anansi's inaccessibility took the form of two nonclosing objects. In this environment the inner speech symbol *and they wanted* activated and altered to include the concrete image of two nonclosing objects. Such thinking evolved out of the preceding narrative context, which included all the dramatis personae plus the critical event that Anansi had been swallowed by the fish. The inner speech symbol in turn classified the image of two nonclosing objects and gave meaning to the absence of contact. The image of nonclosing objects and the inner speech symbol in which two things are related as one "wanting" the other thus formed the initial synthesis of two kinds of thinking. Out of this framework the syntax implied by *and they wanted* could begin to pull apart various segments of meaning. Nothing in this description can be called the "input."

The concept of an "input" is totally different from and has no place for the concept of mutual interaction between two forms of thinking. A memory gap was the input that triggered an operation in the tic-tac-toe machine that had *if . . . you would have* as output. This memory gap was a stimulus, a trigger. It played no part in the operation of the machine, was not altered by the machine, and the output of the machine was in no sense the memory gap in linear-segmented form. An "appropriate environment," however, is selected by the symbol, is carried along with the symbol, and then becomes part of its operations. An example of an appropriate environment for the counterfactual mode of thinking is an image of something that "might have been but was not" (Curme, 1931); such images are possible (an example of one appears in Figure 7.11). *If . . . you would have* selects this aspect of thought and takes it into the forefront of consciousness, and thus becomes this image in new form.

Other Forms of Information Processing

New developments of parallel processing might enable the proponents of the IP approach to conceptualize a synthesis of thinking and speaking. This would enrich both IP and our understanding of thinking/speaking. The proponents of a parallel viewpoint think in terms of dynamic interactions among components. Waltz and Pollack (1985) write, for example:

> All these phenomena indicate the need for a theory of language processing which posits, instead of the simple passing of semi-complete results between processing components, strong interactions between those components; so strong, in fact, that all decisions are interdependent. We believe that most theories of language processing advanced over the years have been seriously flawed because they have drawn on a limited set of computational ideas which cannot effectively deal with interdependent decisions, and because of peculiarities of English and the history of linguistics research which have led to the assumption of the autonomy of syntax in natural language processing" (pp. 53–54).

Whether parallel-processing models can avoid input-output logic and synthesize thinking with speaking remains to be seen, but the sentiments expressed here are certainly in accord with the arguments presented earlier in this chapter (also see McClelland and Rumelhart, 1985). At the end of this book (Chapter 8) I will again consider the topic of parallel processes and their possible relation to social context and linguistic actions.

To give an idea of what a theory that avoids input-output logic looks like, and incidentally to set up an ideal of theoretical understanding in the absence of input-output logic, I will next describe a meta-theory, "autopoiesis," that originally was designed to explain the biological concept of a living organism. (Waltz and Pollack also recognize the appropriateness of the parallel of linguistic with living systems.)

Autopoiesis: A Machine Without Inputs or Outputs

Maturana and Varela (1980) have devised an in-principle machine in which there is no decomposition and no inputs or outputs. They call this an autopoietic machine and propose that it embodies the essential characteristic of a living system: "An autopoietic machine continuously generates and specifies its own organization through its operation as a system of production of its own components, and does this in an endless turnover of components under conditions of continuous perturbations and compensation of perturbations. Therefore, an autopoietic machine is an homeostatic (or rather relations-static) system which has its own organization (defining network of relations) as the fundamental variable which it maintains constant" (Maturana and Varela, 1980, p. 79).*

Man-made machines have a dynamic organization that is profoundly different from this autopoietic organization. Rather than self-organization and self-maintenance, the tic-tac-toe machine and other IP artifacts are logically what Maturana and Varela call nonautopoietic dynamic machines. Such machines are structured in terms of concatenations of processes but do not constitute a unity, because the components of the machine are produced by outside processes that are independent of the organization of the machine. A car, for example, is a concatenation of processes, but the components of the car are manufactured elsewhere (in a factory), not within the network of processes that constitute the car itself. The parsers and production devices that have been proposed assume an outside agent for their organization and continued operation, not just because programmers and users are a practical necessity but because, in principle, these nonautopoietic dynamic machines cannot generate their own components. This limitation explains the fact that parsers and IP production machines cannot

---

*The "official" definition goes into more detail: "Autopoietic machines are homeostatic machines. Their peculiarity, however, does not lie in this but in the fundamental variable which they maintain constant. An autopoietic machine is a machine organized (defined as a unity) as a network of processes of production (transformation and destruction) of components that produces the components which: (i) through their interactions and transformations continuously regenerate and realize the network of processes (relations) that produced them; and (ii) constitute it (the machine) as a concrete unity in the space in which they (the components) exist by specifying the topological domain of its realization as such a network" (Maturana and Varela, 1980, pp. 78–79).

model their own inputs/outputs. "Thought" and "meaning" are necessarily external. They must be fed into the machine (a la Fromkin's and Garrett's speech production devices). In contrast, linguistic thinking develops and maintains its own components of structure.

In our ideal of understanding psycholinguistics, we would like to conceive of the linguistic processes underlying words, phrases, and sentences also as like biological systems (autopoietic machines). The principal biological property of symbols is that as they undergo environmental perturbations they maintain their own identity. The zone of sense referred to by Vygotsky (1962) as "meaning" is not permanently altered by the addition of imagery and context in a given linguistic act, even though these additions have a decisive effect during the act. This dialectic is an autopoietic property of "smart" symbols.

SPEECH ERRORS

Errors are failures of processes. For this reason they are valuable to linguists and psycholinguists. From the occurrence of the failure one can reason backwards to find out what is normal. More frequently than we realize, errors take place as we speak, and the abnormal reveals the normal.

The first major systematic studies of spontaneous errors of speaking were those by Meringer (Meringer and Mayer, 1895; Meringer, 1908), who collected face-to-face examples from his often exasperated colleagues in Vienna, and Freud (1908), who generally took examples from his practice and his own life. Speech errors were not studied again until recently. Thanks must go to Fromkin (1971, 1973*a*) for reviving interest in this topic. In addition to publishing original observations of her own and pointing out the linguistic significance of speech errors (1971), Fromkin assembled two volumes of contributions by herself and others on the topic of speech errors (1973*b*, 1980). The following examples are mostly taken from these works. The examples are chosen to illustrate the different types of error that have been observed.

Sound Metathesis (Spoonerism)

kinquering kongs   [conquering kings]   (Potter, 1980)

Inner Speech Sound Metathesis

lung yawyer   [young lawyer]   (personal experience
                                                    of the author)

Word Metathesis

a gas of tank   [a tank of gas]   (Fromkin, 1973*a*)

Sound Anticipation

twenty-pive percent   [twenty-five percent]   (Shatuck-Hufnagel and
                                                    Klatt, 1980)

Sound Perseveration

you can tell Ten   [you can tell Ken]   (Shattuck-Hufnagel
                                                     and Klatt, 1980)

Misplaced Syllable Stress

the noise sort of   [envélops you]   (Cutler, 1980)
énvelopes you

Excess Analysis of Meaning

why did this be done? [why was this done?]   (Fay, 1980)

Double Framing of Meaning

are those are for the   [are those for the   (Fay, 1980)
taking   taking?]

Double Trouble

Rosa always date   [Rosa always   (Fromkin, 1971)
shranks   dated shrinks]

Paradigmatic Word Blend

omnipicent   [omnipotent +   (Fromkin, 1973*a*)
                          omniscent]

Syntagmatic Haplology

muddle   [mud puddle]   (Fromkin, 1973*a*)

Other types of speech errors can be found (some of which will be mentioned below), but these are the main categories.

Theory of Speech Errors

Quite complex models have been proposed to explain various details of speech errors (e.g., Shattuck-Hufnagel, 1979). All errors, nonetheless, arise from the same basic problem facing the speaker. In speech only one dimension is available; this is the dimension of surface time. Multidimensional meanings are broken down into segments and the segments arranged in time (Saussure, 1959). In this dialectic the speaker separates unitary undivided ideas into time-parts, and this separation can go awry. Either the separation does not go far enough (meaning elements are not completely separated), or it goes too far (separate syntactic ideas compete over the separation). Errors of both types are represented in the preceding list. Despite their surface differences, speech errors are all ultimately traceable to time-parts that have become confused in time. The ultimate source of error is the tension between unitary undivided thinking and syntactic thinking that is the essence of the unpacking process. This is a tension that is always present and sometimes is not resolved. At such times speech errors can occur. Speech errors are therefore a probabilistic by-product of the process of unpacking imagistic meanings by means of linear linguistic segments. Related explanations of speech errors utilizing the idea of competition have been put forth by Bowerman (1978, in press); also see MacWhinney (1978).

The self-activation of two noncombinable inner speech symbols means the speaker is attempting to think with two cognitive tools at the same time. Here segmentation attempts to go too far. Errors of this type include what have been called transformational errors—for example, *Why did this be done?* and *Are those are for the taking?;* semantic blends, such as *omnipicent;* and the celebrated example, *Rosa always date shranks.* Transformational errors show the competition of two "smart" symbols, *why did* _____ and _____ *be done.* The crucial question is whether symbols are combinable. For example, *why did* _____ and *have to be* _____ are combinable into *why did this have to be done?,* and *they wanted* _____ and *get* _____ are combinable into *they wanted to get* _____. But in the errors recorded the symbols are not combinable and conceptual confusion was implicit in the error.

Errors that reveal an appropriately activated "smart" symbol are metatheses; for example, *a gas of tank,* as well as the *kinquering kongs* example already mentioned. Here segmentation has not gone far enough. Such errors arise from the incomplete use of a cognitive tool. In the word level metathesis, *of* implies a syntax that requires segmentation of two concepts, *tank* and *gas,* but these segments were not completely resolved into time-slots and the two words ended up reversed. The sound metathesis also could have resulted from incomplete resolution of time-slots with an appropriately activated "smart" symbol. However, since the context of the error was not recorded, we do not know what this symbol was. If the inner speech symbol implied a syntax that provided no more than one position for both *conquering* and *kings*—that is, one syntactic position that had to be mapped onto two time-slots—these words could have been forced to compete with one another for which would appear in the first time-slot of the frame.

The metathesis error of *kinquering kongs* differs in that a part of each word appears in each of the time-slots, whereas in *a gas of tank* the whole of each word appears in a different time-slot, but in the wrong time-slot in each case. An explanation for this difference will be considered later. Let us now examine the different types of speech error and see how they might have occurred.

Analysis of Examples

The first important observation is that speech errors can take place only in inner speech. The *lung yawyer* example cited above did not occur during speech production; rather it occurred when I was thinking about someone who was a "young lawyer." Inner speech said *lung yawyer*—a sound metathesis on the internal circuit. The context of the error, insofar as I can recall, included a "smart" symbol *is,* and had a single frame slot into which *young* and *lawyer* had to fit (if it had been articulated as a complete sentence, it would have been something like "she's a young lawyer"). This error is therefore similar to the overt spooner-ism, *kinquering kongs,* except that Spooner's own error had, as was characteristic of him, a whimsical tone (other examples are *you hissed all my mystery lectures, the queer old dean,* and *you tasted the whole worm*—for intended sentences readers should be able to work out for themselves).

In both the internal and external sound exchange errors, the initial sounds of two grammatically related words exchanged places, or were "metathesized." In *lung yawyer,* this was because I did not fully separate into time-slots the unitary undivided concept of the person I was thinking of and assign to each time-slot just one of her focused-upon properties. Whereas syntagmatically there were two components, I never quite gave up the initial concept of just one undivided person. Inner speech expressed this state of affairs in the form of a metathesis in which each word appeared in each time-slot. This overlap in time in fact accurately reflected the inadequate resolution I had achieved. Had I been generating external speech I would then have had a verbal plan that actually called for the metathesis. We can assume the same was true when *kinquering kongs* was produced. The unitary undivided image of conquering kings was incompletely segmented and, reflecting this, part of each word appeared in each time-slot. The speaker was then truly *thinking* in terms of "kinquering kongs," a hybrid chimeric idea, and this verbal plan was converted faithfully into speech.

Metathesis also takes place with larger bits of speech. The example given above was *a gas of tank.* I have not yet observed a comparable inner speech error, but this could merely reflect lack of opportunity if most of my inner speech symbols happen to be single words and simple phrases. Again, there was a unified undivided concept of something—a tank of gas (or an empty tank)—which had to be broken into time-slots. I will give an argument below that explains meta-theses and other types of error, such as sound anticipations and perseverations, as all being inner speech metatheses that differ in whether they are externalized through fast or slow media. Each of these types of error can be regarded as arising from the activation of appropriate "smart" inner speech symbols that incorrectly select the words engaged in the error.

Sometimes metatheses create new sound environments and speech errors change to fit the new environment. Here is an example (from Fromkin, 1973*a*):

an arrent curgument   [a current argument]

in which the initial sound segments of two words exchanged places. The exchange put the indefinite article before a vowel, whereas in the intended utterance it was before a consonant, and the form of the article changed to fit the vowel context. This phenomenon is usually taken to indicate that phonological adjustments are later occurrences in the generation of utterances than the metathesis itself (Fromkin, 1973*a*). This may well be the case, but it does not follow deductively. As would be expected from the observation that inner speech usually is devoid of number and person inflections and articles, an error of inner speech would not specify a phonetic environment. The phonological shapes of articles or inflections are thus free to adjust to the new environment that the error creates, rather than reflecting the sound adjustments that would have been appropriate in the intended environment. However, a person who thought in terms of inner speech symbols with articles and inflections attached would *also* produce the same data, but in this case the phonological adjustment would have taken place in thought before the final motor programming of the speech musculature. In other words, the mere observation of a phonological adjustment of *a* to *an* is inadequate for establishing the order of processing steps.

The example of a sound anticipation was *twenty-five percent.* The opposite kind of error is *sound perseveration; you can tell Ten* [you can tell Ken]. In both anticipations and perseverations a fragment of one word appears in two time-slots. As with a metathesis there is a unified undivided meaning corresponding to telling the person named Ken something and this meaning is incompletely separated into time-slots. But in an anticipation or perseveration only one symbol appears in both time-slots; the other symbol that would be necessary to create a metathesis has managed to preserve its identity.

Metatheses appear to be more common in the fast output media of thinking and speaking. In the slow media, writing and typing, anticipations and perseverations seem more common. If the speed of the medium is taken into account, errors of metathesis, anticipation, and perseveration can be seen to be fundamentally the same. All can be linked to the same source of error where an appropriate "smart" symbol incorrectly selects two words. For example, the same imperfect resolution in inner speech that resulted in the metathesis of *lung yawyer* can result in other kinds of error as well if the medium is slowed down. The sketch on the right in Figure 5.6 shows an incomplete linguistic segmentation combined with a rapid medium; the result is metathesis. The sketch on the left shows incomplete linguistic segmentation combined with a slow medium; the result is a perseveration.

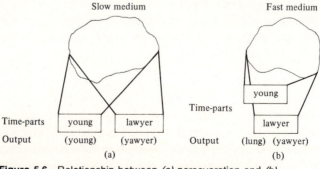

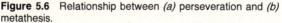

Figure 5.6   Relationship between *(a)* perseveration and *(b)* metathesis.

In these drawings time runs from left to right. The speed of the medium is relevant since, when it is fast, selection of the second word can have started while selection of the first word is still taking place. Since the segmentation is imperfect, each of the time-slots picks some part of each linguistic segment, resulting in a metathesis, *lung yawyer.* But when the speed is slow, selection of the second word is delayed and starts after the first has been selected. Since the segmentation is again imperfect, both time-slots pick up some of the initial segment. However, the first time-slot no longer can pick up anything from the second, resulting in a perseveration, *young yawyer* (in this illustration). In order to produce an anticipation—*lung lawyer*—the two time-slots both must pick up some of the second linguistic segment. This supposes that the word which is uttered second *(lawyer)* was selected first and the word uttered second was selected second *(young)*. Artificially induced errors with nonsense syllable sequences, in fact, occur particularly when a later more heavily stressed syllable is produced too early (MacKay, 1971). Stressing later words would have the effect of encouraging early selection. This is particularly likely in actual speech in that heavy stress can reflect semantic prominence in the context of speaking. Thus the same incomplete segmentation in inner speech that produces a metathesis could also produce a perseveration or anticipation error depending on the speed of the medium and the relation of speech to the context of speaking.

It probably is not the case that all metatheses take place in rapid speech and all anticipations or perseverations in slow speech or writing, but since the rate of output is rarely recorded in speech error observations, it is hard to know (Reich and Dell, 1980). Artificially induced metatheses require that subjects produce speech under considerable time pressure (Motley, 1980; Baars, 1980). To have a rough contrast between fast and slow media we can compare *slips of the tongue* (Fromkin, 1973a) to *slips of the pen* (Potter, 1980). Most slips of the pen (the slow medium) appear to be anticipations or perseverations, and certainly metatheses are very rare. In speech, on the other hand, there are perseverations, anticipations, and large numbers of metatheses. Potter lists anticipatory errors in Spooner's writing (such as *whitless,* which he changed to *whirlwind,* and finally to *whirlpool*). However, the spectacular metatheses to which Spooner involuntarily gave his name all apparently took place only while he was speaking. Inner speech is plausibly the fastest medium of all and in it, as far as my own experience goes, only metatheses occur. There are handwriting errors in which adjacent letters exchange positions, but these are not necessarily counterexamples to the fast-medium hypothesis: adjacent letters are close together in time even though the medium is slow. There are, as far as I am aware, no metatheses in writing where the letters come from different words, let alone where the words come from different parts of phrases.

If sound-level metatheses are produced by squeezing two words into one time-slot, there should be, besides exchanges of initial sounds, all sorts of other exchanges of sounds (this implication was pointed out to me by C. Miller). Fromkin (1973a) lists more than a half-dozen types of sound-level metathesis:

Initial consonants: *t*eep a *c*ape [keep a tape]

Initial consonant-vowels: *ca*ssy *pu*t [pussy cat] (like *kinquering kongs*)

Initial vowels: *o*dd ha*ck* [ad hoc]

Initial vowel after a consonant: W*i*ng's b*a*bliography [Wang's bibliography]

Medial consonant in a consonant cluster: f*r*ish gotto [fish grotto]

Medial vowel: a h*unk* of j*eep* [heap of junk]

Final consonant: ta*p* sta*b*z [tab stops]

There is, therefore, a considerable variety of sound mixtures produced—a picture consistent with words competing for the same time-slots. However, there also are important restrictions on forming these mixtures (Fromkin, 1973*a*): (1) There are no errors in which consonants and vowels exchange places. (2) The same syllabic position is exchanged (e.g., *hunk of jeep* is an exchange of the words' middle positions, *teep a cape* of words initial positions, *tap stabz* of words' final positions, etc.). (3) The stress pattern does not change—for example:

sickle and hámmer [hammer and síckle] (not síckle and hammer)

kínquering kongs [cónquering kings] (not kinquering kóngs)

Within the restriction that when words combine they exchange consonants with consonants (vowels with vowels) in corresponding syllables, without disturbing the stress pattern of the phrase, it appears that the speech sounds of two words trying to occupy the same time-slot do intermingle in almost every place where they can.

Metatheses that are structurally equivalent to *kinquering kongs* and *lung*

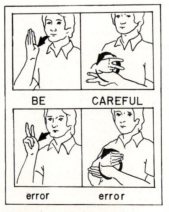

Figure 5.7 Metatheses in American Sign Language. (From Newkirk et al., 1980, p. 175.)

yawyer also occur in the manual sign language of deaf people (called ASL, a description of which can be found in Chapter 7). The phenomenon is not limited to vocal output. The drawing in Figure 5.7 illustrates an error in sign production that is equivalent to a sound-level metathesis. The hand configurations of two signs switched positions, exactly the same way the initial phonemes of *young* and *lawyer* switched positions. The speed of the ASL medium is comparable to the speed of the speech medium (Klima and Bellugi, 1979) and the same explanation of the metathesis can be invoked. A metathesis of hand configuration (or other property) indicates that two signs were competing for the same time-slots and that segmentation of the speaker's unified undivided idea was imperfect. As a result each part of each sign occurred in each time-slot.

Some errors are so fast that they occur without interacting with the correct word. This situation can initiate what is then called a "repair"—that is, an error in which the correct word occurs *after* the error has been produced. Levelt (1983) has carried out an extensive study of repairs, focusing in particular on how and where the correction is made. The circumstances under which repairs occur ought to be the same as for metatheses, perseverations, and anticipations: either an inappropriate "smart" symbol self-activates, or an appropriate "smart" symbol self-activates but makes errors in its selection of other symbols. The most common type of repair in Levelt's study (38 percent of repairs) was the "L-repair" (lexical repair). To judge from the examples cited, these often were the result of the self-activation of inappropriate "smart" symbols; the following are three examples (the subjects were speaking Dutch).

linksaf naar . . . rechtsaf herstel   naar
(left   to . . . right   correction to)
 ↑   ↑

(viz., "to the left . . . correction, to the right")

ga dan naar de Ø verkeer . . . naar de andere kant
(go then to   the Ø wrong . . . to   the other side)
              ↑   ↑

(viz., "then go to the, wrong . . . to the other side")

sla   linksaf bij knooppunt, naar knooppunt blauwz,
(turn left   at node,   to   node   blue
              ↑   ↑

(viz., "turn left at node, to the blue node")

In the context of Levelt's experiment (where the subjects were describing networks of interconnected colored dots) terms such as "left," "right," and "other" would be context-sensitive to the as yet uncoded conceptual environment. These errors are therefore possibly due to "smart" symbols self-activating inappropriately. (In this context even such normally "dumb" words as the names of the colors might be sufficiently sensitive and capable of classifying the conceptual environment to self-activate, thus becoming, for the moment, "smart.")

One way that inappropriate self-activation could occur in this experiment is through unwitting shifts of origo. Consider the following layout and repair (Levelt, p. 43):

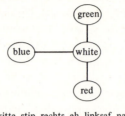

van   witte stip rechts eh linksaf naar blauwe stip
(from white dot right uh left   to   blue   dot)

Rechts ("right") could have self-activated if the speaker, without realizing it, shifted his or her origo from the white dot to the blue dot after saying *witte stip.* This would be a natural tendency, since the gaze would plausibly shift over to the blue dot after the white dot had been referred to.

In examining repairs several points need to be studied. Starting from the word (or other linguistic element) that is to be repaired, there is (1) a delay (measured in number of syllables) before there is the interruption; (2) the optional presence of an editing phrase (such as *uh, wrong, correction,* etc.); and (3) any amount (measured in number of syllables) of the original utterance before the interruption point that the speaker repeats while making the repair. Regarding number one above, Levelt found some repairs that were instantaneous:

straight through to the yel . . ., to the orange node

but many other repairs were delayed one or more syllables (as in the examples already shown). For both kinds of repair the interruption point tended weakly, but significantly, to be the end of a grammatical constituent (NP or PP). Levelt gives arguments that this is the point at which the speaker first *notices* the error. Thus, noticing the error in these cases of repair is associated with having completed a syntagmatic value, which is wrong for unpacking the relation of which the speaker is thinking. This may be a consequence of the error being fast relative to the appropriate symbol: the erroneous word has time to unpack itself into a constituent before the appropriate symbol has self-activated.

Once the error has been noticed the repair itself commences. Regarding number two above, about half of the interruptions were announced by a special editing term that signals an upcoming cohesive linkage of the repair to the element being repaired. For English speakers these are such expressions as *uh, that is, rather, I mean,* etc., whose pragmatic contexts differ (James, 1972, 1973; Du Bois, 1974), and there is a parallel array in Dutch.* The type of repair in

---

*For instance, *that is* has a cohesive function of introducing an explicit NP that specifies an earlier inexplicit referring form: *he hit Mary . . . that is . . . Bill did. Rather* links a word that replaces an earlier word which is felt to correspond to the intended message less well: *I'm trying to lease, rather, sublease an apartment.* (These examples are from Du Bois, 1974.)

Levelt's data depended on the delay variable: the shorter the delay, the more likely to say *uh*. This noise thus seems to convey that the cohesive link will be very short because the error is still going on.

The repair itself often includes some of the original utterance that leads up the substituted word or phrase (Yngve, 1973). The repair commences at a phrase boundary, some of which is repeated from the earlier utterance; for example:

right to a yellow, to a blue

which retains the PP structure of the original with the error corrected. This again suggests that the speaker was thinking in terms of unpacking his or her image of the layout with a completed syntagmatic value, in part the same value as before.

Errors of misplaced syllable-stress, such as *énvelopes you* for *envélopes you*, arise when a derivationally related word appears in the surface sentence in place of the appropriate word (Cutler, 1980). The stress shift is not random. In the example given, the noun form of the basic meaning appeared instead of the verb form. The conceptual meaning that underlies both words was segmented in an inappropriate manner. This type of error was explained by reference to cohort theory in the extension of cohort theory to the recognition of inner speech symbols. It is expected by this use of cohort theory that misplaced syllable-stress errors should be perfectly symmetrical between noun, verb, and adjective stresses. This is because the same cohort (that which contains the noun and verb forms of *envelope,* for example) would be awakened regardless of whether the N form or the V form had self-activated. The statistics from Cutler (see page 126) could in fact hardly be more symmetrical (e.g., the intended stress was that of a noun 20 times and the erroneous stress was that of a noun 18 times, and similarly for verb and adjective stresses).

The three error types that involve larger structures can also be seen to be products of an unresolved tension between global and syntactic modes of thinking. In these errors the competition is between two "smart" symbols that self-activated in an appropriate environment. One of the examples listed was *why did this be done?*, for an intended *why was this done?* (Fay, 1980). The conceptual confusion in this error is excessive analysis of meaning. The syntactic organization of the intended surface sentence states that the stative and past-tense parts of the meaning should be combined into the single time-slot *was*. In the error, however, the components of this unified concept of a past-time state were separated into two time-slots via the tenseless verb *be,* and the semantically vacuous past-tense auxiliary *did*. There exist surface sentences in which this particular separation produces a grammatical pattern—for example, *why did this have to be done?* The excessive analysis of the error example could have arisen from an inappropriate activation of this syntactic pattern.

The example of double framing of meaning, *are those are for the taking?* (rather than *are those for the taking?*), also demonstrates competition in fitting a surface form to a global meaning. There was confusion between complex symbols with different pragmatic functions: a formal interrogative, *are those_____?,* and an informal interrogative, *those are* _____? (marked intonationally). These differ in their customary social contexts and pragmatic functions.

Finally, Fromkin's (1971) example, *Rosa always date shranks,* shows that two noncombinable "smart" inner speech symbols can mutually provide an implicit syntax for one another; hence the name "double trouble" given to this error. The name also suggests the view of the error taken by theoreticians. The *Rosa* error has been a source of great puzzlement (Garrett, 1980, wishes that it had never occurred), and the ability of the theory proposed here to explain it should therefore count in the theory's favor.

What should have been a noun, *(a) shrink,* and therefore a "dumb" symbol, self-activated as a "smart" verb out of the /ænk/ paradigm. The small size of this paradigm could have been a factor in the self-activation. The information load on *shrank* is smaller than on *shrink* as a verb or on *dated,* the intended past tense verb. Thus, rather than being a dependent effect of the error (the assumption made by Garrett, Fromkin, and virtually all others), the past-tense "shift" to *shrank* could actually have been a condition for this word's self-awakening as a "smart" symbol.

It is not irrelevant to the explanation of this error that $shrink_N$ is close in meaning to $shrink_V$ as a metaphor for reducing the size of something immaterial, such as a neurosis. The metaphor apparently derives from popular beliefs about physical head shrinking. In terms of any unitary undivided image of Rosa's dating habits, *shrink* as a verb is not much more remote than *shrink* as a noun.

The decisive evidence of the proximity of the noun and verb forms of *shrink* is the presence of *s* on *shrank.* The plural noun inflection on a verb shows that both the verb and noun forms of *shrink* were active at the same time. Similarly, though there is not such persuasive inflectional evidence, *date* (in the meaning of courtship practice/ritual) also could occur both as noun and verb in the sentence. By chance *date* has the same form both as a noun and a verb.

In this error, then (to give the explanation), there were two "smart" symbols capable of self-activation, $date_V$ and $shrink_V$, that also selected each other as "dumb" nouns. Thus the two inner speech symbols competed over which one provided a frame for the other. The fact that $shrink_V$ and $shrink_N$ are equally capable metaphors for psychiatry, and that *date* happens to have the same form as a noun and a verb were both necessary mechanical components, but the real source of this remarkable utterance would have been conceptual confusion over which symbol should be the predicative element (Rosa's dating or the psychiatrist's shrinking).

Fay (1980) interpreted the excess-analysis and double-framing errors that he discovered as evidence that speakers carry out transformations during linguistic acts. *Why did this be done?* shows, within itself, the paradigmatic contrast between question syntax, *why did?* and nonquestion syntax, *this be done.* This contrast is what the transformation of subject-auxiliary inversion states (Chomsky, 1957). In Fay's interpretation the error shows that this transformation was used during speech production, but the transformation on this occasion failed to work properly. Insofar as the transformation is regarded as a formal statement of a paradigmatic contrast between complex symbols, one could argue that the error does not imply that the transformation was applied incorrectly, but rather that it was incorrect to apply it at all. It was exactly because the speaker was confused between two contrasting "smart" symbols and could not resolve the competition between them that he or she was led into the error.

Returning to metatheses, it turns out empirically that the larger the constituent that is imperfectly resolved, the larger the segment moved in the error. Garrett (1980) pointed out that word exchanges span greater distances within their sentences than do sound exchanges. The latter tend to stay within the same phrases, whereas the former tend to pass between different phrases (both types remain within their clauses). For example:

Sound Metathesis

heft lemisphere   [left hemisphere]   (Fromkin, 1973*a*)

Word Metathesis

I left a briefcase
in my cigar   [I left a cigar   (Garrett, 1976)
                      in my briefcase]

Garrett (1975, 1980) regarded this difference as evidence in support of his theory that the large-scale and the small-scale metatheses take place on different levels of processing—one syntactic and the other morphological (the "functional" and "positional" levels, respectively).

However, these large- and small-scale errors can be regarded as products of word competitions on the same level but differing in the conditions of competition. In this way multiplication of levels is avoided. When one frame slot of a "smart" symbol must be divided into two time-slots, there is a chance for this process to fail and for each of the words that the symbol selects to enter the frame slot at the same time. The two words will then have to compete for the same time-slot and conditions exist in which they might combine *(heft lemisphere)*. The rhythmic pattern of the intended phrase *left hemisphere,* which the error preserved, could have guided the syllable components of the words as they subdivided and merged. On the other hand, when a "smart" symbol has two frame slots, as in ____ in ____ or ____ of ____, there is not this risk of one time-slot for two words. Implicit in the syntax are two time-slots and a metathesis is therefore less likely to result in combining the words. Even if there is imperfect unpacking, each of the words that the symbol selects will still have a separate time-slot; in this case there is no error-generated way the words can merge *(a briefcase in my cigar)*. Thus there is the correlation that Garrett reported.

Two remaining types of error produce word distortions. In one type two paradigmatically contrasting words are selected to perform a meaning segmentation and try to squeeze into a single time-slot. This also is a case of conceptual confusion. Presumably the two words self-activated. The result is a blend, the example of which was *omnipicent* (blend of *ominpotent* and *omniscent*). Blends can readily be seen as imperfect segmentations. In a list of blends provided in Fromkin (1973*b*) virtually all are combinations of paradigmatically related words. The speaker finds the paradigmatic class that provides the desired segmentation but fails to select a unique word from it. The blend, although not a word, therefore still has some recognizable semantic connection with the context. In this respect word blends differ from erroneous word substitutions, or "malapropisms" (Fay and Cutler, 1977); for example, *white Anglo-Saxon prostitute* (for *Protestant;* example from Fromkin, 1973*a*).

In the other type of word distortion two syntagmatically contrasting words are telescoped into one word, a result known as "haplology." Haplologies arise when the speaker combines two grammatically related segments into the same time-slot. The example was the telescoping of an NP *mud puddle* into *muddle.* In a list of haplolgies in Fromkin (1973*b*), all are of the kind in which there is a telescoped syntagmatic combination. Other examples include *shrig souffle* (telescoping an NP, *shrimp and egg souffle*) and *extinguish your seat belts* (from a VP, *extinguish your cigarettes and fasten your seat belts*). Unlike paradigmatic blends, haplologies, even when by chance they make a word or phrase, are not semantically relevant to their contexts. This lack of relevance follows from the syntagmatic source of haplologies. Syntagmatic value depends on how elements are combined, and information about combinations is exactly what haplology removes. Paradigmatic blends, as long as they remain within their paradigmatic contrast field, are assured of at least general semantic relevance.

The theory of speech errors put forth in this chapter has, it seems to me, two main advantages: (1) it relates speech errors to sentence generation in a uniform and organic way, and (2) it explains all the major types of error as coming from the same processes that are inevitably a by-product of segmenting unified undivided thinking.

METAPHOR

The final major topic to be considered in this chapter is metaphor. This topic is a bridge to the following chapter on linguistic determinism, or the Whorfian hypothesis. While metaphors perform rhetorical functions, they also perform an essential role in speech production and understanding. Metaphor connects to the preceding discussion, in that metaphors produce images for abstract, or nonimageable, thinking. Metaphor can be considered under various headings, among them that metaphor is a new meaning made up out of the interaction of related components (Richards, 1936), metaphor is an ornamental substitution of a figurative term for a literal term (a traditional view), or that metaphor is comparison —a form of simile shortened by suppression of the adverb *like* (Miller, 1979)— "society is a sea, from "society is like a sea." But here the emphasis will be on the image-producing power of metaphor. This function is crucial (not ornamental) for ordinary speaking/thinking. Metaphors provide images for nonimageable abstract concepts. Thus, despite the abstractness of such concepts, syntactic thinking still synthesizes with imagistic thinking. Metaphors also help to categorize the conceptual environment of self-activating "smart" symbols. It is not necessary for the thinker/speaker to utilize a specific verbal metaphor as the inner speech symbol to generate an image of an abstract concept. This function of producing images is performed not only by specific verbal metaphors like "torpedo the argument" or "foundations of physics," but also by metaphoric schemas like ARGUMENT IS WAR or A THEORY IS A BUILDING (Lakoff and Johnson, 1980). (Following Lakoff and Johnson's practice, I will show the metaphoric schemas in capital letters; the resulting oracular style suggests a reverberant voice that is appropriate to such pronouncements.) Metaphoric schemas imply a family of related images that can adapt to circumstances and provide specific images for abstract concepts.

In the Anansi example, for instance, the image was of two nonclosing objects. This image is a projection onto the personage of Anansi and his sons of a PERSONALITIES ARE OBJECTS schema. Two nonclosing objects is a specific image belonging to this family of images. It was classified by *and they wanted* as Anansi and the sons and captured the idea of inaccessibility. Even though the speaker did not linguistically formulate a statement about two objects, but rather utilized *and they wanted* as the cognitive tool, the syntax of this tool meshes well with the image of two nonclosing objects. The basis for this "meshing" is quite deep in the linguistic system. (Chapter 6 discusses this question.)

Theories of Metaphor

Ricoeur (1978) concluded that the pictorial aspect of imagery provides a concrete scene in which to detect similarities between the two concepts that the metaphor brings together. To have an image is not merely to have a mental picture but rather it is to display logical relations in a "depicting mode." It is this "depicting mode" that meshes with the syntactic mode of thinking. An analysis of the two terms of a metaphor shows how they are able to produce images of concepts. A straightforward definition is that metaphor is *understanding one thing in terms of something else* (Lakoff and Johnson, 1980). Lakoff and Johnson give this example of a metaphoric scheme: ARGUMENT IS WAR. The concept of an argument is understood in terms of the concept of war. This schema produces various images; for example:

He outflanked his opponent.

He torpedoed my argument.

In the first example the abstract idea of an argument is presented in terms of a movement, and in the second in terms of sinking beneath a surface. The movement is not just any movement, however, but a movement categorized by the concept of warfare. The sinking in the second metaphor is not just any sinking (such as the sun sinking beneath the horizon) but a sinking that leads to destruction. The images are specific to the family of images produced by the warfare schema.

Yet these images are not exactly warfare images either. In the outflanking movement little troopers are not included, and the surface beneath which the argument sinks is not water but an unspecified kind of surface just for sinking arguments. This mutual adjustment of the abstract concept and the image produced by the metaphor has caught the attention of metaphor theorists.

Most often cited as a theory of the way metaphor functions is I. A. Richards's "interanimation theory" contained in his *Philosophy of Rhetoric* (1936). This theory in turn has been extended and renamed the "interaction theory" by Max Black (1962, 1979). According to the version originally proposed by Richards, a metaphor consists of three elements: (1) the *topic* of the metaphor, which is the concept to be presented in terms of something else; (2) the *vehicle* of the metaphor, which is the image or other idea in terms of which the topic is presented; and (3) the common *ground* of the metaphor, which is the dimension on which the topic and vehicle are deemed to be similar. There is a two-way "interanimation" between the topic and vehicle and this develops their common ground. Thus in the metaphoric schema ARGUMENT IS WAR, the topic is ARGUMENT, the vehicle is WAR (and the various images evoked by this), and the ground is the set of concepts having to do with strategy, attack, victory, defeat, and so on, that are regarded as similar between arguing and warring. The metaphor, by linking words with the verb *is* for equation, brings to life ("interanimates") the similarities in the common ground. The metaphor emphasizes the aspects of argument and war that are held in common and deemphasizes the aspects that are unique.

In Black's extension and explication of this theory the ground is described as a set of "associated implications" of the vehicle, which is now called the "secondary subject." The associated implications of the secondary subject are projected onto the "primary subject," or topic, of the metaphor. Black (1979) writes, "The maker of a metaphoric statement selects, emphasizes, suppresses, and organizes features of the primary subject by applying to it statements isomorphic with the members of the secondary subject's implicative complex" (p. 29). This process takes place both in the maker of the metaphor and the receiver of it.

The interaction that gives Black's theory its name occurs between the primary and secondary subjects. Both subjects must be altered *in parallel* by the metaphor. The following example will illustrate what this means (recorded from a lawyer speaking in a rural southern courtroom):

> They got us where they want us. They holding us up with one hand, their good sharp fishin' knife in the other, and they sayin', 'you jes set still, little catfish, we're *jes* gonna *gut* ya' (cited by Booth, 1978).

The secondary subject is the idea of a catfish and the primary subject the lawyer's client, a local company. The metaphor creates an image of the primary subject (the company) as a catfish and projects onto the company the associated implications of the catfish concept (e.g., that it is small and helpless in the hands of a much larger entity, and facing disembowelment while still alive). But to understand the metaphor it is necessary to project selectively the associated implications of a catfish. The projected implicative complex contains only the catfish properties that are parallel to those of the primary subject, the abstract concept of the lawyer's company. The catfish concept, in other words, has to be changed in parallel with the changes introduced in the company concept. The element of interaction is therefore at the center of the functioning of the metaphor.

The same would be true of metaphors in inner speech. If *gut* was the inner speech symbol the speaker would at all stages have been utilizing a suitably altered concept of gutting for thinking about the relation between the opponent and his client. For a speaker whose experience prominently included fishing imagery, *gut* could have turned on spontaneously in this environment of thinking about the client and its relation to a larger company. Once activated it could have produced an image of the primary subject as a helpless catfish in the hands of the fisherman. The inner speech verbal symbol and the image it produced would have developed together.

Metaphors project associated implications together with an image that depicts the logical relations among these implications. Through the metaphor, the speaker generates a unitary undivided image of the abstract concept with which syntactic thinking can synthesize. The image and the associated implications are both altered to fit the primary subject. Together the image and the primary and secondary subjects constitute an analogical symbol of which the image is the signifier half. A gesture can recreate this signifier with the meaning it has in the metaphor (as seen in the Anansi gesture).

In the ARGUMENT IS WAR metaphoric schema there is a family of projected meanings and images that belong to the well-established cultural concept of warfare (very little of which however is based on direct experience of most people). Specific metaphoric expressions pick out one or another of these images. The images are always altered in parallel with the changes introduced in the primary subject of WAR. *I'll torpedo your argument* adds a nautical flavor and the image of something sinking. One could also produce *I'll spear your argument* or even *I'll cutlass your argument.* In keeping with the concept of interaction each of these metaphors selects and exhibits a different image of argumentation: *torpedo* when we imagine removing the primary subject from view, *spear* when we imagine hitting a specific point, and *cutlass* when we imagine a wild slashing attack. On the other hand, the requirement of interaction limits the metaphors we can produce. We cannot so easily generate *I'll total-industrial-effort your argument* or *I'll hauberk your argument.* These are properties of the secondary subject (war) that are too remote or too obsolete in themselves to undergo parallel changes to those of the primary subject (argument). In these unsuccessful metaphors it is unclear what aspect of their associated implicative complexes should be projected onto the primary subject. These metaphors fail because they are signifiers without signifieds. In a successful metaphor such as *we'll jes gut ya,* on the other hand, along with the image of a catfish in relation to the fisherman, a rich implicative complex of properties is projected.

A given primary subject can appear in different metaphoric schemas. The different schemas provide the speaker with a choice of metaphoric analogical symbols and a flexible means of adjusting to the context of speaking. There is for argument, for example, AN ARGUMENT IS A BUILDING (Lakoff and Johnson, 1980):

> We've got the *framework* of a *solid* argument.
>
> If you don't *support* your argument well, it will *collapse.*
>
> He's trying to *buttress* his argument, but it is so *shaky* that the whole thing *falls apart* under the *weight* of criticism.
>
> With the *groundwork* you've got, you can *construct* a *strong* argument.

AN ARGUMENT IS A JOURNEY is another source of images:

> *So far* we haven't *covered much ground.*
>
> A *roundabout* argument.
>
> *At this stage* I can't see *where we are going.*

AN ARGUMENT IS A CONTAINER creates still other images:

> There are good ideas *in* the argument.
>
> A *transparent* argument.
>
> The *solid core* of the argument.
>
> *Go into* the argument *further.*

These different schemas project different images and different implications from the ARGUMENT IS WAR metaphor, and this fact provides alternative avenues for unpacking the abstract concept of an argument into speech. In thinking about *buildings* one has ready access to patterns of thinking that will unpack the image in the use of words such as *foundations, support,* and the like. The schemas are not mutually exclusive. The *go into the argument further* metaphor, for instance, projects two schemas—both a container and a journey. All these schemas, in turn, are special cases of a very general metaphoric schema in our culture in which abstract concepts are presented in terms of the schema IDEAS ARE PHYSICAL OBJECTS (buildings, containers, paths). (This general schema is discussed further in Chapter 6.)

Lakoff and Johnson believe that the secondary subject refers to immediate perceptual and actional experience. Thus buildings are things of which we have more direct perceptual and actional experience than theories, their argument goes, and we structure our understanding of theories on the basis of our understanding of buildings. In other metaphoric schemas the secondary subject also appears to be the thing of which we have more direct experience. For example, COMMUNICATION IS SENDING *(I got your message)* or IDEAS ARE FOOD *(a tough idea to swallow)* present abstract ideas in terms of more concrete experiences. Holland (1983), in a review and commentary on Lakoff and Johnson's work, points out, however, that even seemingly concrete physical experiences are culturally interpreted; that is, also "presented" to us. What we regard as a building, or as sending, or as food are good illustrations, in fact, of cultural concepts, no less than what we take to be theories or ideas. Moreover, cultural variation exists over whether a given experience is coded as "physical" (Habermas, 1970): "Physicality cannot provide an anchor, a formal grounding, for the definition of a metaphor if the same experience can be construed as 'physical' in one culture, 'nonphysical' in a second culture, and as both 'physical' and 'nonphysical' in a third" (Holland, p. 292).

This criticism seems to me valid. As Holland points out, WAR IS ARGUMENT would be a more plausible metaphor by the criterion of direct experience than Lakoff and Johnson's attested example of ARGUMENT IS WAR. Few people have had direct physical experience of war, but virtually everyone experiences arguments. Yet WAR IS ARGUMENT (while conceivably true) is a poor metaphor. In many other metaphors there is a similar asymmetry. BUILDINGS ARE THEORIES or FOOD IS IDEAS are poor metaphors (and poor jokes) and this reflects an asymmetry that depends, I will argue, on the higher image potential of the concept of a building or food. Image potential, however, does not depend on having had direct experience with the referent. All terms of a metaphor are culturally conditioned concepts, and in this regard all are "presented," but the choice of secondary subject reflects the comparative image-generating potential of the two subjects. In keeping with the "depicting mode" mentioned by Ricoeur (1978), terms with greater potential for producing an image become secondary subjects.

This asymmetry is advantageous in terms of the metaphor's role in producing speech. The metaphor provides imagery with which syntactic thinking can synthesize. To place a term with low image potential into the secondary subject would be disruptive to speech. If an experience is classified in one culture as "physical" and in a different culture as "nonphysical," I would guess this means that the concept of the experience in the two cultures has different image-producing potential and would be less likely to provide images for synthesis in the "nonphysical" culture. Although most people have merely a culturally stereotyped concept of war, it is a concept rich with images based on stories, reports, movies, and so forth. WAR IS ARGUMENT is not a successful metaphor because it does not exhibit logical relations in a *depicting* mode, but rather seems to present the logical relations of conflict in terms of a purely verbal definition.

In the metaphors listed by Lakoff and Johnson the secondary subject always has the greater image-producing potential:

ARGUMENT IS WAR

ARGUMENT IS A BUILDING

ARGUMENT IS A CONTAINER

COMMUNICATION IS SENDING

IDEAS ARE FOOD

TIME IS A MOVING OBJECT

GOOD IS UP

Metaphors are *essential* tools for thinking and speaking about abstract concepts. Without them speech and thinking beyond the concrete level would be impossible. Hadamard (1954), in his book on the psychology of mathematical invention, reproduced a statement written many years ago by Roman Jakobson that sums up the central role of these analogical symbols in human thinking, and incidentally foreshadows the distinction drawn in this book between intrinsic and pure linguistic value (which Jakobson calls "personal" and "conventional"; for "symbol" Jacobson uses the term "sign"):

> Signs are a necessary support of thought. For socialized thought (stage of communication) and for the thought which is being socialized (stage of formulation), the most usual system of signs is language properly called; but internal thought, especially when creative, willingly uses other systems of signs which are more flexible, less standardized than language and leave more liberty, more dynamism to creative thought. . . . Amongst all these signs or symbols, one must distinguish between conventional signs, borrowed from social convention and, on the other hand, personal signs which, in their turn, can be subdivided into constant signs, belonging to general habits, to the individual pattern of the person considered and into episodical signs, which are established ad hoc and only participate in a single creative act. (Quoted by Hadamard, 1945, pp. 96–97, ellipses in Hadamard's quotation.)

Experimental Studies of Metaphor

The first experiment I will describe in this section demonstrates the use of metaphoric images during reasoning. This is an important illustration of a major assertion in the preceding argument: the function of metaphor is to produce images in thinking. By projecting one family of images but not another, the metaphor can influence reasoning. Such an influence has been demonstrated experimentally by Gentner and Gentner (1983). They taught either of two metaphors to students who had very little prior understanding of electricity or electrical circuits. For one metaphor the students were told to think of circuits in terms of a hydraulic system (ELECTRICITY IS A FLOWING STREAM), and for the other to think in terms of a moving crowd (ELECTRICITY IS A TEEMING CROWD—mice, in fact). These analogies were chosen because they emphasize different aspects of electrical circuits. Via the effect on water flow of linking two reservoirs in series, one above the other, the hydraulic analogy conveys the idea that linking two batteries in series increases electrical current. Via the effects on the number of mice passing by when there are two narrow gates to get through instead of just one, the moving crowds analogy conveys the idea that having two resistors in parallel increases the current. Each analogy is also capable of presenting the other's strong concept but does not do so very compellingly (in the hydraulic analogy a resistor corresponds to a narrowness in the pipe, and in the moving crowds analogy pressure corresponds to shouting more encouragement to the mice; the image of doubling the shouting in series or of a second narrowness in parallel however is not particularly striking). It turned out that Gentner and Gentner's subjects could do better on questions about parallel resistances in electrical circuits if they had been taught to think in terms of moving crowds, and better with questions about batteries in series if they had been taught to think in terms of flowing water. According to the metaphor chosen there were selective enhancements and limitations of reasoning effectiveness.

A metaphoric schema such as ELECTRICITY IS A TEEMING CROWD or ELECTRICITY IS A FLOWING STREAM can through training be built into the word *electricity* and can provide operations by which the person reasons, but with attendant restrictions. Similarly, selective enhancements and restrictions of reasoning power can arise from other metaphoric schemas. Syntactic thinking readily unpacks these images with corresponding phrases such as *increases the number of electrons passing,* which unpacks the crowd image or *doubles the pressure,* which does so with the liquid image. Thus the metaphors restrict not only thinking but also the diachronic development of the sentences that unpack the images.

A remarkably large number of experimental studies of the psychological aspects of metaphor use has been carried out in recent years. Hoffman (1984) and Hoffman and Kemper (1985) have written comprehensive reviews. In the remainder of this discussion I will focus on the specific problem of metaphor interpretation and look at the question: When a hearer understands a metaphor, is the process one of direct comprehension of the metaphor or does the sentence first receive a nonmetaphoric interpretation?

One theory about understanding metaphors is that the hearer first tries to treat the sentence as a literal statement; that is, tries to treat the secondary subject as if it were the intended propositional content, without regard to the primary subject. If it is *we're jes gonna gut ya,* the sentence's literal interpretation fails any number of Gricean maxims in the context of speaking (a courtroom). The hearer accordingly implicates a metaphorical interpretation. Thus understanding the metaphor passes through two steps. In one version of this theory the logically separable steps are thought to be distinct and chronological (e.g., Clark and Clark, 1977; Kintsch, 1975). However, such an identification of logically distinct steps with temporal succession is not a necessary conclusion (Miller, 1979).

Miller's (1979) proposal was that the implicated interpretation reconstitutes the literal statement as an analogy: instead of "the company is a catfish," the hearer thinks (in effect) "the big company is to the little company as the fisherman with a knife is to a catfish." This proposal explicates our sense of similarity between the primary and secondary subjects of the metaphor. The interaction between these subjects is then a later step in this theory.

Logically, some role of the literal meaning of the secondary subject in metaphor understanding seems undeniable. The interaction of primary and secondary subject requires it, and the mere perception of the words and grammatical structure of a metaphor leaves room for perceiving a literally false or contextually weird statement as well (e.g., "the company is a catfish"). The real issue is whether the interaction required by the interaction theory appears during a second, subsequent step or the primary and secondary subjects are psychologically fused from the beginning of the metaphor interpretation. Either alternative is conceivable a priori. The view that the literal meaning appears and then becomes altered is one obvious possibility. Another view holds that the interaction and parallel modification of the words in the metaphor is the essence of sentence understanding in general and interaction takes place from the start. Such interaction also resolves ambiguities; *he laughed all the way to the bank, and then fell in,* for instance, involves an interaction between distinct parts of the sentence. *The foundations of physics* likewise involves an interaction—in this case between primary and secondary subjects—and this interaction is simply part of all the other interactions going on from the start during sentence understanding. The question of whether the interaction of primary and secondary subject takes place from the beginning of understanding or during a later step is thus an empirical one.

A series of experiments by Glucksberg, Gildea, and Bookin (1982) and Gildea and Glucksberg (1983) has shown that in appropriate contexts metaphors are understood so quickly that they are capable of interfering with the recognition of the literally false statements that provide the secondary subject of the metaphor. This result certainly corresponds to one's intuitions. "This little company is a catfish" appears to be recognized immediately as a metaphor in the context described earlier, whereas if it were not seen as a metaphor it would certainly be false.

The method of these experiments is the equivalent with metaphors of the Stroop color-word interference test (1935). In the original Stroop test, subjects saw words printed in different colored inks that named colors. The word *red* might be printed in blue ink, the word *blue* in brown ink, and so forth. The subject's task was to say the color of the ink but not to read the word. Nonetheless, the tendency to read the word interfered with the attempt to say the color of the ink. In the metaphor version of the Stroop experiment, the test items were sentences that could be read either as metaphors or as literal statements. As metaphors they might be regarded as true, but as literal statements they were definitely false. For example, *some jobs are jails* is literally false but might be considered metaphorically true. If the subject has to decide that it is literally false, disregarding the metaphoric meaning, would there be interference from the metaphoric meaning? This would show that the metaphoric meaning came to the subject quickly and involuntarily, even though it was a cause of interference. The result of the experiment was that it took subjects longer to say that metaphoric statements, like *some jobs are jails,* were literally false than it took to say that literally false statements that presumably are not metaphors, like *some jobs are snakes,* were false (although with a determining context one can certainly get a metaphoric interpretation here, too). The difference was about 7 percent of the subjects' average reaction time for the judgments. Thus there was evidence of the metaphoric meaning coming to the subject involuntarily. In Gildea and Glucksberg (1983) the metaphors—for example, *some marriages are iceboxes*—were ones that pretesting had demonstrated would not produce this kind of interference unless an appropriate context was first introduced. This "context" could be the word *cold* used in either its thermal or its personality-trait sense and also could be a word in the same semantic paradigmatic class but with opposite polarity—*warm,* used in its thermal or personality-trait sense (e.g., *some summers are warm*). Subjects got the context sentence *some summers are warm* and then, out of the blue, *marriages are iceboxes.* Despite the lack of any cohesion between the "context" and the test sentence, subjects' judgments that *some marriages are iceboxes* is false was slower than the same judgment of the sentence without the "context." The size of the effect was the same for each type of paradigmatic word (*warm* or *cold,* thermal or personality trait). Thus the metaphoric meaning in which a judgment of "true" was possible was immediately available after just mentioning a word from the same semantic field. The interaction of primary and secondary subjects evidently takes place immediately, in parallel with other context–sentence interactions that may at the same time be going on to get rid of ambiguities.

Idioms

Idioms are often contrasted with metaphors. However, *to kick the bucket, to spill the beans,* and other idioms are not completely arbitrary forms for "dying" or "divulging secrets." The inclusion of *bucket* in *kick the bucket* projects an implicative complex of a container onto the primary subject of "life," and the inclusion of *kick* projects a manner of dying that is casual if not jaunty (the idiom often seems to be used to distance the speaker from the idea of death).* Likewise, *spill the bean* (singular) would seem to be a less successful referring form than *spill the beans,* the implicative complex of the plural evidently having something to do with the idea of a large quantity of information being divulged.

What distinguishes idioms from metaphors is that idioms, despite their apparent internal syntactic structure, do not participate in the full range of paradigmatic contrasts of normal phrase structures, whereas sentences that contain metaphors do participate in this full range. Fraser (1970) proposed a hierarchy of idioms based on the transformations—that is, paradigmatic contrasts— they will not accept. *Kick the bucket,* for example, forms a contrast only with adjunctions such as *Churchill's kicking the bucket,* but not with other transformational oppositions (e.g., passives: *the bucket got kicked by Churchill* no longer has the idiomatic meaning). There is experimental evidence (Swinney and Cutler, 1979) that all idioms, regardless of the number of paradigmatic contrasts they enter into, are treated by subjects as single complicated words. Subjects can tell that the idiom *kick the bucket* is acceptable in a sentence faster than they can tell that the phrase *kick the ball* is acceptable—though both are indeed acceptable. Cutler (1982) has found that the number of transformations an idiom will tolerate is inversely proportional to the length of time it has existed as an idiom.

---

*This interpretation is not meant to suggest the idiom's etymology. This is quite different from the projected implicative complex—apparently it refers to hanging (see Wentworth and Flexner, 1960). Nonetheless, the implicative complex may suggest why such an unpromising expression has lasted for two centuries.

Moreover, old idioms, at an earlier stage of their history, entered into a wider variety of transformational contrasts. *To build castles in the air,* when the idiom was first used (sixteenth century), could be passivized: *many castles were built in the air,* a contrast now denied it. There is some historical process evident here, in which phrases that take on idiomatic status gradually withdraw from their paradigmatic contrasts, which makes them seem to speakers more wordlike. Thus idioms can serve the function of producing images that syntactic thinking can unpack. Since they provide their own syntax for this synthesis as well, it is easy to see why the use of idioms is so characteristic of casual speech.

Summary

To answer the question with which we started—does the process of metaphor understanding start with separate understanding of the secondary subject or literal meaning of the metaphor?—we cannot deny that the secondary subject meaning is an essential element of the metaphor itself. However, while metaphoric meaning is mediated it can also be immediate in a temporal sense—performed as a single mental step (Miller, 1979). In the highly familiar metaphoric schemas described by Lakoff and Johnson the logically separable steps of metaphor understanding may have fused into single mental steps. In fresh metaphors the logically separable steps might also be psychologically separate.

Presumably inner speech metaphors are so well established that they are understood immediately once recognized. Thinking that utilizes symbols like *foundations* and evokes metaphoric schemas creates its own corresponding images. It is thinking that is, accordingly, readily unpacked into a surface sentence. Metaphoric and idiomatic thinking should be a source of psychological *ease* during speech. Being well established, such thinking is automatic as well as transparent—unconsciously projected onto reality. It tends to conceal itself from the speaker/hearer, who might never notice that he or she is thinking and speaking metaphorically/idiomatically.

chapter 6

Linguistic Determinism: The Whorfian Hypothesis

To account for the spontaneous generativity of speech, I have proposed that inner speech symbols self-activate in appropriate conceptual environments. At the same time, inner speech symbols categorize these environments, giving additional meaning to them, and, in the process, connecting and emphasizing some aspects of the environment while suppressing and disconnecting others. In having these effects on flow of thinking, inner speech symbols seem to impose on thinking an implicit theory of reality, or world view. The speaker who said *it was a Sylvester and Tweetie cartoon* showed in his gesture that the cartoon was conceived of as a bounded object with a spatial locus. Such thinking implies a theory in which the concrete objects of the world include works of art such as cartoons. Speakers are not necessarily aware of this or other metaphors in their thinking; believing that the world of objects includes abstract ideas, speakers project the image of an object onto the idea of the cartoon, and do not notice that they are connecting two areas of reality—abstractions and physical entities. The belief that a cartoon (or other abstract idea) is a concrete object is an example of a cultural model, or world view. According to linguistic determinism, cultural models are embodied in linguistic symbols, including inner speech symbols, and utilized in the organization and interpretation of experience. Other cultures may, however, draw upon different models for inner speech symbols.

The hypothesis of linguistic determinism, commonly termed the Whorfian hypothesis (after Benjamin Lee Whorf, 1956), holds that the grammatical and categorical patterns of language embody these kinds of cultural models. Language, according to the Whorfian hypothesis, contains an implicit classification of experience, and the language system as a whole embodies a world view that speakers of the language accept and project onto reality. Speakers of different languages might therefore classify experience in different ways that can be explained by reference to the world views built into the languages they speak. The Whorfian hypothesis which states there is a force bending back onto thinking from language. This is known as linguistic determinism.

The Whorfian hypothesis is that the synchronic patterns of a language—the limited but obligatory choices it requires—constitute a distinctive thought world (Lucy, 1985). Under the influence of the alternatives laid out by the language, including many that are covert (Whorf, 1946), the members of a culture develop habitual ways of organizing their ideas, segment their experiences of the world, connect events, and in a most general sense arrive at a way of thinking about reality. How, then, can the Whorfian hypothesis be related to the concept of inner speech? A paper by Lucy and Wertsch (in press) addresses this exact question. They point out that in one sense Whorf and Vygotsky are each concerned with the phenomenon of linguistic influence of thought, but have quite different perspectives on this influence. For Whorf the framework is synchronic-contrastive, as noted above, and for Vygotsky it is dynamic-temporal. Discovering how to combine these opposite ideas in the context of Whorf and Vygotsky's common theme of linguistic determinism captures the problem of the synthesis of intrinsic and pure linguistic value in microcosm. The solution proposed below will rely on the arguments introduced earlier in this book.

Whorf is part of an intellectual tradition having roots in the structuralism of Saussure (1959) and stemming directly from Boas (1911) through Sapir (1924, 1928, 1931) and on to Whorf. Along this line there was an accumulation of shared assumptions while the hypothesis of linguistic determinism became more pointed. Lucy (1985) summarizes this history, and the exposition below of Whorf's ideas follows his insightful analysis. The essential concept of the hypothesis of linguistic determinism as it was developed by Whorf in a decade-long series of papers (gathered together and published posthumously in Whorf, 1956) is that linguistic categories are part of a "vast pattern-system" that embodies a cultural world view and guides habitual thought. If a category in a certain language combines meanings, speakers can unwittingly come to regard these meanings as intrinsic to the primary experience. The language does not make its speakers blind to obvious facts of the world but rather suggests associations that are not necessarily part of reality. The proof of this hypothesis for Whorf was the existence of other languages that do not connect the same meanings to the experience. In other words, the connection of meanings is linguistically determined, not a product of experience with the world itself.

The linguistic categories that are most powerful in guiding the habitual thought of speakers are those that are obligatory in the language and are transparent: When the speaker chooses categories that are transparent he or she thinks the associated meanings are part of reality and does not see that they are part of language. These are illusions to which everyone succumbs. For example, in English we have expressions like *the newspaper says . . . ,* in which an action is attributed to an inanimate object. This expression includes a verb choice of a type that English obliges us to make (if not *says,* we would have to use *states, writes, informs,* or some other verb that implies an animate agent). If the choice of *says* is transparent, we may be led to think—if we are not careful—that newspapers truly can make statements. In Japanese such expressions do not occur. One is not obliged in this language to use animate verbs which attribute actions to inanimate objects. In Japanese what is attributed is a state—one says the equivalent of . . . *is written in the newspaper* (which in Japanese is an active sentence with a nonpassive stative suffix). Since there is a language, viz., Japanese, in which inanimate objects are not the subjects of animate verbs, the idea that seems embodied in English—that inanimate objects like newspapers can "speak"—is not therefore *entailed* by experience with reality; the actional idea is *projected onto reality* from the pattern-system of English (this is the classic form of Whorf's argument).

To demonstrate a habitual association of ideas not connected in reality that linguistic categories have engendered, Whorf offered time nomenclature of English (1956, pp. 139–140). English pluralizes nouns that denote concrete bounded objects, such as pencils or apples. In the plurals of these words the categorization has a clear physical meaning of a group of more than one simultaneously present member of the category. English, however, also uses this same grammatical pattern to refer to intervals of time that can be experienced only successively. We say *ten hours* on the same pattern as *ten apples,* yet only apples can be experienced simultaneously as a group of ten. It is not physically possible to experience successive hours simultaneously. The very idea is a self-contradiction. The Whorfian hypothesis holds that the linguistically conveyed meaning of a group of simultaneously present members of a category is projected onto an aspect of reality that is fundamentally not a group. We do not balk at regarding ten hours as a group of hours. For example, if we think ten hours is too long for some tedious task, it is not by thinking of a particular individual hour that was the last hour that we could stand, but by thinking of the group of all the hours as a whole as too large. This way of thinking follows the associated meaning of the plural pattern, as if hours could be simultaneously present in numbers greater than one. Such a pattern is not an entailment of the experience of time; this is shown by comparison with a language where the experience of time is categorized differently. In Hopi the metaphor of time is not a collection of objects, but rather the idea of repeated appearances—like the same person coming to visit over and over. In the Hopi scheme of things there is no sense in which successive time intervals can form a group; no more than there is a sense in which two visits by the same person constitute a group of two people. In the Hopi language, furthermore, there are linguistic patterns that embody this cultural model of time. The words for "come" and "go" in Hopi refer to a process of "eventuating" (an English neologism being required to convey this idea). "Come" translates into Hopi as *pew'i,* but more accurately the Hopi word implies "eventuates to here." "Go" translates as *anggo,* which implies "eventuates from it" (examples from Whorf, 1956, p. 60). These verbs signify not motion, but manifestation. In the Hopi cultural model, a time interval "eventuates," it does not move like a physical object (the implication of the cultural model embodied in the English verbs). For time intervals, Hopi uses ordinal number terms (rather than ten hours, they say the Hopi equivalent of the eleventh hour, meaning the eleventh manifestation of "hour"), a pattern that avoids the associated meaning of a group and that, on the contrary, specifies a succession.

In English and other languages of Western (or as Whorf called it, Standard Average European or SAE) culture, the world view embodied in time nomenclature is that articulated in the Aristotelian distinction between form and substance. Time (regarded as substance) is divided into days, hours, and so forth (regarded as forms), and the forms can thus be grouped and regrouped. The form-and-substance division is part of the "vast pattern-system" embodied in other parts of the language as well. For example, such expressions as *a cup of milk* or *a moment of your time* present reality as a form containing a substance. We have also encountered form and substance in earlier contexts of this book. Metaphoric gestures in which abstract concepts such as works of art are presented as if they were bounded objects is one illustration. According to Whorf these interpretations are suggested by the obligatory grammatical choices of SAE languages that are the embodiments of this basic idea. If Whorf's interpretation of Hopi is correct, such images ought to be quite alien to the Hopi way of thinking.*

Whorf supposed that children who experience the passage of time do not have any a priori way of organizing time into either repetitions of the same interval (the Hopi way) or collections of different intervals (the SAE way). If any grouping is more "natural" it would seem to be the Hopi's. Children's experience with other parts of their language, however, can suggest a structure for time. If language suggests a conception of the world in terms of objects and form-and-substance, children will extend this conception analogically to the experience of time. In Hopi the overall structure of language suggests a conception in terms of cycles and "eventuating"—a concept of becoming and transition that the Hopi world view utilizes with a scope comparable to the SAE use of the static idea of form-and-substance (Whorf, 1956, p. 147)—and the child extends this conception. So the "vast pattern-system" of a language is a crucial link in the Whorfian hypothesis, since it provides the analogies by which speakers form new concepts of reality.

The chief problem in conceptually relating the Whorfian hypothesis to the idea of inner speech is that, in contrast to the Whorfian hypothesis, the concept of inner speech as developed by Vygotsky is fundamentally noncontrastive and temporal. The Whorfian hypothesis is phrased in terms of the synchronic axis, whereas the inner speech concept is expressed in terms of a diachronic, or temporal, axis (Lucy and Wertsch, 1985). Whereas Whorf compared different languages regarded as steady-states, Vygotsky studied developing states within a single language (for example, a child's developing knowledge of language or the development of linguistic ability as a general capacity of human beings). A further

---

*In an exhaustive study, Malotki (1983) has demonstrated for Hopi a rich (probably richer than SAE) system of time metaphors based on forms whose primary references are spatial. These discoveries provide, as Comrie (1985) puts it, a "thorough refutation" of some of Whorf's more extreme ideas about Hopi. Nonetheless, such temporal metaphors in themselves do not seem inconsistent with a world view in which time is cyclic and things in the world "eventuate."

difference is that Vygotsky regarded language as enriching thought by making it social and by permanently altering it, whereas Whorf considered language as limiting thought by guiding it in some directions and not in others. Lucy and Wertsch point out correctly that the Whorfian hypothesis and the inner speech hypothesis are not contradictory but complement one another. The problem is to see how to combine them. They conclude their paper with this statement:

> In summary, we can see that although the views of Vygotsky and Whorf are quite different, their approaches are, on the whole, more complementary than contradictory. Through an investigation that integrates the strengths of Vygotsky's diachronic, historical-developmental approach with Whorf's synchronic, comparative-interpretive approach, a more adequate understanding of the role of language in human thought can be achieved (Lucy and Wertch, in press, ms. p. 28).

The problem of how to combine the Vygotskean and Whorfian approaches is the same problem we have dealt with throughout this book: How to synthesize intrinsic with pure linguistic values. To see such a synthesis depends on taking into account the diachronics of speaking. This has been the chief conclusion of previous discussion. Whorf's and Vygotsky's views are applicable at different moments in time; time is the key to integrating them. In the microdevelopment of linguistic actions, we find enriching and limiting effects successively. At the beginning, a "smart" symbol self-activates in a imagistic environment and categorizes and takes in this environment; these effects of language on thinking are enriching: no commitment to a single linguistic pattern has yet been made. There is, rather, a new *potential* syntactic idea; the not-before categorized image gains meaning from the symbol; and the symbol gains sense from the image. At the end, when thinking is segmented and linearized and thought has acquired socially constituted value, the effect of language is limiting: All choices have been realized; some ideas have been excluded and others linked together in accord with the cultural model embodied in language; and the image has been categorized and filtered through the choices required by the linguistic system. The dynamics of the speaking process thus show how linguistic determinism channels verbal thinking.

The following quotations from Whorf (1956), along with many others, state the hypothesis that language determines thought.

> We cut up and organize the spread and flow of events as we do, largely because, through our mother tongue, we are parties to an agreement to do so, not because nature itself is segmented in exactly the same way for all to see (p. 240).

That is, the segmentations that we believe we find in the world and merely denote with language symbols, may in fact be determined by prior "agreements" built into our language. Our language is the embodiment of these agreements.

Whorf (1956) also puts forth the idea that the whole system of language-patterns is determined by culture and determines habitual thought by connecting some ideas and disconnecting others.

> And every language is a vast pattern-system, different from others, in which are culturally ordained the forms and categories by which the personality not only communicates, but also analyzes nature, notices or neglects types of relationships and phenomena, channels his reasoning, and builds the house of his consciousness (p. 252).

Thus in the example of time experience we assimilate the external reality of passing time to the pattern-system ordained by the form-and-substance dichotomy as it is embodied in the pluralization patterns of English, and other patterns such as *a cup of milk* that parallel time expressions like *a moment of your time.*

The next passage asserts that one's experiences of obvious realities are not destroyed but are subsumed under other kinds of concepts.

> The psychic experiences that we class under these headings (time, velocity, matter) are, of course, not destroyed; rather categories derived from other kinds of experiences take over the rulership of the cosmology and seem to function just as well (Whorf, 1956, p. 216).

That is, the Hopi (about whom this was written) present to themselves the universal experiences of time, velocity, and matter in terms of a different system of linguistic and associated meaning patterns and this creates their distinctive cosmology.

THE LOGIC OF THE WHORFIAN HYPOTHESIS

The Whorfian hypothesis makes three interlocking claims regarding habitual thought:

1. *Linguistic determinism:* The grammatical and lexical patterns of a language are transparent and projected onto reality, and this guides habitual beliefs and attitudes about reality.
2. *Linguistic relativity:* If one language has a certain pattern and associated meaning and a second language has a contrasting pattern and associated meaning, the projections onto reality of the people who speak these languages will be different in ways predictable from the linguistic pattern contrasts.
3. *World view:* Linguistic patterns embody a world view, or model of the world. This embodied model constitutes a distinctive thought world. It is accepted by speakers as the construction of the world. Thus the culture reaches into the habitual thought patterns of its members.

To illustrate these claims with Whorf's example of English and Hopi time nomenclature, we can say that *ten days,* like *ten stones,* is projected onto reality to suggest the existence of groups of simultaneous days as well as groups of simultaneous stones. This is claim number one (above) of linguistic determinism. Further, the plural pattern embodies the form-and-substance world view that days, stones, and so forth belong to categories of groupable objects and induces this culturally relevant belief in English speakers—claim number three of world view. Finally, Hopi speakers project a different model of reality, in particular one in which days and stones belong to different categories of objects in reality. This illustrates claim number two of relativity. These claims are the key to any test of the Whorfian hypothesis. The most dramatic predictions and convincing tests of this hypothesis involve linguistic relativity. However, the world view and determinism claims are more basic and, for the reason given in the following paragraph, the world view claim should be regarded as primary. Thus any proposed test of linguistic relativity should rest on a progression of arguments establishing $(3) \rightarrow (1) \rightarrow (2)$.

An important conclusion that follows from the world view claim is that languages can differ in form at certain points but not project different models of reality. This implication in fact follows from the Whorfian hypothesis. The same models can be embodied in different forms in two languages and, according to the Whorfian hypothesis, the effects of the different forms on thought should be the same. This argument removes a class of apparent counterexamples to the Whorfian hypothesis. Between French and English, for example, are many differences of form. These differences, however, do not necessarily lead to different habitual thought-patterns unless they also embody differences of world view. For this reason, tests of the Whorfian hypothesis should begin their test with claim number three. In addition to locating form contrasts between languages it is also necessary to demonstrate that the languages in question embody in these forms different world views. If linguistic contrasts embody different world views, and yet the habitual thought-patterns are the same (however indexed), then evidence could be said to exist against the Whorfian hypothesis.

ATTEMPTS TO TEST THE WHORFIAN HYPOTHESIS

Experimental tests of the Whorfian hypothesis have been restricted to a few cognitive areas—memory (and only recognition memory, at that), logical inference, and judgments of similarity. Until recently, there have been no attempts to study the effects of linguistic categories on reasoning and the linking and separating of elements of reality. Tests of the Whorfian hypothesis have been devised in a way that reflects the concern of experimenters to work with definable independent and dependent variables, but there is the risk in this of a narrowness that omits most of Whorf's original concepts.

A longstanding tradition has attempted to test the Whorfian hypothesis by utilizing color as the external reality and color vocabulary as the linguistic variable. The color vocabulary of a language could be projected onto reality to convey the idea that there are just those basic colors in the world and all the other distinguishable shades of color are simply variations of these two, three, four, or other number of colors. While this approach might seem to combine Whorf's crucial concepts with the interests of experimenters, in fact the field has developed in quite the reverse direction. There is now an autonomous field of color and color terminology that is disconnected from the Whorfian hypothesis, although it started out from attempts to test it; I will present this field as an autonomous area later in the chapter.

The Color Tests

The use of color words reflects both psychophysiological and cultural factors. There are constraints on the use of color terminology that arise from the nature of human color vision. There are other quite separate constraints that arise from which objects in a culture are regarded as prototypes of color categories—the physical sources of color are powerful determinants of which colors are grouped together and which are kept separate (N. B. McNeill, 1972). The Whorfian hypothesis, as it is applied to color, would add language itself as another factor affecting the use of color terms. In retrospect we must wonder at the wisdom of choosing color as the domain of experience in which to seek tests of linguistic determinism. The color domain has built-in sources of alternative color classifications, both from psychophysiological factors and from cultural factors, such as the availability of prototype color sources, that may mask any linguistic effects.

Applying the Whorfian hypothesis to the color domain, we would predict that linguistic color categories are projected by speakers onto the experience of color. Speakers should believe that physical reality contains just those colors, as their linguistic system contains just those categories of color. If two languages contain different color categories, the speakers of these languages should think that reality has different colors in it. Every language must categorize the color spectrum. Linguistic determinism implies that speakers do not regard the spectrum as a spectrum, however, but as a set of classes. This categorization might alter a person's perception or memory of color, but the primary "Whorfian effect" should be on how speakers habitually think about color as a domain of experience.

The history of Whorfian tests in the color domain reflects an approximate balance of psychophysiological and linguistic/cultural factors in this area of experience. Researchers initially found what was taken to be evidence for linguistic factors altering color memory (Brown and Lenneberg, 1954; Lantz and Stefflre, 1964). Then evidence was found for psychophysiological factors underlying color categorization (Berlin and Kay, 1969; Kay and McDaniel, 1978). Recently there has been renewed interest in linguistic factors (Lucy, 1985; Lucy and Shweder, 1979; Kay and Kempton, 1983). Opinion of researchers in the field has moved back and forth accordingly (my impression is that there is, currently, after a decade of skepticism and hostility, renewed sympathetic interest in Whorf's ideas).

The existence of two or three factors influencing the same conceptual domain is not necessarily contradictory. Color memory or perception could plausibly reflect psychophysiological processes as well as the pull of cultural prototype colors and linguistic categories. Since the Whorfian hypothesis does not refer to psychophysiology at all, and might arguably be distinguished from cultural prototypes too, these factors add confusion to any tests of the Whorfian hypothesis in the color domain. Whether psychophysiology is a stronger influence than language categorization is obviously not important at all for the correctness of the Whorfian hypothesis. A predominant psychophysiological factor, however, would make observation of linguistic-cultural factors difficult to achieve. In a nutshell that sums up the color tests of the Whorfian hypothesis: "observations difficult to achieve." If there is but weak support for linguistic determinism in the experimental literature this must be at least in part the fault of having selected, in the first place, an unpromising place to look for it.

Among the first efforts to test the Whorfian hypothesis experimentally was Brown and Lenneberg's (1954) study of color memory. Brown and Lenneberg defined a new variable that they called "codability" (later modified and renamed "communication accuracy" by Lantz and Stefflre, 1964). Codability or communication accuracy is a property projected onto things in the world—in the case of Brown and Lenneberg's experiment, a property projected onto colors—from language. No language has the infinity of color terms that would be needed to give a unique name to every discriminable shade of color. However, all languages have categories of colors. Any particular chromatic shade may be near or far from the center of its category. This distance from the center is what produces the variable of codability. A given color is codable to the extent that it is namable by the categories of the language. Colors close to the center of a category are high on codability, whereas colors far from the center are low on the variable. Thus a perfect "red" is highly codable and an "off-red" is less so. Communication accuracy differs from codability in that it measures the ability of subjects to make use of the communicative context in designating colors. It is a measure that gives a higher score to colors whose identity can empirically be conveyed more accurately to a receiver. A reddish color that has low codability because it is far away from the center of the red category could still have high communication accuracy if, for instance, it was the only red utilized in the experiment, all the other colors being blues, greens, yellows, and so forth. This concept, however, seems rather remote from Whorf's ideas in that speakers' projecting linguistic meanings onto reality is replaced with the interpersonal concept of effectiveness at getting information across to one's addressee.

The logic of codability or communication accuracy allows one form of linguistic determination to be tested within a single language. Rather than comparing languages with the same colors, Brown and Lenneberg compared colors within a single language (English) by testing whether the codability projected on a color affected how well it is remembered. They presented between one and four colors and after a short delay tested the ability of subjects to recognize the colors in a large array of colors covering all areas of the spectrum. The following table from Brown and Lenneberg (1954, p. 461) shows the correlation coefficients between codability and recognition accuracy for four conditions (with discriminability of the colors statistically held constant).

Condition	Codability $\times$ Recognition
1 color, immediate	.248
4 colors, immediate	.426
4 colors, delayed 30 sec	.438
4 colors, delayed 3 min	.523

For four colors, regardless of delay, there was a significant positive correlation between the codability value of the color and the recognition score (only the correlation of .248 was not significant). Brown and Lenneberg took this result to be evidence of the influence of language (the codability value it confers) on an aspect of visual cognition. A possible mechanism they proposed for this would be if subjects named the original colors and later decoded the names to find the colors. If the color was highly codable this process would lead to a correct choice more reliably than if the color was not highly codable. It is important to note that Brown and Lenneberg had no direct evidence of such naming. This explication, moreover, does not clarify how the *appearance* of highly codable colors could be affected by their projected category membership.

The effects of psychophysiological determination on the formation of color categories appeared from a cross-cultural investigation by Heider (1972). Her experiment paralleled Brown and Lenneberg's but used for subjects the Dani, a New Guinea tribe whose color lexicon is indeed limited. The Dani have only two basic color words: a word for light colors and another word for dark colors. Visiting New Guinea, Heider tested the ability of Dani speakers to remember colors that in English belong to different categories but to which the Dani language gives the same color name; for example, colors that in English are called brown, orange, and red might, in Dani, be called the same. Heider found that some colors referred to by the same Dani name are more easily remembered than others. Remarkably, the most easily remembered colors were the same focal colors that Brown and Lenneberg had found English-speaking North American subjects most able to remember. While the Dani subjects recognized fewer colors than Brown and Lenneberg's subjects, they showed the same relative peak of accuracy on focal colors. Further, Heider was able to teach her Dani subjects new artificial color words more easily when these words referred to the best examples of the English color categories. When the colors were focal *in English* the Dani made on average 7.3 errors before learning the new words, compared to 9.9 errors when the colors were "internominal" (halfway between two color categories of English). (The new color terms were Dani kin-terms not previously associated with color.)

Far from linguistic relativity, this experiment shows linguistic universality. Rather than projecting their own two categories onto the world of color, the Dani projected, somehow, the categories of the English color lexicon, a lexicon of which they knew nothing. These results at first glance seem to border on the miraculous, but in fact suggest that the factor underlying placement of the English color categories is psychophysiological. Such a factor exists with the Dani even though their color lexicon is much simpler. This psychophysiological factor could also have played a major part in producing Brown and Lenneberg's correlation between codability and color memory. If psychophysiological factors cause some colors to be more perceptually salient, the colors might, for this reason, be the best examples of their categories—that is, have the highest codability—and for the same reason also be the easiest colors to recognize. Thus there would be a correlation between codability and recognition accuracy that arises because these variables are correlated with the third factor of saliency.

The conclusion reached by Lucy and Shweder (1979), however, who again conducted a color recognition experiment in the monolingual style of Brown and Lenneberg, is that psychophysiological saliency is not the entire story. With discriminability equated, communication accuracy was a predictor of recognition accuracy and this was so whether the color was salient or not (correlation of .58; also not a strong relation: about 33 percent of the variance). If memory is conceived of as communicating with oneself over time, this correlation implies a role of cultural factors in color memory that exists in addition to the psychophysiological factor of color saliency.

Again, however, the experiment leaves unclarified the question of whether colors that have the same category projected onto them appear more similar than colors that have different categories projected onto them. Fundamentally, the memory experiment appears to be inappropriate for answering this question; some perceptual index is required instead.

The only study I have seen in which perceptual similarity has been tested is by Kay and Kempton (1983) and the result is unclear. They compared the judged similarity of blues and greens for two samples of subjects, English speakers and Tarahumara speakers. The latter is a language of northern Mexico that does not have separate linguistic categories for blues and greens, using *siyoname* for this range of hues. An identical set of blue and green colors were judged as less similar by English speakers than by Tarahumara speakers. Moreover, it would appear to have been the judgments by English speakers that were altered by linguistic categorization: Tarahumara similarity judgments correlated more closely than English judgments with the number of jnds (the jnd is the number of just-noticeable-differences between two colors as determined by careful psychophysical methods) between shades of colors that in Tarahumara are called by the same name but in English are called by different names.

Kay and Kempton argue, however, that this effect does not imply that colors belonging to the different linguistic categories of English had altered perceptual appearances. If distinct color *names* were utilized by English-speaking subjects to make the decision of which colors were most similar this "naming strategy" could produce the English language judgments as recorded. Kay and

Kempton were able to get English-speaking subjects to judge color similarities in direct proportion to jnd differences in a second experiment where subjects were discouraged from utilizing a naming strategy. Colors were judged in successive pairs; in the successive pairs, one color appeared twice and the subjects knew this. This common color was greener than the other color in one of the pairs and was bluer than the other color in the second pair. The subjects had to say which difference involving the common color was larger: greenness or blueness. In this experiment naming the common color would not be a differentiating factor and judgments of similarity followed jnd distance.

However, this experiment depended on the subject's *memory* for color, whereas the first experiment was perceptual. If memory for color depends on remembering names, the effects of linguistic categorization could have been reduced in the second experiment even though in the first experiment there might have been an effect of categorization on perceptual similarity. The situation therefore remains murky.

The investigation of linguistic factors in color perception or memory would be much easier if strongly contrasting language codes for color are found and exploited. In Ainu, for example, the language of the indigenous people of the Japanese islands, there is one word that refers to *both* red and green objects, and another word that refers to *both* yellow and blue objects (N. B. McNeill, 1972). *Siwnin,* for example, combines with object words to refer to both blue and yellow things:

siwninus	blue mildew
siwninrit	blue lines (veins)
siwninsame	blue shark
siwninonkerax	yellow phlegm
siwninmarewrew	yellow butterfly
siwninarake	jaundice

Other languages also have basic color words that refer to complementary colors. In Daza (a language of eastern Nigeria) *zedo* means blue and *zede* means yellow, and for some informants *zede* means both bright yellow and violet. Utilizing this type of color terminology, which contrasts strongly to English and other Western-culture languages, one could ask whether complementary colors are perceptually or mnemonically more similar for Ainu or Daza speakers than for speakers of languages such as English in which complementary colors are kept in separate linguistic categories. Perhaps the very sense of complementarity of color itself is a projection of a linguistic contrast onto colors. (The existence of color words that refer to complementary colors was declared "impossible" by Bickerton, 1980.)

The languages that have been studied in the color domain contrast in terms of their color lexicons, but the color lexicon is a rather narrow basis for drawing conclusions about the effects of world view on habitual thought. While it is true that the world view of the Dani with respect to colors is that there are only two colors, and of the Ainu that blue and yellow are the same color, this kind of cultural classification is not a compelling illustration of a "vast pattern-system" built into language. Other languages have hooked the domain of color to wider cultural concerns, and these languages would appear to be more appropriate for looking for effects of world view in the color domain. In Navaho, for example, color words are structured as elements of ceremonies for the diagnosis and cure of diseases (Kluckhohn and Leighton, 1946), and in Hanunoo, a language of the Philipines, color words are organized in terms of contrasts of dryness and wetness (Conklin, 1955). In these cultures there may be a "vast pattern-system" of which the color lexicon is a part. Categories of disease or wetness-dryness that are built into the color vocabulary may, because of transparency, be projected onto the reality of color, and alter the cognitive experience of this domain. At the same time, the categories of color in these languages may be projected onto the reality of disease or wetness-dryness, and alter the cognitive experience of these domains.

The Psychophysiological Factor

There is a sizable body of research relating to the influence of psychophysiological factors on color terminology. This research has developed as an offshoot of the color tests of the Whorfian hypothesis and is of interest in its own right, but has relatively little to do with the Whorfian hypothesis directly. This section of the chapter interrupts the discussion of linguistic determinism to consider this topic.

Shortly before Heider carried out her experiments with the Dani, Berlin and Kay (1969) published their now famous cross-linguistic study of color terminology. They, like Heider, found evidence of universality in the color domain. For example, English with 11 basic color words and Ibibio (a language of Nigeria) with 4 basic color words, have the same focal colors wherever their respective color words overlap.* The best example of the English red color category is approximately the same color as the best example of the Ibibio red category *(ndaidat),* and likewise for white, black, and green—these being the four overlapping color categories of these two languages. This type of convergence between languages held for 20 languages from various parts of the world for which Berlin and Kay could obtain direct native speaker judgments. This much suggests some influence over the central colors of color categories that operates the same way in all languages.

The next finding suggests a common line of historical development that all languages follow as they build up more complex color lexicons. Berlin and Kay argued that languages add color categories in an orderly sequence, retaining the best-example colors of languages with a smaller number of categories, and agreeing with the best-example colors of other languages that have the same number

---

*The basic color words of English are considered to be black, white, red, green, yellow, blue, brown, purple, pink, orange, and grey. In Berlin and Kay's usage a "basic color word" (1) applies to objects in general, (2) is not composed morphologically out of parts, (3) is not included in any other color word, and (4) refers to a color that is perceptually salient. The English basic color words meet these conditions.

of basic color categories. As a result, the best-example colors of a language are predictable from the number of color categories in the language. Languages with two basic color categories have black and white as best examples; languages with three basic color categories have black, white, and red; languages with four basic color categories have black, white, red, and green or yellow, and so forth. There is a sequence in which later stages contain earlier stages (from Berlin and Kay):

I	II	III	IV	V	VI	VII
black ⎤ ⎥ → red →		green ⎯→ yellow ⎤ ⎥		→ blue → brown →		⎡ purple pink
white ⎦		yellow ⎯→ green ⎦				orange grey ⎦

(This sequence is based on secondary sources and is derived from many more languages than the 20 for which Berlin and Kay had direct native speaker judgments.) The two tracks through stages III and IV represent alternative sequences: stage III languages have green or yellow and stage IV languages have both green and yellow. The implication is that stage IV languages added the reciprocal color in passing out of stage III.

Heider's (1972) results with Dani (a stage I language) suggest that all the best examples of the Berlin-Kay sequence through stage VII were accessible to Dani speakers, although the language itself had introduced only the first pair of contrasting categories. Her subjects remembered best examples of red, green, yellow, etc., and when they learned new color words they could learn these more easily if the words referred to the best-example colors from the sequence. Thus Heider's results imply a basis for the Berlin–Kay sequence that appears independently of cultural experience with color classification.

Kay and McDaniel (1978) have devised a theory that accounts for universal best-example colors. Their theory is formulated in terms of the opponent-process theory of color vision (Hurvich and Jameson, 1955). Four of the focal colors—red, yellow, blue, and green—are located at wavelengths of light where one of the two opponent-process channels is inactive because it is crossing the zero-level from one state to the other. In the opponent-process theory there are two separate color channels, one for yellow-blue and one for red-green. Each of the color responses is the result of a distinct state of its channel. If one state is designated + and the other −, a given channel can be in just one state, + or −, at a time. The specific state depends on the wavelength of the light stimulating the eyes. At most wavelengths both channels are in one state or the other (+ or −) and the resulting color experience is a mixture of the outputs of both channels. At four unique points along the spectrum, however, one of the channels is at the zero-level, switching from one state to the opposite state, whereas the other channel is completely in its + or − state. At these points the ratio of activity between the channels is maximal and the focal colors are predicted to appear at these maximum ratios. The locus of focal blue should be where the red-green channel is crossing from one state to the other while the yellow-blue channel is in the blue state. The absolute level of the blue response is not important and may be less than at other wavelengths. Because there is no red or green this wavelength will still provide the purest sensation of blue. There are unique zero-crossings that would produce in this way pure blue, yellow, red, and green.

The basic color words of any language should gravitate to these pure colors. The reasoning is the same as in explaining other psychological categories that are centered around prototypical examples (Rosch, 1973; Rosch et al., 1976). When Heider (later Rosch) was able to get the Dani to learn new words denoting colors these were presumably colors at or close to the optimal colors predicted by the Kay–McDaniel theory.

The Berlin–Kay sequence is not without its critics. What has particularly drawn fire is their idea that color vocabularies develop through an evolutionary sequence (Selby, 1970; Durbin, 1972). Many researchers object to the logic of reconstructing the historical sequence of any one language from synchronic comparisons of many languages. This criticism of the Berlin-Kay sequence seems valid. It is, however, a criticism that is easy to overstate. The logical problem with reconstruction means that we cannot know, from the Berlin-Kay sequence itself, whether or not there was an evolutionary sequence. However, it also does not prove that such a sequence did not exist. The question is not settled in either direction, but should remain open.

Durbin put forth an additional criticism. He observed that the stages of the Berlin-Kay sequence are concentrated in a few geographical regions of the world. The stages could therefore be due to cultural diffusion. For example, 7 out of 9 stage I languages are in New Guinea; 17 out of 21 stage II languages are in Africa south of the Sahara; 6 out of 9 stage III languages with yellow are in the Pacific other than New Guinea; 13 out of 18 stage IV languages are in the Americas; and 5 out of 8 stage V languages are in Africa; only stages VI and VII appear throughout the world. While this geographical concentration suggests cultural diffusion, cultural diffusion and an evolutionary sequence are not mutually exclusive. The locus of an evolutionary stage can be an entire cultural area, not an individual language. Moreover, cultural diffusion cannot explain the fundamental fact of the Berlin-Kay sequence that when a language has $n + 1$ basic color categories the best examples of these categories are the same best examples that appear in some other language with just n basic color words. These languages can be on opposite sides of the world, as happens for the stage III languages of the Pacific that include the best examples of the stage II languages of Africa, the stage IV languages of the Americas that include the best examples of languages in Africa and the Pacific, and so on. Berlin and Kay's synchronic evidence remains consistent with an evolutionary sequence despite the likelihood that there has been cultural diffusion of color terms.

A different kind of limitation on the Kay–McDaniel hypothesis arises from cultural prototypes of color. Historically, color terms are initially taken from the words for objects that are sources of the color in the culture (N. B. McNeill, 1972). In ancient Japan, for example, the word for red, *akane*, was the name of the root used to make red dye. How to make this dye is still known (Uemura, 1943) and the color is far from the pure zero-crossing red predicted by the Kay and

McDaniel hypothesis (it is orangish). Similarly, the word for blue, *hanada,* was the name of the plant that produced blue dye and the color was again far from an optimal zero-crossing blue (it is turquoise). The ancient Japanese color lexicon was centered on these colors (the words for which would have been classified as "basic" by the four Berlin–Kay criteria). Here was a lexicon that was not centered at the psychophysiologically optimal ratios, and this was no accident. The uses and sources of color terms and their history in a culture are factors that can overshadow psychophysiological functioning in establishing prototype colors. Only in cultures like our own, where the original object denotations of basic color words have been forgotten (*orange* alone is still an object word), would we expect prototype colors to approximate psychophysiologically optimal colors. (For the history of color terminology in a wide range of languages, see N. B. McNeill, 1972.)

The Problem of Differentiation

The Kay–McDaniel hypothesis (1978) explains the locus of focal colors (in a language like English) but does not explain the sequence of color categories discovered by Berlin and Kay (1969). A zero-crossing is a zero-crossing. Why should green and yellow, for example, be established as categories after red and before blue? Some property of color other than the responsiveness of the color vision system to various wavelengths evidently is responsible for this and other sequences.

This section of the chapter presents a new hypothesis for the Berlin-Kay sequence. For reasons that will be clear, I will refer to the hypothesis after Goethe. The proposal is that the sequence of color categories corresponds to how the colors of objects change when the intensity of light falling on them changes. This is a universal human experience that could influence all cultures in a uniform way regardless of whether they have linguistically distinguished the categories implied by the focal colors. Thus all cultures could follow a common path as color categories are differentiated.

Goethe's (1840) approach to color emphasized its phenomenological aspects: how colors appear to observers, and the laws of change of their appearance. While this theory is completely incorrect in terms of the physics of color (for example, white to Goethe was the source, not the result, of all color) it accurately describes color appearance and is still in use by painters and others for whom color appearance is crucial. Any object will appear white if the light is bright enough, regardless of its "true" color. If the light is very slightly darkened the object appears yellow. A milk-white object turns yellow as the light falling on it dims. Simultaneously on its shadowed side the same object looks blue or bluish-green. Between yellow and blue is what Goethe called a "chasm of nature." The change from white to yellow takes place on the yellow or light side of the chasm while on the blue or dark side there is a change from blue-green to blue and finally to black. As the amount of light falling on objects changes, the colors on the two sides of the chasm turn into other colors in orderly sequences. The changes take place separately on the blue and yellow sides. The same white object passes through the white-yellow series as the light falling on it dims, whereas on the dark side the object is blue turning into black. Green is on the dark side of the chasm and is connected to blue by lightening it.

Red is unique in that it can appear in either sequence: it is the point at which the two sides meet. Red is the darkest member of the light sequence and the lightest member of the dark sequence. This special status of red appears in various guises. The word for red in many languages derives from the word for blood, and thus has special significance as a cultural and personal symbol, and the words for various red colors are the first color words children learn (Miller and Johnson-Laird, 1976; Barlett, 1978).

Turning now to language, within a semantic field terms are introduced to mark new contrasts. If a culture wants to add a new color term it must determine what colors contrast with the colors that it has already categorized. In the case of stage I the rule is simple: light colors versus dark colors. One way of selecting further contrasting colors would be to separate the complementary colors—red versus green and yellow versus blue. This procedure would apply to some of the Berlin-Kay sequence but not to all of it. One place it could not apply is stage III with yellow. Yellow is not the complementary of any of the already existing categories (black, white, or red).

Another way to select contrasts is to use the opposition of dark versus light. This opposition is on a different axis from that of chroma and applies to every color. In fact, combining the light-dark and the complementary color contrasts in the appropriate way produces the Berlin-Kay sequence through stage V.

The central place of white in the experience of color suggests that white or a word for "light" is the place where the differentiation of linguistic categories starts. This implies a stage zero in which there is only a word for light or for the experience of sight itself. The first division would be the bifurcation implicit in the experience of light between light and the absence of light. This introduces the "chasm of nature" between light and dark colors into the color lexicon from the start. Because of their close connection yellow would appear with white; all other colors would be dark. Red might appear on either the light side or the dark side and which side it appears on has consequences for later parts of the sequence. In either position, red would be the starting point of color differentiation. If it is on the dark side it would be the lightest of the dark colors; if on the light side it would be the darkest of the light colors. In both positions it would be the most contrastive color, and the first color to be set up as a separate category. (See Figure 6.1.)

If the process of darkening is repeated on the dark side—that is, if the lightest of the remaining dark colors is removed and set up as a new category—there would be a new set of remaining colors that is still darker. If on the light side there is the equivalent process but in the reverse direction—lightening the category by removing the darkest of the colors—there will be two series generated, each of which contrasts light and dark. What is light and dark, however, constantly changes in this series. (Figure 6.1 assumes that red is placed with the dark colors. An equivalent diagram could be made with red on the light side.)

Since yellow is on the light side of the primeval light-dark division and green is on the dark side, yellow and green differentiate independently. This produces

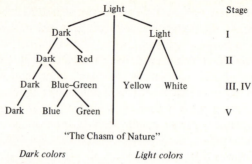

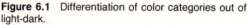

Figure 6.1 Differentiation of color categories out of light-dark.

the two tracks through stages III and IV, depending on whether blue-green on the dark side or white-yellow on the light side splits first. A single blue-green category appears in some of Berlin and Kay's stage III languages.

The red-green complementarity would play a role in selecting the upper track at stage III. Red is the lightest of the dark colors and would be separated at stage II while green is still among the dark colors. Red could therefore select green as the next contrast to initiate stage III (upper track).

If red is initially classified with the light colors, it is the darkest of the light colors and again would be separated at stage II. However, in this case red cannot select green, since red and green are now on opposite sides of the "chasm of nature." After removal of red from the light colors at stage II, yellow is the darkest of the light colors and can next separate from white among the light colors; this gives the lower track of stage III. The choice of the two tracks through stages III and IV therefore can be traced back to the initial classification of red as a dark or light color.

The yellow-blue complementarity, unlike red-green, cannot play a role until stage V. This can be seen by working out the effects of yellow when it appears. On the bottom track of stage III yellow cannot select blue because blue and green are still unseparated. On this track green separates from blue only at stage IV. At that point yellow can select blue, and this produces stage V. On the upper track green is separated from blue by stage III, but yellow is not separated from white until stage IV. Thus again yellow cannot select blue until stage V. Regardless of the track followed, blue always appears as a distinct category at stage V.

In this way the Goethean hypothesis explains the Berlin-Kay sequence through stage V. It is the result of the successive marking of the light-dark contrast as this appears to observers under varying conditions of illumination, supplemented with the red-green and yellow-blue complementary contrasts.

There is apparently no direct way to test this hypothesis in its natural area of application, since the historical changes to which it applies are lost in the mists of history, particularly the unwritten histories of languages long since lost. Conceivably the color terms, if any, of pidgin languages would trace out, as they are converted into real languages through "creolization" (Bickerton, 1981), a sequence of steps that could be compared to those predicted by the Goethean hypothesis.* However, I can find no appropriate reports to verify this.

Children's learning of color terms might be another avenue to test the Goethean hypothesis, although it is not proposed as anything other than a hypothesis about the cultural evolution of color. In order to extend it to children's language learning one would have to assume that the dominant color experience to which children attend is *change* of appearance of color as light changes. On the development of color names in English there are good data (Bartlett, 1978) but children are not cooperative.

The first six color words learned by children (English-speaking) are variants of red. In terms of the diagram above, these are subdivisions of one node: pink, orange, purple, and brown (in order of the frequency with which these terms were among the first six learned; reported on p. 95 of Bartlett's paper of 1978). That is, the first six terms are exactly those to which the Goethean hypothesis does not apply at all. Moreover, when children form color categories that are not those of the adult language, they rarely utilize light-dark as the basis of differentiation. Bartlett discovered that children often combined desaturated colors into the same category. For example, for children, white-grey-black might be one category and all be called by the same name. Children also tended to group into the same categories colors that are adjacent in the spectrum. For example, pink with purple, red with orange, and (very telling) *yellow with green.* On the other hand, except for grouping two dark colors together (black and brown) there was no appreciable tendency to form categories out of light or dark colors. Bartlett (1978), writing about the original Berlin-Kay sequence, concluded:

> Our results conflict with ethnographic studies . . . [when] we consider that, historically, the first colour terms to enter a language are those which refer to the dimension of brightness . . . then we would have expected our children readily to conceive of grouping colours along the dimension of brightness. That they did not do so is surprising and suggests, once again, that we cannot assume any simple relation between historical and developmental processes (p. 103).

Children may be insensitive to the changing appearance of objects, and thus do not really take in the light-dark opposition. For the things children do pay attention to, saturation and hue may be the most evident color properties.

The Counterfactual Tests

A new line of research on the Whorfian hypothesis has been opened up by A. Bloom (1981). Unlike the color tests, Bloom tested the effect of a linguistic

---

*"Creolization" is a term originally used to refer to the linguistic amalgamation of unrelated languages with French, but is now used to refer to the historical situation in which any two unrelated languages come into contact and a new language emerges; the word is no longer limited to situations in which one of the source languages is a Romance language; see Bickerton (1981).

form that is comfortably distant from the psychophysiological restrictions in the color domain and plausibly does belong to a "vast pattern-system" of English. The linguistic form is the English subjunctive mood, as illustrated in this example:

> If he had been to Paris, he would have seen the Eiffel Tower.

The correlated meaning of the subjunctive is that something is unreal or contrary to concrete reality, but is conceivable (Curme, 1931). When used in a conditional sentence the subjunctive sets up a false proposition as if it were true and from this proposition draws a conclusion; the conclusion is also false but is set forth as though true. However, no one is fooled by this stage play. The above example is such a conditional subjunctive that presupposes (since it includes the subjunctive mood) that the character referred to has not been to Paris and has not seen the Eiffel Tower, but presents both of these propositions as if they were true.

This type of statement is called a *counterfactual,* a statement that commits the speaker to the falsity of the proposition with which it appears (Lyons, 1977, p. 795). Bloom's approach was to compare the English subjunctive coding of counterfactuality to the coding of counterfactuality in Mandarin Chinese, in which there is no subjunctive form. To make statements contrary to fact in Chinese one can use adposition of clauses with no special marking (examples from Comrie, 1983):

> Zhangsan he jiu, wo ma ta
>
> (= (literally) "Zhangsan drinks wine, I scold him," but with a counterfactual implication in context)

Alternatively, one can add words for "if" and "then," but these are not obligatory:

> ruguo Zhangsan he jiu, wo jiu ma ta
>
> (= "if Zhangsan drinks wine, then I scold him," again with a counterfactual implication in context)

It is also possible to add a word only for the antecedent or p term of the $p \rightarrow q$ relation (the "protatis"), leaving unmarked the consequent (the "apodosis" or q term):

> ruguo Zhangsan he jiu, wo ma ta
>
> (= "if Zhangsan drinks wine, I scold him," counterfactuality again implied in context)

The converse also is possible (adding only a word for the apodosis or q term). Chinese has still other forms that convey hypotheticality, possibility, or probability, but in the counterfactual tests of the Whorfian hypothesis the above have been the most important.

Bloom presented American English speakers and Chinese speakers with

brief stories (in their respective languages) in which counterfactuality was featured. In the English-language version of the story conditional subjunctive sentences were used to code counterfactuality, whereas in the Chinese-language version some form of *if-then* was used. In some contexts the English and Chinese
text specified that p was not the case. In Chinese this type of negative preface is
one of the devices for conveying the counterfactuality of subsequent *if p, then q*
statements. The exact form of the code in Chinese is important and we will return
to it. Bloom's expectation was that the subjunctive, being a compact embodiment
of the counterfactual concept, would enable English speakers to reason on the
basis of a counterfactual assumption, whereas the Chinese reliance on *if-then,*
even when the context makes clear that a counterfactual situation is being talked
about, would be less efficient and more prone to error. A difference in reasoning
proficiency between Chinese and English speakers might be expected with sufficiently complex counterfactual reasoning problems. To this end Bloom composed
a short exposition of a hypothetical eighteenth-century European philosopher
named Bier who ". . . could not read Chinese, but if he had been able to read
Chinese he would have found . . .," viz., various things that were presented in
later parts of the exposition via other counterfactual clauses (e.g., ". . . he would
certainly have been influenced by it, have synthesized it with Western philosophy,
and have created a theory which not only explained natural phenomena as
individual entities, but which also made clear their interrelationships") (from A.
Bloom, 1981, p. 98). The subjects, after reading the exposition of Bier's lost career
(in English or its Chinese translation), had to answer questions about the truth
or falsity of the "apodosis" or q terms of the counterfactual conditionals. All but
one of these q terms are false under a counterfactual interpretation.

Whereas nearly all of Bloom's English-speaking subjects gave correct answers to these questions, that is, judgments of "false," only 55 percent of his
Chinese-speaking subjects gave correct answers (this is the average level of
Bloom's, 1981, Table 1, p. 30). Both the Chinese and American subject samples
were adults. With a different version of the Bier story the contrast was even more
dramatic—nearly all the English speakers responded correctly and less than 10
percent of the Chinese speakers did so.

Rarely has such a clear-cut result proved to be nonrepeatable; but such is
the case here. Au (1983), using the same Bier story, obtained much higher
performance from Chinese-English bilinguals in Hong Kong. She argues that it
was not their grasp of English that explains this outcome—young subjects who
had studied English but were not able to produce the English subjunctive still
showed significant levels of correct response to counterfactual reasoning problems.

There are complications, however. As noted, Au did not use monolingual
Chinese speakers, but rather Hong Kong students in English-language schools;
her adult subjects had been studying English for 12 years in some cases. Second,
the story given to children who did not know the English subjunctive was not the
Bier story but a new story (called "Human Broth"—the exciting implications of
which readers can check for themselves) which, as Bloom (1984) points out in
his reply to Au, is more concrete and therefore probably less demanding than the
Bier story. A further confusing problem in reading this literature is that there are

several versions of the Bier story. Bloom used two versions, and Au used both of these and two other versions that were rewritten improvements of Bloom's versions. As a native speaker, Au found the original Bier stories to be not fully idiomatic (although Bloom had relied on native Chinese speakers to render the story from the English original) and rewrote them to make them read better. These rewritten versions are called by the same names as Bloom's versions. Au used the original Bloom stories as well as her own rewritten stories and obtained significant levels of counterfactual understanding with all versions, so the changes she introduced do not explain the different results.

Liu (1985) has used the identical Bloom story (version three) and Au's more idiomatic version and also was able to show significant levels of counterfactual understanding. Among Liu's subjects who demonstrated counterfactual understanding, moreover, were some who had been exposed to English for only a few years (in contrast to Au's, who had been studying English for 12 years in some cases), and had not encountered English conditional constructions at all at the time of testing. These subjects were both significantly superior to Bloom's Chinese subjects and not significantly different from Bloom's American adult subjects (Liu's subjects who were most comparable to Bloom's in age averaged 82 percent correct on Bloom's Chinese version of the same version three story, compared to Bloom's Chinese subjects' average of 55 percent).

In view of these findings there is no doubt that Chinese-speaking subjects can perform as well as English-speaking subjects on counterfactual reasoning problems. How then are we, the spectators, to understand all of this? The difficulty here is not just a matter of interpreting a specific set of experiments, but rather an illustration of a general problem that any investigator must face in experimentally testing the Whorfian hypothesis. To see this problem we should return to the linguistic differences between Chinese and English in the counterfactual realm and look at these differences more closely. Then we must ask what exactly the Whorfian hypothesis predicts of the effects of such differences on thought and what the experiments have in fact tested.

A clear demonstration of the differences between Chinese and English with respect to the counterfactual can be obtained with the help of the following diagram (this sort of chart is from Haiman, 1978; the terminology is based on Lyons, 1977):

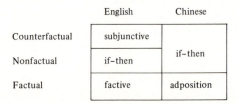

	English	Chinese
Counterfactual	subjunctive	if–then
Nonfactual	if–then	
Factual	factive	adposition

The terms along the left of the chart are interpreted as follows. *Counterfactual* means that the speaker is committed to the falsity of the proposition; this is conveyed with English subjunctives, especially in the past tense—for example, *if he had been in Paris, he would have seen the Eiffel Tower* (this example and the next two are from Lyons, 1977, p. 795). English speakers exposed to such sentences and later tested for their memory often think they have actually heard the negation of the protatis and apodosis; that is, that they have heard *he has not been in Paris* and *he has not seen the Eiffel Tower* (Fillenbaum, 1974). *Nonfactual* means the speaker is committed to neither the falsity nor the truth of the proposition; this is the case with English *if-then* conditionals *(if he went to Paris, he saw the Eiffel Tower)*. *Factual* means the speaker is committed to the truth of the proposition; this is the case with "factive" verbs (Karttunen, 1973) such as *know (he knows Bill went to Paris* commits the speaker to the truth of *Bill went to Paris)*.

The bare Chinese adposition, *Zhangsan he jiu, wo ma ta* ("Zhangsan drinks wine, I scold him"), covers the full range of possibilities in this chart; context alone tells whether a factual, nonfactual, or counterfactual meaning is intended. Addition of *ruguo* ("if") and/or *jiu* ("then") excludes the factual meaning as a possibility (L. Liu, personal tutorial). Thus *ruguo Zhangsan he jiu, wo jiu ma ta* could mean either the speaker is committed to the falsity of the proposition that Zhangsan has been drinking and the speaker has been scolding, or that the speaker is not committed to either the truth or the falsity of these propositions. Excluded is the possibility that the speaker is committed to the truth of the proposition. Chinese does not have a form, like the subjunctive, that commits the speaker to the falsity of these propositions. Context again must decide; that is, the context must contain sufficient clues to push the interpretation toward the top of the chart above, if a counterfactual interpretation is to be made. It is this process of contextual "pushing" and its inherent uncertainty that I believe contains an explanation of the contrasting results of Bloom's, Au's, and Liu's experiments. Comparison of experimental materials shows that Bloom's materials contained fewer clues and that what Au added, in order to make the Bier story more readable, were additional clues, pushing the interpretation of *if-then* sentences toward the counterfactual end of the continuum.

In Bloom's original Chinese translation of the Bier story there is the expression *yiding* that was used for the English word *certainly* (which in the English version appeared as follows: *If Bier had read Chinese philosophy he would certainly have been influenced by it*). Au replaced this expression with *jiu* ("then"). To a Chinese speaker the change results in greater fluency and naturalness. But this change also more clearly indicates an interpretation that favors the counterfactual end of the continuum. In the open-ended counterfactual situation of Chinese the effect of *yiding*, "certainly," apparently was to move the interpretation more toward the factual end (that it has no such effect in English is, of course, irrelevant). Thus Bloom's subjects, trying to solve the reasoning problem he set them, would have been led toward the factual end to answer "yes" to such questions as "Did Bier lead European philosophy closer to Chinese philosophy?" Conversely, one could argue that Au's subjects, also trying to solve the reasoning problem, were more strongly pushed to the counterfactual end. These are relative motions and there is no absolute standard for what is "right."

Liu's result with the identical Chinese story that Bloom had used also showed clear counterfactual response by Chinese subjects. Her procedure (in contrast to Bloom's), however, included having each subject read both the Bier story and the more concrete "Human Broth" story that Au had composed. It is possible that Liu's subjects were, by this procedure, made more aware of the relevance in the experiment of counterfactual reasoning. This is another form of context that could be capable of pushing interpretations of *if-then* to the counterfactual end.

It is crucial to point out that the methodology of these experiments does not test the Whorfian hypothesis as such. That hypothesis would say of English speakers that they project the subjunctive and its associated meaning of counterfactuality onto reality. These experiments, in contrast, are designed to measure reasoning proficiency. All of the variables that can influence reasoning proficiency are accordingly important. One such variable is the possibility of automatic reasoning in the counterfactual mode that the subjunctive can provide; this is what Bloom was counting on. But many other factors are also relevant and may overwhelm automaticity in experimental contexts.

Herein lies the moral of this conflict. When attempting to test the Whorfian hypothesis within some kind of experimental paradigm, the process under test is necessarily an experimentally accessible process, like reasoning or memory. Such processes, however, can be controlled by variables that have nothing to do with the Whorfian hypothesis. In the case of the counterfactual tests there were such variables that influence reasoning proficiency. Such things as whether clues in the material push the experimental subjects more to one end or the other of the chart given earlier have nothing to do with whether English and Chinese speakers project false propositions onto reality as a category. The importance of variables that affect reasoning as such in the counterfactual tests is made clear in another part of Liu's experiment, in which she found that factors like specific knowledge and the format of the problem played a decisive role in producing correct counterfactual response by Chinese-speaking subjects.

As far as the Whorfian hypothesis is concerned, the counterfactual tests remain quite unclear at the moment. It is established beyond doubt that Chinese speakers reason correctly in the counterfactual mode. But whether they habitually categorize the world in terms of true versus false propositions that remain plausible is still not known; by the same token, we are equally in the dark about whether English speakers do this as well!

The Whorfian hypothesis thus remains untested through experimental methods. Much of the experimentation has been carried out in an unpromising domain—color—and all of the experimentation, including the recent counterfactual tests, can be challenged on the ground that it does not test the habitual classification of reality by speakers, but rather other processes (memory, perception, reasoning efficiency) whose connection to the classification of reality is indirect. It should not be overlooked that Whorf did provide empirical (not experimental) tests of the relativity hypothesis. English speakers project the concept of an object into an area of experience in which it is not entailed (time experience); that it is not entailed by the primary experience of time is demonstrated by the existence of Hopi conceptions of time as cyclic. This demonstration, however, does not prove linguistic determinism to everyone's satisfaction. Some argue that there are nonlinguistic forms of cognition that affect linguistic structure as well as nonlinguistic cognition (Au, 1984b, for example, appears to argue this way). The only way to be safe from this argument is to show, prior to demonstrating linguistic determinism or relativity, that language forms embody a form of thinking not entailed by experience.

The following sections present cultural models that appear to be built into language forms. These are appropriate places to look for determining effects of language on thought. I have not, however, attempted to provide response measures that might be used to show experimentally that these forms have a determining effect.

HOW TO TEST THE WHORFIAN HYPOTHESIS

The Whorfian hypothesis should be tested in three logically ordered steps, corresponding to the priority order of the tenets of the hypothesis:

1. Identify an aspect of world view.
2. Determine specific linguistic patterns that embody this world view.
3. Ask whether these patterns and the associated world view are included in subjects' interpretations of reality. If posing this question proves impossible, then test memory, perception, reasoning, or whatever else the clever experimenter can devise, that appears to be a sensitive reflection of interpretations of reality.

Previous efforts to test the Whorfian hypothesis have usually jumped straight to number three (above), omitting numbers one and two. One exception is an experiment by Lucy (1981) in which all three logical steps can be found. Although Lucy does not present his investigation in the following terms, I will describe it so that the three steps can be seen:

1. Two world views are being tested: on the one hand, the form-substance distinction mentioned earlier in connection with time nomenclature in SAE and, on the other, a distinction between alive and nonalive things.
2. A linguistic form that may embody these aspects of reality is the morphological process of pluralizing nouns. In English this process is different for references to bounded objects and to unbounded substances (so-called mass nouns, such as gold, water, sand, etc.). Lucy compared the process utilized by English to that in Yucatec Maya, the Native American language of the Yucatan Peninsula still in use in that part of modern Mexico, where the pluralization process is different for nouns that denote animate versus inanimate objects. Without entering into details, in English, nouns that refer to naturally bounded objects are pluralized in the straightforward manner of affixing the plural (e.g., *cat* + *s*)—whereas nouns that refer to naturally unbounded substances are pluralized via a construction in which boundaries are supplied through a second noun (e.g., *two bar* + *s of gold*). In Yucatec there is

an equivalent straightforward plural for animate nouns, but for objects that are inanimate Yucatec employs a construction that specifies the inanimacy of the substance; for example, "two inanimate paper" (whereas aliveness is implicit in the noun for "man" and it is possible to say, straightforwardly, the counterpart of "two men"). In the continuum of different kinds of objects and substances in reality, English and Yucatec Maya thus treat nonalive bounded objects (barrels, stools, etc.) in opposite ways. To English they are bounded and can be pluralized in the straightforward way. To Yucatec they are not alive and can be pluralized only via a construction that specifies the lack of life. Thus the same objects are classified in different ways, and this difference maps onto aspects of world view—form-and-substance or alive-versus-not-alive—that are built into the respective linguistic systems.

3. Rather than pose questions about the interpretation of reality, Lucy tested judgments of similarity for pairs of objects. In the critical case of bounded inanimate objects (barrels and the like) he found that similarity judgments followed the underlying linguistically coded dimensions. For example, to English speakers inanimate and animate objects with boundaries—such as a barrel and a person—were judged to be more similar to each other than either was to an inanimate unbounded substance—meat or sand. To Yucatec speakers the pairings were reversed—objects such as barrels (bounded and nonalive) and substances such as meat or sand (also nonalive) were judged more like one another than either is to an alive and bounded object such as a person.

The linguistic forms described in the next section appear to embody what can be called, using the term introduced by Quinn (in press), "cultural models." Each cultural model is a way of organizing some part of the experience of reality and is, according to the Whorfian hypothesis, embodied in linguistic structure.

EXAMPLES OF LINGUISTIC FORMS THAT (MIGHT) EMBODY CULTURAL MODELS

Navaho Color Terms

Unlike the color terms of English, Navaho color terms are connected to a wider system of concepts—concepts for the diagnosis and healing of diseases. The basic color terms of the language correspond approximately to English as follows (N. B. McNeill, 1972):

lagai (white)

lidzin (black)

lichi (red)

ditl'ish (blue-green)

litso (yellow)

These words are also the names of minerals used in religious ceremonies. The fundamental factor in the selection of color words by Navaho appears to have been ceremonial. Navaho color terms thus offer an opportunity to test the effect of color terminology on color perception or memory when they connect to a wider cultural sphere than the color world itself. "Hand-trembling," for instance, is an important divination ceremony which goes through several steps each of which is identified by one of the basic colors. For example: "Black Gila monster, I want you to tell me what is wrong with this patient. Do not hide anything from me. I am giving you a jet bead to tell me what the illness of this patient is" (Kluckhohn and Leighton, 1946, p. 148). This prayer is given for each finger, with a different colored bead to go with each one, and addressed to a correspondingly colored Gila monster. In this language color categories embody a world view connected with disease and categories of disease. The ability to distinguish and remember colors might be different for Navaho speakers in ways that can be traced to this world view.

Nominal Compounds of English

The distinction between form and substance has already been emphasized as an important aspect of the SAE world view. The "entification" of abstract concepts (A. Bloom, 1981) is a product of this world view in which concepts are regarded as localized within a container or other object. Entification is embodied in a wide range of linguistic forms of English including, in particular, the specialized grammatical form of the nominal compound (Lees, 1960; Gleitman and Gleitman, 1970). The semantic effect of the nominal compound is to make a process, event, condition, purpose, and so forth, into a bounded conceptual entity. Although it appears in sentences as an NP its meaning derives from a full proposition. The form of jargon known as "space speak" (itself a nominal compound) is full of this grammatical form (far more frequent than other rhetorical figures such as metaphors and metonyms). The longest specimen I could find in a survey occurred (perhaps not surprisingly) in the Congressional Record (McNeill, 1966):

> liquid oxygen liquid hydrogen rocket powered single stage to orbit reversible boost system

This entire structure functioned grammatically as a single noun. The associated meaning is that there is in the world a corresponding *bounded entity* with the properties listed in the compound. The Whorfian hypothesis predicts that this entity meaning is projected onto reality so that English speakers tend to think of all the disparate components and processes listed in the compound as a bounded object in reality.

The method for creating nominal compounds is to start with a sentence or phrase and arrange the referring terms in reverse order. For the Congressional Record example, the source is a phrase approximately as follows:

> a reversible system for a boost to orbit in a single stage rocket that is powered by liquid hydrogen and liquid oxygen

In this form of description the various components of the system are presented more or less as separate elements. Comparing the nominal compound to the source phrase, the Whorfian hypothesis predicts that what is added is the perception of a bounded entity.

Although the form-and-substance world view permeates English as a "vast pattern-system," popular enthusiasm for matters technological seized on the nominal compound as a particular linguistic outcropping of form-and-substance in the 1960s when I carried out my survey. Computer jargon appears to play a similar role at present (for examples, see Turkle, 1984). Political and sociological factors doubtlessly played a part in selecting this single grammatical process. For technical writers and speakers the nominal compound provided a method for coining new technical terms, but for the nontechnical the nominal compound also became a kind of shibboleth for appearing technologically knowledgeable without having any particular technological knowledge. To study this latter phenomenon I computed a "Pomposity Index," or PI, and compared several groups in terms of their PI values. The PI compared lengths of compounds in samples of speech or writing to standard NASA dictionaries. I found that technical users (persons in the space program) used fewer long compounds than nontechnical users. The differences were quite large and grew larger the longer the compound: in a magazine there were 220 percent more five-word compounds and 300 percent more six-word compounds than in the dictionary. Since a legitimate referential use of a long nominal compound could mean only that there was increased specificity of reference, the abundance of very long compounds in nontechnical contexts where precision has no particular importance would seem to be clear examples of "pomposity."

Assonance-Rime Combinations in English

While the phonological structure of single-syllable words would not at first glance seem a promising place to look for the embodiment of cultural models, in fact such combinations, in English at least, follow models of the internal structure of everyday objects. We can thus extend the range of linguistic determinsim to the phonological patterning of words.

Assonance-rime is the name given by Rhodes and Lawler (1981) to the semantic structure of single-syllable words. "Assonance" refers to the initial consonant or consonant cluster of the word, and "rime" (so spelled) to the vowel nucleus plus final consonant(s); these terms were first used by Bolinger (1950). Rhodes and Lawler discovered semantic associations for different assonances and rimes. The associations reflect concepts of objects and parts of objects. For example, the word *loop* is a combination of the *l-* assonance, which conveys that something is connected (as in *link, latch, lock*), together with the *-oop* rime, which means that something is curved (as in *hoop, droop, swoop*). A connected curve is a loop. Thus the construction of the very word shows how, according to a certain model built into the structure of the word, a loop is constructed in reality. Another example is the word *snatch,* made out of the *sn-* assonance (meaning something quick: *snap, snag, snip*) plus the *-atch* rime (meaning something held: *catch* and *latch*). To snatch something is to quickly hold onto it. Again, the construction of the word is a model for the internal organization of the referent.

There seems to be a degree of phonetic symbolism running through these examples; that is, symbolism in which movements of the mouth or sensory impressions of sound iconically represent the outer world (see Sapir, 1924, and Paget, 1930, for early discussions of this idea; and Newman, 1933, for positive experimental results; see Taylor and Taylor, 1965, for more recent discussion). The *l-* assonance, meaning that something is connected, is formed by pushing the tongue back and up so that it connects the two sides of the mouth, and the *-oop* rime, meaning that something is curved, is made by forming a curve with the lips. The *sn-* assonance, meaning quick, requires a rapid alteration of the shape of the tongue between the *s* and *n* positions, and the *-atch* rime, meaning to catch, requires pressing the tongue behind the front teeth in a way that could be said to depict catching. The trouble with such phonetic symbolism interpretations is that it is almost impossible not to see semantic connections in every direction. For example, while *sn-* can be seen to "naturally" depict quickness, *s-* could be said to depict slowness because there is a gradual release of air pressure. If slowness and quickness combine, the result should be medium speed rather than quickness.

The assonance-rime hypothesis explains otherwise arbitrary word choices in terms of metaphors that extend the object composition model. For example, why do we say a play "flopped" but not that it fell, dropped, or sat down (all denotationally equivalent)? The *fl-* assonance means something that is inadequate *(flunk, flaw, flimsy)* and the *-op* rime means that something abruptly ceases operation *(stop).* The flop of a play is a combination of these ideas: the play is (commercially) inadequate and abruptly ceases operation (Rhodes and Lawler, 1981).

Rhodes and Lawler found that about half of English monosyllablic words could be analyzed as systematic assonance-rime combinations whose meanings as words are predictable from their parts. Typically these are words whose etymologies dictionary-makers have regarded as obscure—which is not surprising if such words actually are composed out of parts.

Noun Classifiers in Various Languages

Nouns themselves categorize objects presumed to exist in the world; noun *classifiers* categorize how people *interact* with the objects in the world (Denny, 1976). If a classifier is sufficiently transparent and its associated meaning is projected onto reality, speakers could think there are categories of objects in reality organized in terms of how people interact with them. The cultural models embodied in noun classifies can be recognized as deriving from different traditional technologies. Where the technologies are different the models, and the classifier systems in which they are embodied, are also different. Denny gives these examples of noun classifiers from Ojibway, an Algonquian language spoken in the

Northern Great Lakes region, where the technology is based on fashioning artifacts by hand, and the classifier system implies categories of objects that differ in terms of how they are manipulated:

apikk	Hard inorganic objects like rocks that require chipping and grinding
attik	Rigid organic objects like poles used to make frames for canoes and wigwams
ek	Flat organic objects like sheets of bark or hide for covering canoes or wigwams
apik	Flexible organic objects like rawhide cords to tie these things together

Denny observes that the same or similar classifier categories occur in other languages associated with manual technology. In cultures where the technology is more complex there are also classifiers for objects used in other ways, like planks and bricks. For instance, in Tzeltal, a Mayan language, there is a classifier for flat and rigid objects, like paving stones *(pehc)*. Sometimes the categories of objects implied by the classifier system are highly diverse from a physical viewpoint. In Gilbertese there is the classifier *kai* used for trees, plants, land sections, and fish hooks. All are objects essential for life. In English there is a very limited noun classification system that reveals a separation of man from the natural world: *one* is used for humans (in *someone, anyone, no one, everyone*) and *thing* for natural objects (in *something, nothing, everything*). If these are transparent and projected onto reality English speakers could habitually think (as they might) that two completely different orders of beings exist, humanity and "everything" else.

Cryptotypes in English, Spanish, and Atsugewi

In the following examples of English motion verbs, an abstract structure (a "cryptotype" in Whorf's terminology, 1946) embodies a cultural model in which there is a single category of motion formed by combining the fact of motion with the manner or cause of motion (Talmy, 1985):

motion + cause: The bone pulled loose from its socket.

That is, the bone moved and the cause of it was an outward pressure. English combines these meanings into a single category associated with *pull.* An example of the fact of motion combined with manner is the following:

motion + manner: The rock bounced down the hill.

That is, the rock moved and its motion was bouncy. The verb *bounce* combines these ideas into one category.

It is common in English for verbs of movement to combine the fact of motion with the cause or manner of motion into a single category. The combination is obligatory and for most speakers probably is transparent (projected onto reality). This situation may result in a perception of motion classes that are differentiated according to cause or manner.

Spanish embodies a different cultural model of motion. The combined concepts here are the fact of motion and the path (path in English, in contrast, is usually specified separately, as in *bounce DOWN the hill*). For example:

meti	el barril	a la bodega	rodandolo
(I moved-in)	(the keg)	(into the storeroom)	(by rolling)

The verb *meti* conveys both the fact of motion itself and the direction of motion. Again the combination of meanings is obligatory and for most speakers probably transparent.

English also has a few verbs that blend path and motion. Talmy lists *enter, exit, pass, rise, demand, return, circle, cross,* and *separate*—all, however, (except *rise*) are verbs that originally came from Romance stock. When these verbs are used the sentence has to specify separately the usually fused elements of cause and manner:

The horse crossed at a trot (specifying manner)

The Northern California Hokan language of Atsugewi shows a third pattern, in which the fact of motion is differentiated according to the different kinds of objects that are in motion (called "figures" by Talmy). A few English verbs also combine concepts in this way—*to rain* combines the figure of rain with the kind of motion typical of rain, and *to spit* does likewise. But in Atsugewi, distinguishing and classifying motion according to the type of figure is fundamental. Talmy gives the following verbs from a much larger set (all are infixes, or morphemes, that fit inside other morphemes):

-lup-	motion of small shiny spherical objects
-t-	motion of small planar objects
-caq-	motion of slimy lumpish objects
-swal-	motion of limp linear objects suspended at one end
-qput-	motion of loose dry dirt
-staq-	motion of runny icky stuff

The following example illustrates the use of one of these, *-staq-;* the complete sentence is *sma.taqc^ha* (and of the pragmatic situation one can only make a wild guess):

s-w-	-ma-	-staq-	-cis-a
	caused by the foot	motion of runny icky stuff	into the fire

(e.g., "I kicked the guts into the fire"). In other words, the language imposes a combination of meanings such that a unified category is formed of the motion of runny-icky-(gutsy)-stuff.

These examples illustrate differences in cultural models of the kind that Whorf proposed as the determining forces in producing culturally different habitual thought patterns. Between English and Atsugewi there are major differences in the way motions are categorized and, assuming the Whorfian hypothesis, corresponding major differences in the way English and Atsugewi speakers habitually experience the world of moving objects. For example, what to an English speaker are similar motions (kicking guts and kicking potatoes into the fire) to an Atsugewi speaker should seem fundamentally different. Conversely, to an Atsugewi speaker kicking guts and throwing guts should seem like the same motions but to an English speaker should seem fundamentally different. Both speakers are projecting transparent linguistic categories onto reality, according to the Whorfian hypothesis.

Metaphors

Metaphors have already been discussed in Chapter 5 as inner speech symbols. They are also examples par excellence of cultural models, a fact emphasized by Lakoff and Johnson (1980). Metaphors, by their very nature as projections of secondary onto primary subjects, connect separate ideas into single concepts. They are perfect illustrations of meanings being connected by virtue of linguistic patterns but that are not necessarily connected by experience. In addition to the metaphors described in Chapter 5, the following metaphoric schemas for the mind and mental products and for time are offered as places to test the Whorfian hypothesis.

THE MIND IS A MACHINE

We're trying to *grind out* a solution.

My mind isn't *working* today.

After coffee *the wheels began to turn.*

I'm a little *rusty* at it.

After five hours of it they *ran out of gas.*

His conversation was just *a memory dump.*

THE MIND IS A BRITTLE OBJECT

A fragile ego.

Handle him with care.

He's easily *crushed.*

A *shattering* experience.

Among the associated implications of the MACHINE metaphor, Lakoff and Johnson list the following: the mind has an on-off state, a level of efficiency, a productive capacity, a source of energy, and an operating condition. Facts of mental life that we sense to be machinelike will tend to be facts that are formulatable in concepts like these. (The IP theory appears to be an effort to make scientifically explicit some implications of the MACHINE metaphor.)

The BRITTLE OBJECT metaphor, on the other hand, provides a way of describing mental strength and irreversible changes of mental state. Psychological illness can be described by either metaphor, but the projected implications are different:

He broke down (machine)

He cracked up (brittle object)

If the illness is of the wild catastrophic kind the BRITTLE OBJECT metaphor seems more appropriate for describing what is happening, whereas if it is of the lethargic nonfunctioning kind the MACHINE metaphor seems more appropriate. The point is, in either case, the phenomenon of mental illness is not interpreted directly as "it is," but indirectly via the cultural models embodied in such linguistic expressions as *break down* and *crack up*.

Other metaphoric schemas that apply to the "life of the mind" embody a world view based on the production and consumption of goods.

IDEAS ARE FOOD

It left *a bad taste.*
Half-baked ideas.
His statement was hard *to swallow.*

IDEAS ARE PRODUCTS

Turning out new ideas.
Taking the rough edges off the idea.

IDEAS ARE RESOURCES

He *ran out of gas.* (also the MACHINE metaphor)
Don't *waste* your ideas.

IDEAS ARE MONEY

Put in my *two cents' worth.*
A treasure trove of ideas.

IDEAS ARE FASHIONS

That idea *went out of style.*

The Freud *craze.*

These metaphor schemas embody the general SAE model and several present ideas as kinds of substance—food, products, resources, money—and others suggest forms into which substances can go—*two cents' worth,* for example.

The form-and-substance world view seems not to be well entrenched in the Japanese language, and Japanese lacks all of the above metaphors except the last, IDEAS ARE FASHIONS. Thus the set of metaphors in English organized around the cultural ideal of consuming substances is lacking from Japanese as nearly a whole set. Japanese, however, utilizes other metaphors for ideas that exist in English as well. For example:

IDEAS ARE PROGENITORS

The *father* of genetics

A *fertile* mind

IDEAS ARE CUTTING INSTRUMENTS

An *incisive* mind

A *cutting* remark

Whether Japanese speakers consider the connection of ideas with substances (food, resources, etc.) to be intelligible only tests could reveal. Unless these metaphoric schemas are now entering Japanese, however, the Whorfian hypothesis would predict that English speakers but not Japanese speakers should project onto the world of ideas the metaphors of food, resources, products, and so on.

A metaphoric schema for time described by Lakoff and Johnson is TIME IS A MOVING OBJECT:

The time *will come* (the future approaches us)

The time has long since *passed* (time has moved behind us)

If we face in the direction of time we can also can get:

Coming up in the weeks ahead

Looking *forward* to the trip

Conceiving of time as a moving object or as a flowing substance (the "river of time") again implies the SAE world view of form and substance. When time is conceived of in this world view as a moving object it acquires a deictic front-back orientation. If time is an object with a front and back, it has an origo and can be oriented with respect to other times. Thus (the word denoting the origo is indicated ⊕):

Next week and the week *following* it (= ⊕)

in which *follow* refers to the time that will come along after the origo; or with respect to oneself:

Next week and the weeks *ahead* of us (= ⊕)

in which *ahead* refers to the time that is approaching the origo.

The same model of time as a moving object creates what, at first glance, appear to be contradictory lexical choices in the words *following* and *ahead.* This contradiction can be resolved by taking into account the implied origos. The future "follows" the backside of the moving object of time; the future is "ahead" of us as we look at the approaching frontside of time. Both orientations can appear in a single sentence, if the appropriate origos are implied or mentioned:

We're (= ⊕) looking *ahead* (just now (= ⊕)) to the *following* weeks.

in which *we* is the origo for *ahead* and the implicit *just now* is the origo for *following:*

$$
\text{just now } (= \oplus_2)
$$
$$
\downarrow
$$

we (= $\oplus_1$)→   the moving object of time   *weeks*

(is "ahead")   (are "following")

English speakers should organize their experiences of time according to images of moving forms as well as collections of forms into simultaneous groups (as Whorf emphasized). Each of these ways of organizing temporal experience is a manifestation of the form-and-substance world view.

Gestures As Evidence

English speakers produce gestures in which the hands appear to create objects. The cartoon gesture mentioned in earlier chapters (where the speaker said *it was a Sylvester and Tweetie Bird cartoon* while his hands appeared to support an object) is an example (see Figure 7.10, p. 230). One quality of this gesture is its boundedness. The object that the gesture created and that stood for the abstract idea of the cartoon was not only a substance but a bounded substance. The gestures of speakers in some other cultures lack this feature of boundedness.

Figure 6.2 illustrates a gesture produced by a Turkana tribemember (the Turkana live in northwestern Kenya) who, while he produced the gesture, was

toditarite ngitunga   lu na kilna yoka   - - nith!
(they–extract people) (this–here knowledge
                        our–inclusive)

Figure 6.2 Gesture in Turkana that presents, as the image of an abstract concept, a substance *without* form. This example was originally cited in Stephens and Tuite (1983) and was taken from a film by MacDougall and MacDougall (1977). The transcription and English translation were performed for our research by R. Dyson-Hudson.

discussing knowledge (see McNeill, 1985*a,* for further discussion of this example). The speaker was saying the Turkana equivalent of "these people (i.e., foreigners) want to extract all our knowledge—pft!," and made the gesture shown. As in the English example an abstract concept is "entified," but in the Turkana gesture there is no boundary given to the object. The speaker seems to pluck "knowledge" from his brow and then releases it—"knowledge" rises of its own accord and vanishes. The gesture makes the abstract concept into a substance *without* form, a wisp of vapor with a motion all its own. Gestures in which there are boundaries around physical objects appear in the Turkana film, but not gestures that create boundaries for objects that exhibit abstract concepts. Here, then, is evidence in the gesture realm of a different world view. To "entify" may be a universal tendency of human thought, but to provide entities with shapes may be the product of a grammatical pattern that embodies the form-with-substance world view. In order to pursue the Turkana example in any depth we would obviously need, in addition to this gestural evidence, independent sources of insight into Turkana cultural models. In particular, it would be crucial to know if the world view of substance-without-form is embodied in the grammatical patterns of the Turkana language. Gestures, nonetheless, are a source of data that can be compared to the linguistic evidence.

In a recent linguistic analysis of Turkana (Dimmendaal, 1983) I have found in the system of number inflection a suggestion of a parallel linguistic pattern. In SAE one uses locutions such as *a moment of time* on analogy with the treatment of words like *sand* that refer to formless substances that can be localized only in bounded objects. Turkana grammar lacks these analogies, using instead a category of "intrinsically plural" substances, some of which (like water) are, semantically speaking, unbounded masses (Dimmendaal, 1983). There are also "intrinsically singular" substances that from the SAE point of view are equivalently unbounded masses (e.g., sand). Thus their method for pluralization does not embody the form-with-substance idea but seems consistent with a concept of form that is inherent in some substances (like containers being inherent in water) and not inherent in others (like sand). Whether this should be interpreted as a world view in which the concept of substance prevails over that of form, or something else less accessible, this cultural concept could lead to gestures in which there is no urge to indicate form. All of these noncountable Turkana nouns are deemed inherently plural: *na-kile,* "milk"; *na-akot,* "blood"; *na-kipi,* "water"; *na-kiilir,* "sweat"; and *na-lupu,* "soil"; whereas these are inherently singular: *a-kure,* "thirst"; *a-koro,* "hunger"; *a-pidi,* "bile"; *a-suji,* "snuff"; and *a-siloni,* "sand." What seems to characterize the inherently plural *na-* words is that (with the apparent exception of sweat) the words denote substances that the Turkana keep in containers, whereas the *a-* words (again with a presumed exception, snuff) denote substances that they do not keep in containers.

Perhaps the meaning of inherent plurality, as derived from the Turkana's practices and embodied in the linguistic patterns of their language, is projected onto experiences of the world to suggest the world view of substance-without-form, and Turkana gestures reflect this world view.

chapter 7

Gestures and Signs

In this book spontaneous gestures have been utilized as a source of information about mental operations during thinking and speaking. Such gestures have been used to open a second channel of observation onto mental processes (the first channel being speech itself). By examining gesture production we can see, in comparatively pure, undistorted form, the mental operations of speakers as they utilize the linguistic code. One of the purposes of this chapter is to present an explanation of why gestures are able to "mirror" mental processes in this way.

Two interlocking reasons can be given for the privileged status of gesture production: (1) gestures and sentences share a stage of development before speech takes on its socially constituted form; and (2) gestures exhibit this stage without distortion because they lack direct social regulation. Whereas in the case of spoken sentences the morphological and phonological levels stand between mental processes and speech, in the case of gestures there are no such levels that alter the display of mental processes. These two reasons together explain how spontaneous gestures are able to exhibit the sentence in its early diachronic stages.

The various ways in which gestures exhibit mental processes will lead us in this chapter into a discussion of the varieties of gesture. Part of the argument that gestures do not have intervening phonological and morphological levels involves comparing gesture to ASL signs where such levels exist; thus we will also examine this manual linguistic system.

ARGUMENTS THAT SPEECH AND GESTURE SHARE A STAGE OF DEVELOPMENT BEFORE SPEECH TAKES ON CONTRASTIVE VALUE

The arguments are the following: (1) gestures synchronize with speech in the sense that for each clause there is one and only one gesture; and (2) they also anticipate speech in the sense that the first evidence of the meaning exhibited by speech and gesture appears in gesture form.

Gestures Synchronize with Speech

This was demonstrated in Chapter 1. The synchrony of gestures with clauses implies that each gesture and each clause tend to exhibit a common source of meaning in the speaker's thinking. Synchronization of gesture with speech even occurs when the speech is from one person and the gesture from a listener. Such gestures are very rare, but one is illustrated in Figure 7.1. As the speaker (facing the camera) said *these are all in order* and produced a gesture moving to his left, the listener (not speaking) simultaneously produced a similar gesture to *his* left —in the opposite direction of the speaker's movement. The fact that the listener moved in the opposite absolute direction and prepared to make a gesture at the same time suggests that the listener was not just copying the speaker. Rather, the listener was separately programming a gesture movement to synchronize with his understanding of the speaker's sentence. The listener's gesture thus exhibits an on-line process of comprehension in terms of an image that ran in synchrony with the speaker's similar image.

The second point, discussed below, does not contradict the claim of synchrony, but shows that this common source of meaning first finds its way to the outside in gesture form.

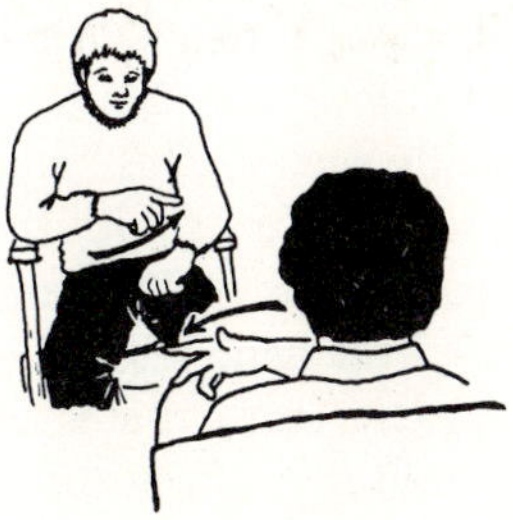

(speaker: these are all in order the way I've described them)

listener: ok

Figure 7.1 Gesture by a listener (near figure) synchronized with speaker's utterance and gesture.

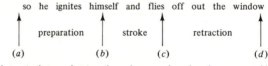

Figure 7.2 Preparation, stroke, and retraction phases of an iconic gesture. Numbers indicate time (unit = ⅟₆₀th second). Beneath each panel is an oscilloscope trace of the speech sound being uttered at that instant.

Gestures Anticipate Speech

The anticipation is very slight but still significant, for it shows unquestionably that the speaker's thinking is initially in imagistic form. Figure 7.2, based on video records, illustrates a gesture synchronized with a clause that also anticipates the meaning expressed linguistically. The concurrent sentence was *So he ignites himself and flies off out the window,* and the gesture exhibited both flying out and a simultaneous expansion in space that might express the idea of igniting oneself, something like a fireball. The arrows below show the point in the speech stream at which each picture was taken. Kendon (1972) divided "gesticulations," or G-phrases, into three prototypical components. Kendon called the middle movement the "stroke" phase of the gesture. This is an accented movement that gives the appearance of having been made deliberately with some tension or *effort.* The stroke is the part of the gesture that most obviously carries semantic content. In addition, however, the hands begin to move in such a way that the stroke can be executed before the stroke itself actually occurs. This "preparatory" phase would not occur if there were not a gesture occurrence with the meaning that is seen most clearly in the stroke. The preparation is the first evidence that the hand is taking on symbolic value. In Figure 7.2 the hand rising to the rear is the preparatory phase. Moving the hand up and to the rear—that is, in the opposite direction —only makes sense in terms of the need to perform the forward-moving stroke. Thus the real point at which the gesture first revealed the unitary undivided image of the character rocketing out in a burst of flames was in the preparation phase that coincided with the discourse conjunction *so*—that is, before the speaker had started to encode any segment of the propositional content of the image in the linguistic stream.

The preparatory component in the flying-out gesture began exactly as the speaker started to say *so.* The stroke phase began later as he started to say *-self.* This stroke also anticipates the linguistic expression of the specific meaning that it exhibits. Kendon's (1972) rule for the timing of the stroke was that it either just precedes or exactly coincides with the phonologically most prominent syllable of the utterance but never follows it. In the above example the most prominent syllable in terms of phonological effort was the second syllable of *ignites*. It was here that the stroke began, however, rather than ended. The forward movement of the stroke depicted flying out and in fact ended at the word *flies*. This syllable was the second most prominent in the utterance, far more prominent than *off* or *out*, which followed it. Kendon's rule therefore appears to require an additional clause which states that the stroke ends with the most prominent syllable of *the semantically parallel* linguistic segment. The effect of this revised rule is that the stroke always anticipates its semantically parallel linguistic segment. Thus both the preparatory component and the stroke component of the gesture first show the meaning that speech then expresses in linear and segmented form, the stroke ending with the specific speech segment that we infer (since it and the stroke remained together) was the inner speech symbol. Anticipation is a key reason for treating the image exhibited in gestures as revealing the meaning also expressed in the sentence at an early diachronic stage.

In the case of the flying-out example, we would infer that this primitive form of meaning included the image of the character exploding in flames and rocketing outward. This image would be an environment in which the inner speech symbols *flies* and *ignites* turn on. In turn, these symbols would categorize the image displayed in the gesture and would be altered by this image: the uncurling of the hand is given the meaning of "igniting" and shows this igniting to be sudden and explosive; the movement of the hand is "flying out" and shows this flying out to be upward. The gesture and speech jointly exhibit the inner dialectic of the sentence as it develops.

ARGUMENTS THAT GESTURES DO NOT HAVE MORPHOLOGICAL OR PHONOLOGICAL LEVELS

The preceding argument establishes the likelihood that gestures and speech have a common mental source. The next argument establishes that gesture exhibits the speaker's mental operations in relatively undistorted form. This privileged status of gesture derives from the absence of social standards for the performance of gestures. In contrast to the linguistic expression of mental operations there is in gesture production neither a phonological nor a morphological level standing between the mental operations of the speaker and the expression of these operations in gesture form.

The consequences of social control are clear from a study of the linguistic system of ASL, the manual-visual language of deaf people in North America (see the final section of this chapter for more discussion). In this language a phonological structure is undeniably present (Newkirk et al., 1980); one bit of evidence for this was presented in Chapter 5 (Fig. 5.7)—a speech error in which there was a metathesis of hand configurations. Hand configurations are one aspect of the system of phonological contrasts maintained in ASL (Newkirk et al. list 19 configurations). A given sign will typically consist of one of these 19 configurations combined with a movement (circular, rotational, vertical, etc.) and place of articulation (the other hand, the cheek, etc.). Movements and places of articulation also are regulated and drawn from specified sets of contrasts. Such phonological "primes" are crucial for the well-formedness of signs in ASL and can be regarded as both the instruments and the products of social regulation by the community of ASL users.

A striking illustration of morphological structure in ASL is the method for incorporating intensification. This is accomplished by combining morphemic constituents, one of which is the sign for the quality and the other for intensification. For intensification the signer performs the sign for the quality more quickly and with a larger movement. Such a combination can reduce the iconicity of certain signs. The ASL sign meaning "slow" is made by drawing one hand slowly across the back of the other hand; the sign meaning "very slow" is this same movement only made more *quickly* (Klima and Bellugi, 1979)—a clear consequence of morphological combination. In a spontaneous gesture for something moving very slowly the gesture would be made still more slowly: this is because in contrast to the socially constituted signs of ASL the gesture is under direct mental control and there is no level of morphological structure standing between gesture form and mental operations.

To say that spontaneous gestures lack a phonological or morphological level is the equivalent of saying that there is no composition out of parts. The gesture exhibits a meaning as a whole. It is not constructed by combining one element that means "a person" with another than means "climbs," and these with a third element meaning "upward." Rather, the gesture globally shows, in one indivisible symbol, the meaning of "person-climbs-upward." Figure 7.3 (page 218) shows drawings of different speakers narrating the same event from a cartoon (from McNeill, 1985a). The gestures have in common the fact that they exhibit the upward movement of an object. In some gestures the destination of the movement is also shown (pointing finger). The common features of gesture form clearly derive from the meaning that is common to the gestures—upward motion of the character referred to. Other than this constraint of meaning there is apparent no other standard of form: one speaker has her palm facing down, another up; one speaker flexes her hand to the rear, the others extend their hands forward or do not move their hands in relation to the wrist; and so forth. This flexibility on the signifier side of gestures follows from the absence of any socially constituted standards of gesture performance. Speakers and hearers are generally unaware of gesture form, may be only vaguely conscious that gestures are being made, and have no inkling of what a "well-formed" iconic gesture should look like (only major deviations from iconicity stand out).

There is a type of gesture for which socially constituted standards exist. These gestures were called "emblems" by Ekman and Friesen (1969). Emblems are quite different in form and function from iconic gestures (emblems are used to comment on and control interpersonal behavior in contrast to the propositional function of iconic gestures; see the section on emblems below).

Not having a level of socially constituted phonological or morphological structure, iconic gestures can directly exhibit mental operations.

COUNTERARGUMENTS AND REPLIES

Three counterarguments to the use of gestures as evidence of speech processes that might have occurred to the reader are the following: (1) gestures are merely like photographs that are held up while speaking, (2) gestures are translations of speech into a different medium, and (3) the shared computational stage of gestures and speech is already a complete linear-segmented verbal plan. These counterarguments and the following replies are from McNeill (1985*a*).

Gestures Are Like Photographs

Just as holding up a photograph would have nothing to do with the process of speaking, performing a gesture could have nothing to do with it either. The first point to make in reply to this argument is that, unlike a photograph, a gesture is something the speaker is creating on-line while speaking. Second, the gesture is very closely connected to the sentence temporally, semantically, and pragmatically, and all of these connections point to a coordination of gesture and sentence that is internal—totally different from holding up a photograph. Finally, gestures compensate for linguistic meaning and this results in a division of meaning between the channels. Gestures are not called forth, as a photograph might be held up, to repair an otherwise interrupted message. For example, we do not observe

so he . . .

(gesture to complete the idea)

but rather,

so he chases her out again

(gesture to show the means)

These points reduce to a single reply: gesture and speech are integrated *within.* They share a common development and source.

Gestures Translate Sentences

The counterargument in this case runs as follows. The visual-action medium of the gesture has its own qualities, but these do not characterize the psychological process of producing the sentence. There are in fact two quite separate psychological processes. In the sentence medium the process is linear and segmented (built on pure linguistic values) and this process is translated into the gesture medium, where it acquires a different set of qualities (global and synthetic). There are two replies to this counterargument. First, it has difficulty explaining the fact that gestures anticipate the semantically parallel linguistic segment; if gestures are a translation of the sentence into a different medium the temporal order should be the reverse. Second, it can be shown that the fundamental assumption of this counterargument is false: gestures do *not* impose their own characteristic structure. The gesture medium is capable of reflecting different kinds of mental representations. The following are two cases (among many that could be cited) which demonstrate that the gesture medium is not inherently global and synthetic. One is that in ASL, a manual-visual language, segmentation and linearity are fundamental properties (see the section on ASL at the end of the chapter). The other is the behavior of hearing subjects (naive to ASL), who are required to narrate stories without the use of speech. Under these circumstances the subjects spontaneously subdivide meanings into idea segments by making different gestures for each segment (R. Bloom, 1979). To convey the meaning of an entire event, the subject concatenates gestures into a linear sentencelike succession. The following is an illustration from R. Bloom's (1979) study; these five gestures formed a single statement:

> Gesture for "queen" (itself a composite made out of a gesture for "crown" and a gesture for "breasts")
>
> Gesture for "smiling"
>
> Gesture for "frowning" plus head-shake (negation)
>
> Gesture for "smiling" plus head-nod (affirmation)
>
> Gesture for "queen"

In words this translates as "the queen was smiling, not frowning, smiling—the queen." The order of segments is free and repetitious (queen-property-property-queen), and there is simultaneous indication of negation or affirmation with the indication of the properties, but segmentation and linearization of segments is unmistakable.

Evidently the minimal communicative use of gestures in this situation, no more than simply forcing gestures to stand alone and getting the subject to attend to them as the channel of expression, was enough to bring out a number of basic linguistic properties.

In contrast to spontaneous speech-accompanying gestures, gestures in Bloom's situation functioned in a morphemelike way. There were gestures with fixed meaning and there was compositionality out of parts, and there were also paradigmatic contrasts. The gesture for "queen" was a composite of "crown" (for royalty) and "breasts" (for feminine attribute). This contrasted with the gesture for "king," which was made with the same "crown" gesture combined with a gesture for "muscles" (for masculine attribute). (This narration shows many other interesting properties, particularly in connection with the creation and maintenance of a gesture lexicon. Morphemic combinations such as "king" (muscles + crown) and "queen" (breasts + crown) tended to become monosyllabic —performed as single smooth gestures with just vestigial references to the separate gesture components—and remarkably enough this smoothing occurred after no more than about six repetitions of the combination.)

Thus the gesture modality is perfectly capable of revealing linear-segmented representations when these exist. That gestures do not take a linear-segmented form in the case of spontaneous gesture production is therefore a meaningful phenomenon: the gesture is revealing a nonlinear image that is copresent with the sentence generation process.

Gesture and Speech Share the Same Linear-Segmented Verbal Plan

According to this counterargument spontaneous gestures, too, are generated from a verbal plan:

There are three replies to this argument. First, from this theory one cannot explain the global-synthetic form of gestures. They should be linear-segmented if they are produced from a covert linear-segmented verbal plan. Second, from this theory we cannot explain the compensatory relation of gestures and linguistic structure. If there is a meaning in the gesture channel it must have come from the covert verbal plan and should also be present in the speech channel. Finally, the image exhibited in the gesture can *itself* be regarded as the verbal plan at an early stage of development, which has been argued in this book.

TYPES OF GESTURE

Different types of gesture show imagistic mental operations that perform different functions. The following sections describe the major types of gesture.

Iconic Gestures

In iconic gestures the hands function as symbols that depict in their form and manner of movement a meaning that is relevant to the concurrent linguistic meaning. This relation is the essence of an "iconic" gesture. The five drawings in Figure 7.3 show iconic gestures by subjects who were (independently) describing the same scene from a cartoon. The common feature of "upward motion" in the gestures of five different people is a convincing demonstration of symbolic functioning: the hands exhibit something other than themselves, and do this in essentially the same way in different individuals. The gestures, while differing in detail, have in common an upward motion of the hand that is in accord with the verbally expressed descriptions. Such congruence is the defining property of iconic gestures.

A way of studying iconic gestures is to describe movement profiles of the gestures that accompany different linguistic meanings. This was the goal of a study based on the narrations of the subjects depicted in Figure 7.3 (McNeill and

he tries going up the inside of the drainpipe   he tries climbing up the drainspout of the building

and he goes up through the pipe this time   this time he tries to go up inside the raingutter

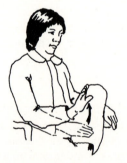

as he tries climbing up the rain barrel

Figure 7.3 Similar gestures by five speakers describing the same event.

Levy, 1982). Each subject viewed a cartoon and then immediately afterwards told the story of the cartoon from memory to a listener. The narrative performance was recorded on videotape. We used 44 movement features to describe the form of the gestures, of which the following are a few examples: Were the fingers curled or extended? Was the index finger extended? Was the palm turned down, up, to the right or to the left, toward the self or the front? Was the movement of the hand upward, downward, horizontal, in an arc? The stroke shown in Figure 7.2 would have been coded as first having the fingers curled and in a fist and then extending; the palm facing downward; movement from back to front and upward; and everything taking place in the right half of central gesture space.

To describe the concurrent linguistic meaning we utilized 37 "meaning features" based on verbs. The inspiration for this type of analysis came from Miller and Johnson-Laird (1976). Some examples of verb meaning features and sentences in which they occurred are:

Verb	Meaning Feature
Swallows (he swallows the bowling ball)	Entrance
Comes down (he comes down the pipe)	Downward
Runs ahead of (he runs ahead of it)	Horizontal
Catch up to (it catches up to him)	End state

A single verb can have several meaning features, just as a single gesture can have several movement features. The question we asked was whether there was an empirical correlation between the meaning features and movement features of concurrent gestures.

McNeill and Levy demonstrated the nonarbitrariness of iconic gestures by constructing a matrix in which the 37 rows represented meaning features and the 44 columns represented gesture movement features (a portion of the matrix is reproduced in Table 7.1). By looking along a given row we can see the total gesture movement profile for that meaning feature. In general, different features have distinct gesture profiles, with peaks and valleys appearing at various places. The matrix shows, for example, that the gestures accompanying verbs with the end-state feature tend to be two-handed, whereas gestures accompanying the longitudinal feature tend to be one-handed. The meaning of an end-state verb entails achieving a particular final state (Vendler, 1967) and a two-handed gesture allows the speaker to symbolize the attainment of that end state. Thus *catch up to,* an end-state verb, entails that something *was* caught up to, whereas *run along,* a longitudinal verb, does not mean anything other than simply the activity running along—an activity without a specific end state. By recreating the image of one thing catching another thing, two hands show the achievement of the final state by letting one hand come into proximity with the other. A similar analysis can be made of the two-handed gestures that accompany *swallow* and other verbs that carry the entrance/exit feature (where 90 percent of the gestures were made with two hands). Examples of gestures for the "catching up with" and "running ahead of" meanings are shown in Figure 7.4.

Such differences between iconic gestures convince one of their symbolic status. In the ability to convey a meaning other than themselves they are quite comparable to the symbols of socially constituted linguistic systems.

Changes in the form of iconic gestures are not restricted to just those movement features that directly reproduce semantic features. An example of a direct reproduction is the horizontal gesture movement accompanying verbs that

Table 7.1 CORRELATION OF GESTURE FEATURES WITH VERB FEATURES FOR ICONIX (SHOWS PERCENTAGE OF GESTURES IN EACH ROW THAT HAVE GIVEN GESTURE FEATURE)

Verb features	RH	BH	Fist	Fs curled	Fs extended	IF extended	Palm down	Palm self	BH same	Up	Down	L–R	St line	Redup	Number of gestures
Entrance/exit	0	90	0	70	10	20	10	40	30	0	50	60	20	10	10
Downward	62	31	8	62	8	15	31	15	0	0	54	23	31	0	13
Horizontal	30	57	8	43	24	5	30	19	35	8	16	73	13	35	37
Rotation	58	42	8	50	17	8	17	17	17	17	8	67	25	25	12
Longitudinal	52	35	4	48	17	22	22	22	9	4	22	61	30	30	23
End state	29	67	17	50	25	21	17	17	17	0	46	42	0	21	24
Closure/contact	54	45	27	36	36	18	18	18	0	9	36	9	18	18	11
Use feet successively	14	57	21	29	21	0	7	7	29	21	21	64	29	43	14
Number of gestures	30	37	10	38	12	13	18	13	14	11	21	36	15	21	—

Gesture features

Key: RH means right hand alone; *BH* means both hands; *F* means finger; *IF* means index finger; Palm *self* means palm facing self; *BH same* means both hands moving in the same direction or alternating; *L–R* means movement left to right; *St line* means movement in a straight line; *Redup* means reduplication of movement.

Source: McNeill and Levy (1982, Table 1, p. 277).

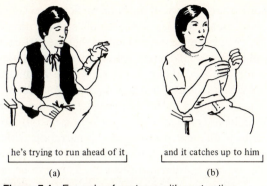

he's trying to run ahead of it | and it catches up to him

(a)   (b)

Figure 7.4 Example of gestures with contrasting meaning features. *(a)* Not End-State; *(b)* End-State.

described horizontal motions exclusively, such as *runs ahead of.* Iconic gestures also exhibited the speaker's memory of *entire scenes* and included aspects of meaning that were not entailed by the single verb segment whose meaning feature was recorded in the row of the matrix. For example, the downward verb meaning feature was accompanied by curled fingers in more than 60 percent of the gestures in our subjects' narrations. The use of curled fingers is often associated with the idea of passivity (old rhetoric manuals recommended curled fingers when the speaker wished to emphasize passivity; for instance Austin's book on rhetoric, 1806). In the cartoon narration, downward motion was invariably due to the influence of gravity and not the efforts of the character exhibiting the motion. The downward meaning feature also did not appear with gestures whose meanings were the opposite of passivity, such as upward gestures with the fingers extended (according to Austin this should be used to convey activity). Downward also did not appear in gestures where both hands were moving in the same direction, a gesture movement that signified parallel motion of two objects. Parallel motion is not logically opposed to downward motion, but in the cartoon narrations happens not be be combined with downward motion. Also, the downward meaning feature did not appear with reduplicated gestures, again because the meaning that was conveyed with reduplication (rapid locomotion) was not combined in the cartoon narrations with downward motion. This pattern of associations between particularities of gesture form and downward meaning suggests a coherent picture in which there is downward physical movement, passivity, one object moving at a time, and motion other than locomotion. This gesture model quite accurately reflects the situations the narrators were remembering and describing, in which the character being described was constantly falling passively and involuntarily from great heights; thus the gesture exhibited entire scenes, not the movement equivalent of single analytic meaning features.

Beats

In contrast to iconic gestures, where the form of the gesture exhibits a meaning relevant to the concurrent linguistic meaning, beats are constant in form and do not change with different propositional content. A typical beat is a simple up-and-down or back-and-forth movement of the hand made somewhere in the periphery of the gesture space, usually the lap. Beats emphasize the discourse function of the concurrent speech. They appear with clauses that are performing an extranarrative role—introducing new characters, setting scenes, summing up or anticipating the story but not actually adding to the story line. Adding to the story line is the function of clauses that iconic gestures accompany. Iconic gestures occur when clauses are performing a narrative role—actually describing the events of the narration. A hallmark of clauses that perform a narrative role is that they cannot be moved to a different position in the narration without signalling a different sequence of the narrated events (Hopper, 1979). Clauses performing an extranarrative role are not restricted in this way. They can be placed in another position without affecting the sequence of events in the narration.

Thus beats accompany extranarrative statements and do so with small uniform movements whose own content is minimal. Iconics accompany narrative statements and do so with typically large diverse movements that have their own content.

Figure 7.5 shows, in a sequence of drawings, three beats that were performed successively during a narration of a film. Each movement co-occurred with each new item of information presented: (1) the character mentioned had a girlfriend (this was the first mention of the girlfriend); (2) her given name was Alice; and (3) her surname was White. All of these items were of extranarrative importance.

Beats also occur with statements *about* language—metalinguistic statements—such as comments on word definitions (by a 5-year-old):

"execute" # it's something else
         |_____|
         (hand rises up and down (3 ×) on armrest of chair)

(The # indicates a brief hesitation).

These examples illustrate the generalization that beats exhibit not the propositional content of the concurrent speech (this is what iconics do), but the *relational functions* of speech. These include the relation of speech to the rest of a narration (extranarrative role) and the relation of speech to the language code itself (metalinguistic role). Despite their simplicity as movements, beats are participants in complex conceptual-linguistic patterns.

The noncorrelation of beats with propositional content is shown with another 37×44 matrix of the kind described above for iconics (McNeill and Levy, 1982); a portion of this second matrix is shown in Table 7.2. Whereas in the iconics matrix rows were differentiated from one another—showing that each meaning feature has its own gesture profile—in the beats matrix the rows look much the same. There is in this matrix only one pattern of peaks and valleys, more or less the same regardless of the specific verb meaning, since for these gestures movements do not change with different propositional meanings.

Beats do not exhibit the propositional content of their clauses and so there is no reason not to produce more than one per clause. Both illustrations above

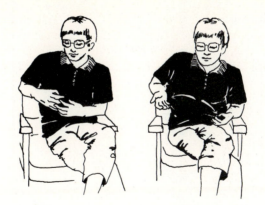

his girlfriend #
⎵

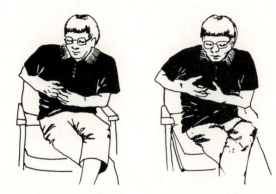

⌐Alice¬

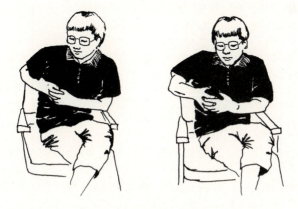

Alice ⌐White¬

Figure 7.5 Example of beats produced with successive increments of information in a sentence introducing a character, his gírlfriend # Álice # Alice Whíte.

Table 7.2 CORRELATION OF GESTURE FEATURES WITH VERB FEATURES FOR BEATS (SHOWS PERCENTAGE OF GESTURES IN EACH ROW THAT HAVE GIVEN GESTURE FEATURE)

Verb features	Gesture features															
	RH	LH	BH	Fs curled	Fs extended and separated	Palm down	Palm self	Palm rotates	Up	Down	L–R	Redup	Slight	Fs extend	Fs spread	Number of gestures
End state	33	56	11	44	41	67	4	33	37	52	30	15	15	26	19	27
Activity	14	71	14	52	38	86	10	38	52	24	48	14	38	19	10	21
Goal directed	30	50	21	42	34	50	3	39	39	39	34	18	37	16	13	38
Complex action	27	47	27	33	27	40	0	13	40	13	20	20	20	13	0	15
Cognitive state/ process	46	54	0	54	38	77	0	31	31	38	46	15	15	15	15	13
Stative	14	79	7	0	36	93	0	43	64	29	50	7	14	21	7	14
Number of gestures	20	44	12	34	27	47	10	28	28	26	22	14	27	14	10	—

Key: RH means right hand; *LH* means left hand; *BH* means both hands; *F* means finger; *Palm self* means palm facing self; *Palm down* means palm facing down; *L–R* means left to right; *Redup* means reduplicated movement; *Slight* means a movement of small extent.
Source: McNeill and Levy (1982, Table 4, p. 286)

show multiple beats within one clause. Since beats arise when the extranarrative content of a clause is emphasized, it is also possible to superimpose beats on iconic gestures. Superimposition could occur when one aspect of the propositional content is exhibited in the iconic gesture and another aspect of the proposition that is not emphasized is left over; the beat can then emphasize this deemphasized aspect without creating a second iconic gesture for the same clause. The very fact that the beat lacks content of its own provides a way of emphasizing the deemphasized. In this way more gestures than one per clause can occur with iconics—an iconic plus one or more beats. Here is an example:

and you see him drawing up # lots of blueprints
         L_____J

(appears to be holding up blueprints
and simultaneously)
L_____JL_____J

(moves hands (moves hands
up and down) up and down)
(1×)   (3×)

There is a blueprint gesture that is primary. There is a beat for the the act of drawing before the hesitation #, and three beats for the quantity of blueprints after this hesitation. Beats add emphasis without adding images to the clause. A beat or iconic arises depending on what the speaker thinks the important function of the sentence is. Beats and iconics co-occur when narrative and extranarrative functions are performed together. The clause as a whole serves to advance the story line and simultaneously to set the scene.

Cohesives

Cohesive gestures were described in Chapter 4. They are discourse gestures that make use of iconic gestures. Such gestures are called "cohesive" on the model of Halliday and Hasan's (1976) use of this term as described in Chapter 4. Like cohesive linguistic devices, cohesive gestures tie together separate parts of the discourse. Figure 7.6 is an illustration from one of the cartoon narrations. The speaker had reached a point in the story where she had to introduce a bit of antique technology, at least in most U.S. cities—the electrically powered streetcar. Interrupting her story, she broke off an iconic gesture that illustrated the overhead wires on which the action of the cartoon was taking place and made the gesture shown in the second drawing. This second gesture depicted the streetcar pantograph and how it connects with the wire. The side-comment about the pantograph was clearly extranarrative in function and its content was expressed primarily in gesture form.

The resumption of the narration was accompanied by resumption of the network-of-wires gesture. This cohesive gesture coincided with the start of its clause and anticipated the linguistic indication of the cohesive link in the *these wires,* showing that the speaker's feeling of cohesiveness attached to the clause

the network of wires that hooks up the cable car | um you know the trolley (listener: oh a c–)

right and there's a whole network of there wires

Figure 7.6 Example of cohesive gestures utilizing form.

as a whole. The gesture indicates in a visible symbol to what clause in the past narration the referential linkage should be made (viz., where the image of criss-crossing wires was last invoked).

Space can be used to indicate referential cohesiveness as well. This is a spontaneous gesture usage that is similar to American Sign Language (discussed later in this chapter). The example of a cohesive gesture given in Chapter 4 included spatial cohesion, in that one action stream (holding the newspaper) was made to the left, whereas the other action stream (the person entering the room as seen in the mirror) was made to the right. Figure 7.7 demonstrates another instance of spatial cohesion. This diagram is a map of the speaker's gesture space as viewed from above. Successive gestures were performed in different sectors (both to the right of the midline) for verbal references to different characters in a narrative. The verbal references are indicated on the map in the order in which they occurred. References *(a)* and *(b)* are to a character named Alice; the accompanying gestures were made to the extreme right. Reference *(c)* was to an artist; the accompanying gesture was performed more to the front. Reference *(d)* was again to Alice and the accompanying gesture was once more to the far right. References *(e)* and *(f)* were again to the artist and the gestures returned to the

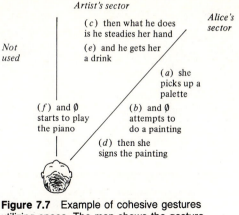

Figure 7.7 Example of cohesive gestures utilizing space. The map shows the gesture space as seen from above. The letters indicate the temporal order in which the clauses occurred. Each clause was accompanied by a gesture that the speaker performed in the sector of space shown on the map.

front. The speaker had established a reference space for each character and could link successive references to a given character by performing gestures in its particular space. The references *(a)–(d)* were all at the same physical locus in the film, and thus an iconic depiction of the film layout cannot explain the partitioning of the gesture space.

Cohesive gestures, like beats, show that gestures are parallel to speech at "off-propositional" levels as well as the propositional level. If gestures and linguistic processes have a common mental source where all functions—semantic, syntactic, and pragmatic—are mentally active at the same time and interact with imagistic thinking, these parallels would be produced.

Deictics

Deictic gestures were also discussed in Chapter 4. They function in many speech acts as part of the speaker's effort to structure the discourse. Pointing gestures appear at the beginnings of conversations and the start of new narrative episodes both when aimed at and when not aimed at physically existing targets (Marslen-Wilson et al., 1982; Levy, 1984). The speaker, wishing to set up a chain of coreferring forms, seems compelled to point at something. In this section I will discuss these gestures in relation to the idea that they are a form of iconic gesture. This idea can explain the occurrence of deictic gestures at the beginning of coreferential chains as well as the systematic shifting of the origo depending on speaker-viewpoint that was described in Chapter 4.

Figure 7.8 shows speakers A and B in the Amana conversation excerpt discussed in Chapter 4 pointing at, in a physical sense, "nothing." But this "nothing" is very much something. There is an abstract target of the gestures that

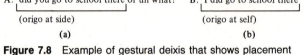

A: did you go to school there or uh what? B: I did go to school there

(origo at side) (origo at self)

(a) (b)

Figure 7.8 Example of gestural deixis that shows placement of origo to correspond with viewpoint of sentence *(a)* Other's viewpoint; *(b)* own viewpoint. (Repeated from Figure 4.3.)

corresponds to the deictic word *there,* namely, the gesture in *(b)* indicates a place off in the distance while that in *(a)* indicates a place near at hand. The actual physical locations that speakers A and B referred to were unrelated to the places pointed at (*there* was not defined in relation to the room where A and B were seated, but was a general milieu they were talking about, that is, a discourse specified *there;* it seems to have been Iowa to which A and B were evidently not physically pointing).

Hands (or other organs, including mechanical extensions like sticks) iconicially depict a line between the origo and the reference object. If the indicated object is abstract, like a new reference point for discourse, there is still a line connecting it to the origo. In the examples given in Figure 7.8, the origo of A's gesture (for which B's past history is the reference object) was off to the side, while the origo of B's gesture (which has the same reference object) was B's own locus. The lines connecting these origos with the target locus is what the pointing hand exhibits iconically.

To see the iconic aspect of pointing gestures we must take into account the speaker's sense of "empathy" (Kuno, 1976) that allows him or her to adopt different viewpoints toward reference objects. Deictic gestural reflection of empathy depends on there being an origo that can be abstracted away from the speaker's own physical locus. By shifting the origo away from the primary origo (the speaker's own locus), empathy for the viewpoint of another person can be registered through contrast with the primary origo. The two pointing gestures in Figure 7.8 demonstrate this kind of contrast. In *(a)* the speaker took the point of view of the addressee and moved the origo away from his own locus, whereas in *(b)* the speaker was adopting his own point of view and kept the origo at his own locus. This movement of the origo is understandable if the deictic gesture is regarded as a type of iconic gesture.

Regarded as an iconic gesture exhibiting a line between an adopted origo and an imaginary reference object, deictix are expected when the *relation* between the origo and reference object is the meaning the speaker is emphasizing. Thus there is a compulsion to produce deictic gestures at the beginnings of conversational or narrative episodes; it is there that this relationship is problematic. The speaker at such points is trying to establish or alter the relationship between the speaker, the listener, and the thematic reference point of the discourse.

That pointing gestures should be regarded as iconic can be traced to the development of deictic and iconic gestures by children. A number of studies of the gesture production of infants have described pointing gestures as occurring for the first time at the onset of intentional symbol use, usually thought to be between 9 and 14 months of age (see Bates et al., 1983, for a review). Pointing movements themselves occur much earlier (see Trevarthen, 1977, for examples). The earliest pointing movements that are symbolic gestures are used to indicate existing concrete reference objects. It is not known whether babies can understand pointing gestures with origos not at their own locus. Evidence suggests they cannot, but the data are not conclusive. Murphey and Messer (1977) tested the ability of children to follow adult pointing gestures that had targets in different relative positions. The different target positions also introduced a variation in origo. The data show that 9-month-old babies would follow pointing gestures more reliably the nearer the origo was to the child's own locus. This effect implies that the the baby understands an origo as his or her own locus. Gestures with origos not at this locus tend to be ignored. Murphey and Messer's method intentionally introduced another variable, however, which could have had a similar effect. The origo-different gestures pointed at targets that were on the opposite side of the baby's midline, creating a tracking problem for children of this age (Kaye, 1982). Thus the ability of babies to understand origos other than their own locus remains an open question.

These first *pointing* gestures may also be the first *iconic* gestures of children. That is, iconic reenactment and deictic indication may not be initially distinct. Pointing may be simultaneously the deictic indication of objects *and* the iconic display of acts of reaching, manipulation, and so forth. This hypothesis requires that the earliest pointing gestures should be, like iconix, related to object manipulation. Figure 7.9 shows a child at 6 months (on the left) and the same child at 12 months (from Lock, 1980, p. 59). In both drawings there is an effort to obtain or explore an object, but whereas the 6-month-old reaches, the 12-month-old points. The hypothesis is that the gesture on the right is not only a deictic

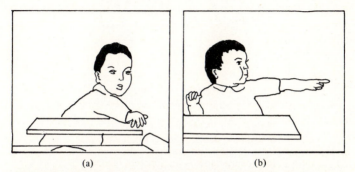

(a)   (b)

Figure 7.9 Development of deictic gesturing. *(a)* Child is 6 months old and reaches for a desired object. *(b)* At 12 months, the same child points at a desired object. The latter gesture is both deictic and iconic for the act of reaching. (From Lock, 1980, p. 59.)

indication of an object but also an iconic reenactment of the type of practical movement on the left that could be made with respect to the object. If pointing gestures and the first iconic gestures are not distinct, the type of children's iconix at 2 to 5 years of age, which also appear to be reenactment of actions (see the section on children's gestures below), could be traced back to the very start of the iconic gesture mode. How might iconicity and deixis become differentiated? After a heroic study of more than seven thousand pointing gestures, Lock et al. (1985) concluded that the development of true deictic pointing gestures arises out of the social interaction between baby and mother. Adults play a part in the baby's initial attempts at object exploration, and out of this interaction the concept of deixis emerges. This conclusion is compatible with the first deictix also being the first iconix. Under socialization the deictic-iconic gestural indication of the origo-object line becomes standardized and socially regulated into a fixed posture that performs as a deictic indicator. Outside this kind of socialization (with no special socialization) the movement is not regulated and remains free to reflect new understandings as children grow, and this is the path that becomes expressive and iconic. In this way, the path to deictix and the path to iconix reflect different histories of *socialization,* and this may help explain how it is that iconix are, in older children and adults, semiconscious movements subject to general cultural shaping but devoid of any specific system of social regulation. Deictix, while they may be used unwittingly (as the gestures in Fig. 7.8 seem to have been), are definitely regulated in form.

Metaphorics

The final category of gesture that occurs only during speech is the metaphoric gesture. These gestures exhibit images of abstract concepts. Metaphoric gestures

it was a Sylvester and Tweetie cartoon

(a)   (b)

Figure 7.10 Example of a conduit metaphoric gesture during a narration. *(a)* Synchronized with the deictic pronoun *it,* the gesture creates an apparent object and *(b),* synchronized with the predicate expansion *was a Sylvester and Tweetie cartoon,* breaks the object open.

are like iconic gestures in that they depict a meaning relevant to the concurrent linguistic meaning, but differ from iconics in that the meaning they exhibit is not itself picturable. These gestures exhibit, rather, a picturable vehicle of a metaphor for the abstract meaning. A number of examples of this type of gesture have already been given. The "Anansi" gesture of Chapter 5 was a metaphor for the abstract ideas of pursuit and inaccessibility. An example mentioned in Chapter 1 is pictured in Figure 7.10. This gesture-created object is a metaphoric vehicle (secondary subject) for the abstract concept of a cartoon (the primary subject). The metaphor in Figure 7.10 is one of the family of entity metaphors; that is, the cartoon is presented as an object that the speaker is holding before the hearer. Among the projected implications of the metaphor is that an abstract concept is a bounded object that can be supported in the hands. Metaphors in which abstract meanings are presented in this way are very widespread. Reddy (1979) was the first to identify these metaphors and he coined the term "conduit" to refer to them, a term also used by Lakoff and Johnson (1980). The conduit metaphor underlies the entification of the abstract that is prominent in SAE thinking (Whorf, 1956; A. Bloom, 1981) and that apparently is lacking from the habitual thought patterns of other cultures. For comparison, the reader should return to the Turkana substance-without-form gesture that was illustrated in Figure 6.2 on page 208. Absent from the Turkana gesture is the image of a bounded and manipulated object, so conspicuous in the American substance-with-form (conduit) gesture.

According to the conduit metaphor, language "objects" are containers, meaning is a substance ("content") that goes into the language-containers, and communication requires passing language-containers filled with substance back and forth along a conduit. There are familiar gestures that accompany each step of this metaphor:

> I want to ask a question.
> └─────────────────────┘
> (hand forms a cup)

This corresponds to the language-is-a-container metaphor. The open hand could be interpreted, alternatively, as extended to receive the answer. This is also an illustration of a conduit metaphoric gesture—in this case, the metaphor that the answer (meaning) is a substance. Another example showing the meaning-is-a-substance metaphor is:

> That book is packed with meaning.
>   └─────────────────────┘
>   (one hand pushes against the palm of the other)

The conduit portion of the conduit metaphor is presented in a gesture such as:

> I've got to tell you something.
> └────────────────────────────┘
> (palm-up hand moves toward hearer)

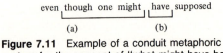

(a)   (b)

Figure 7.11 Example of a conduit metaphoric
gesture for the concept of "what might have been
but was not" (past subjunctive mood).

A virtuosic conduit gesture is shown in Figure 7.11, where the hands appear
to create an image for (no less than) the idea conveyed by the subjunctive past
tense. The cup shapes are metaphoric images of containers of meaning; the
spreading-out-of-the-hands images of the idea of possibility (cf. an "anything-
goes" gesture), whereas the sudden closure of the cup shapes an image of nonex-
istence. All of this exhibits the idea of a possibility that did not in fact obtain,
the essence of the subjunctive concept in English according to Curme (1931). This
interpretation is supported by the timing of the gesture. The hands closed just as
the speaker said the linguistic element *have* to start the coding of the subjunctive
itself. A final example is a movement very commonly seen when people say *I can't
believe it.* The two hands appear to pull something out of the speaker's head and
vigorously fling this substance onto the ground—the place where the incredible
goes (thanks to W. Eilfort for this example).

The production of metaphoric gestures was attributed to Zeno by Montaigne (1958) in the following passage, which suggests that conduit gestures have
been in existence for at least 2300 years (and certainly for the 400 years since
Montaingne wrote):*

Zeno pictured in a gesture his conception of this division of the faculties of the
soul: the hand spread and open was appearance; the hand half shut and the
fingers a little hooked, consent; the closed fist, comprehension; when with his
left hand he closed his fist still tighter, knowledge (Montaigne, 1958, p. 372).

The entification of abstract ideas also appears in the technical discussions
of mathematicians. Figure 7.12 shows gestures for the concept of a dual. In this
concept one relation is replaced by the converse relation; for example, if the

*I am grateful to J. Stern for bringing this wonderful passage to my attention.

and this gives a complete duality

Figure 7.12 Example of metaphoric gesture for the concept of a mathematical dual.

relation is "above," the dual is "below." The dual gestures are made with the hand alternating between two positions, the analogical equivalent of the dual concept.

Other gestures exhibit images for the concepts of limits, both inverse and direct. For references to direct limits the hand moves along a straight line (Figure 7.13), whereas for inverse limits it loops downward and back up (Figure 7.14). These gestures end in a tensed-stop, or "end-marking," which is a metaphor for the idea of a limit; the directness of the movement that comes to a tensed-stop corresponds to the idea of a direct limit and the looping or inverted movement to an inverse limit.

The concept of a quotient and the related concept of factoring were represented in gestures where a plane was created and a hand sliced through this plane. Figure 7.15 illustrates a quotient gesture. The concept of a mapping was associated with a gesture in which the hand carried out an upward loop (opposite to the inverse movement), as seen in Figure 7.16. A final example is the gesture for the concept of a relation that holds "over" a structure. This was translated into the spatial relation of one thing being over something else (Figure 7.17). The gesture depicts the locatum of the "over" relation, while the sentence refers to the location. The gesture in Figure 7.17 is thus another illustration of a compensatory relation between gesture and speech.

If metaphoric gestures are under direct mental control they could be a less transformed version of thinking than speech. They should thus be open to fewer sources of error. At one point in the mathematics discussion there was a speech error in which one of the speakers said *inverse* although *direct* was intended. (The other speaker caught the mistake and corrected it.) What was striking about this error is that the synchronized gesture was a *gesture* for a direct limit. The speech error evidently took place after the shared computational stage of gesture and speech. The entire example is shown in Figure 7.18. A similar phenomenon is seen in the gestures of aphasics, as described below.

is gonna be a ˌdirect limitˌ

Figure 7.13 Example
of a metaphoric gesture
for the concept of a
direct limit.

it'sˌan inverse limitˌ

Figure 7.14
Example of a
metaphoric
gesture for the
concept of an
inverse limit.

that means thatˌthe quotientˌ

Figure 7.15 Example of a
metaphoric gesture for the
concept of a quotient.

Homˌinto G_mˌ

Figure 7.16
Example of a
metaphoric
gesture for the
concept of
mapping one
function into
another.

ˌover this topological ringˌ

Figure 7.17 Example
of a metaphoric gesture
for the concept of
mathematically "over."

an inverse limit . . . of . . .   (listener) it's a direct limit
└─────────────────┘   └───────────────┘
   direct limit gesture   direct limit gesture

I mean a direct limit
└────────────┘
direct limit gesture

Figure 7.18   Speech error accompanied by a semantically correct gesture.

Even deictix can be metaphors. An entification of abstract ideas underlies the use of deictix for introducing reference points in narrations and conversations. To point at a space implies a concrete materialization of the theme. The gesture space functions, moreover, as a kind of metaphoric image of the common ground shared by the participants in the discourse. In Figure 7.8, speakers A and B were locating the concrete image of B's origins (the thematic reference point) in a space that represented, by its shared quality, their "common ground".

Emblematics

In contrast to the gestures that have been heretofore described, emblems (as they were called by Ekman and Friesen, 1969) are regulated by a social code. Emblems have a different relation to speech, often replacing speech (whereas iconics, metaphorics, beats, and deictics pointing at abstract objects occur only with speech), and have a nonpropositional function. Nonetheless, emblems are the gestures of popular imagination. When someone says the French or Italians are good gesturers, whereas the English or Scandinavians gesture very little, they probably have emblems in mind. (Casual observation confirms that U.K. and Scandinavian speakers produce idiosyncratic gestures in quantity.) An example of an emblem widely understood in America is the "OK" sign (the "ring"). This has the socially constituted meaning of being adequate for some function, is made in accord with socially regulated standards of performance, and can replace the word *okay* without gain or loss of meaning. In all these respects it differs from the spontaneous gestures described earlier.

Morris et al. (1979) tested the interpretation of 20 emblems by speakers in different European countries. Some emblems received quite different interpretations while others tended to be understood in the same way everywhere, and several were known only in one or two countries (and then with possibly different meanings). This kind of variation is expected with socially regulated gestures. A good example of the cultural conditioning of meaning is the "hand purse" gesture, which is made by placing the fingers and thumb together and pointing up. This has three major, completely unrelated meanings: query in Italy; good in Greece; and fear in France, Belgium, and Portugal. Note the potential for misunderstanding with this gesture and others, such as the "ring", which means "OK" in most places but threat in Tunisia.

Kendon (1983) has observed that the emblem can be shared with the same meaning over a wider geographical area than spoken language. An emblem also may remain more or less unchanged for thousands of years. Almost all emblems have been in use with unchanged meaning for at least 400 years. In a survey of gestures from South America, the United States, East Africa, southern Italy, France, and Iran, Kendon (1981) found that the most frequent function served is interpersonal control. These are emblems of greeting, command, request, insult, threat, and protection. A second less frequent class of functions is comments on the behavior of others (e.g., the cheek screw with the "crazy" interpretation). A third class is performatives—gestures whose execution accomplishes an act (e.g., curses). Emblems that have propositional content with respect to objects or actions are virtually nonexistent. Thus between the two kinds of gesture—socially-constituted and spontaneous—there is a sharp division of labor, and this is additional justification for treating emblematics separately from iconics, metaphorics, and so forth.

GESTURES OF CHILDREN

Bates et al. (1983) and others have observed deictic gestures in use by infants as young as 9 months. This gesture type is well established by 14 months. As suggested earlier, these first deictix may also be regarded as the first iconics, as the distinction between the two forms has not yet been clearly established.

Iconic gestures during narrations have been observed in children as young as 2½ years (McNeill, in press). This is the youngest age studied, but iconics for actions and objects are most likely present at younger ages; how they emerge out of the original iconic-deictic situation is unknown.

A broad description of children's linguistic development would show it passing through three overlapping stages: (1) an initial emphasis on denoting concrete objects and performing simple acts of possession and transfer. These are possible with very simple expressions, single words and simple combinations of words, provided there is a detailed context of speaking shared by the child and the others with whom it interacts, as invariably there is. This first stage typically occupies the first two years of life and part of the third. (2) Gains in flexibility achieved through the construction of grammatically organized word strings. These early sentences can express relations—spatial, temporal, causal, interpersonal, and so on—between objects and persons. This second stage occupies the third, fourth, and fifth years, approximately. (3) The emergence of text coding such as the appropriate use of anaphoric and other devices for indicating cohesiveness. This stage occupies the rest of primary language acquisition.

The earliest deictic-iconic gestures correspond to the first stage of this progression: they denote objects and are modeled on acts of possessing and transferring objects. The iconic gestures of very young children exhibit the same relational information that the simple sentences of this developmental stage are built upon, a fact that implies an ability to unpack imagistic thinking with syntactic thinking from the beginning of children's grammatical development (this point is discussed further in Chapter 8).

Werner and Kaplan (1963) described linguistic growth in terms of increasing "distance" between signifiers and signifieds. The production of gestures follows a developmental path parallel to this speech development. Young children act as if properties of the signifier must reproduce properties of the signified. In speech the lack of "distance" is shown by children's use of onomatopoeias. For instance, a French-speaking child coined a verb *boom-er* (with the French verbal suffix *-er*) for the meaning of something falling down. A German-spaking child came up with *whee-en* (with the German verbal suffix *-en)* for the meaning of going down a slide. The lack of distance in such examples of onomatopoeia also exists in children's iconic gestures.

In the iconic gestures of adults the same posture and movement of the hands can be correlated with new references. The hand postures can be the same, or very nearly so, and yet different meanings may be expressed. In these cases there are small extra movements that mark the separation of one gesture from the next (an example of this was given in Chapter 1: *and as he's coming up and the bowling ball's coming down* [right hand depicts Sylvester] — *he swallows it* [right hand depicts Sylvester's alimentary canal], where an extra movement occurred at the —).

The iconic gestures of young children are less flexible; the limits on new meanings are less wide. The child's hands tend to play only the part of the character's *hands.* If they have to play the part of something else, the child includes extra movements to exhibit the nonhand properties that differentiate the gesture from a hand. Children's gestures tend to be more detailed and less abstract than the corresponding gestures of adults. This shows the lesser distance that children can accept between the form of the gesture and the scene it exhibits.

Children's gestures tend to be *enactments.* The entire body and all of its relevant parts reproduce the movements of the character whose acts are being described. Body parts of the character tend to be played by the corresponding body parts of the child (if nonhands are played by the hands, movements are added to simulate the real thing); the gestures are large, like real actions, and the space of gesture movement, like the space of real actions, centers on the child. The examples in Figures 7.19 to 7.22 illustrate these qualities. Figure 7.19 shows a gesture made with the whole body that reenacts the posture of a character hiding inside a mailbox. Figure 7.20 shows the engagement of the child's hand, arm and leg to reenact the process of clambering. Figure 7.21 shows the gesture

⌊Sylvester the cat was hiding in the mailbox⌋

Figure 7.19 Example of a child's whole-body gesture.

⌊he climbed⌋ _⌊up_⌋ it _⌊from the outside_⌋

(1)   (2)   (3)

Figure 7.20 Example of child's multiple repetitive gestures utilizing different body parts.

space extended above the child's head. Figure 7.22 shows the gesture space centered on the child's own position. The reference to "there" in this example is a place in the cartoon, not a physical location in the room in which the child sat. It is the child's *reference* space that "wraps around" her in this way. The development of the more highly symbolic gestures of adults out of such enactments parallels the increasing distance that appears in the linguistic domain, in Werner and Kaplan's sense, between signifiers and signified.

The third stage of linguistic development, text coding, is accompanied by the first occurrence of beats. Although beats require little in the way of movement control, they are complex conceptually and do not occur in the gestures of young children. The cognitively and linguistically complex relations among sentences that beats code are absent until the third stage (Karmiloff-Smith, 1980; also see Chapter 4 of this book). The earliest beat we have seen was the example mentioned on page 222 *('execute' # it's something else),* which was produced by a 5-year-old.

th– this mail it's a whole bunch of boxes put together

Figure 7.21 Example of child's oversize gesture.

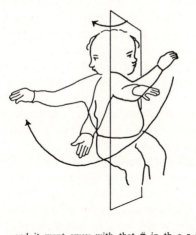

and it went away with that, # in th–e–r–e

(turns body to rear)

Figure 7.22 Example of child's gesture
space that includes the speaker.

Metaphoric gestures also appear for the first time in the third stage. The earliest examples are conduits, which can be seen by 5 or 6 years of age. Original metaphorics do not appear until later; the Anansi gesture (Chapter 5) was one of the earliest of these (the child was 9 years old). Like the development of other gesture types, the emergence of metaphoric gestures also parallels the development of the corresponding linguistic ability. Studies of children's ability to interpret metaphors shows this also to be a late development (Winner et al., 1976).

Children's iconic gestures show a peculiarity of gesture space that also

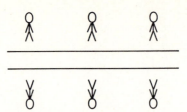

Figure 7.23 Local orientation of human figures.

appears in their drawings. This is the property of "local orientation" (Arnheim, 1969), in which the vertical and horizontal are defined with respect to local surfaces, not with respect to an external system of coordinates. In drawings with local orientation people standing on the opposite sides of a road can be placed as shown in Figure 7.23. Each row of people is standing upright with respect to its own side of the road (a local horizontal).

Local orientation reveals a form of spatial cognition (Piaget and Inhelder, 1967) that appears in the construction of children's gesture space as well. Rather than use a general system of coordinates (the walls of the room), the child creates temporary local coordinates and with these defines horizontal and vertical in the gesture space. Figures 7.24 and 7.25 contain two examples. In Figure 7.24 a 6-year-old child was describing a character pacing back and forth, and made a gesture in which her hand moved to the rear (this direction of movement, incidentally, also reveals a gesture space centered on the child herself). The aspect of the gesture that shows local orientation was the fact that as the hand moved to the rear it rotated so that the palm remained upright—as if the character were *on* the hand and in danger of falling off. To define the upright position required that the palm be upright. The resulting rotation is an awkward movement that in fact was omitted when the child repeated the gesture a moment later. The gesture in Figure 7.25 was made while a child was describing how to construct a teeter-totter and shows how to place a horizontal board over the fulcrum. This fulcrum was a crate that had already been described both verbally and gesturally. The gesture shows the board curving around the sides of the crate-fulcrum, the definition of "horizontal" being locally defined as the top and side surfaces of the crate.

GESTURES AND BRAIN FUNCTION

Studies by Kimura (1973a, b) suggest that the cerebral hemisphere that is dominant for linguistic production (typically the left hemisphere for right-handed people) also controls gesture production. However, this is true only for iconics and metaphorics (Stephens, 1983). Kimura found that while self-touching movements (nongestures) might be carried out with either the right or the left hand and might occur during nonspeech, gestures are made with the person's dominant hand in other manual performances and occur only during speech. Stephens found a similar preference for the dominant hand with iconic and metaphoric gesture production but not with beat production. Beats tend to be produced with

(n' then he was walking around y'know)
this way . . . and then this way

Figure 7.24 Example of local orientation in child's gesture space.

puts the board on top of it

Figure 7.25 Example of local orientation in child's gesture space.

either hand, and with some speakers even preferentially with the subordinate hand (McNeill and Levy, 1982). Hand preference is thus not an automatic consequence of the dominant hand being used more frequently in general.

Iconic gestures are also more complex as motor movements, and this could be the reason they are performed with the dominant hand (Kimura and Archibald, 1974). Beats, in contrast, because they are simple movements, could be controelld by either hemisphere. Stephens, however, found that motorically simple metaphoric gestures (conduits) were preferentially made by the dominant hand; this shows that the presence of content is a crucial factor in determining hand preference.

Aphasia is the linguistic impairment that follows damange to the speech areas of the dominant hemisphere. There are many types of aphasia, but the two classic categories are anterior (Broca's) and posterior (Wernicke's) aphasia. Broca's aphasia consists of an almost total loss of ability to construct word sequences, but retention of the ability to divide meaning complexes into meaning-ful segments. Such patients produce utterances that consist of single words, especially referring words—nouns, verbs, and adjectives. Wernicke's aphasia consists of a very serious loss of the ability to form semantic plans, but retention of the ability to produce word sequences. Their speech is often described as semanti-cally empty.

While gestures would seem to be a way of compensating for the linguistic losses of aphasia in fact these patients suffer a parallel loss of gesture ability (Cicone et al., 1979; Delis et al., 1979). Patients with Broca's aphasia make numerous iconic gestures that refer to objects and actions, comparable to their single words, but no beats or other gestures that depend on a sensitivity to the interrelations of linguistic segments. Patients with Wernicke's aphasia move a great deal while they speak but make make very few interpretable gestures of any kind. They do, however, make some movements when there are major semantic discontinuities in their speech (insofar as this can be judged). If these are beats in function (if not form) perhaps it is because such gestures are less dependent on the dominant hemisphere (Stephens, 1983).

A paraphasia is an unmotivated speech error produced by aphasics. An example is *and he went up through the pillow* for the cartoon scene where a character was seen climbing up inside a drainpipe (gestures by normal speakers for this scene appear in Figure 7.3). Gestures with paraphasias provide striking illustrations of the relative immunity of gestures to error (L. Pedelty, in prepara-tion); such gestures clearly exhibit the appropriate meaning. The gesture in Figure 7.26 accompanied the "pillow" paraphasia; it shows nothing like a pillow but appropriately indicates the pipe, its vertical position, and the relevance of its

and he went through the pillow

Figure 7.26 Example of semantically correct gesture accompanying paraphasic speech.

interior zone. The gesture points down unlike those produced by normal speakers describing the same scene in Figure 7.3, but still is semantically relevant.

AMERICAN SIGN LANGUAGE

American Sign Language refers to the system of manual communication used by the deaf of North America. American Sign language, or ASL, is not the same as finger spelling, nor is it the substitution of manual signs for English words. American Sign Language is a distinct linguistic system with its own structure, history, and community of users (henceforth I will write "speakers") that is learned as a native language by children. It seems comparable to spoken language in expressive power, having metaphoric (Marschark et al., 1986) and poetic resources (Klima and Bellugi, 1979). Part of the interest in ASL, as far as this chapter is concerned, is to compare ASL to spontaneous gesture production. This comparison makes it possible to observe the consequences of introducing socially constituted standards into a symbolic mode. It is not possible to make such observations with speech. Speakers do not produce evidence in the spoken mode comparable to spontaneous gestures—virtually everything spoken is socially regulated, and a socially unregulated set of spoken symbols with which to compare speech does not exist. To the socially constituted system of ASL signs and grammar, however, meaningful comparisons are possible with the spontaneous individually constituted gestures of hearing persons.

Klima and Bellugi (1979), Supalla (in press), and others who have studied the linguistic system of ASL have taken pains to compare this system to spoken language. However, a three-way comparison that includes spontaneous gestures is possible:

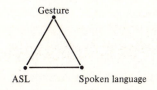

Something is to be learned from each of these comparisons, and all three are part of what must be grasped in order to understand fully the consequences of introducing socially constituted rules into symbolic modes of every kind. The ASL "gesture" leg, in particular, is important for seeing the effects of social control in a symbolic mode.

We may suppose that ASL operates in the same way spoken language does —as an unpacking of intrinsic values by pure linguistic values—and that intrinsic values arise from unitary undivided meanings. However, we cannot observe the intrinsic imagistic content of ASL sentences. This may seem paradoxical, but actually it is quite predictable. ASL symbols with contrastive (pure linguistic) value are themselves manual-visual. This fact preempts the manual-visual space in which gestures could occur. I am told (by D. Metlay, personal communication) that virtually every manual movement is systematic. Metlay informs me that deaf people produce gestures with facial expressions and (very interestingly) vocalizations; however, these seem to be mainly emotive. Such vocalizations and facial gestures might correspond to expressive intonation but not to iconic and metaphoric gestures in which the function is propositional.

Very Brief History

It is somewhat unclear just how ASL came into being. Frishberg (1975) believes that ASL is an evolved descendant from French Sign Language (FSL), which was brought to North America early in the nineteenth century. French Sign Language was in turn developed by Epée in the eighteenth century, who first introduced standard signs into the Parisian deaf community, based partly on spontaneous signs used by two deaf sisters and partly on spoken French; the result was an amalgamation that one could term "signed French" (Lane, 1980). If this is the history, then ASL would be related to FSL (which in turn is related to spoken French), and French and American deaf people retain to the present some degree of mutual intelligibility (Stokoe, 1972). In contrast, the sign language in use in Britain is quite unrelated to ASL (British and U.S. deaf communicate via their knowledge of a second language—written English). However, others have argued that modern ASL is the result of a creolization process; that is, the product of an initial contact between historically unrelated sign languages. One of these languages was FSL and the other (or others) were one or more native homegrown sign languages that had arisen in the United States before Gallaudet and Clerc brought FSL to this country in 1816 (Woodward, 1978). If ASL is a creole it is not a lineal descendant of FSL but a new language. Evidence in favor of the creolization hypothesis includes the very rapid divergence of ASL from FSL during the past 160 years. If creolization was the origin of ASL, rapid change was to be expected when the language took on its own form. The limited mutual intelligibility of French and American deaf people would be explained by the retention of occasional cognate signs, but would not imply that ASL is an evolved version of FSL. The history of FSL and ASL are both described in detail by Lane (1981), who also describes the alternating attitudes of the hearing world toward this and other sign languages (that they are languages in their own right vs. dialects of the local spoken language), attitudes that the deaf community has also, on occasion, internalized.

Structure of ASL

Modern analysis by a devoted group of linguists and psycholinguists, both hearing and (especially important) deaf, has established beyond reasonable doubt that ASL, whatever its history, is an independent language with its own structure. As already pointed out earlier in this chapter, ASL has the critical characteristics of all human linguistic systems. These characteristics are both the product and the instrument of social control by the community of ASL users: it has contrastive value, a morphology, and a phonology; it also has an elaborate syntactic system of linearization that is in many ways unique.

The main point I wish to make is that we see in ASL all the properties that in spoken languages exist in order for the community of users to establish and maintain standards of well-formedness. In these respects ASL stands in complete contrast to spontaneous gesture. American Sign Language signs contrast morphologically. The distinction mentioned earlier between "slow" and "very slow" (p. 214) is paralleled by the distinction between "fast" and "very fast": in both sets the intensified version is made more rapidly and energetically (this creates a more iconic sign for "very fast" as well as a less iconic sign for "very slow"). The linguistic value of these intensified combinations is the same: a syntagmatic combination of two morphemes (which happen to be performed at the same time).

As in spoken languages, sentences in ASL are constructed out of basic grammatical categories—Ns, Vs, and others—that appear in certain orders (Supalla, in press). Depending on the type of verb the order is SVO (subject-verb-object) or OSV. Verbs signed on the body and not articulated in space—for example, the verb for "like" (which is made by moving the hand away from the chest with the "mid-finger hand"; see Figure 7.27)—appear in SVO sequences. Verbs in OSV sequences are ones that include what Supalla calls "classifiers" of location in the verb itself. In addition to this classifier that is built into the verb, the location of the action is signed first and this creates an OSV sequence. Supalla gives the example, "the car crashes through the fence," which is signed in the following order: *fence move-through-fence* (the last all one sign, with "fence" appearing in the verb, performed by moving one hand past the "fence" hand, as a classifier). These exemplify some of the regular grammatical features of ASL sentences.

The hand in ASL is constrained to adopt particular shapes. Figure 7.27 (from Klima and Bellugi, 1979) shows a number of these identified in the notation introduced by Stokoe (1960, 1965). Hand shapes are comparable to the sound structure (phonology) of spoken languages. Combined with a certain movement and a certain place of articulation the basic hand shapes make words. Figure 7.28 shows four such words, all made with the same hand shape (the "mid-finger hand") moving in different ways and coming into contact with different articulating surfaces. The metathesis speech error demonstrated earlier in Figure 5.7 consisted of such phonological features exchanging places between words, and implies that when two signs try to fit into the same time-slot they break down into the features of hand shape, movement, and place of articulation.

These few examples should suggest that in ASL there are operations of segmentation and linearization. Signs and sentences are composed out of parts, and the resulting combinations have linguistic value in the same sense described for spoken language. Quite comparable observations have been made by Kendon (1980*a, b, c,*) for the manual sign language communication of the deaf of the Enga Province in the New Guinea Highlands.

The production and understanding of ASL and other manual sign languages we suppose proceeds according to an unpacking process that is basically the same as that utilized in spoken language. The medium should not make any difference for this process. In both ASL and speech a unitary undivided meaning, which in ASL as well as speech can be an image, contains the germ of a fully

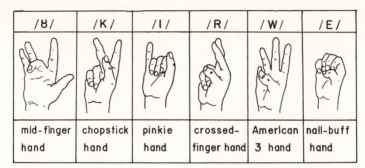

/8/	/K/	/I/	/R/	/W/	/E/
mid-finger hand	chopstick hand	pinkie hand	crossed-finger hand	American 3 hand	nail-buff hand

Figure 7.27 Different "phonological" categories in ASL. (From Klima and Bellugi, 1979, p. 46.)

Figure 7.28 Morphemic contrasts in ASL utilizing the same midfinger hand configuration. *Left*-to-*right,* these signs mean "taste," "smart," "touch," and "contact-each-other". (From Klima and Bellugi, 1979, p. 48.)

articulated linguistic structure and unpacks itself through the introduction of linguistic values. ASL does not appear to pose any qualitatively new problems for this process, although the absence of iconic and metaphoric gestures from ASL means that (an apparent paradox) we cannot directly observe the existence of imagistic thinking by ASL speakers, as I have already pointed out.

The introduction of social controls into the manual-visual modality has wide-ranging effects. Some of the consequences include contrastive paradigms, segmentation and linearization of meaning complexes, grammatical classes (Ns, Vs, etc.), morphological and phonological levels of structure, and others. All of these make possible the maintenance of social standards of well-formedness.

It is striking that many of the same linguistic properties are observed in the spontaneous manual communication systems worked out by young deaf children who are not taught ASL or any other socially constituted manual system (Goldin-Meadow, 1982). In order to communicate with their hearing parents these children work out a system of manual signs which the parents also adopt (thus there is a social unit that employs the language system). Their gestures come to have morphology and grammar. Moreover, segmentation and linearization, the most fundamental of linguistic properties, appeared within minutes in the gestures of R. Bloom's (1979) hearing adult subjects who were forced to tell a story to their listeners without speaking to them, and morphological combinations appeared just as quickly. It is striking that listeners, although not proscribed from speaking, also began to utilize this impromptu manual language (to ask questions, for example). Clearly, there was a nearly instantaneous effect on the gesture mode when it was transported from a private to a social plane. Among the social factors that might play a part in this sudden emergence of linguistic properties are the attention the participants pay to gestures when they are used as a deliberate communicative channel and the requirement that the same gestures must be recycled, without losing recognizability, for successive descriptive statements. These join the more psychological factor of the need to store and retrieve gestures as a force for standardization. The linguistic properties we find in ASL and every socially constituted linguistic system are evoked by these experiences, but the process by which this is accomplished is quite unclear at present.

COMPARISON TO GESTURES

Despite the profound effects of social control over the gesture modality, ASL shows similarities to the spontaneous gesture production of hearing persons. Describing some of these similarities will sharpen our perception of the differences. The following sections offer two illustrations.

Modulation of Actions

In ASL there is *aspectual marking* of verbs to show how an action is distributed in time and space—whether it goes to one recipient, to several, to all at once, to all in succession, and so forth (Klima and Bellugi, 1979). Figure 7.29 is taken from Klima and Bellugi's book and shows the ASL sign for "give." On the left is the citation, or dictionary form of the sign, and on the right this sign is modified to indicate the meaning of "he gave something to each of them"—what Klima and Bellugi call the "allocative determinate inflection."

Angiolillo-Bent (n.d.), in an unpublished paper, describes the performance

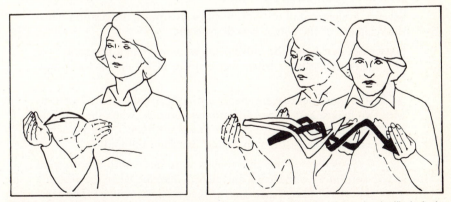

Figure 7.29 Aspectual modulation of "give" in ASL (the "allocative determinative"). *Left,* the basic sign; *right,* the aspectual modification. (From Klima and Bellugi, 1979, p. 286.)

Figure 7.30   Four different stages in the aspectual modulation of a gesture by a hearing subject, not familiar with ASL, using the sign for "give". The subject was conveying the meaning of "I give something to each of them" (allocative determinative).

of hearing persons who are taught such citation forms of ASL signs as "give" and then, without further instruction, are asked to produce in whatever manner they feel appropriate gestures utilizing this sign to express aspectual meanings. Figure 7.30 illustrates four stages of one of these gestures (recorded in a seminar at the University of Chicago). The spontaneously introduced modification of the basic sign by the hearing subject in several respects matches the inflectional modification of ASL. In other respects it differs. The most noticeable resemblances are the iteration or "bumpiness" of the hand movement, the use of two hands in unison, and the trajectory of the hand which proceeds right to left in front of the body (although, as described below, two-handed gestures were not produced for this aspect by the majority of Angiolillo-Bent's subjects). Two hands may have been an iconic depiction of plurality. The similarities clearly relate to the concept of giving something to multiple recipients—this explains both the direction of motion and the iterative quality of motion.

Angiolillo-Bent showed several other iconic features in the aspectual modulations of hearing subjects. Some of these are revealed in the following statistics:

Eighty-four percent of the movements were away from the gesturer when the meaning was of a first-person subject doing something to a second- or third-person recipient.

Seventy-five percent of the movements were toward the gesturer when the recipient of the action was first-person.

Sixty-eight percent of the movements were made in a horizontal arc in front of the gesturer when the recipient of the action was plural ("them").

All of the movements were made with a horizontal arc, 67 percent with two hands, and 79 percent *without iteration,* when the meaning was "apportionative" (e.g., *I give the group something*). The use of two hands enabled the gesturer to spread out from the midline.

Sixty-seven percent of the movements were made with a horizontal arc, 75 percent with one hand, and all *with iteration* when the meaning was "allocative" (e.g., *I give each of the group something*). The presence of iteration is connected to the idea of doing something individually to all the members of a group. The use of one hand seems to convey the idea of performing the action serially.

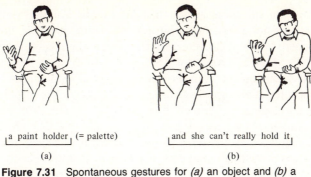

| a paint holder | (= palette) | and she can't really hold it |
            (a)   (b)

Figure 7.31 Spontaneous gestures for *(a)* an object and *(b)* a correlated action.

Actions and Objects

American Sign Language has a procedure for deriving Ns from Vs in which the noun-verb paradigmatic contrast is marked by a gesture-movement contrast. The noun is made with the same movement as the verb but is reduplicated and made more "tightly," taking up less space (Supalla and Newport, 1978). This occurrence of reduplication and smaller space in the nominal sign is probably the result of the sign for the object being performed with more muscular tension. The kinesthetic experience of confining the verbal sign in space to make the nominal sign is the primary contrast (E. Newport, personal communication). In spontaneous gesture production a similar process takes place in which gestures that depict actions and gestures that depict the objects utilized in actions are made in such a way that the object-gesture is performed with greater muscular tension. This tension manifests itself in the object-gesture being smaller and tighter than the action-gesture and in the action-gesture being made with more movement (whereas the object-gesture tends to be static). Figure 7.31 shows two sets of drawings of spontaneous gestures, the first of a speaker who was trying to remember the word *palette* and said *paint holder?* as a substitute, and the second of the same person immediately afterwards while he was saying *she can't really hold it.* The object-gesture is a reduced version of the action-gesture. The occurrence of movement in the action-gesture, even though the action being described is the "action" of not doing something, is an illustration of the classification of action of any kind as kinetic. This classification of action as kinetic is, in SAE, the cultural contrast to the notion of entification as a bounded substance (another observation due to Whorf). Thus the ASL properties introduced in the derived noun-sign to create the impression of constraint appear in spontaneous object-gestures that contrast with action-gestures, to create the same effect. There is a superficial difference between ASL and spontaneous gesture in that reduplication in ASL exists to induce the quality of an object conceived of as space with boundaries, whereas in spontaneous gesture it occurs as an iconic depiction of action. But underlying this difference in how reduplication performs as a symbol we can see the same SAE concepts of objects as bounded spaces and actions as unbounded kinesis.

There are, therefore, parallels between ASL sign production and naïve gesture production and these suggest that the choices of movement features in ASL signifiers are not completely arbitrary. The iconic parallels, however, provide the context in which to interpret the nonparallels between spontaneous gesture and the social institution of ASL.

The most fundamental of the nonparallels is that spontaneous gestures and socially constituted ASL signs have opposite relations to the diachronic axis of the internal development of speech. The fact that signs in ASL are used in a self-conscious manner by a cohesive social group and that they are under social control and regulated by the need to preserve effective social communication means that signs in ASL are segments of sentences that are socially constituted and possess full linguistic value as grammatical constructions. A fascinating question, the answer to which I have not a notion, is what is the form of inner speech for users of ASL. One supposes that for the deaf, as for the hearing, the initial stage of sentence production is dominated by imagistic thinking that utilizes inner speech symbols as cognitive tools. Are these tools representations of ASL signs, including hand shapes?*

The difference in the psycholinguistic significance of spontaneous gestures and ASL signs has an effect on the way ASL signs are produced, since they are subject to forces of social control to which gestures are not. Thus, in ASL we can find examples of reduced iconicity, such as the way "*very* slow" is conveyed through a more rapid performance. Semantic modification of spontaneous gestures always increases iconicity because the modification is under the direct control of the speaker's mental operations.

The differences between the socially constituted linguistic system of ASL and spontaneous gestures also affect the timing of signs. Like spoken words, signs are arranged syntagmatically in time. A given semantic unit requires several signs in succession. In contrast, gestures occur at the very beginning of their meaning units and there is only one gesture per unit.

In small isolated communities of signers something like a system halfway between spontaneous gesture and a full-fledged langue appears. This may also reflect the importance of social experience for the emergence of linguistic properties. There is, for example, departure from strict segmentation and linearization among signers on Providence Island (off the Caribbean coast of Colombia)—an island of small, scattered villages in which the deaf live in partial isolation from each other (Washabaugh, 1980). In these communities the deaf make successive signs but the signs are imperfect segments. The form and meaning of the signs are not constant but signs interact fluidly with each other in the same utterance —linearization, therefore, without fixed segmentation. Thus an intermediate linguistic situation exists under these conditions of partial isolation. The deaf of Providence Island are working out a common language. However, at this early stage they may remain closer to a communication process that is based on intrinsic value.

---

*I have observed deaf people moving their lips *and* their fingers when buried in thought during exams. These acts seemed simultaneous, but I could not tell whether English words and ASL signs were being produced, nor what meaning relations between signs and words there might be (e.g., the same meanings, complementary meanings, or something else).

chapter *8*

Action, Thought, and Language

At the beginning of this book we looked first at the contrast between intrinsic and socially constituted values and, second, at the statement that a quintessential psycholinguistic problem is the relation of individual linguistic thinking and action (contributing to intrinsic value) to the social institution of language (contributing to socially constituted value). This social institution is the permanent social and environmental context of all linguistic actions that is built into the system of langue itself. When a linguistic action meets the standards of performance laid down in this system it acquires recognizable "pure" linguistic value that makes the action interpretable to others. Thus linguistic action is social in a fundamental way. The individual's contribution is to carry out linguistic actions that have a natural basis in the speaker's thinking, purposes and goals, and consciousness, and a sense of cohesiveness with the context of speaking. All of these factors have been analyzed in this book. Now I want to return to the themes introduced at the beginning of the text to consider the relation between intrinsic value and socially constituted value in action, thought, and language.

I want in particular to consider the implications from gesture data that linguistic actions are performed with two qualitatively different forms of thinking at once. Why is imagistic thinking unpacked by syntactic thinking during linguistic actions? I offer four reasons which zero in on the necessity of imagistic thinking and its synthesis with syntactic thinking.

First, the deep time axis is an *essential* factor in the sentence, not a mechanical by-product of performance. It is only through change in time that the speaker realizes synchronic choices. This change implies a form of thinking different from syntactic thinking.

A second reason is that society cannot directly control imagistic thinking, but does control this type of thinking indirectly through linguistic categories and their linearization. Thus to have imagistic thinking that is intersubjective, a synthesis of syntactic and imagistic thinking is essential.

A third reason concerns the development of language in children. Imagistic thinking is a (perhaps *the*) predominant form of thought when initial language acquisition takes place. Children must learn, among other things, to unpack the imagistic mode of thinking that is available to them prelinguistically by means of the syntactic mode. Because of this learning, imagistic thinking remains locked in as an integral part of the linguistic process. One might say that for adult speakers the syntactic thinking of inner speech *creates* a need for imagistic thinking. This creation of imagery is revealed most clearly in metaphor. As described in this book, a cognitive function of metaphor is to generate images of abstract, otherwise nonimageable concepts with which syntactic thinking can synthesize.

A fourth and surely ultimate reason for a synthesis of two forms of thinking during speech is that there is an innate capability, evolved in our species, for a new form of thinking. In this new form of thinking there is the ability to subdivide and linearize images without losing sight of the global whole; that is, to create and maintain a *synthesis* of global and syntactic categorical thinking. This capability is essential to our capacity for culture and for forming social institutions. Without this ability there could be no culturally conditioned learning. It could therefore have been selected along with the emergence of a cultural form of life.

In this chapter I will discuss these explanations of the synthesis of imagistic and syntactic thinking. At the end of the chapter I will comment on the relation between linguistic action and a theory of consciousness formulated by Johnson-Laird (1983) in order to show, for the problem of consciousness, the importance of including the relation between individual linguistic action and the social context.

WHY A SYNTHESIS?

Time Is Essential

Linguistic value depends on contrasts, or choices. A basic concept of a linguistic description is that all alternatives are simultaneously present; this is the primary concept of synchronic description. To see the contrasts of a symbol all the other symbols that contrast with it must be taken into view at the same time. This idea extends to complex symbols and underlies the notion of a transformation. As a model of linguistic actions, however, a synchronic conception leads to rather absurd results. Taken directly as a model it is necessary to assume that the speaker/hearer carries out not one but an indefinite number of linguistic actions —one for each different contrast. *It was a Sylvester and Tweetie cartoon,* for example, embodies the choice of the subject pronoun *it,* rather than *that,* which in a purely synchronic model must be assumed to have been an active part of the sentence generation process that came up just to be rejected—giving value to *it.*

Similarly, *he keeps getting electric shocks* embodies the choice of a passive sentence structure; but to give value to the passive an active sentence must also be assumed to have been part of the process. It would have come up only to be rejected.

The implication that there are shadow words and sentences running alongside the person's linguistic choices is required by a purely synchronic model, since otherwise it cannot generate linguistic value. The addition of a diachronic axis avoids absurd consequences of this kind.

One illustration of a diachronic axis in the speech process was described previously in cohort theory. In this theory the recognized word is the survivor of a winnowing process in which the word's contrasts have been sequentially rejected. The recognition of the word produces contrastive value arising from what the word was not. The process necessarily extends in time. In cohort theory the deep diachronic axis of the process and the surface axis of speaking time coincide, but these are distinct axes. The addition of a diachronic axis allows the process to unfold as a kind of action in which linguistic value is developed over time.

A similar line of thinking justifies the addition of a diachronic axis to other linguistic processes, in particular to sentence generation/understanding. The diachronic axis of the sentence is the sentence changing from being predominantly imagistic to being predominantly syntactic and can be conceptualized as linguistic choices guided by the image with which the choices are attempting to synthesize. In the Anansi example we saw this taking place in detail. From the initial self-activation of *and they wanted* plus the image of two unclosing objects, the diachronic path went to *get* and to *where Anansi was.* Each choice produced a change; this was the merger of the synchronic and diachronic axes that occurs on the microgenetic time-scale of sentence production and understanding.

This diachronic dimension of the sentence entails a qualitatively different kind of thinking than the syntactic thinking embodied in the linguistic contrasts. The diachronic path first led to *get* for two reasons: (1) *wanted* opened up a syntactic context for *get,* and (2) *wanted* plus *get* together unpacked the image of two unclosing objects. This shows the roles played by both syntactic and nonsyntactic thinking.

Society Controls Only Overt Actions

Individual thinking is free to be imagistic, but such thinking cannot be directly socially regulated. There is no way for social others to know when images occur or what form they take. Yet society has an interest in the imagistic thinking of individuals. It is this kind of thinking, particularly when it involves metaphoric imagery, from which habitual and predictable aspects of individual mental actions derive. By forcing imagistic thinking to synthesize with socially constituted syntactic thinking, imagistic thinking is made intersubjective; it is seen by others as definitely present and taking the right form. Gestures exhibit imagistic thinking directly but escape social regulation. In fact, the regulation is already achieved through synthesized imagistic thinking and syntactic thinking. This principle is recognized in the law, where overt acts are codified and regulated, but influence over conscience and morality are actually at stake. The social institution of language is similar. Through a network of linguistic values society controls the surface aspects of linguistic acts. The Whorfian hypothesis expresses this concept in a grand manner. The world view built into linguistic acts can affect imagistic thinking if images synthesize with syntactic thinking. Images of substance-with-form meet the embodied world view of English grammar in a synthesis with syntactic thinking.

Utilizing gesture evidence, the imagistic thinking that is part of the linguistic action is seen to be visual-kinesthetic and (in our culture) oriented toward the manipulation of objects. It can be demonstrated that these images are not directly regulated by social controls by a comparison of the regulated form of manual signs in ASL to the unregulated form of spontaneous gestures. Unlike ASL, spontaneous gestures have no linguistic structure of their own that would imply social standards of form. There are no gesture roots with fixed meanings that combine with other morphemes to form complex gestures whose meanings are a function of the combination. Again unlike ASL, there are no movement features (corresponding to phonemes) that have been set up as standardized ways of forming gesture signifiers. Morphemes and phonemes are necessary means for the social regulation of linguistic systems. They provide *limited* and *anticipatable* variations in linguistic form. These are the kinds of variation that can be regulated by social consensus. The absence of limited and anticipatable categories from spontaneous gestures suggests a lack of direct social regulation of both the gestures themselves and the images they exhibit. This kind of thinking remains noncompositional, global, and synthetic and is controlled only through its synthesis with socially constituted syntactic thinking.

Children Learn to Unpack Imagistic Representations

The primary mode of thinking in young children at the onset of language appears to be global and imagistic (Piaget, 1954; Werner, 1961). The cognitive operations at this stage are in terms of thought-entities and thought-actions (to use terms from Haskell, 1985). Sensory-motor and global-synthetic thought is the earliest manifestation of the form of thinking that is also part of the linguistic actions of adult and older child speakers.

Unpacking these images into word and morpheme segments and simple linearizations of words are the first steps of language learning at ages 1 to 2 years. Children at this age are learning how to think syntactically. Their learning *presupposes* sensory-motor images: the synthesis of syntactic thinking with children's primary modus operandi of sensory-motor images is the step taken with the first one-, two-, and three-word unpackings. The implication of this observation is that, with older children and adults, the utilization of inner speech creates a need for imagistic sensory-motor thinking. Syntactic thinking requires not only a socially constituted linguistic code but *also* imagistic thinking. Children's language will be discussed further in a later section.

Innate Capability to Perform the Synthesis

There is a form of thinking that is qualitatively different from both thinking carried out in terms of images and thinking in terms of syntactic structures alone: thinking that consists of a synthesis in which images are subdivided and linearized without losing sight of the global whole. We realize intuitively that the syntactic thought is the same as the global whole but subdivided and linearized (see the discussion of the Anansi example in Chapter 5). Thinking in language is not simply subdividing into segments—this replaces a global whole, but does not synthesize with it. Imagistic thinking is an essential component of syntactic thinking. Thinking that synthesizes imagistic and syntactic thought is comparable in its unconscious nature to our ability to perceive three dimensions in space. It seems automatic, unavoidable, and unlearned. Indeed, the entire phenomenon of language as a socially constituted system depends on this ability, but does not teach it. The synthesis of global and syntactic thinking that we observe in each act of speaking draws on this new form of thinking; and this synthesis appears in the earliest stages of linguistic development.

Many organisms are probably capable of remembering and thinking in terms of images (Griffin, 1976). There are also examples that suggest that animals other than humans are capable of segmenting images (Griffin, 1984). For example, adult female vervet monkeys in East Africa normally respond to screams of juveniles by looking in the direction of the sound. If, however, the ethologist arranges to play a tape recording of a particular juvenile's scream when the juvenile is out of sight and away from its mother, adult females respond by looking not at the loudspeaker but at the juvenile's *mother*. The screams might globally be associated with danger, but the vervet females extract the segment of this complex that connects specifically to an individual mother.

The ability of apes to produce and understand symbolic references is demonstrated convincingly by chimpanzees and gorillas instructed on natural and artificial linguistic systems (Premack, 1976; Patterson, 1978). The chimpanzee named Washoe, for example, first learned to use the ASL sign *open* for doors, but later used it for boxes, drawers, briefcases, books, and so on (Gardner and Gardner, 1971). The chimpanzee named Austin was able to request from another chimpanzee a tool needed to obtain food by means of a symbol presented on a computer keyboard (Savage-Rumbaugh et al., 1978); the symbol evidently referred to something other than the key itself.

However, experiments in which chimpanzees have been taught to use ASL signs show that thinking with two simultaneous forms of representation, if it exists at all, is developed to a rudimentary degree in these animals and may be lacking altogether. Crucial observations appear in an extensively reported chimpanzee-language investigation (Terrace, 1979).

The chimpanzee described by Terrace, named Nim Chimpsky, in the hope of parallel achievements, was assiduously taught ASL for a number of years. Success comparable to that achieved by Washoe was evident in the areas of language development having to do with vocabulary and the ability to produce sequences of signs. These successes demonstrate a symbolic capacity in chimpanzees and an ability to divide events into meaningful segments. These are the first steps toward syntactic thinking. However, the chimpanzee's development of a form of thinking that consisted of the synthesis of imagistic and syntactic thinking can be seriously doubted. Human children, in contrast, spontaneously adopt this mode of thinking without teaching. Goldin-Meadow (1982) observed fundamental properties of spoken languages in the invented signs of deaf children not exposed to ASL. These children, not instructed in sign, organize their own signs into contrastive sets and convey complex meanings compositionally in linear sign-combinations that interrelate propositions.

Many observers have noted that when ASL-trained chimpanzees and gorillas produce multiple-sign sequences the extra length is accompanied by a large amount of repetition of signs. For example, Nim produced these combinations (Terrace, 1979, pp. 212–213):

Play me (= play with me)

Play me Nim

Play me Nim play

The two-sign combination could be the unpacking of a global image; this interpretation is not implausible on the surface. The redundant three- and four-sign combinations, however, suggest that in producing these longer sequences Nim was not synthesizing a global image of "playing" with linear and segmented versions of the same image. The additional words do not unpack the image into a larger number of parts, and if we force ourselves to interpret the long sequences as wholes we cannot see how they unpack an image of any kind. Nim's long sequences are utterly unlike the long sequences of deaf children. What the long sequences look very much like, in fact, are words separately evoked by the image of playing, but not by syntactic thinking about playing synthesized with this image.

The longest utterance that Nim was observed to make (16 signs) consisted of repeated segmentations of the same image: *give orange me give eat orange me eat orange give me eat orange give me you* (Terrace, 1979, p. 210). In contrast, as the utterances of deaf children not exposed to ASL expand, the utterance extracts different information. Here is an example from one of these children (named David) recorded under circumstances more or less comparable to Nim's: *Lisa* [+ *head shake*] *eat David* [+ *head nod*] *eat;* that is, "Lisa will not eat, David will eat" (Goldin-Meadow, 1982, p. 59). We see in this example syntactic thinking, including syntagmatic combinations and interrelation of propositions.

Terrace doubts that even the words in Nim's two-sign sequences were related to one another. Nim (and also Washoe) had preferences for performing signs in certain orders. For instance, *more* + *X* and Verb + *X* were more common than their opposite orders. However, these sequences were restricted to a few specific words; as "ways of thinking" they would be exceedingly narrow. Furthermore, careful examination of videotaped recordings of Nim's sign production showed that a large proportion of Nim's signs were copies of signs that his human trainers had just previously performed. A preference for, say, *give* + *X* could thus reflect a tendency to produce *give* and one of the signs the teacher had just produced, not syntactic thinking synthesized with an image. Lieberman (1984) has pointed out, however, that chimpanzees other than Nim produce signs when the possibility of imitation has been excluded. Washoe, for instance, made signs to herself, and other chimpanzees have made signs to humans who do not know ASL. Whether these unimitated signs were parts of sign sequences is not clear, however.

For our purposes a more significant discovery is that the average length of Nim's multiple-sign sequences was unchanged over a 12-month period in which his total vocabulary size increased significantly. In contrast, children, as their vocabularies expand, exhibit orderly increases in utterance length. As they learn to think syntactically they also are able to unpack more and more complex details of thinking. The unchanging length of multiple-sign sequences on Nim's part, on the other hand, suggests that he was not able to use word sequences as tools for thinking.

Griffin (1976) raises a revolutionary question: What do animals think about, and what is the form of their thought? We can probably conclude that it does not include the new form of thinking evolved by our species in which we think in terms of segments while synthesizing these segments with a global whole. If this form of thinking is present in chimpanzees and other animal species it is very rudimentary. Griffin gives arguments that behavior and mental experiences, like morphological and physiological attributes, are acted upon by natural selection. Mental images confer adaptive advantages for animals that are capable of thinking in terms of them. The further step of thinking in terms of images that are synthesized with linearly arranged segments of the image—a syntax—could also confer adaptive advantages for animals that think in this way. A highly significant advantage of this new form of thinking is that it creates, not a narrow linguistic capacity, but a form of thinking that is necessary for culture and a mechanism for the brain's storage of cultural information. It is true that language itself must have played a crucial part in the emergence of cultural existence, but apart from this contribution due to language as such, the mental abilities that underly syntactic thinking seem similar to those required of cultural existence in general. Division into segments and the linear recombination of segments is the key to the social regulation of all cultural practices, not only language. It is this syntactic mode of thinking that makes possible predictability and requires acceptance. The capacity for culture and for syntactic thinking may thus have developed together in our species. Here we can apply Whorf's insights into linguistic determinism. By embodying a culture's theory of the world in language, the categories of culture combine with those of language and it becomes possible to utilize syntactic thinking and language directly on cultural thinking.

OTHER PHENOMENA OF CHILDREN'S LANGUAGE

If children are learning to unpack imagistic thinking with syntactic thinking, some other phenomena of children's language also fall into place. I would like to mention a few of these.

Lack of Coordination in Syntactic Thinking

The following examples all seem to reveal a lack of coordination between different syntactic elements that are used to break up unitary undivided meanings (Bowerman, 1985, 1986):

> to smoothen (= to smooth)
>
> to unopen (= open)
>
> to untake off (= to take off)
>
> feets, ated
>
> make die (= kill)
>
> make my shoe come on my foot (= put my shoe on . . .)

The child who said *unopen,* for example, double coded the image of something closed that she wanted to be open. Each component, *un* and *open,* segments the desired undoing but there is insufficient coordination. The other examples reveal the same sort of poor coordination. *To smoothen* was unable to suppress the *-en* that is used to unpack ideas involving causation. *To untake off,* like *to unopen,* unpacks an idea with two segments that perform the same job and are used without proper coordination. What the child appeared to have done was apply *take off* for the idea of getting rid of something and to apply *un-* for the same idea; these were independent moves of thought that combined in speech. *Feets* and *ated* are similar with respect to ideas involving plurality and past tense. The two periphrastic examples, *make die* for "kill" and *make come on* for "put on" are straightforward illustrations of unpacking with syntactic thinking; the child did not take into account or did not know the verbs that are in quotes.

Different Imagistic and Syntactic Thinking

If children are developing two forms of thinking, imagistic and syntactic, then the possibility of representing reality in different and perhaps inconsistent ways is inherent in this situation. Church and Goldin-Meadow (1986) have found that children performing conservation tasks (e.g., Piaget, 1965) can display, in gestures, different forms of understanding from what is apparent in their verbal explanations. More often than not, the level exhibited in the gesture is higher. A disparity in favor of gesture was found to be particularly likely with children whose insight into conservation is changing. For example, a child might deem two sticks the same length after one of them has been rotated 90 degrees but may inadequately explain this verbally. Yet, at the same time, the child's gesture might present the information for an adequate explanation based on identity. Thus, a child might explain, inappropriately, "that [the transformed] stick is going down and the other [the untransformed stick] is going across" but point carefully at the two ends of the vertical stick and then do the same on the ends of the horizontal stick (i.e., indicating the identical length of both sticks).

What appears to underlie this very interesting discovery is an inadequate coordination of two forms, imagistic and syntactic, in which the conservation experiment could be thought about. Children must master this coordination in order to unpack their grasp of equivalence into a socially constituted explanation of the equivalence relation and meet the criterion of verbally stated conservation reasoning. The absence, seen by Church and Goldin-Meadow, of coordinated imagistic and syntactic thinking is explicable in terms of unpacking: children have developed an intuitive imagistic comprehension of the equivalence relation and have partial understanding of this relation in a linear-segmented syntactic mode, but still have to work out how to unpack the one form of reasoning by reasoning that takes place in the other form and achieve a synthesis of the two forms of thinking. True understanding of conservation would seems to consist of reasoning in both forms and achieving this synthesis.

Alternative Syntactic Thinking

In McNeill (1975) I linked the primitive form of thinking that I presumed to be part of every linguistic action to the performance of object-oriented motor movements. These movements were taken to be a source of sensory-motor schemas, the organizing structures of children's thinking when language development begins (Piaget, 1954). I sought parallels between how young children constructed object-oriented motor movements and how they constructed their first sentences. For example, placing an object in a location is necessarily carried out such that reaching the location is the last thing that happens. If the movement sequence of placing an object in a location is a model for sentence organization, children's sentences would be expected to follow a corresponding word order sequence— action-location or entity-location. This in fact is the preferred order in the speech of some children in describing dynamic situations. The following examples and others from Bowerman (1973) are all in the entity-location order:

> Kendall bed (= is in the bed)
> Kendall water
> Lotion tummy
> Towel bed

On the other hand, when the entity is not something that can be moved, there appears to be no word order preference: *ear outside* and *mess here* (from the same child) are in the entity-location order, whereas *there cow* and *here mess* are in the location-entity order. These parallels of movement sequences with word order sequences support the idea that movement sequences are models for the construction of sentences by young children, and when there is no movement order inherent in reaching the location, sentences are constructed in word orders that vary.

What this interpretation lacks, however, is the following. First, there is no appreciation that syntactic structure is a form of thinking in its own right that must interact with global-synthetic forms of thinking. Hunting for parallels implies that there is just one form of thinking—sensory-motor—which is revealed in the word order sequence. The idea of semiotic extension (McNeill, 1975, 1979) thus remained linear with no room for dialectic synthesis. Second, it also lacks a natural way of introducing the concept of inner speech, which has been the key to explaining the unpacking of imagistic thinking and synthesis with syntax. Third, it has a much too restricted view of the imagistic aspects of thinking, limiting images to motor sequences. A way to overcome all of these problems has been one of the results of this book.

Slobin (1982) pointed out what appears to be a very precocious development of semantic case relations by children whose initial language is Turkish. He found that Turkish children master these cases by age 2. The systematic use of case endings releases Turkish sentences from any specific linear word order as the means of unpacking relations between verbs, agents, and patients. Thus *the squirrel scratches the dog* versus *the dog scratches the squirrel* in Turkish could come out with the same word order, since the nouns have distinctive endings. (Word order in Turkish is used for emphasis and pragmatic coding.) Evidently word-endings of the systematic and transparent type used in Turkish are more salient than word order sequences for synthesis with imagistic thinking.*

The interpretation that I would now make of these results is that both English word-order and Turkish word-endings are examples of (different) socially constituted syntactic thinking patterns. Children must learn how to synthesize imagistic thinking with whatever syntactic thinking their language provides. Thus English-speaking children utilize motor actions as models of the organization of sentences (such as object-location), because in their language linear word order is a major part of the syntactic thought pattern they are learning to utilize for thinking. Turkish-speaking children on the other hand would not utilize these kinds of models since in their language the syntactic thinking that focuses on the relations between verbs, agents, and patients is segmental rather than linear.

MISCLASSIFICATIONS OF "SMART" SYMBOLS

Children do not necessarily learn immediately what "smart" symbols their language provides. A child may initially try to use symbols that are treated as "dumb" in place of "smart" self-activating symbols. There is, in fact, some gesture evidence of nouns performing as inner speech symbols with children as old as 5 years of age. From adults the comparable gesture evidence invariably points to verbs and prepositions as inner speech symbols. Utilizing the methodological assumption that has previously guided us, that the gesture on the surface synchronizes with the word or phrase that was the inner speech symbol, we can compare children's and adults' inner speech symbols. Examining a phenomenon I termed the occurrence of "holophrastic" words in the context of grammatical

---

*However, not every form of inflectional morphology is more salient: Serbo-Croatian inflections posed great difficulties for children learning that language, as found in another study reported by Slobin (1982). In Serbo-Croatian the inflection that appears for a given semantic relation is not constant. The form changes depending on the gender, number, and animacy of the root word, rather than occurring as a constant predictable addition to the word—which is the method of Turkish.

clauses (McNeill, 1985*b*), I noticed that, for children 5 and 6 years old, gestures that exhibit entire events can synchronize with single nouns and noun phrases. These are not gestures for the noun alone, but for the event described by the clause containing the noun. Yet the gesture exhibiting the event synchronizes with the single noun. We should conclude, following our assumption, that the noun was the child's inner speech symbol. The following is an example from a 6-year-old:

> Granny # called up this man.
> |⎽⎽⎽⎽⎽|
> (right index finger points at ear as hand moves in circle)

The speaker shows in somewhat stylized manner a dialing motion and points to his ear—clearly the meaning conveyed in the clause as a whole. We infer that the proper noun *Granny* was the cognitive tool with which the global meaning of "calling" was unpacked (not the verb *called up*). The use of a cohesive referring form *(this)* with *man* suggests that, of the two references, the reference to the man was not the psychologically new element, and that Granny and the act of telephoning were more focal at the moment. In contrast, all such "holophrastic" examples from adults suggest that inner speech symbols are verbs or prepositions. Here are some examples (the first from Chapter 7):

> He tries going up inside the drainpipe.
> |⎯⎯⎯⎯⎯⎯⎯⎯⎯⎯⎯|
> (hand rises and points upward)

In this example, the inner speech symbol appears to have been a preposition or prepositional phrase. In the next example it was a verb synchronized with an image of thinking about a range of questions (McNeill, 1985*b*):

> Think about a whole range of questions.
> |⎯⎯⎯⎯⎯⎯|
> (hand moves in large arc)

In learning to unpack imagistic thinking children may therefore initially develop inappropriate "smart" symbols, nouns in particular, that will have to be reclassified and demoted to "dumb" status. This is the equivalent of learning a different form of categorization of conceptual environments, shifting from initial classifications in terms of object references to later classifications in terms of relations and actions of various types. The latter are clearly superior in terms of their ability to select further linguistic symbols, the other direction in which "smart" symbols must be context-sensitive.

Although there is evidence that young children can classify objects on the basis of similarities and contrasts (thus placing people and babies into the same group; see Huttenlocher and Smiley, 1985, for evidence and discussion), early demonstrations by Inhelder and Piaget (1964) showed that children as old as 4 to 5 years would form groups of objects that were dissimilar but were functionally and spatially related (e.g., babies grouped with a crib rather than with nonbaby people). Children's free word associations likewise display a preponderance of noun–verb and noun–adjective associations (called, for obvious reasons, "syntagmatic") up to age 6 or so, and thereafter only gradually shift to a predominance of "paradigmatic" associations (noun–noun) (the predominant type for adults). These indications of nouns performing some "smart" and other relational functions suggest that, for children prior to school age, nouns have the "smart" symbol power of codifying thinking.

LINGUISTIC CONSCIOUSNESS

Philip Johnson-Laird concludes his book *Mental Models* (1983) with a chapter on consciousness. I can think of no better way to end this book than on the same note and relate the concept of a linguistic action to Johnson-Laird's discussion of consciousness.*

Johnson-Laird considers the problem of consciousness in artifacts within the following hierarchy:

1. "Cartesian machines" that do not employ symbols and lack awareness.
2. "Craikian machines" (after K. Craik, 1943) that construct models and are aware of the world in the way "babies and other animals are aware." The models (not necessarily verbal) are mental representations of reality but the machine lacks self-awareness.
3. Self-reflective machines that construct models of reality and can embed models within models, so that they can model their own mental operations. The concept of an autopoietic machine—that is, one capable of self-generation and self-maintenance—is similar (Chapter 5); and indeed many have concluded that a necessary component of consciousness is self-awareness (for example, the chapters in Oakley, 1985). Self-aware machines are able to act and communicate intentionally rather than merely as if they were acting intentionally (of which Craikian machines are capable). This is because they can create a model of a future reality and a model of themselves deciding that this reality should come into being. Self-aware artifacts might be said to have some of the qualities of "consciousness" in an adult human sense (at least, their qualitites of intentionality and self-awareness are among those necessary for adult human consciousness).

A linguistic action *creates* self-aware consciousness. Linguistic actions do not have self-awareness as a condition, but instead are a source of self-awareness. Built into inner speech is a process of self-knowledge. Inner speech is an instrument of the person's awareness of his or her own mental operations. Unlike an artifact at level three of Johnson-Laird's hierarchy, however, which would seem to be able to construct models of any arbitrary kind, the models constructed by human minds are fundamentally social. Self-activating "smart" inner speech symbols imply the presence of an "other." The symbols of inner speech can be

---

*However, I am not participating in Johnson-Laird's insistence on "effective procedures" as a rite of passage for concepts; this doctrine inhibits thinking and is all too easy for an author to use against concepts that for one reason or another he or she dislikes.

viewed either actively, in which case the "other" appears as the addressee, or passively, in which case the "other" speaks to us. In both cases there is the utilization of inner speech to form a social model of our own mental operations as involving more than one person. The self-referring quality of consciousness produced by inner speech appears to us on a social plane. *We become linguistically conscious by mentally simulating social experience.* Human consciousness is so-cial, a property which appears even in monologic thinking. Even though the addressee and addresser are identical, we simulate an "other" through inner speech. The apparent inescapability of the "other" is explained by the argument that thinking utilizes inner speech. This form of human consciousness would thus seem to be more specialized and more narrowly adapted than the consciousness envisioned for artifacts.

The conception of consciousness as fundamentally social was an aspect of George Herbert Mead's profound theory of the self. Significant symbols implicitly arouse in the person who makes them the same response that they explicitly arouse in others (Mead, 1974, p. 47). Self-awareness is due to the person's ability to take the attitudes of these others into his or her own mental life (p. 175)—"the organization of the social act has been imported into the organism and becomes then the mind of the individual" (p. 178). What language in particular accom-plishes is to make inevitable this transferral of the external social act into the internal conduct of the individual. We experience the external social act in the form of inner speech symbols addressed either to the "other" or addressed to us by the "other." (Vygotsky's theory of consciousness also emphasized this social character.)

In his writings Mead draws a well-known distinction between the "I" and the "me" aspects of the self. The "me" is the self of which we are most aware. The "I" is the self that we are uncertain about. It is the "I" that reacts, and its reaction is always slightly unpredictable, since it reaches out to the future from the present. In viewing inner speech actively, it is the "I," the unpredictable element, that addresses the inner speech symbol to the known "me"; whereas when viewing it passively, it is the stable "me" that addresses inner speech to the "I." This distinction accounts for the feeling of uncertainty that prevails when inner speech is regarded actively, compared to the more certain feeling of being dictated to, when it is regarded passively. Whether these opposite feelings corre-spond to anything more than an active or passive attitude (e.g., whether there are differences of actual clarity) is unknown and may be unknowable. In either case the linguistic action, by utilizing inner speech to simulate a social interaction in thinking, creates consciousness in the sense of Johnson-Laird's level three—the product of the social simulation is self-awareness, as Mead explained.

Returning to Johnson-Laird's development of the artifact metaphor of consciousness, an artifact at the third level, ideally constructed, combines serial and parallel processes. These he suggests correspond to conscious and uncon-scious processes. The artifact has a serial processor to perform overall control and monitoring, and a large number of lower parallel processors that carry out special tasks. Although Johnson-Laird does not mention Maturana and Varela (1980) I assume that this kind of machine, if it could actually be designed, would necessarily have some of the qualities of an autopoietic machine. Johnson-Laird does claim for this kind of machine certain autopoietic properties—in particular, flexibility in the presence of environmental change, immunity to degradation, and rapidity of response to disruptions of equilibrium. Presumably natural selection would have led to a similar autopoietic combination of serial and parallel processors in the human brain. Johnson-Laird identifies the contents of consciousness with the parameters that govern the computations of the serial processor. The parallel processors, on the other hand, correspond to the vast unconscious field of concurrent mental operations that are unknowable by the serial processor. Instead, the parallel processors report to the serial processor in the kind of serial terms with which it can operate. An illustration of this distinction is the clinical syndrome known as "blindsight," in which patients report blindness for part of the visual field but still make use of information from this part of the field (Weiskrantz et al., 1974). "They see without being conscious of what they see" (Johnson-Laird); or, in terms of the metaphor of serial and parallel processes, their serial processor does not appropriately handle information from the parallel processors corresponding to that part of the visual field.

The self-activation of images and "smart" symbols would correspond in this metaphor to the product of parallel processes, and the person's self-awareness produced with inner speech, in which there is invoked an "other," to the operation of the serial processor. Inner speech symbols are the type of information that the serial processor can assimilate but the unconscious self-activation of inner speech symbols would be the outcome of parallel processes.

The synthesis in linguistic actions of imagistic and syntactic modes of thinking is experienced in consciousness by the serial processor, but its sources are deep within unconscious parallel operations. Socially categorized thought is what we are aware of, but the source of this awareness is initial imagistic thinking utilizing inner speech symbols that corresponds, in Johnson-Laird's terms, to unconscious parallel processes. The serial processor is satisfied with a flow of socially constituted linguistic values, a flow that brings to perfection its simulation of a social interaction. Much of speech therefore seems automatic and preconscious from the viewpoint of the self. Only the final linear-segmented linguistic product in its external spoken form appears to be the product of deliberation. However, this is illusory since most of this external form is determined by the form of the sentence when it is imagistic-cum-inner speech. The active attitude in which the "speaker" of the inner speech symbol is attributed to the "I" of the self corresponds to the attempt by the serial processor to decide that the parallel processors should move in a certain direction. The passive attitude in which the inner speech symbol appears to be spoken by the "me" to the "I" corresponds to a willingness by the serial processor to "listen" to the parallel processors as they move in whatever direction they happen to go in. Stravinsky said of *Le Sacre du Printemps* that it composed itself, that he merely took dictation. This is the passive attitude of the self-aware conscious mind toward the "other," and when the unconscious is as fertile as Stravinsky's it is not always an attitude to be condemned.

References

Anderson, J. R. 1978. Arguments for representations for mental imagery. *Psychological Review* 85: 249–277.

Angiolillo-Bent, J. (n.d.). Non-conventional forms in American Sign Language: Universals of expressive gesture. Unpublished paper, Department of Behavioral Sciences, University of Chicago.

Arnheim, R. 1969. *Visual thinking.* Berkeley: University of California Press.

Au, T. K.-F. 1983. Chinese and English counterfactuals: The Sapir-Whorf hypothesis revisited. *Cognition* 15: 155–187.

———. 1984. Counterfactuals: In reply to Alfred Bloom. *Cognition* 17: 289–302.

———. (in press). Language and cognition. In *Language perspectives II,* L. L. Lloyd and R. L. Schiefelbusch (eds.). Baltimore: University Park Press.

Austin, G. 1806. *Chironomia, or a treatise on rhetorical delivery.* London: Cadell and Davies.

Austin, J. L. 1962. *How to do things with words.* Cambridge, MA: Harvard University Press.

Baars, B. J. 1980. On eliciting predictable speech errors in the laboratory. In *Errors in linguistic performance: Slips of the tongue, ear, pen, and hand,* V. A. Fromkin (ed.). New York: Academic Press, pp. 307–318.

Baddeley, A. and Wilson, B. 1985. Phonological coding and short-term memory in patients without speech. *Journal of Memory and Language 24:* 490–502.

Barrett, M. D. 1982. The holophrastic hypothesis: conceptual and empirical issues. *Cognition 11:* 47–76.

Bartlett, E. J. 1978. The acquisition of the meaning of colour terms: A study of lexical development. In *Recent advances in the psychology of language: Language development and mother-child interaction,* R. N. Campbell and P. T. Smith (eds.). New York: Plenum Press, pp. 89–108.

Bates, E.; Bretherton, I.; Shore, C.; and McNew, S. 1983. Names, gestures, and objects: Symbolization in infancy and aphasia. In *Children's language,* vol. 4, K. E. Nelson (ed.). Hillsdale, NJ: Erlbaum, pp. 59–123.

Benjamin, J. D. 1946. A method for distinguishing and evaluating formal thinking disorders in schizophrenia. In *Language and thought in schizophrenia,* J. S. Kasanin (ed.). Berkeley: University of California Press, pp. 65–88.

Berlin, B. and Kay, P. 1969. *Basic color terms: Their universality and evolution.* Berkeley: University of California Press.

Berwick, R. C. and Weinberg, A. S. 1983. The role of grammars in models of language use. *Cognition* 13: 1–61.

Bever, T. G. 1970. The cognitive basis for linguistic structures. In *Cognition and the development of language,* J. R. Hayes (ed.). New York: Wiley, pp. 279–362.

Bickerton, D. 1981. *Roots of language.* Ann Arbor, MI: Karoma Press.

Black, M. 1962. *Models and metaphors.* Ithaca, NY: Cornell University Press.

———. 1979. More about metaphor. In *Metaphor and thought,* A. Ortony (ed.). Cambridge: Cambridge University Press, pp. 19–43.

Bloch, B. 1947. English verb inflection. *Language* 23: 399–418.

Block, N. (ed.) 1980. *Imagery.* Cambridge, MA: MIT Press.

Bloom, A. H. 1981. *The linguistic shaping of thought: A study in the impact of language on thinking in China and the West.* Hillsdale, NJ: Erlbaum.

———. 1984. Caution—the words you use may affect what you say: A response to Au. *Cognition* 17: 275–287.

Bloom, R. 1979. *Language creation in the manual modality: A preliminary investigation.* Unpublished paper, University of Chicago.

Boas, F. 1911. Introduction. In *Handbook of American Indian Languages,* F. Boas (ed.). Bureau of American Ethnology Bulletin 40, part I), Washington, DC: Smithsonian Institution, pp. 1–83.

Bolinger, D. 1950. Rime, assonance, and morpheme analysis. *Word* 6: 117–136.

Booth, W. C. 1978. Metaphor as rhetoric: The problem of evaluation. In *On metaphor,* S. Sacks (ed.). Chicago: University of Chicago Press, pp. 47–70.

Bowerman, M. F. 1973. *Early syntactic development: A cross-linguistic study with special reference to Finnish.* Cambridge: Cambridge University Press.

———. 1978. Systematizing semantic knowledge: Changes over time in the child's organization of word meaning. *Child Development* 49: 977–987.

———. 1985. Beyond communicative adequacy: From piecemeal knowledge to an integrated system in the child's acquisition of language. In *Children's language,* vol. 5, K. E. Nelson (ed.). Hillsdale, NJ: Erlbaum, pp. 369–398.

———. (in press). What shapes children's grammars? In *The cross-linguistic study of language acquisition,* D. I. Slobin (ed.). Hillsdale, NJ: Erlbaum.

Bresnan, J. 1978. A realistic transformational grammar. In *Linguistic theory and psychological reality,* M. Halle, J. Bresnan, and G. A. Miller (eds.). Cambridge, MA: MIT Press, pp. 1–59.

Brown, R. and Lenneberg, E. H. 1954. A study in language and cognition. *Journal of Abnormal and Social Psychology* 49: 454–462.

Bucci, W. 1984. Linking words and things: Basic processes and individual variation. *Cognition* 17: 137–153.

Bybee, J. L. 1984. The lexical representation of morphologically complex words. Unpublished paper, Department of Linguistics, State University of New York, Buffalo.

———. 1985. *Morphology: A Study of the Relation Between Meaning and Form.* Amsterdam: Benjamins.

Bybee, J. L. and Slobin, D. I. 1982. Rules and schemas in the development and use of the English past. *Language* 58: 265–289.

Caplin, D. 1972. Clause boundaries and recognition latencies in sentences. *Perception and Psychophysics* 12: 73–76.

Catlin, J. 1969. On the word frequency effect. *Psychological Review* 76: 504–506.

Chafe, W. L. 1976. Givenness, contrastiveness, definiteness, subjects, topics, and point of view. In *Subject and topic,* C. N. Li (ed.). New York: Academic Press, pp. 25–55.

Chafe, W. L. 1980. The deployment of consciousness in the production of a narrative. In *The pear stories: Cognitive, cultural, and linguistic aspects of narrative production,* W. L. Chafe (ed.). Norwood, NJ: Ablex, pp. 9–50.

Charniak, E. 1983. Passing markers: A theory of contextual influence in language comprehension. *Cognitive Science* 7: 171–190.

Chomsky, N. 1957. *Syntactic structures.* The Hague: Mouton.

———. 1965. *Aspects of the theory of syntax.* Cambridge, MA: MIT Press.

———. 1968. *Language and mind.* New York: Harcourt, Brace & World.

———. 1977. Questions of form and interpretation. In *Essays on form and interpretation,* N. Chomsky (ed.). New York: North-Holland, pp. 25–59.

———. 1980. On binding. *Linguistic Inquiry* 11: 1–46.

Chomsky, N. and Halle, M. 1968. *The sound pattern of English.* New York: Harper & Row.

Chomsky, N. and Lasnik, H. 1977. Filters and control. *Linguistic Inquiry* 8: 425–504.

Church, R. B. and Goldin-Meadow, S. 1986. The mismatch between gesture and speech as an index of transitional knowledge. *Cognition* 23: 43–71.

Cicone, N.; Wapner, W.; Foldi, N. S.; Zurif, E.; and Gardner, H. 1979. The relation between gesture and language in aphasic communication. *Brain and Language* 8: 324–349.

Clancy, P. M. 1980. Referential choice in English and Japanese discourse. In *The pear stories: Cognitive, cultural, and linguistic aspects of narrative production,* W. L. Chafe (ed.). Norwood, NJ: Ablex, pp. 127–202.

Clark, H. H. 1979. Responding to indirect speech acts. *Cognitive Psychology* 11: 430–477.

Clark, H. H. and Clark, E. V. 1977. *Psychology and language: An introduction to psycholinguistics.* New York: Harcourt Brace Jovanovich.

Clark, E. V. and Clark, H. H. 1979. When nouns surface as verbs. *Language* 55: 767–811.

Clark, H. H. and Sengul, C. J. 1979. In search of referents for nouns and pronouns. *Memory and Cognition* 7: 35–41.

Comrie, B. (in press). Conditionals: A typology. In *On conditionals,* E. Traugott, C. A. Ferguson, J. S. Reilly, and A. ter Meulen (eds.). Cambridge: Cambridge University Press.

———. 1985. *Tense.* Cambridge: Cambridge University Press.

Conklin, H. C. 1955. Hanunoo color categories. In *Language in culture and society,* D. Hymes (ed.). New York: Harper & Row, pp. 189–192.

Cowart, W. 1986. Evidence for structural reference processes. In *Papers from the 22d meeting of the Chicago Linguistic Society,* A. Farley, P. Farley, and K.-E. McCullough (eds.). Chicago: The Chicago Linguistic Society, pp. 307–317.

Craik, K. 1943. *The nature of explanation.* Cambridge: Cambridge University Press.

Curme, G. 1931. *Syntax.* New York: D. C. Heath.

Cutler, A. 1980. Errors of stress and intonation. In *Errors in linguistic performance: Slips of the tongue, ear, pen, and hand,* V. A. Fromkin (ed.). New York: Academic Press, pp. 67–80.

———. 1982. Idioms: The colder the older. *Linguistic Inquiry* 13: 317–320.

D'Andrade, R. and Wish, M. 1985. Speech act theory in quantitative research on interpersonal behavior. *Discourse Processes* 8: 229–259.

Darden, B. J. 1984. Report to the Sloan Foundation, Center for Cognitive Science, University of Chicago.

Davey, A. C. and Longuet-Higgens, H. C. 1978. A computational model of discourse production. In *Recent advances in the psychology of language: Formal and experimental approaches,* R. N. Campbell and P. T. Smith (eds.). New York: Plenum Press, pp. 125–136.

Davison, A. 1975. Indirect speech acts and what to do with them. In *Syntax and semantics. Speech acts,* vol. 3, P. Cole and J. L. Morgan (eds.). New York: Academic Press, pp. 143–186.

Delis, D.; Foldi, N. S.; Hamby, S.; Gardner, H.; and Zurif, E. 1979. A note on temporal relations between language and gestures. *Brain and Language* 8: 350–354.

Dell, G. S. and Reich, P. 1980. Toward a unified model of slips of the tongue. In *Errors in linguistic performance: Slips of the tongue, ear, pen, and hand,* V. A. Fromkin (ed.). New York: Academic Press, pp. 273–286.

Denes, P. B. and Pinson, E. N. 1963. *The speech chain: The physics and biology of spoken language.* New York: Garden State/Novo.

Denny, J. P. 1976. What are noun classifiers good for? In *Papers from the 12th regional meeting of the Chicago Linguistic Society,* S. K. Mufwene, C. A. Walker, and S. B. Steever (eds.). Chicago Linguistic Society, pp. 122–132.

de Groot, A. M. B. 1983. The range of automatic spreading activation in word priming. *Journal of Verbal Learning and Verbal Behavior* 22: 417–436.

de Villiers, P. A. 1974. Imagery and theme in recall of connected discourse. *Jornal of Experimental Psychology* 103: 263–268.

Dimmendaal, G. J. 1983. *The Turkana language.* Dordrecht, Holland: Foris.

Du Bois, J. W. 1974. Syntax in mid-sentence. In *Berkeley studies in syntax and semantics,* vol. I. Berkeley: Department of Linguistics, pp. 1–25.

Duncan, S. and Fiske, D. W. 1977. *Face-to-face interaction. Research, methods, and theory.* Hillsdale, NJ: Erlbaum.

Durbin, M. 1972. Basic color terms—off color? *Semiotica* 6: 257–278.

Eco, U. 1976. *A theory of semiotics.* Bloomington: Indiana University Press.

Einstein, A. 1945. Quoted in J. Hadamard, *The psychology of invention in the mathematical field,* Princeton, NJ: Princeton University Press, p. 142.

Ekman, P. and Friesen, W. V. 1969. The repertoire of nonverbal behavioral categories—origins, usage, and coding. *Semiotica* 1: 49–98.

Fay, D. 1980. Transformational errors. In *Errors in linguistic performance. Slips of the tongue, ear, pen, and hand,* V. A. Fromkin (ed.). New York: Academic Press, pp. 111–122.

Fay, D. and Cutler, A. 1977. Malapropisms and the structure of the mental lexicon. *Linguistic Inquiry* 8: 505–520.

Fillenbaum, S. 1966. Memory for gist: Some relevant variables. *Language and Speech* 9: 217–227.

———. 1967. Verbal satiation and the exploration of meaning relations. In *Research in verbal behavior and some neurophysiological implications,* K. Salzinger and S. Salzinger (eds.). New York: Academic Press, pp. 155–165.

———. 1974. Information amplified: Memory for counterfactual conditionals. *Journal of Experimental Psychology* 102: 44–49.

Fillmore, C. J. 1971. Lectures on deixis. Unpublished paper. Department of Linguistics, University of California, Berkeley.

Fodor, J. A. 1975. *The language of thought.* Cambridge, MA: Harvard University Press.

————. 1980*a*. Methodological solipsism considered as a research strategy in cognitive psychology. *The Behavioral and Brain Sciences* 3: 63–73.

————. 1980*b*. *Modularity of mind.* Cambridge, MA: MIT Press.

Fodor, J. A.; Bever, T. G.; and Garrett, M. F. 1974. *The psychology of language: An introduction to psycholinguistics and generative grammar.* New York: McGraw-Hill.

Fodor, J. D. 1984. Learnability and parsability: A reply to Culicover. *Natural Language and Linguistic Theory* 2: 105–150.

Fodor, J. D. and Frazier, L. 1980. Is the human sentence parsing mechanism an ATN? *Cognition* 8: 418–459.

Forster, K. I. 1976. Accessing the mental lexicon. In *New approaches to language mechanisms,* R. J. Wales and E. Walker (eds.). Amsterdam: North-Holland, pp. 257–287.

Fortes, M. 1940. Children's drawings among the Tallensi. *Africa* 13: 293–295.

Fowler, C. 1977. *Timing control in speech production.* Bloomington: Indiana University Linguistics Club.

Fraser, B. 1970. Idioms within a transformational grammar. *Foundations of Language* 6: 22–42.

Frazier, L. and Fodor, J. D. 1978. The sausage machine: a new two-stage parsing model. *Cognition* 6: 291–325.

Freud, S. 1958. *Psychopathology of everyday life* (A. A. Brill, trans.). New York: New American Library. (First German edition, 1901.)

Frishberg, N. 1975. Arbitrariness and iconicity: Historical change in American Sign Language. *Language* 51: 696–719.

Fromkin, V. A. 1971. The non-anomalous nature of anomalous utterances. *Language* 47: 27–52.

————. 1973*a*. Introduction. In *Speech errors as linguistic evidence,* V. A. Fromkin (ed.). The Hague: Mouton, pp. 11–45.

Fromkin, V. A. (ed.) 1973*b*. *Speech errors as linguistic evidence.* The Hague: Mouton.

Fromkin, V. A. (ed.), 1980. *Errors in linguistic performance: Slips of the tongue, ear, pen, and hand.* New York: Academic Press.

Gardner, B. T. and Gardner, R. A. 1971. Two-way communication with an infant chimpanzee. In *Behavior of non-human primates,* vol. IV, A. M. Schrier and F. Stolnitz (eds.). New York: Academic Press, pp. 117–184.

Garnham, A.; Oakhill, J.; and Johnson-Laird, P. N. 1982. Referential continuity and the coherence of discourse. *Cognition* 11: 29–46.

Garrett, M. F. 1976. Syntactic processes in sentence production. In *New approaches to language mechanisms,* R. J. Wales and E. Walker (eds.). Amsterdam: North-Holland, pp. 231–256.

————. 1980. The limits of accommodation: Arguments for independent processing levels in sentence production. In *Errors in linguistic performance: Slips of the tongue, ear, pen, and hand* V. A. Fromkin (ed.). New York: Academic Press, pp. 263–272.

Garvey, C.; Caramazza, A.; and Yates, J. 1975. Factors influencing assignment of pronoun antecedents. *Cognition* 3: 227–243.

Gazdar, G. (1981). Unbounded dependencies and coordinate structure. *Linguistic Inquiry* 12: 155–184.

Gentner, D. (1981). Some interesting differences between verbs and nouns. *Cognition and Brain Theory* 4: 161–178.

Gentner, D. and Gentner, D. R. (1982). Flowing waters and teeming crowds: Mental models of electricity. Report No. 4981, Cambridge, MA: Bolt, Beranek and Newman.

Gernsbacher, M. A. 1985. Surface information loss in comprehension. *Cognitive Psychology* 17: 324–363.

Gildea, P. and Glucksberg, S. 1983. On understanding metaphor: The role of context. *Journal of Verbal Learning and Verbal Behavior* 22: 577–590.

Gleason, H. A. 1955. *An introduction to descriptive linguistics.* New York: Holt.

Gleitman, L. R. and Gleitman, H. 1970. *Phrase and paraphrase: Some innovative uses of language.* New York: Norton.

Glucksberg, S.; Gildea, P.; and Bookin, H. A. 1982. On understanding nonliteral speech: Can people ignore metaphors? *Journal of Verbal Learning and Verbal Behavior* 21: 85–98.

Goethe, J. W. von 1840. *Theory of colours.* London: John Murray.

Goffman, E. (1974). *Frame analysis: An essay on the organization of experience.* Cambridge, MA: Harvard University Press.

———. 1981. *Forms of talk.* Philadelphia: University of Pennsylvania Press.

Goldin-Meadow, S. 1982. The resilience of recursion: A study of a communication system developed without a conventional language model. In *Language acquisition. The state of the art,* E. Wanner and L. R. Gleitman (eds.). Cambridge: Cambridge University Press, pp. 51–77.

Goodwin, C. 1981. *Conversational organization. Interaction between speakers and hearers.* New York: Academic Press.

Gordon, D. and Lakoff, G. 1975. Conversational postulates. In *Syntax and semantics: Speech acts,* vol. 3, P. Cole and J. L. Morgan (eds.). New York: Academic Press, pp. 83–106.

Gough, P. B. 1972. One second of reading. In *Language by ear and by eye: The relationship between speech and reading,* J. F. Kavanagh and G. Mattingly (eds.). Cambridge, MA: MIT Press, pp. 331–358.

Greeno, C. 1981. *Fundamental Axioms of Language Study.* Unpublished paper, University of Chicago.

Grice, H. P. 1957. Meaning. *Philosophical Review* 66: 377–388.

———. 1975. Logic and conversation. In *Syntax and semantics: Speech acts,* vol. 3, P. Cole and J. L. Morgan (eds.). New York: Academic Press, pp. 41–58.

Griffin, D. R. 1976. *The question of animal awareness: Evolutionary continuity of mental experience.* New York: Rockefeller University Press.

———. 1984. *Animal thinking.* Cambridge, MA: Harvard University Press.

Grimes, J. E. 1975. *The thread of discourse.* The Hague: Mouton.

Grober, E. H.; Beardsley, W.; and Caramazza, A. 1978. Parallel function strategy in pronoun assignment. *Cognition* 6: 117–133.

Grosjean, F. (1980). Spoken word recognition processes and the gating paradigm. *Perception and Psychophysics* 28: 267–283.

Grosz, B. 1981. Focusing and description in natural language dialogues. In *Elements of discourse understanding,* A. K. Joshi, B. L. Webber, and I. A. Sag (eds.). Cambridge: Cambridge University Press, pp. 84–105.

Habermas, J. 1970. Toward theory of communicative competence. In *Recent sociology No. 2: Pattern of communicative behavior,* H. P. Dreitzel (ed.). New York: Macmillan.

Hadamard, J. 1945. *The psychology of invention in the mathematical field.* Princeton, NJ: Princeton University Press.

Haiman, J. 1978. Conditionals are topics. *Language* 54: 564–589.

Halle, M.; Bresnan, J.; and Miller, G. A. 1978. *Linguistic theory and psychological reality.* Cambridge, MA: MIT Press.

Halliday, M. A. K. 1967a. Notes on transitivity and theme in English: I. *Journal of Linguistics* 3: 37–81.

————. 1967*b*. Notes on transitivity and theme in English: II. *Journal of Linguistics* 3: 199–244.

Halliday, M. A. K. and Hasan, R. 1976. *Cohesion in English.* London: Longman.

Haskell, R. E. 1985. Thought-things: Levi-Strauss and "the modern mind." *Semiotica* 55: 1–17.

Haviland, E. E. and Clark, H. H. 1974. What's new? Acquiring new information as a process in comprehension. *Journal of Verbal Learning and Verbal Behavior* 13: 512–521.

Heider, E. R. 1972. Universals in color naming and memory. *Journal of Experimental Psychology* 93: 10–20.

Hirst, W. and Brill, G. A. 1980. Contextual aspects of pronoun assignment. *Journal of Verbal Learning and Verbal Behavior* 19: 168–175.

Hockett, C. F. 1958. *A course in modern linguistics.* New York: Macmillan.

Hoffman, R. R. 1984. Recent research on metaphor. In *Discourses in reading and linguistics,* S. White (ed.). *Annals of the New York Academy of Sciences* 433: 137–166.

Hoffman, R. R. and Kemper, S. 1985. What could reaction-time studies be telling us about metaphor comprehension? Unpublished paper, Department of Psychology, Adelphi University, Garden City, NY.

Holland, D. 1983. All is metaphor: Conventional metaphors in human thought and language. *Reviews in Anthropology* 9: 287–297.

Hopper, P. 1979. Aspect and foregrounding in discourse. In *Syntax and semantics. Discourse and Syntax,* vol. 12, T. Givon (ed.). New York: Academic Press, pp. 213–241.

Hopper, P. and Thompson, S. 1980. Transitivity in grammar and discourse. *Language* 56: 251–299.

Howes, D. H. and Solomon, R. L. 1951. Visual duration threshold as a function of word-probability. *Journal of Experimental Psychology* 41: 401–410.

Hurvich, L. M. and Jameson, D. 1955. Some quantitative aspects of an opponent-colors theory. II: Brightness, saturation, and hue in normal and dichromatic vision. *Journal of the Optical Society of America* 45: 602–616.

Huttenlocher, J. and Goodman, J. (in press). The time to identify spoken words. In *The perception and production of speech,* W. Printz, D. MacKay, and A. Allport (eds.). Berlin: Springer.

Huttenlocher, J. and Smiley, P. (in press). Early word meanings: The case of object names. *Cognitive Psychology.*

Jacobson, R. 1945. Quoted in J. Hadamard, *The psychology of invention in the mathematical field.* Princeton, NJ: Princeton University Press, pp. 96–97.

James, D. 1972. Some aspects of the syntax and semantics of interjections. In *Papers from the eighth regional meeting of the Chicago Linguistic Society,* P. M. Peranteau, J. N. Levi, and G. C. Phares (eds.). Chicago: Chicago Linguistic Society, pp. 162–172.

————. 1973. Another look at, say, some grammatical constraints on, oh, interjections and hesitations. In *Papers from the ninth regional meeting of the Chicago Linguistic Society,* C. Corum, T. C. Smith-Stark, and A. Weiser (eds.). Chicago: Chicago Linguistic Society, pp. 242–251.

James, W. 1890. *The principles of psychology,* vol. I. New York: Holt.

Jarvella, R. 1971. Syntactic processing of connected speech. *Journal of Verbal Learning and Verbal Behavior* 10: 409–416.

Jespersen, O. 1942. *A modern English grammar on historical principles, VI: Morphology.* Copenhagen: Munksgaard.

Johnson-Laird, P. N. 1983. *Mental models. Towards a cognitive science of language, inference, and consciousness.* Cambridge, MA: Harvard University Press.

Johnston, J. C. 1978. A test of the sophisticated guessing theory of word perception. *Cognitive Psychology* 10: 123–153.

Karmiloff-Smith, A. 1980. Psychological processes underlying pronominalization in children's connected discourse. In *Papers from the Parasession on Pronouns and Anaphora,* J. Kreiman and A. E. Ojeda (eds.). Chicago: Chicago Linguistics Society, pp. 231–250.

Karttunen, L. 1973. Presuppositions of compound sentences. *Linguistic Inquiry* 4: 169–193.

Kay, P. and Kempton, W. 1983. What is the Sapir-Whort hypothesis? *Berkeley Cognitive Science Report No. 8.* Institute of Human Learning, University of California, Berkeley.

Kay, P. and McDaniel, C. K. 1978. The linguistic significance of the meanings of basic color terms. *Language* 54: 610–646.

Kaye, K. 1982. *The mental and social life of babies: How parents create persons.* Chicago: The University of Chicago Press.

Kempen, G. 1977. Conceptualizing and formulating in sentence production. In *Sentence production: Developments in research and theory.* Hillsdale, NJ: Erlbaum, pp. 259–274.

Keenan, E. O. and Schieffelin, B. B. 1976. Topic as a discourse notion: A study of topic in the conversations of children and adults. In *Subject and topic,* C. N. Li (ed.). New York: Academic Press, pp. 335–384.

Kendon, A. 1972. Some relationships between body motion and speech. In *Studies in dyadic communication,* A. Siegman and B. Pope (eds.). New York: Pergamon Press, pp. 177–210.

———. 1980*a*. A description of a deaf-mute sign language from the Enga Province of Papua, New Guinea with some comparative discussion. Part I: The formational properties of Enga signs. *Semiotica* 32: 1–34.

———. 1980*b*. A description of a deaf-mute sign language from the Enga Province of Papua, New Guinea with some comparative discussion. Part II: The semiotic functioning of Enga signs. *Semiotica* 32: 81–117.

———. 1980*c*. A description of a deaf-mute sign language from the Enga Province of Papua, New Guinea with some comparative discussion. Part III: Aspects of utterance construction. *Semiotica* 32, 245–313.

———. 1980*d*. Gesticulation and speech: Two aspects of the process of utterance. In *The relation between verbal and nonverbal communication,* M. R. Key (ed.). The Hague: Mouton, pp. 207–227.

———. 1981. Geography of gesture. *Semiotica* 37: 129–163.

———. 1983. Gesture and speech: How they interact. In *Nonverbal interaction,* J. M. Wiemann and R. P. Harrison (eds.). Beverly Hills: Sage, pp. 13–45.

Kimball, J. 1973. Seven principles of surface structure parsing in natural language. *Cognition* 2: 15–47.

Kimura, D. 1973*a*. Manual activity during speaking: I. Right handers. *Neuropsychologia* 11: 45–50.

———. 1973*b*. Manual activity during speaking: II. Left handers. *Neuropsychologia* 11: 51–55.

Kimura, D. and Archibald, Y. 1974. Motor functions of the left hemisphere. *Brain* 97: 337–350.

Kintsch, W. 1974. *The representation of meaning in memory.* Hillsdale, NJ: Erlbaum.

Klein, W. 1982. Local deixis in route directions. In *Speech, place, and action,* R. Jarvella and W. Klein (eds.). Chichester: Wiley, pp. 161–182.

―――. (n.d.). The story of a goal. Unpublished paper. Max-Planck-Institut für Psycholinguistik, Nijmegen, The Netherlands.

Klima, E. S. and Bellugi, U. 1979. *The signs of language.* Cambridge, MA: Harvard University Press.

Kluckhohn, C. and Leighton, D. 1946. *The Navaho.* Cambridge, MA: Harvard University Press.

Kosslyn, S. M. 1975. Information representation in visual images. *Cognitive Psychology* 7: 341–370.

Kozhevnikov, V. A. and Chistovich, L. A. 1965. *Speech, articulation, and perception.* Washington, D. C.: U.S. Department of Commerce, Joint Publication Service (JPRS #30,543).

Kučera, H. and Francis, W. N. 1967. *Computational analysis of present-day American English.* Providence, RI: Brown University Press.

Kuhn, T. 1962. *The structure of scientific revolutions,* vol. 2, no. 2, *International Encyclopedia of Unified Science.* Chicago: University of Chicago Press.

Kuno, S. 1976. Subject, theme, and the speaker's empathy—A re-examination of relativization phenomena. In *Subject and topic,* C. N. Li (ed.). New York: Academic Press, pp. 417–444.

Labov, W. and Fanshel, D. 1977. *Theraputic discourse. Psychotherapy as conversation.* New York: Academic Press.

Lakoff, G. and Johnson, M. 1980. *Metaphors we live by.* Chicago: University of Chicago Press.

Lane, H. 1980. A chronology of the oppression of sign language in France and the United States. In *Recent perspectives on American Sign Language,* H. Lane and F. Grosjean (eds.). Hillsdale, NJ: Erlbaum, pp. 119–161.

Lantz, D. and Stefflre, V. 1964. Language and cognition revisited. *Journal of Abnormal and Social Psychology* 69: 472–481.

Lees, R. B. 1960. *The grammar of English nominalizations.* The Hague: Mouton.

Lenneberg, E. H. 1967. *Biological foundations of language.* New York: Wiley.

Leont'ev, A. N. 1979. The problem of activity in psychology. In *The concept of activity in Soviet psychology,* J. V. Wertsch (ed. and trans.). Armonk, NY: Sharpe, pp. 37–71.

Lesgold, A. M. 1972. Pronominalization: A device for unifying sentences in memory. *Journal of Verbal Learning and Verbal Behavior* 11: 316–323.

Levelt, W. J. M. 1982. Linearization in describing spatial networks. In *Processes, beliefs, and questions,* S. Peters and E. Saarinen (eds.). New York: D. Reidel, 199–220.

―――. 1983. Monitoring and self-repair in speech. *Cognition* 14: 41–104.

―――. 1984. Some perceptual limitations on talking about space. In *Limits on perception,* A. J. van Doorn, W. A. van de Grind, and J. J. Koenderink (eds.). Utrecht: VNU Science Press, pp. 323–358.

Levelt, W. J. M.; Richardson, G.; and La Heij, W. 1985. Pointing and voicing in deictic expressions. *Journal of Memory and Language* 24: 133–164.

Levy, E. 1982. Towards an objective definition of "discourse topic." In *Papers from the 18th Regional Meeting of the Chicago Linguistic Society,* K. Tuite, R. Schneider, and R. Chametsky (eds.). Chicago: Chicago Linguistic Society, pp. 295–304.

―――. 1984. Communicating thematic structure in narrative discourse: The use of referring terms and gestures. Unpublished dissertation, University of Chicago.

Liberman, A. M.; Shankweiler, D. P.; and Studdert-Kennedy, M. 1967. Perception of the speech code. *Psychological Review* 74: 431–461.

Licklider, J. C. 1951. Basic correlates of the auditory stimulus. In *Handbook of experimental psychology,* S. S. Stevens (ed.). New York: Wiley, pp. 985–1039.

Lieberman, P. 1984. *The biology and evolution of language.* Cambridge, MA: Harvard University Press.

Linde, C. and Labov, W. 1975. Spatial networks as a site for the study of language and thought. *Language* 51: 924–939.

Lindsay, P. H. and Norman, D. A. 1977. *Human information processing* (2d ed.). New York: Academic Press.

Liu, L. G. 1985. Reasoning counterfactually in Chinese: Are there any obstacles? *Cognition* 21: 239–270.

Lock, A. 1980. *The guided reinvention of language.* London: Academic Press.

Lock, A.; Young, A.; Service, V.; and Chandler, P. 1985. Some observations on the origins of the pointing gesture. Paper given at the meetings of the Society for Research on Child Development, Toronto, Ont.

Lucy, J. A. 1981. An empirical approach to the Whorfian question. Unpublished paper, Committee on Human Development, University of Chicago.

———. 1985. Whorf's view of the linguistic mediation of thought. In *Semiotic mediation: Sociocultural and psychological perspectives,* E. Mertz and R. J. Parmentier (eds.). New York: Academic Press, pp. 73–97.

Lucy, J. A. and Shweder, R. A. 1979. Whorf and his critics: Linguistic and nonlinguistic influences on color memory. *American Anthropologist* 81: 581–615.

Lucy, J. A. and Wertsch, J. V. (in press). Vygotsky and Whorf: A comparative analysis. In *Social and functional approaches to language and thought,* M. Hickmann (ed.). New York: Academic Press.

Lyons, J. (1977). *Semantics,* vol. 2. Cambridge: Cambridge University Press.

MacDougall, D. and MacDougall, J. 1977. *Lorang's way* [film]. Berkeley: University of California Extension Media Center.

Maclay, H. and Osgood, C. E. 1959. Hesitation phenomena in spontaneous English speech. *Word* 15: 19–44.

MacWhinney, B. 1978. The acquisition of morphophonology. *Monographs of the Society for Child Development* 43: Serial No. 174.

Malotki, E. 1983. Hopi Time: A linguistic analysis of the temporal concepts in the Hopi language. Berlin: Mouton.

Marcus, M. P. 1980. *A theory of syntactic recognition for natural language.* Cambridge, MA: MIT Press.

Marschark, M.; West, S. A.; Nall, L.; and Everhart, V. (1986). Development of creative language devices in signed and oral production. *Journal of Experimental Child Psychology* 41: 534–550.

Marslen-Wilson, W. D. 1975. Sentence perception as an interactive parallel process. *Science* 189: 226–228.

———. 1978. Sequential decision processes during spoken word recognition. Paper presented at the Psychonomic Society meetings, San Antonio, TX.

———. 1984. Function and process in spoken word-recognition. In *Attention and performance X: Control of language processes,* H. Bouma and D. B. Bouwhuis (eds.). Hillsdale, NJ: Erlbaum, pp. 125–150.

———. (in press). Parallel processing in spoken word-recognition. *Cognition.*

Marslen-Wilson, W. D.; Levy, E.; and Tyler, L. K. 1982. Producing interpretable discourse: The establishment and maintenance of reference. In *Speech, place, and action,* R. Jarvella and W. Klein (eds.). Chichester: Wiley.

Marslen-Wilson, W. D. and Tyler, L. K. 1980. The temporal structure of spoken language understanding. *Cognition* 8: 1–71.

Marslen-Wilson, W. D. and Welsh, A. 1978. Processing interactions during word-recognition in continuous speech. *Cognitive Psychology* 10: 29–63.

Maturana, H. R. and Varela, F. J. 1980. *Autopoiesis and cognition. The realization of the living.* Dordrecht: D. Reidel.

McClelland, J. L. and Rumelhart, D. E. 1985. Distributed memory and the representation of general and specific information. *Journal of Experimental Psychology: General* 114: 159–188.

McNeill, D. 1966. Speaking of space. *Science* 152: 875–880.

———. 1975. Semiotic extension. In *Information processing and cognition. The Loyola symposium,* R. L. Solso (ed.). Hillsdale, NJ: Erlbaum, pp. 351–380.

———. 1979. *The conceptual basis of language.* Hillsdale, NJ: Erlbaum.

———. 1985*a*. So you think gestures are nonverbal? *Psychological Review* 92: 350–371.

———. 1985*b*. Holophrastic noun phrases *within* grammatical clauses. In *Children's single-word speech,* M. D. Barrett (ed.). Chichester: Wiley, pp. 269–285.

———. 1985*c*. Temaniotics, or the wisdom of the hands. Paper presented at the 1985 Eastern States Conference on Linguistics, State University of New York, Buffalo.

———. 1986. Speech-gesture synthesis, or natural acts. In *Papers from the 22d meeting of the Chicago Linguistic Society,* A. Farley, P. Farley, and K.-E. McCullough (eds.). Chicago: The Chicago Linguistic Society, pp. 286–306.

———. (in press). Iconic gestures of children and adults. *Semiotica.*

McNeill, D. and Levy, E. 1982. Conceptual representations in language activity and gesture. In *Speech, place, and action: Studies in deixis and related topics,* R. Jarvella and W. Klein (eds.). Chichester: Wiley, pp. 271–295.

McNeill, N. B. 1972. Colour and colour terminology. *Journal of Linguistics* 8: 21–33.

Mead, G. H. 1974. *Mind, self, and society.* Chicago: University of Chicago Press.

Mehler, J. 1963. Some effects of grammatical transformations on the recall of English sentences. *Journal of Verbal Learning and Verbal Behavior* 2: 346–351.

Meringer, R. 1908. *Aus dem Leben der Sprache.* Berlin: B. Behr.

Meringer, R. and Mayer, K. 1895. *Versprechen und Verlesen.* Stuttgart: Goshen.

Meyer, D. and Schvanevelt, R. W. 1971. Facilitation in recognizing pairs of words: Evidence of dependence between retrieval operations. *Journal of Experimental Psychology* 90: 227–234.

Miller, G. A. 1965. Some preliminaries to psycholinguistics. *American Psychologist* 20: 15–20.

———. 1979. Images, models, similes and metaphors. In *Metaphor and thought,* A. Ortony (ed.). Cambridge: Cambridge University Press, pp. 202–250.

Miller, G. A.; Heise, G.; and Lichten, W. 1951. The intelligibility of speech as a function of the context of the test materials. *Journal of Experimental Psychology* 41: 329–335.

Miller, G. A. and Johnson-Laird, P. N. 1976. *Language and perception.* Cambridge, MA: Harvard University Press.

Mitchell, D. C. and Holmes, V. M. 1985. The role of specific information about the verb in parsing sentences with local structural ambiguity. *Journal of Memory and Language* 24: 542–559.

Monsell, S. (in press). Programming of complex sequences: Evidence from the timing of rapid speech and other productions. In *Generation and modulation of action patterns: Experimental brain research (Supplement),* C. Fromm and H. Heuer (eds.). New York: Springer.

Montague, R. 1974. *Formal philosophy: Selected papers.* New Haven, CT: Yale University Press.

Montaigne, M., de. 1958. *The complete essays of Montaigne* (D. Frame, trans.). Stanford, CA: Stanford University Press.

Morris, D.; Collett, P.; Marsh, P.; and O'Shaughnessy, M. 1979. *Gestures, their origins and distribution.* New York: Stein and Day.

Morton, J. 1969. Interaction of information in word recognition. *Psychological Review* 76: 165–178.

———. 1979. Facilitation in word recognition: Experiments causing change in the logogen model. In *Processing of visible language,* vol. 1, P. A. Kolers, M. E. Wrolstad, and H. Bouma (eds.). New York: Plenum Press, pp. 259–268.

Motley, M. T. 1980. Verification of "Freudian slips" and semantic prearticulatory editing via laboratory-induced Spoonerisms. In *Errors in linguistic performance: Slips of the tongue, ear, pen, and hand,* V. A. Fromkin (ed.). New York: Academic Press, pp. 133–148.

Murphey, C. M. and Messer, D. J. 1977. Mothers, infants and pointing: A case study of a gesture. In *Studies in mother-infant interaction,* H. R. Schaffer (ed.). London: Academic Press, pp. 325–354.

Neisser, U. 1967. *Cognitive psychology.* New York: Appleton-Century-Crofts.

Newkirk, D.; Klima, E. S.; Pedersen, C. C.; and Bellugi, U. 1980. Linguistic evidence from slips of the hand. In *Errors in linguistic performance: Slips of the tongue, ear, pen, and hand,* V. A. Fromkin (ed.). New York: Academic Press, pp. 165–198.

Newman, S. S. 1933. Further experiments in phonetic symbolism. *American Journal of Psychology* 45: 53–75.

Norris, D. 1982. Autonomous processes in comprehension: A reply to Marslen-Wilson and Tyler. *Cognition* 11: 97–101.

Oakley, D. A. (ed.) 1985. *Brain and mind.* London: Methuen.

Paget, R. 1930. *Human speech.* New York: Harcourt, Brace & Company.

Paivio, A. 1971. *Imagery and verbal-processes.* New York: Holt.

Palmer, S. E. and Kimchi, R. (1986). The information processing approach to cognition. In *Approaches to cognition: contrasts and controversies,* T. J. Knapp and L. C. Robertson (eds.). Hillsdale, NJ: Erlbaum, pp. 37–77.

Patterson, F. G. 1980. Innovative uses of language by a gorilla: A case study. In *Children's language,* vol. II, K. Nelson (ed.). New York: Gardner Press, pp. 497–561.

Pechmann, T. and Deutsch, W. 1980. From gesture to word and gesture. Paper presented at the 12th Stanford Child Language Research Forum, Stanford University.

Pedelty, L. (in preparation). Gestures in aphasia. Department of Behavioral Sciences, University of Chicago.

Piaget, J. 1954. *The construction of reality in the child,* M. Cook (trans.). New York: Basic Books.

———. 1965. *The child's conception of number.* New York: Norton.

Piaget, J. and Inhelder, B. 1967. *The child's conception of space,* F. J. Langdon and J. L. Lunzer (trans.). New York: Norton.

Pillsbury, W. B. 1897. The reading of words: a study in apperception. *American Journal of Psychology* 8:315–393.

Postman, L. and Rosenzweig, M. R. 1957. Perceptual recognition of words. *Journal of Speech and Hearing Disorders* 22: 245–253.

Potter, J. M. 1980. What was the matter with Dr. Spooner? In *Errors in linguistic performance: Slips of the tongue, ear, pen, and hand,* V. A. Fromkin (ed.). New York: Academic Press, pp. 13–34.

Potter, M. C. and Faulconer, B. A. 1979. Understanding noun phrases. *Journal of Verbal Learning and Verbal Behavior* 18: 509–521.

Premack, D. 1976. *Intelligence in ape and man.* Hillsdale, NJ: Erlbaum.

Pylyshyn, Z. 1973. What the mind's eye tells the mind's brain: A critique of mental imagery. *Psychological Bulletin* 80: 1–24.

———. 1980. Computation and cognition: Issues in the foundation of cognitive science. *The Behavioral and Brain Sciences* 3: 111–132.

Quinn, N. (in press). Introduction. In *Cultural models in language and thought,* N. Quinn and D. Holland (eds.). Cambridge: Cambridge University Press.

Radford, A. 1981. *Transformational syntax. A student's guide to Chomsky's extended standard theory.* Cambridge: Cambridge University Press.

Reddy, M. 1979. The conduit metaphor—a case of frame conflict in our language about language. In *Metaphor and thought,* A. Ortony (ed.). Cambridge: Cambridge University Press, pp. 284–324.

Reicher, G. M. 1969. Perceptual recognition as a function of meaningfulness of stimulus material. *Journal of Experimental Psychology* 81: 275–280.

Reichman, R. 1978. Conversational coherency. *Cognitive Science* 2: 283–327.

Reinhart, T. 1983. *Anaphora and semantic interpretation.* London: Croom Helm.

Rhodes, R. A. and Lawler, J. M. 1981. Athematic metaphors. In *Papers from the 17th regional meeting of the Chicago Linguistic Society,* R. A. Hendrick, C. S. Masek, and M. F. Miller (eds.). Chicago: Chicago Linguistic Society.

Richards, I. A. 1936. *The philosophy of rhetoric.* New York: Oxford University Press.

Ricoeur, P. 1978. The metaphorical process as cognition, imagination, and feeling. In *On metaphor,* S. Sacks (ed.). Chicago: University of Chicago Press, pp. 141–157.

Rosch, E. 1973. On the internal structure of perceptual and semantic categories. In *Cognitive development and the acquisition of language,* T. E. Moore (ed.). New York: Academic Press, pp. 111–144.

Rosch, E.; Mervis, C. B.; Gray, W. D.; Johnson, D. M.; and Boyes-Braem, O. 1976. Basic objects in natural categories. *Cognitive Psychology* 8: 382–439.

Ross, J. R. 1967. Constraints on variables in syntax. Unpublished doctoral dissertation, Department of Linguistics, MIT.

Sachs, J. S. 1967. Recognition memory for syntactic and semantic aspects of connected discourse. *Perception and Psychophysics* 2: 437–442.

Sacks, H.; Schegloff, E. A.; and Jefferson, G. 1974. A simplest systematics of turn-taking for conversation. *Language* 50: 696–735.

Sadock, J. M. 1975. *Toward a linguistic theory of speech acts.* New York: Academic Press.

Sapir, E. 1921. *Language—An introduction to the study of speech.* New York: Harcourt, Brace.

———. 1924. The grammarian and his language. *American Mercury* 1: 149–155.

———. 1929a. A study in phonetic symbolism. *Journal of Experimental Psychology* 12: 225–239.

———. 1929b. The status of linguistics as a science. *Language* 5: 207–214.

———. 1931. Conceptual categories in primitive languages. *Science* 74: 578.

Saussure, F., de. 1959. *Course in general linguistics* (W. Baskin, trans.). New York: Philosophical Library. (Original work published in 1916.)

Savage-Rumbaugh, E. S.; Rumbaugh, D. M.; and Boysen, S. 1978. Linguistically-mediated tool use and exchange by chimpanzees *(Pan Troglodytes). The Behavioral and Brain Sciences* 1: 539–554.

Savin, H. B. 1963. Word frequency effect and errors in the perception of speech. *Journal of the Acoustical Society of America* 35: 200–206.

Savin, H. B. and Perchonock, E. 1965. Grammatical structure and the immediate recall of English sentences. *Journal of Verbal Learning and Verbal Behavior* 4: 348–353.

Schank, R. 1980. Language and memory. *Cognitive Science* 4: 243–284.

Schank, R. and Abelson, R. 1977. *Scripts, plans, goals, and understanding. An inquiry into human knowledge structures.* Hillsdale, NJ: Erlbaum.

Schiffman, R. 1985. Discourse constraints on "it" and "that": A study of language use in career-counseling interviews. Unpublished dissertation, University of Chicago.

Searle, J. R. 1969. *Speech acts. An essay in the philosophy of language.* Cambridge: Cambridge University Press.

———. Indirect speech acts. 1975. In *Syntax and semantics: Speech acts,* vol. 3, New York: Academic Press, P. Cole and J. L. Morgan (eds.). pp. 59–82.

Searle, J. R. 1979. *Expression and meaning. Studies in the theory of speech acts.* Cambridge: Cambridge University Press.

Seidenberg, M. S.; Tanenhaus, M. K.; Leiman, J. M.; and Bienkowski, M. 1982. Automatic access of the meanings of ambiguous words in context: Some limitations of knowledge-based processing. *Cognitive Psychology* 14: 489–537.

Selby, H. A. 1970. Continuities and prospects in anthropological studies. In *Current directions in anthropology,* A. Fischer (ed.), *Bulletins of the American Anthropological Association* 3:35–55 (as cited by M. Durbin, 1972).

Selfridge, O. and Neisser, U. 1960. Pattern recognition by machine. *Scientific American* 203 (August): 60–68.

Shattuck-Hufnagel, S. 1979. Speech errors as evidence for a serial-ordering mechanism in sentence production. In *Sentence processing,* W. E. Cooper and E. C. T. Walker (eds.). Hillsdale, NJ: Erlbaum, pp. 295–418.

Shattuck-Hufnagel, S. and Klatt, D. H. 1980. How single phoneme error data rule out two models of error generation. In *Errors in linguistic performance: Slips of the tongue, ear, pen, and hand,* V. A. Fromkin (ed.). New York: Academic Press, pp. 35–46.

Shepard, R. N. 1978. The mental image. *American Psychologist* 33: 125–137.

Silverstein, M. 1984. On the pragmatic "poetry" of prose: parallelism, repetition, and cohesive structure in the time course of dyadic conversation. In *Meaning, form, and use in context: linguistic applications,* D. Schiffrin (ed.). Washington, D.C.: Georgetown University Press.

Slobin, D. I. 1966. Grammatical transformations and sentence comprehension in childhood and adulthood. *Journal of Verbal Learning and Verbal Behavior* 5: 219–227.

———. 1977. Language change in childhood and history. In *Language learning and thought,* J. Macnamara (ed.). New York: Academic Press.

———. 1982. Universal and particular in the acquisition of language. In *Language acquisition: The state of the art,* E. Wanner and L. R. Gleitman (eds.). Cambridge: Cambridge University Press, pp. 128–170.

Slowiaczek, L. M.; Nusbaum, H.C.; and Pisoni, D. B. 1985. Acoustic-phonetic priming in auditory word recognition. *Research on speech perception. Progress Report No. 10.* Department of Psychology, Indiana University, pp. 33–76.

Sokolov, A. N. 1972. *Inner speech and thought.* New York: Plenum Press.

Sperling, G. 1960. The information available in brief visual presentations. *Psychological Monographs* 74, no. 11 (whole no. 498).

Steedman, M. J. 1985. LFG and psychological explanation. *Linguistics and Philosophy* 8: 359–385.

Steedman, M. J. and Johnson-Laird, P. N. 1980. The production of sentence, utterances and speech acts: Have computers anything to say? In *Language production,* vol. 1: *Speech and talk,* B. Butterworth (ed.). London: Academic Press, pp. 111–141.

Stephens, D. 1983. Hemispheric language dominance and gesture hand preference. Unpublished doctoral dissertation, University of Chicago.

Stephens, D. and Tuite, K. 1983. The hermeneutics of gesture. Paper presented at the symposium on gesture at the meeting of the American Anthropological Association, Chicago, IL.

Sternberg, S.; Monsell, S.; Knoll, R. L.; and Wright, C. E. 1978. *Information processing in motor control and learning.* New York: Academic Press, pp. 117–152.

Sternberg, S.; Wright, C. E.; Knoll, R. L.; and Monsell, S. 1980. Motor programs in rapid speech: Additional evidence. In *Perception and production of fluent speech,* R. A. Cole (ed.). Hillsdale, NJ: Erlbaum, pp. 507–534.

Stokoe, W. C. 1960. Sign language structure: An outline of the visual communication system of the American deaf. *Studies in Linguistics,* Occasional Papers 8. Buffalo, NY: University of Buffalo Press.

———. 1972. *Semiotics and human sign languages.* The Hague: Mouton.

Stokoe, W. C.; Casterline, D.; and Croneberg, C. 1965. *A dictionary of American Sign Language.* Washington, D. C.: Gallaudet College Press.

Stroop, J. R. 1935. Studies of interference in serial verbal reactions. *Journal of Experimental Psychology* 20: 643–662.

Supalla, T. (in press). *Structure and acquisition of verbs of motion in American Sign Language.* Cambridge, MA: MIT Press/Bradford Books.

Supalla, T. and Newport, E. 1978. How many seats in a chair? The derivation of nouns and verbs in American Sign Language. In *Understanding language through sign language research,* P. Siple (ed.). New York: Academic Press, pp. 91–132.

Swinney, D. A. 1979. Lexical access during sentence comprehension: (Re) consideration of context effects. *Journal of Verbal Learning and Verbal Behavior* 18: 645–660.

Swinney, D. A. and Cutler, A. 1979. The access and processing of idiomatic expressions. *Journal of Verbal Learning and Verbal Behavior* 18: 523–534.

Talmy, L. 1985. Lexicalization patterns: Semantic structure in lexical forms. In *Language typology and syntactic description, vol. III: Grammatical categories and the lexicon,* T. Shopen (ed.). Cambridge: Cambridge University Press, pp. 57–149.

Tanz, C. 1980. *Studies in the acquisition of deictic terms.* Cambridge: Cambridge University Press.

Taylor, I. K. and Taylor, M. M. 1965. Another look at phonetic symbolism. *Psychological Bulletin* 64: 413–427.

Terrace, H. S. 1979. *Nim.* New York: Knopf.

Thorndike, E. L. and Lorge, I. 1944. *A teacher's wordbook of 30,000 words.* New York: Teachers College, Columbia University.

Trevarthen, C. 1977. Descriptive analysis of infant communicative behavior. In *Studies in mother-infant interaction,* H. R. Schaffer (ed.). London: Academic Press, pp. 227–270.

Turkle, S. 1984. *The second self. Computers and the human spirit.* New York: Simon and Schuster.

Tyler, L. K. and Marslen-Wilson, W. D. 1982. Conjectures and refutations: A reply to Norris. *Cognition* 11: 103–107.

Tyler, L. K. and Wessels, J. 1984. Quantifying contextual contributions to word-recognition processes. *Perception and Psychophysics* 34: 409–420.

Uemura, R. 1943. *Manyosenshoku no Kenkyu* (Studies in the Manyo dyes). Tokyo: Kobunsha.

Ullmer-Ehrich, V. 1982. The structure of living space descriptions. In *Speech, place, and action,* R. J. Jarvella and W. Klein (eds.). Chichester: Wiley, pp. 219–250.

Vendler, Z. 1967. *Linguistics in philosophy.* Ithaca, NY: Cornell University Press.

Vygotsky, L. S. 1962. *Thought and language,* E. Hanfmann and G. Vakar (trans.). Cambridge, MA: MIT Press.

———. 1978. *Mind in society: The development of higher psychological processes,* M. Cole, V. John-Steiner, S. Scribner, and E. Souberman (eds. and trans.). Cambridge, MA: Harvard University Press.

———. 1984. *Vygotsky's collected works, vol. 2: Problems of general psychology.* R. Rieber and A. Carton (series eds.); N. Minick (prelim. trans.). New York: Plenum Press.

Waltz, D. L. and Pollack, J. B. 1985. Massively parallel parsing: A strongly interactive model of natural language interpretation. *Cognitive Science* 9: 51–74.

Wanner, E. 1980. The ATN and the sausage machine: Which one is baloney? *Cognition* 8: 209–225.

Warren, R. M. 1970. Perceptual restoration of missing speech sounds. *Science* 167: 392–393.

Warren, R. M. and Obusek, C. J. 1971. Speech perception and phonemic restorations. *Perception and Psychophysics* 9: 358–363.

Washabaugh, W. 1980. The manu-facturing of a language. *Semiotica* 29: 1–37.

Wason, P. C. 1965. The contexts of plausible denial. *Journal of Verbal Learning and Verbal Behavior* 4: 7–11.

Wason, P. C. and Reich, S. S. 1979. A verbal illusion. *Quarterly Journal of Experimental Psychology* 31: 591–597.

Weiskrantz, L.; Warrington, E. K.; Sanders, M. D.; and Marshall, J. 1974. Visual capacity in the hemianopic field following a restricted occipital ablation. *Brain* 97: 709–728.

Wentworth, H. and Flexner, S. B. 1960. *Dictionary of American slang.* New York: Crowell.

Werner, H. 1961. *Comparative psychology of mental development.* New York: Science Editions.

Werner, H. and Kaplan, B. 1963. *Symbol formation: An organismic-developmental approach to language and the expression of thought.* New York: Wiley.

Whorf, B. L. 1945. Grammatical categories. *Language* 21: 1–11.

———. 1956. *Language, thought, and reality: Selected writings of Benjamin Lee Whorf,* J. B. Carroll (ed.). Cambridge, MA: MIT Press.

Winner, E.; Rosenstiel, A. K.; and Gardner, H. 1976. The development of metaphoric understanding. *Developmental Psychology* 12: 289–297.

Winnick, W. A. and Daniel, S. A. 1970. Two kinds of response priming in tachistoscopic recognition. *Journal of Experimental Psychology* 84: 74–81.

Winograd, T. 1972. Understanding natural language. *Cognitive Psychology* 3: 1–191.

Woodward, J. 1978. Historical bases of American Sign Language. In *Understanding language through sign language research,* P. Siple (ed.). New York: Academic Press, pp. 333–348.

Yngve, V. H. 1970. On getting a word in edgewise. In *Papers from the sixth regional meeting of the Chicago Linguistic Society.* Chicago: Chicago Linguistic Society.

———. 1973. I forget what I was going to say. In *Papers from the ninth regional meeting of the Chicago Linguistic Society* C. Corum, T. C. Smith-Stark, and A. Weiser (eds.). Chicago: Chicago Linguistic Society, pp. 688–699.

Subject Index

Name Index